Taste *of* Home.
Celebrations

TASTE OF HOME BOOKS • RDA ENTHUSIAST BRANDS, LLC • MILWAUKEE, WI

© 2021 RDA Enthusiast Brands, LLC.
1610 N. 2nd St., Suite 102, Milwaukee, WI 53212-3906
All rights reserved. Taste of Home is a registered trademark
of RDA Enthusiast Brands, LLC.

Visit us at **tasteofhome.com** for other Taste of Home
books and products.

International Standard Book Number: 978-1-62145-710-7
Library of Congress Control Number: 2021931568

Executive Editor: Mark Hagen
Senior Art Director: Raeann Thompson
Editors: Amy Glander, Hazel Wheaton, Christine Rukavena
Art Director: Courtney Lovetere
Senior Designer: Jazmin Delgado

Deputy Editor, Copy Desk: Dulcie Shoener
Copy Editor: Sara Strauss

Cover Photography: Taste of Home Photo Studio

Pictured on front cover: Blue Ribbon Red Velvet Cake,
p. 29; Butter Cookies, p. 28; Midnight Cocktails, p. 266;
Easter Bunny Treats, p. 81; Broken Glass Dessert,
p. 362; Argyle Cake, p. 362; Sock Monkey Cookies,
p. 363; Moist Turkey Sausage Stuffing, p. 295; Juicy
Roast Turkey, p. 297; Almond Broccoli Salad, p. 291;
Hot Cider, p. 292

Pictured on title page: Honey Champagne
Fondue, p. 435; Champagne Blondies, p. 439;
Mango Bellini, p. 434

Pictured on back cover: Ocean Punch, p. 130; BB-8 Cake, p. 317;
Wookiee Cookies, p. 318; Lightsaber Pretzels, p. 313; Ham & Cheese
Biscuit Stacks, p. 436; Christmas Elf Cake Pops, p. 343; Three-Green
Salad, p. 87; Apricot-Glazed Ham, p. 90; Guinness Float, p. 56;
Traditional New Orleans King Cake, p. 41; Grilled Cherry-Glazed Chicken
Wings, p. 189; Mother's Day Spa Basket, p. 113; Football Cake Pops,
p. 333

Printed in China
1 3 5 7 9 10 8 6 4 2

It's time to celebrate!

Celebrating means being with the ones you love the most. Whether it's an annual holiday feast with all the trimmings or a warm-weather party with a laid-back vibe, there is nothing like family and friends gathered around the table, smiling, laughing and eating delicious homemade food.

From backyard barbecues and birthday bashes to festive Yuletide gatherings and cozy potlucks, the perfect party planner is at your fingertips with *Taste of Home Celebrations*. Divided by the four seasons, this enticing collection of recipes and entertaining tips takes your social gatherings from ordinary to extraordinary.

LOOK INSIDE FOR:

- 400+ recipes including holiday classics as well as innovative crowd pleasers destined to become new party faves. Tested and approved by the *Taste of Home* Test Kitchen, these surefire winners make every event memorably delicious.

- Complete menus and handy timelines for major holidays and other seasonal events that call for joyous celebrations.

- Easy decoration ideas, take-home treats, stocking stuffers, party games, hosting tips and more inspiration for creating an unforgettable affair.

More than just a collection of menu ideas, *Celebrations* features hundreds of gorgeous photos, step-by-step instructions, nutrition facts, clever kitchen tips and illustrated how-to's for making the most of your culinary creations. Let the celebrations begin!

MORE WAYS TO CONNECT WITH US:

Spring Gatherings

Summer Bashes

Autumn Gatherings

Holiday Celebrations

Spring Gatherings

Galentine's Day

What is Galentine's Day? "Oh, it's only the BEST day of the year," according to Leslie Knope, the overachieving deputy director of the Pawnee, Indiana, Parks and Recreation Department on TV's *Parks and Recreation*. "Every February 13, my lady friends and I leave our husbands and our boyfriends at home, and we just come and kick it breakfast-style." Here's how to throw an epic Galentine's Day celebration of your own.

FRESH STRAWBERRY SYRUP

One summer our garden yielded 80 quarts of strawberries! What to do with them all? We preserved a good portion as strawberry syrup and treat ourselves to this sweet, warm mixture over waffles or pancakes.
—Heather Biedler, Martinsburg, WV

TAKES: 15 MIN. • **MAKES:** 2 CUPS

- ¼ cup sugar
- 2 tsp. cornstarch
  Dash salt
- 2 cups chopped fresh strawberries
- ½ cup water
- ½ tsp. lemon juice

In a small saucepan, combine the sugar, cornstarch and salt. Stir in strawberries, water and lemon juice until blended. Bring to a boil. Reduce heat; simmer, uncovered, until mixture is thickened and strawberries are tender, 2-3 minutes.

¼ cup: 40 cal., 0 fat (0 sat. fat), 0 chol., 19mg sod., 10g carb. (8g sugars, 1g fiber), 0 pro.

PEANUT BUTTER MALLOW TOPPING

Looking for the perfect ice cream topping? You've found it! This tasty topper can also be drizzled over sliced apples, bananas or brownies.
—Sandy DeCosta, Vineland, NJ

TAKES: 10 MIN. • **MAKES:** 2 CUPS

- 1 jar (7 oz.) marshmallow creme
- ½ cup chunky peanut butter
- ¼ cup hot water
- 1 Tbsp. chocolate syrup

In a mixing bowl, combine all the ingredients; beat until blended.

2 Tbsp.: 93 cal., 4g fat (1g sat. fat), 0 chol., 49mg sod., 10g carb. (9g sugars, 1g fiber), 2g pro.

BUTTERMILK PECAN WAFFLES

These golden waffles are a favorite for breakfast, so we enjoy them often. They are just as easy to prepare as regular waffles, but their distinctive taste makes them truly exceptional.
—Edna Hoffman, Hebron, IN

PREP: 10 MIN. • **COOK:** 5 MIN./BATCH
MAKES: 7 WAFFLES

- 2 cups all-purpose flour
- 1 Tbsp. baking powder
- 1 tsp. baking soda
- ½ tsp. salt
- 2 cups buttermilk
- 4 large eggs, room temperature
- ½ cup butter, melted
- 3 Tbsp. chopped pecans

1. In a large bowl, whisk flour, baking powder, baking soda and salt. In another bowl, whisk buttermilk and eggs until blended. Add to dry ingredients; stir just until moistened. Stir in butter.

2. Pour about ¾ cup batter onto a lightly greased preheated waffle maker. Sprinkle with a few pecans. Bake according to manufacturer's directions until golden brown. Repeat with remaining batter and pecans.

1 waffle: 337 cal., 19g fat (10g sat. fat), 159mg chol., 762mg sod., 31g carb. (4g sugars, 1g fiber), 10g pro.

TEST KITCHEN TIP

If you don't have buttermilk on hand, you can make a quick substitution by stirring vinegar or lemon juice into regular milk—a tablespoon of the acid per cup of milk. Let stand for 15 minutes, allow the milk to curdle and presto! Homemade buttermilk!

MARBLED MERINGUE HEARTS

Pretty pastel cookies are a fun way to brighten any special occasion. Replace the vanilla with a different extract, such as almond or raspberry, for a change of flavor.
—Laurie Herr, Westford, VT

PREP: 25 MIN. • **BAKE:** 20 MIN. + COOLING
MAKES: ABOUT 2 DOZEN

- 3 **large egg whites**
- ½ **tsp. vanilla extract**
- ¼ **tsp. cream of tartar**
- ¾ **cup sugar**
  Red food coloring

1. Place egg whites in a large bowl; let stand at room temperature for 30 minutes. Line baking sheets with parchment.
2. Preheat oven to 200°. Add vanilla and cream of tartar to egg whites; beat on medium speed until soft peaks form. Gradually beat in sugar, 1 Tbsp. at a time, on high until stiff peaks form. Remove ¼ cup and tint pink. Lightly swirl pink mixture into the remaining meringue. Fill a pastry bag with the meringue. Pipe 2-in. heart shapes 2 in. apart onto prepared baking sheets.
3. Bake until the meringue is set and dry, about 20 minutes. Turn oven off; leave the meringues in oven until the oven has completely cooled. Store in an airtight container.

1 meringue: 27 cal., 0 fat (0 sat. fat), 0 chol., 7mg sod., 6g carb. (6g sugars, 0 fiber), 0 pro.

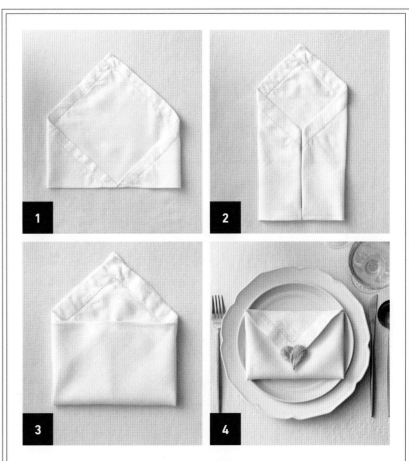

HOW TO MAKE A NAPKIN ENVELOPE

Give your table setting some love with this easy envelope napkin fold.

STEP 1
Fold a napkin in half diagonally, set with the point facing up. Then take the bottom corners and fold them so they meet in the middle.

STEP 2
Fold the outer edges in once again so they meet in the middle.

STEP 3
Fold the bottom half up until it meets the base of the triangle.

STEP 4
Fold the triangle flap down. Top with a meringue heart.

HONEY POPPY SEED FRUIT SALAD

The subtle honey sauce in this salad steals the show. The colorful dish pairs well with any morning entree and takes just 10 minutes to assemble.
—Dorothy Dinnean, Harrison, AR

TAKES: 10 MIN. • **MAKES:** 8 SERVINGS

    2 medium firm bananas, chopped
    2 cups fresh blueberries
    2 cups fresh raspberries
    2 cups sliced fresh strawberries
    5 Tbsp. honey
    1 tsp. lemon juice
    ¾ tsp. poppy seeds

In a large bowl, combine the bananas and berries. In a small bowl, combine the honey, lemon juice and poppy seeds. Pour over fruit and toss to coat.
¾ cup: 117 cal., 1g fat (0 sat. fat), 0 chol., 2mg sod., 30g carb. (23g sugars, 5g fiber), 1g pro.

HOW TO PLAN A GALENTINE'S DAY

This Feb. 13, make your female friends feel special by throwing a party that celebrates your cherished friendships.

ASSEMBLE THE SQUAD
Galentine's Day is a day to kick back with the girlfriends who make life wonderful, so be as inclusive as your budget allows. You could even ask each of your friends to invite a friend.

SERVE PINK DRINKS
A pink and frothy drink is so befitting of a Galentine's Day bash. You can bet the Cotton Candy Champagne Cocktails on page 15 will be a hit.

TURN ON FABULOUS MUSIC
Make a playlist that includes classic, upbeat friendship-themed tunes like Cyndi Lauper's "Girls Just Want to Have Fun," Sister Sledge's "We Are Family" and Queen's "You're My Best Friend."

BREAK OUT THE CHOCOLATE
Girlfriends and chocolate go together like chocolate and, well, everything. Serve chocolate desserts or set out a bowl filled with Hershey's Hugs and Kisses.

GIVE OUT VALENTINES
Since Valentine's Day is right around the corner, give each of your ladies a handwritten note saying why her friendship is meaningful to you.

RASPBERRY SOUR CREAM COFFEE CAKE

Coffee and cake are like a wink and a smile. You'll take one without the other, but given a choice, you want the pair. This fresh and fruity breakfast pastry is perfect for brunch. A drizzle of icing adds a nice finishing touch.
—Debbie Johnson, Centertown, MO

PREP: 20 MIN. • **BAKE:** 30 MIN. + COOLING
MAKES: 8 SERVINGS

- 1 cup fresh raspberries
- 3 Tbsp. brown sugar
- 1 cup all-purpose flour
- ⅓ cup sugar
- ½ tsp. baking powder
- ¼ tsp. baking soda
- ⅛ tsp. salt
- 1 large egg, room temperature
- ⅔ cup sour cream
- 3 Tbsp. butter, melted
- 1 tsp. vanilla extract
- ¼ cup sliced almonds

ICING
- ¼ cup confectioners' sugar
- 1½ tsp. 2% milk
- ¼ tsp. vanilla extract
  Additional raspberries, optional

1. Preheat oven to 350°. In a small bowl, toss raspberries with brown sugar.
2. In a large bowl, whisk flour, sugar, baking powder, baking soda and salt. In another bowl, whisk egg, sour cream, melted butter and vanilla until blended. Add to the flour mixture; stir just until moistened (batter will be thick).
3. Transfer half the batter to a greased and floured 8-in. round baking pan. Top with the raspberry mixture. Spoon the remaining batter over the raspberries; sprinkle with almonds.
4. Bake for 30-35 minutes or until a toothpick inserted in the center comes out clean. Cool in pan 10 minutes before removing to a wire rack to cool.
5. In a small bowl, mix confectioners' sugar, milk and vanilla until smooth; drizzle over top. Serve warm. If desired, serve with additional raspberries.

1 piece: 238 cal., 10g fat (5g sat. fat), 48mg chol., 154mg sod., 32g carb. (19g sugars, 2g fiber), 4g pro.

COTTON CANDY CHAMPAGNE COCKTAILS

You'll love these whimsical champagne cocktails. The cotton candy melts away, leaving its pretty pink color behind.
—*Taste of Home* Test Kitchen

TAKES: 5 MIN. • **MAKES:** 6 SERVINGS

- 6 Tbsp. raspberry-flavored vodka
- 1 bottle (750 milliliters) champagne, chilled
- 1½ cups pink cotton candy

Add 1 Tbsp. of vodka to each of 6 champagne flutes. Top with the champagne; create a cotton candy garnish for each glass. To serve, stir in cotton candy.

1 cocktail: 125 cal., 0 fat (0 sat. fat), 0 chol., 0 sod., 4g carb. (2g sugars, 0 fiber), 0 pro.

BITTERSWEET DOUBLE CHOCOLATE TRUFFLES

Milk chocolate chips enhance the bittersweet flavor in these decadent treats. Tie a few in pretty ribbons for an easy gift.
—*Taste of Home* Test Kitchen

PREP: 30 MIN. + CHILLING
MAKES: 1½ DOZEN

- 1 cup 60% cacao bittersweet chocolate baking chips
- ¾ cup whipped topping
- ¼ tsp. ground cinnamon
- 1 cup milk chocolate chips
- 1 tsp. shortening
  Optional toppings: Crushed peppermint candies, sprinkles and chopped nuts

1. In a small saucepan, melt bittersweet chips over low heat. Transfer to a bowl; cool to lukewarm, about 7 minutes.
2. Beat in the whipped topping and cinnamon. Place in the freezer for 15 minutes or until firm enough to form into balls. Shape the mixture into 1-in. balls.
3. In a microwave, melt milk chocolate chips and shortening; stir until smooth. Dip truffles in chocolate and place on waxed paper-lined baking sheets. Immediately sprinkle with toppings of your choice. Refrigerate until firm. Store in an airtight container in the refrigerator.

1 truffle: 105 cal., 6g fat (4g sat. fat), 2mg chol., 8mg sod., 12g carb. (10g sugars, 1g fiber), 1g pro.

SPARKLING COCONUT GRAPE JUICE

This sparkling drink is a nice change of pace from the expected lemonade and party punch. The lime, coconut and grape combination is so refreshing. Add a splash of gin if you're feeling bold.
—Shelly Bevington, Hermiston, OR

TAKES: 5 MIN. • **MAKES:** 6 SERVINGS

- 4 **cups white grape juice**
- 2 **tsp. lime juice**
   Ice cubes
- 2 **cups coconut-flavored sparkling water, chilled**
   Optional: Lime wedges or slices

In a pitcher, combine grape juice and lime juice. Fill 6 tall glasses with ice. Pour juice mixture evenly into glasses; top off with sparkling water. Stir to combine. Garnish with lime wedges if desired.

1 cup: 94 cal., 0 fat (0 sat. fat), 0 chol., 13mg sod., 24g carb. (21g sugars, 0 fiber), 0 pro.

MINI SAUSAGE FRITTATAS

These are amazing for breakfast or brunch. While my gal pals love the spicy kick in hot sausage, I like using sage-flavored sausage and substituting Parmesan for cheddar.
—Courtney Wright, Birmingham, AL

PREP: 15 MIN. • **BAKE:** 20 MIN.
MAKES: 1 DOZEN

- 1 lb. bulk pork sausage
- 1 large onion, finely chopped
- 6 large egg whites
- 4 large eggs
- ¼ cup 2% milk
- ¼ tsp. coarsely ground pepper
- ½ cup shredded sharp cheddar cheese
  Additional shredded sharp cheddar cheese

1. Preheat oven to 350°. In a large skillet, cook sausage and onion over medium heat 6-8 minutes or until sausage is no longer pink and onion is tender, breaking the sausage into crumbles; drain.
2. In a large bowl, whisk egg whites, eggs, milk and pepper; stir in sausage mixture and cheese. Fill greased muffin cups almost full; sprinkle with additional cheese.
3. Bake 20-25 minutes or until a knife inserted near the center comes out clean. Cool 5 minutes before removing from pans to wire racks.
2 mini frittatas: 302 cal., 23g fat (8g sat. fat), 175mg chol., 629mg sod., 5g carb. (2g sugars, 0 fiber), 19g pro.

COFFEE BODY SCRUB

Looking for a fun party favor? Mix up this invigorating coffee body scrub.

If you're a coffee lover, the idea of using precious coffee beans in a body scrub might shock you, but give this DIY product a shot!

Coffee scrubs aren't just for exfoliation and boosting circulation. The caffeine in the beans can also plump and tighten your skin, helping to reduce the appearance of cellulite. Plus, the coconut oil will leave your skin silky smooth.

TO MAKE:
Mix ½ cup fresh ground coffee and ½ cup brown sugar. Add ½ cup melted coconut oil, then 1 tsp. vanilla extract. Mix until well combined. Makes 4 applications.

TO USE:
Gently rub the mixture over your body. Leave it on for a few minutes, then rinse thoroughly. (Be careful if using the scrub in the shower; the oil can make the floor slippery.)

SUGARED DOUGHNUT HOLES

These tasty, tender doughnut bites are easy to make. Tuck them in scalloped boxes and tie each with a bow to give as a party favor.
—Judy Jungwirth, Athol, SD

TAKES: 20 MIN. • **MAKES:** ABOUT 3 DOZEN

- 1½ cups all-purpose flour
- ⅓ cup sugar
- 2 tsp. baking powder
- ½ tsp. salt
- ½ tsp. ground nutmeg
- 1 large egg, room temperature
- ½ cup 2% milk
- 2 Tbsp. butter, melted
  Oil for deep-fat frying
  Confectioners' sugar

1. In a large bowl, combine the flour, sugar, baking powder, salt and nutmeg. In a small bowl, combine the egg, milk and butter. Add to the dry ingredients and mix well.
2. In an electric skillet or deep-fat fryer, heat oil to 375°. Drop dough by heaping teaspoonfuls, 5 or 6 at a time, into oil. Fry until browned, about 1-2 minutes, turning once. Drain on paper towels. While still warm, roll doughnut holes in confectioners' sugar.

1 doughnut hole: 47 cal., 2g fat (1g sat. fat), 7mg chol., 68mg sod., 6g carb. (2g sugars, 0 fiber), 1g pro.

RASPBERRY MERINGUE HEARTS

Here's a lovely dessert that your guests will think is almost too pretty to eat! I love the way the raspberry meringue easily drapes into a heart shape.
—Mary Lou Wayman, Salt Lake City, UT

PREP: 30 MIN. + STANDING
BAKE: 35 MIN. + COOLING
MAKES: 6 SERVINGS

- 3 large egg whites
- ¼ tsp. cream of tartar
  Dash salt
- 1 cup sugar
- ⅓ cup finely chopped almonds, toasted
- 1 tsp. vanilla extract

FILLING
- 3 cups fresh or frozen unsweetened raspberries, thawed
- 1 tsp. cornstarch
- ½ cup seedless raspberry jam
- 3 cups raspberry or lemon sorbet
- ⅓ cup sliced almonds, toasted
  Additional fresh raspberries, optional

1. Place egg whites in a small mixing bowl; let stand at room temperature for 30 minutes. Beat egg whites, cream of tartar and salt on medium speed until soft peaks form. Add sugar, 1 Tbsp. at a time, beating on high until stiff peaks form and sugar is dissolved. Fold in chopped almonds and vanilla.
2. Preheat oven to 300°. Drop meringue into 6 mounds on a parchment-lined baking sheet. Shape into 4-in. hearts with the back of a spoon, building up the edges slightly. Bake for 35 minutes. Turn oven off; leave meringues in the oven for 1-1½ hours.
3. For the filling, place the raspberries in a food processor. Cover and process until blended. Strain and discard the seeds. In a small saucepan, combine the cornstarch, pureed raspberries and jam until smooth. Bring to a boil over medium heat, stirring constantly. Cook and stir for 1 minute or until thickened. Cool.
4. To serve, spoon sauce into meringue hearts. Place scoop of sorbet on top. Sprinkle with sliced almonds. Garnish with fresh raspberries if desired.

1 meringue with ¼ cup sauce and ½ cup sorbet: 423 cal., 7g fat (0 sat. fat), 0 chol., 53mg sod., 89g carb. (78g sugars, 6g fiber), 5g pro.

Valentine's Day

It's Valentine's Day and it's red all over—red food, that is!
Red symbolizes love, passion and desire, so what better time
to make a red dish or garnish a sweet with a bit of crimson
flair? Here's a tantalizing lineup that boasts rosy hues,
such as tomato soup and red velvet cake. Incorporate these
dishes as part of a romantic meal for two or a heartfelt
dinner for the entire family. Show loved ones how much
you care, and make it a Valentine's Day to remember.

CHICKEN WITH RED PEPPER SAUCE & SPINACH

This tender moist chicken is dressed up with a savory sauce that combines roasted sweet red peppers, garlic and Italian seasonings. It's simple and pretty.
—Martha Pollock, Oregonia, OH

TAKES: 30 MIN. • **MAKES:** 4 SERVINGS

- 1 large egg white
- ½ cup seasoned bread crumbs
- ¼ tsp. salt
- 4 boneless skinless chicken breast halves (4 oz. each)
- 1 Tbsp. olive oil
- 6 oz. fresh baby spinach (about 7½ cups)
- 1 jar (7 oz.) roasted sweet red peppers, drained
- 1 garlic clove, peeled
- ½ tsp. Italian seasoning
- ½ cup crumbled feta cheese
  Fresh basil leaves, optional

1. In a shallow bowl, whisk the egg white. In another shallow bowl, mix bread crumbs and salt. Dip chicken in egg white, then roll in crumb mixture.
2. In a large skillet, heat oil over medium heat. Add the chicken; cook until a thermometer reads 165°, 4-5 minutes per side. Meanwhile, place the spinach in a steamer basket; place in a large saucepan over 1 in. of water. Bring to a boil; cover and steam just until tender, 3-4 minutes.
3. Process peppers, garlic and Italian seasoning in a food processor until smooth. Transfer to a small microwave-safe bowl; cover and microwave until heated through.
4. Divide spinach among 4 plates. Serve with chicken; top each plate with about 2 Tbsp. red pepper sauce, 2 Tbsp. feta cheese and, if desired, basil.

1 serving: 245 cal., 9g fat (3g sat. fat), 70mg chol., 600mg sod., 9g carb. (2g sugars, 2g fiber), 29g pro. **Diabetic exchanges:** 4 lean meat, 2 vegetable, 1 fat, ½ starch.

READER REVIEW
"This was a really tasty recipe. My husband will not eat red peppers, but he raved about this dish. I felt good serving this to my family."
—AWARE, TASTEOFHOME.COM

CHOCOLATE-DIPPED ICE CREAM CONE CUPCAKES

I created this recipe based on our family's love of chocolate-dipped ice cream cones. Red heart-shaped sprinkles make them fun for Valentine's Day. Vary the sprinkles to match any occasion.
—Jennifer Gilbert, Brighton, MI

PREP: 40 MIN. • **BAKE:** 15 MIN.
MAKES: 2 DOZEN

- 24 ice cream cake cones (about 3 in. tall)
- 1 pkg. French vanilla or yellow cake mix (regular size)

FROSTING
- 1 cup butter, softened
- ½ cup shortening
- 6 cups confectioners' sugar
- ¼ cup 2% milk
- 2 tsp. vanilla extract

GLAZE
- 4 cups semisweet chocolate chips
- ¼ cup shortening
  Colored sprinkles

1. Preheat the oven to 350°. Grease 24 mini-muffin cups. Stand ice cream cones in additional mini-muffin cups.
2. Prepare cake mix batter according to package directions. Fill each greased muffin cup with 1 Tbsp. batter. Divide remaining batter among ice cream cones (scant 2 Tbsp. each).
3. Bake until a knife inserted in center comes out clean, 15-20 minutes. Cool in pans 5 minutes. Transfer both the plain and cone cupcakes to wire racks; cool completely.
4. For frosting, beat the butter and the shortening until blended. Gradually beat in confectioners' sugar, milk and vanilla on medium speed until soft peaks form.
5. To assemble, spread a small amount of frosting on the bottom of each plain cupcake; attach each to the top of a cone cupcake. Spread remaining frosting over tops of the cupcakes, rounding each top to resemble a scoop of ice cream. Freeze until frosting is firm, 5-10 minutes.
6. For glaze, in a large metal bowl over simmering water, melt chocolate and shortening, stirring until smooth. Dip tops of cones in chocolate mixture. Decorate with sprinkles. Let stand until set.

1 cone: 445 cal., 23g fat (10g sat. fat), 44mg chol., 224mg sod., 61g carb. (48g sugars, 2g fiber), 2g pro.

SHRIMP POMODORO

My husband and I have hectic schedules, so I'm always looking for fast meals that have special-occasion appeal. Shrimp with garlic, tomatoes and pasta is a winner.
—Catherine Jensen, Blytheville, AR

TAKES: 20 MIN. • **MAKES:** 4 SERVINGS

8	oz. uncooked thin spaghetti
1	Tbsp. olive oil
¾	lb. uncooked shrimp (26-30 per lb.), peeled and deveined
2	cloves garlic, minced
¼ to ½	tsp. crushed red pepper flakes
1	can (14½ oz.) petite diced tomatoes, undrained
10	fresh basil leaves, torn
½	tsp. salt
⅛	tsp. pepper
¼	cup grated Parmesan cheese

1. Cook the spaghetti according to the package directions.

2. In a skillet, heat oil over medium-high heat. Add shrimp; cook until the shrimp begin to turn pink, 1-2 minutes. Add the garlic and red pepper flakes; cook 1 minute longer.

3. Add the tomatoes; bring to a boil. Reduce heat; simmer, uncovered, until shrimp turn pink, 2-3 minutes, stirring occasionally. Remove from heat; stir in basil, salt and pepper. Serve with spaghetti and cheese.

¾ cup shrimp mixture with 1 cup cooked spaghetti: 357 cal., 7g fat (2g sat. fat), 108mg chol., 653mg sod., 49g carb. (5g sugars, 4g fiber), 24g pro.

BEET SALAD WITH ORANGE VINAIGRETTE

Beets and watercress topped with Gorgonzola and a sweet citrus dressing form a fabulous new blend for a mixed salad. The combination of ingredients may seem unlikely, but I guarantee it will become a new favorite.
—Mary Moskovitz, Ventnor, NJ

PREP: 25 MIN. + CHILLING
BAKE: 40 MIN. + COOLING
MAKES: 8 SERVINGS

- ½ cup orange juice
- 1 Tbsp. olive oil
- 2 tsp. white wine vinegar
- 1 tsp. minced fresh rosemary or ¼ tsp. dried rosemary, crushed
- 1 tsp. chopped shallot
- ½ tsp. grated orange zest
- ⅛ tsp. salt
- ⅛ tsp. pepper
- 4 fresh beets (about ½ lb.)
- 1 bunch watercress
- ¼ cup walnut halves, toasted
- ¼ cup crumbled Gorgonzola cheese

1. For the vinaigrette, place the first 8 ingredients in a jar with a tight-fitting lid; shake well. Refrigerate 1 hour.
2. Preheat oven to 400°. Place beets in a 13x9-in. baking dish; add 1 in. of water. Bake, covered, until tender, 40-45 minutes. Cool; peel and cut beets into thin slices.
3. Just before serving, arrange the watercress on a platter or individual plates; top with beets. Sprinkle with walnuts and cheese. Shake dressing again; drizzle over salad.
1 serving: 68 cal., 5g fat (1g sat. fat), 3mg chol., 110mg sod., 5g carb. (3g sugars, 1g fiber), 2g pro. **Diabetic exchanges:** 1 vegetable, 1 fat.

CHERRY DESSERT LASAGNA

I think it's fun to incorporate pasta into a dessert. Not everyone in my family agrees, but try it! This is a tasty and memorable way to end a meal.
—Linda Cifuentes, Mahomet, IL

PREP: 20 MIN. • **BAKE:** 45 MIN+ STANDING
MAKES: 9 SERVINGS

- 1 container (15 oz.) whole-milk ricotta cheese
- ½ cup sugar
- 1 large egg
- ½ tsp. ground cinnamon
- ¼ tsp. almond extract
- 1 can (21 oz.) cherry pie filling
- 4 no-cook lasagna noodles

TOPPING
- ⅓ cup packed brown sugar
- ¼ cup all-purpose flour
- ¼ cup quick-cooking oats
- ½ tsp. ground cinnamon
- 3 Tbsp. cold butter, cubed
- ½ cup chopped almonds

1. Preheat oven to 350°. Mix the first 5 ingredients. Spread half the pie filling into a greased 8-in. square baking dish. Place 2 noodles on top, cutting to fit into baking dish. Layer with half the ricotta cheese mixture and the remaining noodles. Top with the remaining cheese mixture and pie filling.
2. For topping, mix brown sugar, flour, oats and cinnamon; cut in butter until crumbly. Stir in almonds. Sprinkle over the top. Bake, uncovered, until bubbly, 45-50 minutes. Let stand 30-45 minutes before serving.
1 piece: 314 cal., 9g fat (4g sat. fat), 33mg chol., 191mg sod., 50g carb. (35g sugars, 2g fiber), 8g pro.

QUICK TOMATO SOUP

There's nothing like a steamy bowl of classic tomato soup on a cold February day. The addition of sugar puts a sweet spin on this version. For extra loveliness, top with homemade heart-shaped croutons.
—Jane Ward, Churchville, MD

TAKES: 15 MIN.
MAKES: 6 SERVINGS (1½ QT.)

- ¼ cup butter
- ¼ cup all-purpose flour
- 1 tsp. curry powder
- ¼ tsp. onion powder
- 1 can (46 oz.) tomato juice
- ¼ cup sugar
  Optional: Oyster crackers or croutons

In a large saucepan, melt butter. Stir in flour, curry powder and onion powder until smooth. Gradually add the tomato juice and sugar. Cook, uncovered, until thickened and heated through, about 5 minutes. If desired, serve with the crackers or croutons.
1 cup: 156 cal., 8g fat (5g sat. fat), 20mg chol., 862mg sod., 22g carb. (15g sugars, 1g fiber), 2g pro.

CHOCOLATE TART WITH CRANBERRY RASPBERRY SAUCE

With its rich chocolate and fruity flavors, a little bit of this tart goes a long way. The berry-wine sauce lends an elegant touch.
—Diane Nemitz, Ludington, MI

PREP: 40 MIN. • **BAKE:** 40 MIN. + COOLING
MAKES: 12 SERVINGS

- 1 cup all-purpose flour
- ½ cup old-fashioned oats
- ¼ cup sugar
- ½ cup cold butter, cubed
- 1½ cups unblanched almonds
- ½ cup packed brown sugar
- ½ cup dark corn syrup
- 2 large eggs, room temperature
- 4 oz. bittersweet chocolate, melted
- 2 Tbsp. butter, melted

SAUCE
- 2 cups fresh raspberries, divided
- 1 cup fresh or frozen cranberries, thawed
- ¾ cup sugar
- 2 Tbsp. port wine or water

1. Preheat oven to 350°. Process the flour, oats and sugar in a food processor until the oats are ground. Add butter; pulse until crumbly. Press onto bottom and 1 in. up the sides of an ungreased 10-in. springform pan. Bake until lightly browned, 14-16 minutes. Cool on a wire rack.
2. Process the almonds in a food processor until coarsely chopped. Beat together the brown sugar, corn syrup, eggs, chocolate and melted butter; stir in almonds.
3. Pour into prepared crust. Bake until center is set and crust is golden brown, 25-30 minutes. Cool completely on a wire rack.
4. Meanwhile, in a saucepan, combine 1 cup raspberries, cranberries, sugar and wine. Bring to a boil, stirring to dissolve the sugar. Reduce heat to low; cook, uncovered, until the cranberries pop, 4-5 minutes, stirring occasionally. Remove from heat; cool slightly.
5. Press the berry mixture through a fine-mesh strainer into a bowl; discard seeds. Refrigerate sauce until serving.
6. Remove rim from pan. Serve the tart with sauce and remaining raspberries.
1 slice with 4 tsp. sauce: 462 cal., 24g fat (9g sat. fat), 56mg chol., 115mg sod., 55g carb. (39g sugars, 4g fiber), 7g pro.

BUTTER COOKIES

These classic cookies will melt in your mouth. They're favorites of my nephews, who love the tender texture and creamy frosting. Kids can help decorate, too.
—Ruth Griggs, South Hill, VA

PREP: 25 MIN. • **BAKE:** 10 MIN./BATCH
MAKES: ABOUT 6½ DOZEN

1	cup butter, softened
¾	cup sugar
1	large egg, room temperature
½	tsp. vanilla extract
2½	cups all-purpose flour
1	tsp. baking powder
¼	tsp. salt

FROSTING

½	cup butter, softened
4	cups confectioners' sugar
1	tsp. vanilla extract
3	to 4 Tbsp. 2% milk
	Red food coloring, optional

1. Preheat oven to 375°. Cream the butter and sugar until light and fluffy, 5-7 minutes. Beat in egg and vanilla. In another bowl, whisk flour, baking powder and salt; gradually beat into creamed mixture.

2. Using a cookie press fitted with a heart disk, press dough 1 in. apart onto ungreased baking sheets. Bake until set but not brown, 6-8 minutes. Cool on wire racks.

3. For the frosting, beat the butter, confectioners' sugar, vanilla and enough milk to reach a spreading consistency. If desired, tint with food coloring. Decorate cookies as desired.

1 cookie: 157 cal., 7g fat (4g sat. fat), 24mg chol., 99mg sod., 22g carb. (15g sugars, 0 fiber), 1g pro.

BLUE RIBBON RED VELVET CAKE

This two-layer beauty features a striking red interior. It calls for more baking cocoa than most red velvet cakes, making it extra chocolaty. Feel free to change the color of the food coloring to suit the occasion. I'm proud to say that this recipe won a blue ribbon in the holiday cake division at the 2006 Alaska State Fair. I think this award-winning red velvet cake recipe will be a winner in your house, too!
—Cindi DeClue, Anchorage, AK

PREP: 35 MIN. • **BAKE:** 25 MIN. + COOLING
MAKES: 16 SERVINGS

1½ cups canola oil
1 cup buttermilk
2 large eggs, room temperature
2 Tbsp. red food coloring
1 tsp. white vinegar
2½ cups all-purpose flour
1½ cups sugar
3 Tbsp. baking cocoa
1 tsp. baking soda
FROSTING
1 pkg. (8 oz.) cream cheese, softened
½ cup butter, softened
2 tsp. vanilla extract
3¾ cups confectioners' sugar

1. Preheat the oven to 350°. Line the bottoms of 2 greased 9-in. round pans with parchment; grease parchment. Beat the first 5 ingredients until well blended. In another bowl, whisk together the flour, sugar, baking cocoa and baking soda; gradually beat into oil mixture.

2. Transfer the batter to prepared pans. Bake until a toothpick inserted in center comes out clean, 25-30 minutes. Cool in pans for 10 minutes before removing to wire racks; remove parchment. Cool the cakes completely.

3. Beat the cream cheese, butter and vanilla until blended. Gradually beat in confectioners' sugar until smooth. Using a long serrated knife, trim the tops of cakes; set tops aside. Place 1 cake layer on a serving plate. Spread with ¾ cup frosting. Top with remaining cake layer, bottom side up. Frost top and sides with remaining frosting.

4. Break the cake tops into pieces. Pulse in a food processor until fine crumbs form. Decorate cake with the crumbs as desired.

1 slice: 559 cal., 33g fat (8g sat. fat), 53mg chol., 208mg sod., 64g carb. (48g sugars, 1g fiber), 4g pro.

DID YOU KNOW?
The combination of cocoa, vinegar and buttermilk work together to give red velvet cake a maroon color. A bit of red food coloring is usually added for a deeper crimson hue.

Mardi Gras

Mardi Gras—translated Fat Tuesday—is the ultimate celebration with some of the best party foods around: Cajun and Creole dishes, tropical drinks, paczkis, and the famous king cake—baby included! Full of color, history, tradition, fun and, of course, lots and lots of flavor, New Orleans fare instantly takes get-togethers to crazy new heights. Let this colorful chapter show you how to throw your best Mardi Gras party ever. (See page 34 for some easy hosting ideas.) What a fabulous way to liven up spring!

NEW ORLEANS BEIGNETS

These sweet French doughnuts are square instead of round and have no hole in the middle. They're a traditional part of breakfast in New Orleans.
—Beth Dawson, Jackson, LA

PREP: 25 MIN. + CHILLING
COOK: 5 MIN./BATCH • **MAKES:** 4 DOZEN

1 pkg. (¼ oz.) active dry yeast
¼ cup warm water (110° to 115°)
1 cup evaporated milk
½ cup canola oil
¼ cup sugar
1 large egg, room temperature
4½ cups self-rising flour
Oil for deep-fat frying
Confectioners' sugar

1. In a large bowl, dissolve yeast in warm water. Add milk, oil, sugar, egg and 2 cups flour. Beat until smooth. Stir in enough remaining flour to form a soft dough (the dough will be sticky). Do not knead. Cover and refrigerate overnight.
2. Punch down the dough. Turn onto a floured surface; roll into a 16x12-in. rectangle. Cut into 2-in. squares.
3. In a deep cast-iron or electric skillet, heat 1 in. oil to 375°. Fry the squares, in batches, until golden brown on both sides. Drain on paper towels. Roll the warm beignets in confectioners' sugar.
1 beignet: 104 cal., 5g fat (1g sat. fat), 6mg chol., 142mg sod., 14g carb. (5g sugars, 0 fiber), 2g pro.

RED BEANS & RICE

I take this dish to many potlucks and never fail to bring home an empty pot. I learned about the mouthwatering combination of meats, beans and seasonings while working for the Navy in New Orleans. If you want to get a head start, cover the beans with the water and let them soak overnight. Drain them the next day and continue with the recipe as directed.
—Kathy Jacques, Summerfield, FL

PREP: 15 MIN. + SOAKING • **COOK:** 2 HOURS
MAKES: 10 SERVINGS

1 lb. dried kidney beans
2 tsp. garlic salt
1 tsp. Worcestershire sauce
¼ tsp. hot pepper sauce
1 qt. water
½ lb. fully cooked ham, diced
½ lb. fully cooked smoked sausage, diced
1 cup chopped onion
½ cup chopped celery
3 garlic cloves, minced
1 can (8 oz.) tomato sauce
2 bay leaves
¼ cup minced fresh parsley
½ tsp. salt
½ tsp. pepper
Hot cooked rice

1. Place beans in a Dutch oven; add water to cover by 2 in. Bring to a boil; boil for 2 minutes. Remove from the heat; cover and let stand for 1-4 hours or until softened.
2. Drain beans, discarding liquid. Add the garlic salt, Worcestershire sauce, hot pepper sauce and water; bring to a boil. Reduce heat; cover and simmer for 1½ hours.
3. Meanwhile, in a large skillet, saute ham and sausage until lightly browned. Remove with a slotted spoon to bean mixture. Saute the onion and celery in drippings until tender. Add minced garlic cloves; cook 1 minute longer. Add to the bean mixture. Stir in the tomato sauce and bay leaves. Cover and simmer for 30 minutes or until beans are tender.
4. Discard bay leaves. Measure 2 cups beans; mash and return to the bean mixture. Stir in the parsley, salt and pepper. Serve over rice.
1 cup: 276 cal., 9g fat (3g sat. fat), 27mg chol., 1149mg sod., 32g carb. (4g sugars, 8g fiber), 18g pro.

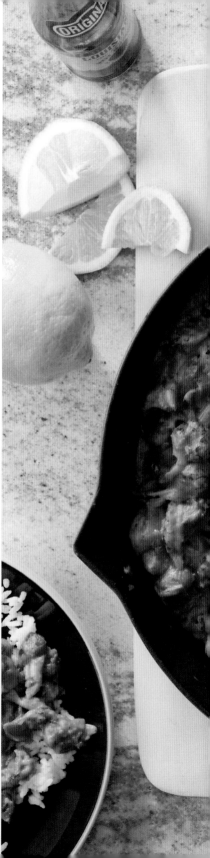

VIRGIN HURRICANES

Revelers of all ages can enjoy a nonalcoholic version of the punchlike refresher that's often called Mardi Gras in a glass. Adults who want a more authentic flavor can simply mix in rum.
—*Taste of Home* Test Kitchen

TAKES: 10 MIN. • **MAKES:** 9 SERVINGS

- 2 cups passion fruit juice
- 1 cup unsweetened pineapple juice
- 1 cup orange juice
- ¾ cup lemon juice
- 2 cups carbonated water
  Ice cubes
  Pineapple wedges
  Maraschino cherries

Combine the juices in a pitcher. Just before serving, stir in carbonated water. Pour into hurricane or highball glasses filled with ice. Garnish with pineapple wedges and cherries.

¾ cup: 61 cal., 0 fat (0 sat. fat), 0 chol., 6mg sod., 15g carb. (12g sugars, 0 fiber), 0 pro. **Diabetic exchanges:** 1 fruit.

THROW A MARDI GRAS PARTY

Mardi Gras is famous for its vibrant colors and delicious Louisiana-inspired cuisine. Even if you're hundreds of miles from New Orleans, it's easy to host a Mardi Gras bash that will bring the celebration to you.

DECORATIONS

Mardi Gras is known for its bright, tricolor decorations. The traditional colors are purple to symbolize justice, green to symbolize faith and gold to symbolize power. Any good party will decorate using this color scheme. Place purple, green and gold balloons in the party area. Or look for a Mardi Gras pinata at your local party store.

FOOD

Good food is a must for Mardi Gras—after all, it literally means Fat Tuesday! You'll definitely want to serve some New Orleans flavor to pay homage to the event's cultural roots. This could be heaping platters of beans and rice, bowls of jambalaya or gumbo, or a delicious seafood dish. And, of course, you can't forget the traditional New Orleans king cake! See page 41 for the perfect recipe.

ACTIVITIES

Keep the party going with these fun Mardi Gras games and activities:

Mask Decorating: Masquerade masks are another Mardi Gras tradition, so why not create a mask-decorating station? You'll need plain masks and decorating supplies like paint, glue, glitter and feathers.

Selfie Contest: Create a list of fun and silly selfies—posing with the king cake baby, wearing at least 10 necklaces, etc. At the end of the party, the person who completed the most selfies gets a prize.

Pin the Mask on the Jester: Put a festive twist on the old-time game of pin the tail on the donkey by purchasing or printing a cutout of a Mardi Gras jester. Blindfold guests and have them take turns pinning the mask on the jester's face.

CRAWFISH ETOUFFEE

I like to serve this Cajun sensation when I entertain. Etouffee is typically served with shellfish over rice and is similar to gumbo. This dish has its roots in New Orleans and the bayou country of Louisiana.
—Tamra Duncan, Lincoln, AR

PREP: 15 MIN. • **COOK:** 50 MIN.
MAKES: 8 SERVINGS

- ½ cup butter, cubed
- ½ cup plus 2 Tbsp. all-purpose flour
- 1¼ cups chopped celery
- 1 cup chopped green pepper
- ½ cup chopped green onions
- 1 can (14½ oz.) chicken broth
- 1 cup water
- ¼ cup minced fresh parsley
- 1 Tbsp. tomato paste
- 1 bay leaf
- ½ tsp. salt
- ¼ tsp. pepper
- ¼ tsp. cayenne pepper
- 2 lbs. frozen cooked crawfish tail meat, thawed
  Hot cooked rice

1. In a large heavy skillet, melt butter; stir in flour. Cook and stir over low heat for about 20 minutes until mixture is a caramel-colored paste. Add celery, pepper and onions; stir until coated. Add broth, water, parsley, tomato paste, bay leaf, salt, pepper and cayenne pepper. Bring to a boil.
2. Reduce heat; cover and simmer for 30 minutes, stirring occasionally. Discard bay leaf. Add crawfish and heat through. Serve with rice.
1 cup: 250 cal., 13g fat (7g sat. fat), 187mg chol., 579mg sod., 10g carb. (1g sugars, 1g fiber), 22g pro.

PACZKI

My mom used to make these when I was growing up. She filled them with raspberry or apricot jam, but prune filling is pretty traditional in Polish and Czech households.
—Lisa Kaminski, Wauwatosa, WI

PREP: 35 MIN. + RISING
COOK: 5 MIN./BATCH
MAKES: 2 DOZEN

- 1¼ cups sugar, divided
- 1 pkg. (¼ oz.) active dry yeast
- 1 tsp. salt
- 3¼ to 3¾ cups all-purpose flour
- ¾ cup 2% milk
- ¼ cup shortening
- ¼ cup water
- 1 large egg, room temperature
  Oil for deep-fat frying
- 1 cup seedless raspberry jam

1. In a large bowl, mix ¼ cup sugar, yeast, salt and 2 cups flour. In a small saucepan, heat milk, shortening and water to 120°-130°. Add to the dry ingredients; beat on medium speed 2 minutes. Add the egg; beat on high 2 minutes. Stir in enough remaining flour to form a soft dough (dough will be sticky).

2. Turn dough onto a floured surface; knead until smooth and elastic, about 6-8 minutes. Place in a greased bowl, turning once to grease the top. Cover and let rise in a warm place until doubled, about 1 hour.

3. Punch down dough. Turn onto a lightly floured surface; roll to ½-in. thickness. Cut with a floured 3-in. round cutter. Place 2 in. apart on greased baking sheets. Cover and let rise in a warm place until nearly doubled, about 1 hour.

4. In an electric skillet or deep fryer, heat oil to 375°. Fry the doughnuts, a few at a time, until golden brown, about 2-3 minutes on each side. Drain on paper towels. Cool slightly; roll in remaining 1 cup sugar.

5. Cut a small hole in the tip of a pastry bag; insert a small pastry tip. Fill bag with jam. With a small knife, pierce a hole into the side of each doughnut; fill with jam.

1 doughnut: 183 cal., 6g fat (1g sat. fat), 8mg chol., 105mg sod., 30g carb. (17g sugars, 1g fiber), 2g pro.

MUFFULETTA

The sandwich, which originated in New Orleans, is named after the round, crusty Sicilian loaf of bread it is traditionally served on. While I favor my own olive salad, there are several very good commercially-produced versions available in most supermarkets.
—Lou Sansevero, Ferron, UT

PREP: 30 MIN. + CHILLING
MAKES: 8 SERVINGS

- 1 cup pimiento-stuffed olives, chopped
- ¾ cup olive oil
- 1 celery rib, finely chopped
- ½ cup sliced pepperoncini, chopped
- ½ cup pitted Greek olives, chopped
- ¼ cup cocktail onions, drained and chopped
- ¼ cup red wine vinegar
- 2 Tbsp. capers, drained
- 3 garlic cloves, minced
- 1 tsp. dried oregano
- 1 tsp. dried basil
- ¾ tsp. pepper
- ½ tsp. kosher salt
- ½ tsp. celery seed
- 1 round loaf (1 lb.) unsliced Italian bread
- ½ lb. thinly sliced Genoa salami
- ½ lb. thinly sliced deli ham
- ½ lb. sliced mortadella
- ½ lb. sliced Swiss cheese
- ½ lb. sliced provolone cheese

1. In a large bowl, combine the first 14 ingredients. Cover and refrigerate at least 8 hours.

2. Cut the bread in half horizontally; carefully hollow out top and bottom, leaving a 1-in. shell (discard removed bread or save for another use). Spoon half the olive mixture over bottom half of bread. Layer with the salami, ham, mortadella, Swiss and provolone; top with remaining olive mixture. Replace bread top. Wrap tightly. Refrigerate at least 3 hours or overnight. Cut into 8 wedges.

1 slice: 762 cal., 59g fat (18g sat. fat), 103mg chol., 2326mg sod., 25g carb. (2g sugars, 2g fiber), 35g pro.

CREOLE-SPICED SHRIMP PO'BOYS

My father is Cajun, and I grew up eating Cajun food. This recipe makes me think of happy childhood memories. Sometimes I use oysters or crawfish in addition to— or instead of—the shrimp.
—Stacey Johnson, Bonney Lake, WA

PREP: 30 MIN. • **COOK:** 5 MIN./BATCH
MAKES: 4 SANDWICHES (1 CUP SAUCE)

- ¾ cup mayonnaise
- ½ cup ketchup
- 1 tsp. prepared horseradish
- 1 tsp. hot pepper sauce
  Oil for frying
- ¾ cup all-purpose flour
- ¾ cup cornmeal
- 1 Tbsp. Creole seasoning
- 1 tsp. salt
- 1 lb. uncooked medium shrimp, peeled and deveined (tails removed)
- 4 French rolls, split
- 2 cups shredded lettuce
- 2 medium tomatoes, sliced

1. In a small bowl, mix the mayonnaise, ketchup, horseradish and pepper sauce. Cover and chill until serving.
2. In an electric skillet, heat ½ in. oil to 375°. In a large shallow dish, combine the flour, cornmeal, Creole seasoning and salt.
3. Add shrimp, a few at a time; toss to coat. Fry shrimp in oil for 2-3 minutes on each side or until golden brown. Drain on paper towels.
4. Spread rolls with some of the sauce. Layer bottoms with lettuce, shrimp and tomatoes; replace tops. Serve with remaining sauce.

1 sandwich: 847 cal., 49g fat (6g sat. fat), 153mg chol., 1889mg sod., 71g carb. (12g sugars, 5g fiber), 29g pro.

NEW ORLEANS-STYLE STEWED CHICKEN

This dish is like a gumbo but with far less liquid and bigger pieces of meat. Don't let the ingredients trick you into thinking it is a difficult recipe to cook. Most of the ingredients are herbs and spices that coat the chicken.
—Eric Olsson, Macomb, MI

PREP: 45 MIN. • **COOK:** 1 HOUR
MAKES: 4 SERVINGS

- 1 Tbsp. dried parsley flakes
- 2 tsp. salt
- 1¼ tsp. pepper, divided
- 1⅛ tsp. dried thyme, divided
- 1 tsp. garlic powder
- 1 tsp. onion powder
- ¼ tsp. white pepper
- ¼ tsp. cayenne pepper
- ¼ tsp. rubbed sage
- 1 lb. chicken drumsticks
- 1 lb. bone-in chicken thighs
- 2 Tbsp. plus ½ cup bacon drippings or olive oil, divided
- ½ cup all-purpose flour
- ½ lb. sliced fresh mushrooms
- 1 medium onion, chopped
- 1 medium green pepper, chopped
- 1 celery rib, chopped
- 1 jalapeno pepper, seeded and finely chopped
- 4 garlic cloves, minced
- 4 cups chicken stock
- 4 green onions, finely chopped
- 5 drops hot pepper sauce
  Hot cooked rice

1. In a bowl, mix parsley, salt, 1 tsp. pepper, 1 tsp. thyme, garlic powder, onion powder, white pepper, cayenne and sage; rub over chicken. In a Dutch oven, brown the chicken, in batches, in 2 Tbsp. bacon drippings; remove the chicken from pan.
2. Add remaining ½ cup bacon drippings to the same pan; stir in the flour until blended. Cook and stir over medium-low heat 30 minutes or until browned (do not burn). Add mushrooms, onion, green pepper and celery; cook and stir for 2-3 minutes or until vegetables are crisp-tender. Add jalapeno pepper, garlic and remaining ⅛ tsp. thyme; cook 1 minute longer.
3. Gradually add stock. Return chicken to pan. Bring to a boil. Reduce the heat; cover and simmer until chicken is very tender, about 1 hour. Skim fat. Stir in the green onions, pepper sauce and the remaining ¼ tsp. pepper. Serve with hot cooked rice.

Freeze option: Place individual portions of cooled stew in freezer containers and freeze. To use, partially thaw the stew in refrigerator overnight. Heat through in a saucepan, stirring occasionally; add a little broth if necessary.

1 serving: 680 cal., 48g fat (17g sat. fat), 131mg chol., 1847mg sod., 23g carb. (5g sugars, 3g fiber), 38g pro.

THE MEANING BEHIND THE KING CAKE

A traditional Mardi Gras celebration isn't complete without a king cake. King cake—also known as three kings cake or *galette des rois* in French—is a sweet pastry made with a cinnamon swirl and coated in thick frosting decorated with colorful sugar sprinkles. But there is something special about a king cake. It has a toy baby inside.

WHY IS THERE A BABY?

The baby inside symbolizes baby Jesus and is a symbol of good luck and prosperity. Only one is hidden in the cake, and the lucky finder is dubbed king or queen for the evening.

THE HISTORY BEHIND THE TOY

The tradition originated centuries ago when wreath-shaped cakes were eaten on King's Day (Jan. 6).

By the 19th century, king cake had become a staple at New Orleans' annual King's Ball. That's when bakers began hiding objects inside the cake, usually a fava bean. Whoever found the hidden treasure was named king or queen of the ball.

Fast forward to the 1940s when a salesman had a surplus of tiny porcelain babies on hand. He suggested hiding them in cakes baked by McKenzie Bakery. The idea stuck, with plastic babies later replacing the porcelain figures.

So choose your slice of king cake carefully. You may end up with a forkful of good luck!

TRADITIONAL NEW ORLEANS KING CAKE

Get in on the fun of king cake. Hide a little toy baby in the cake. Whoever finds it has one year of good luck!

—Rebecca Baird, Salt Lake City, UT

PREP: 40 MIN. + RISING
BAKE: 25 MIN. + COOLING
MAKES: 1 CAKE (12 SLICES)

2   pkg. (¼ oz. each) active dry yeast
½   cup warm water (110° to 115°)
¾   cup sugar, divided
½   cup butter, softened
½   cup warm 2% milk (110° to 115°)
2   large egg yolks, room temperature
1¼ tsp. salt
1   tsp. grated lemon zest
¼   tsp. ground nutmeg
3¼ to 3¾ cups all-purpose flour
1   tsp. ground cinnamon
1   large egg, beaten
GLAZE
1½ cups confectioners' sugar
2   tsp. lemon juice
2   to 3 Tbsp. water
    Green, purple and yellow sugars

1. In a large bowl, dissolve the yeast in warm water. Add ½ cup sugar, butter, milk, egg yolks, salt, lemon zest, nutmeg and 2 cups flour. Beat until smooth. Stir in enough of the remaining flour to form a soft dough (dough will be sticky).

2. Turn onto a floured surface; knead until smooth and elastic, 6-8 minutes. Place in a greased bowl, turning once to grease the top. Cover and let rise in a warm place until doubled, about 1 hour.

3. Punch dough down. Turn onto a lightly floured surface. Roll into a 16x10-in. rectangle. Combine the cinnamon and remaining sugar; sprinkle over dough to within ½ in. of edges. Roll up jelly-roll style, starting with a long side; pinch the seam to seal. Place seam side down on a greased baking sheet; pinch the ends together to form a ring. Cover and let rise until doubled, about 1 hour. Brush with egg.

4. Bake at 375° for 25-30 minutes or until golden brown. Cool completely on a wire rack. For glaze, combine the confectioners' sugar, lemon juice and enough water to achieve the desired consistency. Spread over cake. Sprinkle with colored sugars.

1 slice: 321 cal., 9g fat (5g sat. fat), 73mg chol., 313mg sod., 55g carb. (28g sugars, 1g fiber), 5g pro.

READER REVIEW
"I made this king cake for a friend's birthday because that year it fell on Mardi Gras. I even hid a toy baby inside. It was a hit. Remember, the person who gets the baby also has to make next year's king cake."
—MSB2, TASTEOFHOME.COM

Friday Fish Fry

More of an event than a meal, Friday fish fries are a culinary tradition, especially during the Lenten season when many people eat less meat. While fish is the star of the show, bountiful sides—rye bread, coleslaw, potato pancakes, tartar sauce—round out the feast. Whether you like your fish battered or baked, here's the perfect excuse to get your fry on—any day of the week, any time of the year!

TARTAR SAUCE

You simply can't have fried fish without tartar sauce! Skip the bottled stuff and opt for this creamy homemade version that takes just minutes to mix together.
—Alice McGeoghegan, Willows, CA

TAKES: 5 MIN. • **MAKES:** 1 CUP

- 1 cup mayonnaise
- 1 green onion, finely chopped
- 2 Tbsp. lemon juice
- 1 tsp. dill weed
- 1 tsp. ground mustard
- ½ tsp. paprika
- ½ tsp. pepper

In a small bowl, combine all ingredients. Refrigerate until serving.

2 Tbsp.: 184 cal., 20g fat (3g sat. fat), 2mg chol., 141mg sod., 1g carb. (0 sugars, 0 fiber), 0 pro.

READER REVIEW

"This is a terrific recipe. My family doesn't like pickles, so I was looking for a recipe without relish. Two days later, when the flavors had melded, it was even better. Wonderful combination of flavors."
—FARMERGIG, TASTEOFHOME.COM

MOM'S PICKLED BEETS

Zesty and fresh-tasting, these bright and beautiful beet slices add spark to any meal. My mouth still begins to water when I think of how wonderful they tasted when Mother prepared them.
—Mildred Sherrer, Fort Worth, TX

PREP: 15 MIN. + CHILLING
MAKES: 8 SERVINGS

- ¾ cup sugar
- ¾ cup white vinegar
- ¾ cup water
- 1½ tsp. salt
- ¾ to 1 tsp. pepper
- 1 large onion, thinly sliced
- 2 cans (13¼ oz. each) sliced beets, undrained
  Sliced green onions, optional

1. In a large saucepan, combine the first 6 ingredients; bring to a boil. Reduce heat; cover and simmer for 5 minutes. Remove from the heat; add beets. Let stand at room temperature for 1 hour. Transfer to a large bowl.
2. Cover and chill 6 hours or overnight. Garnish with green onions if desired.

½ cup: 110 cal., 0 fat (0 sat. fat), 0 chol., 626mg sod., 28g carb. (25g sugars, 2g fiber), 1g pro.

LEMON-BATTER FISH

Fishing is a popular recreational activity where we live, so folks are always looking for good ways to prepare their catches. My husband ranks this as one of his favorites.
—Jackie Hannahs, Cedar Springs, MI

TAKES: 25 MIN. • **MAKES:** 6 SERVINGS

- 1½ cups all-purpose flour, divided
- 1 tsp. baking powder
- ¾ tsp. salt
- ½ tsp. sugar
- 1 large egg, lightly beaten
- ⅔ cup water
- ⅔ cup lemon juice, divided
- 2 lbs. perch or walleye fillets, cut into serving-sized pieces
  Oil for frying
  Lemon wedges, optional

1. Combine 1 cup flour, the baking powder, salt and sugar. In another bowl, combine egg, water and ⅓ cup lemon juice; stir into dry ingredients until smooth.
2. Place remaining lemon juice and remaining flour in separate shallow bowls. Dip fillets in lemon juice, then flour, then coat with egg mixture.
3. In a large skillet, heat 1 in. oil over medium-high heat. Fry fillets until golden brown and fish flakes easily with a fork, 2-3 minutes on each side. Drain on paper towels. If desired, serve with lemon wedges.

5 oz. cooked fish: 384 cal., 17g fat (2g sat. fat), 167mg chol., 481mg sod., 22g carb. (1g sugars, 1g fiber), 33g pro.

COCONUT FRIED SHRIMP

These crisp and crunchy shrimp make a tempting appetizer or a fun change-of-pace main dish. The coconut coating adds a touch of sweetness, and the tangy marmalade and honey sauce is excellent for dipping.
—Ann Atchison, O'Fallon, MO

TAKES: 20 MIN. • **MAKES:** 4 SERVINGS

- 1¼ cups all-purpose flour
- 1¼ cups cornstarch
- 6½ tsp. baking powder
- ½ tsp. salt
- ¼ tsp. Cajun seasoning
- 1½ cups cold water
- ½ tsp. canola oil
- 2½ cups sweetened shredded coconut
- 1 lb. uncooked shrimp (26-30 per lb.), peeled and deveined
    Additional oil for deep-fat frying
- ½ cup orange marmalade
- 2 Tbsp. honey

1. In a bowl, combine first 5 ingredients. Stir in water and oil until smooth. Place the coconut in another bowl. Dip shrimp into batter, then coat with the coconut.
2. In an electric skillet or deep-fat fryer, heat oil to 375°. Fry the shrimp, a few at a time, for 3 minutes or until golden brown. Drain on paper towels.
3. In a small saucepan, heat marmalade and honey; stir until blended. Serve with the shrimp.

7 shrimp with about 2 Tbsp. sauce: 906 cal., 40g fat (20g sat. fat), 138mg chol., 1193mg sod., 117g carb. (58g sugars, 4g fiber), 24g pro.

FARMHOUSE APPLE COLESLAW

A friend from church gave me this apple coleslaw recipe that her grandmother handed down to her. The flavors really complement each other well, while the fruit creates a refreshing change of pace from the usual coleslaw.
—Jan Myers, Atlantic, IA

PREP: 20 MIN. + CHILLING
MAKES: 12 SERVINGS

- 4 cups shredded cabbage
- 1 large apple, chopped
- ¾ cup raisins
- ½ cup chopped celery
- ¼ cup chopped onion
- ¼ cup mayonnaise
- 2 Tbsp. lemon juice
- 1 Tbsp. sugar
- 1 Tbsp. olive oil
- ½ tsp. salt
- ⅛ tsp. pepper

In a serving bowl, combine cabbage, apple, raisins, celery and onion. In a small bowl, combine the remaining ingredients. Pour over the cabbage mixture and toss to coat. Cover and refrigerate for at least 30 minutes.

⅔ cup: 87 cal., 5g fat (1g sat. fat), 0 chol., 131mg sod., 12g carb. (8g sugars, 1g fiber), 1g pro. **Diabetic exchanges:** 1 vegetable, 1 fat, ½ starch.

CUTTING CABBAGE

Cut the cabbage in half, then cut a "V" to remove the core. Cut the cabbage halves into wedges, and chop or shred as finely as you wish. Chopped cabbage holds more water and stays crunchier over time. Shredded gets softer as it sits. The choice is yours!

HOW TO MAKE POTATO PANCAKES

Crispy and golden brown, potato pancakes make an ideal side dish.
Here's how to get that perfect texture with a bit of crunch.

STEP 1
Shred peeled potatoes using the disc attachment on your
food processor. If you don't have a food processor,
a box grater works, too.

STEP 2
Once you've shredded 4 cups' worth, rinse the potatoes in
cold water and drain well. Place drained potatoes in a large
piece of cheesecloth and firmly squeeze over a bowl to
release any excess water.

STEP 3
In a large bowl, mix the beaten eggs, flour, diced onion, salt
and pepper. Stir in your drained potatoes well, making sure
every shred is coated. You can also incorporate herbs into
the batter at this stage if you like a little extra flavor. Try dill,
cumin, cayenne and curry powder.

STEP 4
Heat ¼ in. oil in a large nonstick skillet over medium heat.
We recommend canola, vegetable or corn oil because of
their high smoke points (meaning they won't start to smoke
until they hit higher temperatures). Working in batches, drop
the potato mixture by ¼ cupfuls into the oil. Use a spatula to
flatten lightly into a pancake shape.

STEP 5
The pancakes will need a little room to get nice and crispy,
so don't crowd the pan. Use a second spatula to flip the
pancakes so you don't contaminate them with raw egg
from the first spatula.

STEP 6
When golden brown on both sides, drain on paper towels to
soak excess oil. Once drained, they're ready to eat!

PERFECT POTATO PANCAKES

Potato pancakes are a staple at any good fish fry. They make a nice alternative to french fries. When my son and his family visited from Winnipeg, one of the first things they asked for were my potato pancakes!
—Mary Peters, Swift Current, SK

PREP: 20 MIN. • **COOK:** 10 MIN./BATCH
MAKES: ABOUT 16 PANCAKES

- 4 large potatoes (about 3 lbs.)
- 2 large eggs, lightly beaten
- ½ cup all-purpose flour
- ½ cup finely diced onion
- 1 tsp. salt
- ⅛ tsp. pepper
  Oil for frying
  Optional: Maple syrup or applesauce

1. Peel and shred the potatoes; place in a bowl of cold water. Line a colander with cheesecloth or paper towels. Drain potatoes into cloth and squeeze out as much moisture as possible. In a large bowl, combine the potatoes, eggs, flour, onion, salt and pepper.
2. In an electric skillet, heat ¼ in. oil over medium heat. Carefully drop batter by ¼ cupfuls into oil, about 3 in. apart. Press lightly to flatten. Fry until golden brown, about 4 minutes on each side. Drain on paper towels. Repeat with remaining batter. If desired, top with maple syrup or applesauce.

2 pancakes: 287 cal., 12g fat (1g sat. fat), 47mg chol., 324mg sod., 39g carb. (2g sugars, 4g fiber), 6g pro.

HUSH PUPPIES

A fish dinner isn't complete without a side of hush puppies, and my mom is well-known for this recipe. It's the best!
—Mary McGuire, Graham, NC

TAKES: 25 MIN. • **MAKES:** 2 DOZEN

- 1 cup yellow cornmeal
- ¼ cup all-purpose flour
- 1½ tsp. baking powder
- ½ tsp. salt
- 1 large egg, room temperature, lightly beaten
- ¾ cup 2% milk
- 1 small onion, finely chopped
  Oil for deep-fat frying

1. In a large bowl, combine cornmeal, flour, baking powder and salt. Whisk the egg, milk and onion; add to dry ingredients just until combined.
2. In a cast-iron Dutch oven or an electric skillet, heat oil to 365°. Drop batter by tablespoonfuls into oil. Fry until golden brown, 2-2½ minutes. Drain on paper towels. Serve warm.

1 hush puppy: 55 cal., 3g fat (0 sat. fat), 9mg chol., 86mg sod., 7g carb. (1g sugars, 0 fiber), 1g pro.

OLD-WORLD RYE BREAD

Rye and caraway lend to this bread's flavor, while the surprise ingredient of baking cocoa gives it a rich, dark color. I sometimes stir in a cup each of raisins and walnuts.
—Perlene Hoekema, Lynden, WA

PREP: 25 MIN. + RISING
BAKE: 35 MIN. + COOLING
MAKES: 2 LOAVES (12 SLICES EACH)

- 2 pkg. (¼ oz. each) active dry yeast
- 1½ cups warm water (110° to 115°)
- ½ cup molasses
- 6 Tbsp. butter, softened
- 2 cups rye flour
- ¼ cup baking cocoa
- 2 Tbsp. caraway seeds
- 2 tsp. salt
- 3½ to 4 cups all-purpose flour
  Cornmeal

1. In a large bowl, dissolve yeast in warm water. Beat in molasses, butter, rye flour, cocoa, caraway seeds, salt and 2 cups all-purpose flour until smooth. Stir in enough remaining all-purpose flour to form a stiff dough.
2. Turn onto a floured surface; knead until smooth and elastic, 6-8 minutes. Place in a greased bowl, turning once to grease top. Cover and let rise in a warm place until doubled, about 1½ hours.
3. Punch dough down. Turn onto a lightly floured surface; divide in half. Shape each piece into a loaf about 10 in. long. Grease 2 baking sheets and sprinkle with cornmeal. Place the loaves on prepared pans. Cover and let rise until doubled, about 1 hour.
4. Bake at 350° for 35-40 minutes or until bread sounds hollow when tapped. Remove from pans to wire racks to cool.

1 slice: 146 cal., 3g fat (2g sat. fat), 8mg chol., 229mg sod., 26g carb. (5g sugars, 2g fiber), 3g pro.

NEW ENGLAND APPLESAUCE

We once lived next to an apple orchard and used the fresh fruit to make lots of delicious homemade applesauce. This is my own recipe, and people have been telling me for years that it's so good it should be published. I hope you agree!
—Marilyn Tarr, Palos Heights, IL

PREP: 30 MIN. • **COOK:** 20 MIN.
MAKES: 6 CUPS

- 4 lbs. Rome Beauty or McIntosh apples
- 1 cup honey
- 1 cup water
- ½ cup lemon juice
- 1 tsp. grated lemon zest
- ¼ tsp. ground cinnamon
- 2 Tbsp. grenadine syrup, optional

1. Peel, core and cut the apples into wedges. In a large kettle, combine all ingredients except grenadine; bring to a boil. Reduce heat and simmer until apples are fork-tender, 20-25 minutes.
2. Mash apples to a chunky texture or process with food mill for smooth sauce. Stir in grenadine if desired.
½ cup: 161 cal., 0 fat (0 sat. fat), 0 chol., 1mg sod., 43g carb. (39g sugars, 3g fiber), 0 pro.

FREEZING APPLESAUCE

Homemade applesauce can be frozen in serving-sized portions for future use. Freeze cooled applesauce in freezer containers. To use, thaw in the refrigerator overnight. Serve it cold or heat through in a saucepan, stirring occasionally.

CILANTRO LIME COD

My daughter loves to cook and especially likes dishes with Mexican flair. She bakes these wonderfully seasoned fish fillets in foil to keep them moist and to cut down on the cleanup.
—Donna Hackman, Bedford, VA

PREP: 15 MIN. • **BAKE:** 35 MIN.
MAKES: 8 SERVINGS

- 4 cod or flounder fillets (2 lbs.)
- ¼ tsp. pepper
- 1 Tbsp. dried minced onion
- 1 garlic clove, minced
- 1 Tbsp. olive oil
- 1½ tsp. ground cumin
- ¼ cup minced fresh cilantro
- 2 limes, thinly sliced
- 2 Tbsp. butter, melted

1. Place each fillet on a 15x12-in. piece of heavy-duty foil. Sprinkle with pepper. In a small saucepan, saute onion and garlic in oil; stir in cumin. Spoon over fillets; sprinkle with cilantro. Place lime slices over each; drizzle with butter. Fold foil around the fish and seal tightly.
2. Place on a baking sheet. Bake at 375° for 35-40 minutes or until fish just begins to flake easily with a fork.
3 oz. cooked fish: 132 cal., 5g fat (2g sat. fat), 51mg chol., 85mg sod., 3g carb. (1g sugars, 1g fiber), 18g pro.
Diabetic exchanges: 3 lean meat, 1 fat.

STRAWBERRY SHORTCAKE PIE

This fresh fruity pie doesn't last long at our house. The crust is a nice variation from traditional pie crust.

—Jackie Deibert, Klingerstown, PA

PREP: 20 MIN. + CHILLING
BAKE: 10 MIN. + COOLING
MAKES: 8 SERVINGS

- 1½ cups biscuit/baking mix
- 6 Tbsp. cold butter, cubed
- 2 to 3 Tbsp. cold water

FILLING
- 1 pkg. (3 oz.) strawberry gelatin
- 2 cups water, divided
- ⅔ cup sugar
- 2 Tbsp. cornstarch
- 2 qt. fresh strawberries, quartered

1. Place dry biscuit mix in a large bowl. Cut in butter until crumbly. Gradually add water, tossing with a fork until dough forms a ball.
2. Press onto the bottom and up the sides of an ungreased 9-in. deep-dish pie plate. Bake at 450° for roughly 10-12 minutes or until golden brown. Cool on a wire rack.
3. Meanwhile, in a small saucepan, sprinkle the gelatin over ½ cup cold water; let stand for 1 minute. Heat over low heat, stirring until gelatin is completely dissolved.
4. In a large saucepan, combine sugar and cornstarch. Stir in the remaining 1½ cups water until smooth. Bring to a boil. Cook and stir for 2 minutes or until thickened. Remove from the heat; stir in gelatin mixture.
5. Transfer to a large bowl. Cool to room temperature. Add strawberries; stir gently to coat. Spoon into the crust. Refrigerate until set, about 4 hours. Refrigerate leftovers.

1 piece: 319 cal., 11g fat (6g sat. fat), 23mg chol., 327mg sod., 54g carb. (34g sugars, 3g fiber), 4g pro.

LEMON BARS WITH CREAM CHEESE FROSTING

I won a baking contest at Purdue University with this recipe for lemon bars with cream cheese frosting. I think you'll love the dreamy topping.

—Michael Hunter, Fort Wayne, IN

PREP: 20 MIN. • **BAKE:** 20 MIN. + COOLING
MAKES: 2 DOZEN

- 1 cup butter, softened
- 2 cups sugar
- 4 large eggs, room temperature
- 2 tsp. lemon extract
- 1¾ cups all-purpose flour
- ½ tsp. salt
- 1 tsp. grated lemon zest

LEMON CREAM CHEESE FROSTING
- 4 oz. cream cheese, softened
- 2 Tbsp. butter, softened
- 2 cups confectioners' sugar
- 2 tsp. lemon juice
- 1½ tsp. grated lemon zest

1. In a large bowl, cream butter and sugar until light and fluffy, 5-7 minutes. Beat in eggs and extract. Combine the flour and salt; gradually add to creamed mixture and mix well. Stir in lemon zest.
2. Spread into a greased 13x9-in. baking pan. Bake at 350° for 18-22 minutes or until center is set and edges are golden brown. Cool completely.
3. For frosting, in a large bowl, beat cream cheese and butter until fluffy. Beat in confectioners' sugar, lemon juice and zest. Frost bars. Store in the refrigerator.

1 bar: 243 cal., 11g fat (7g sat. fat), 59mg chol., 145mg sod., 34g carb. (27g sugars, 0 fiber), 2g pro.

TEST KITCHEN TIP

These bars don't use baking soda or baking powder, so it's very important to beat the butter and sugar together really well. Doing so actually incorporates air into the batter, which will cause the bars to rise in the oven, so make sure you don't skimp on this step.

St. Patrick's Day

Make your house the place to be on March 17 with this jig-worthy lineup of Irish classics. Whether hosting a bash or simply surprising the family, these over-the-rainbow ideas make it easy to bring a touch o' green (and a pot o' gold) to your table. Turn the page for everything you need for the ultimate feast—snacks and sides, entrees and desserts. These dishes are sure to have everyone's Irish eyes smilin'.

SLOW-COOKER REUBEN SPREAD

My daughter shared this recipe with me for a hearty spread that tastes just like a Reuben sandwich. Serve it from a slow cooker set to warm so the dip stays at its most tasty temperature.
—Rosalie Fuchs, Paynesville, MN

PREP: 5 MIN. • **COOK:** 2 HOURS
MAKES: 3½ CUPS

- 1   can (14 oz.) sauerkraut, rinsed and well drained
- 1   pkg. (8 oz.) cream cheese, cubed
- 2   cups shredded Swiss cheese
- 1   pkg. (3 oz.) deli corned beef, chopped
- 3   Tbsp. prepared Thousand Island salad dressing
     Snack rye bread or crackers

In a 1½-qt. slow cooker, combine the first 5 ingredients. Cover and cook on low for 2-3 hours or until cheeses are melted; stir to blend. Serve warm with bread or crackers.

2 Tbsp.: 69 cal., 6g fat (3g sat. fat), 18mg chol., 203mg sod., 1g carb. (1g sugars, 0 fiber), 3g pro.

READER REVIEW

"My sister sent this recipe to me last year, and I've made it at least a dozen times. The bottom line? Outstanding!"
—RICKSBRO, TASTEOFHOME.COM

ST. PATRICK'S DAY POPCORN

All your friends will have smilin' eyes when they see this candied corn with an Irish twist. The color gives the snack instant appeal.
—Karen Weber, Salem, MO

PREP: 15 MIN. + COOLING • **MAKES:** 6 QT.

- 4   qt. popped popcorn
- 1   cup sugar
- ½   cup packed brown sugar
- ½   cup water
- ½   cup light corn syrup
- 1   tsp. white vinegar
- ¼   tsp. salt
- ½   cup butter
- 8   to 10 drops green food coloring

1. Place popcorn in a large roasting pan; keep warm in a 250° oven. Meanwhile, in a large heavy saucepan, combine the sugars, water, corn syrup, vinegar and salt. Cook and stir over medium heat until the mixture comes to a boil. Cook, stirring occasionally, until a candy thermometer reads 260° (hard-ball stage).
2. Remove from heat; stir in the butter until melted. Stir in the food coloring. Drizzle over warm popcorn and toss to coat. Cool. Break into pieces. Store in an airtight container.

1 cup: 139 cal., 6g fat (3g sat. fat), 10mg chol., 138mg sod., 22g carb. (16g sugars, 1g fiber), 1g pro.

GUINNESS FLOAT

That very first sip of a Guinness is what inspired this quick and easy dessert. The rich, creamy foam that gathers on the top of a freshly poured draft made me think of vanilla ice cream. At that point, I knew I had to combine the two in a Guinness float.
—James Schend, Pleasant Prairie, WI

TAKES: 5 MIN. • **MAKES:** 2 FLOATS

- 1   cup vanilla ice cream, softened if necessary
- 2   cups Guinness or other stout beer
- 2   Tbsp. chocolate syrup

Divide ice cream between 2 glasses. Slowly top with beer; drizzle with chocolate syrup. Serve immediately.

1 serving: 286 cal., 7g fat (4g sat. fat), 29mg chol., 68mg sod., 36g carb. (31g sugars, 1g fiber), 4g pro.

PRESSURE-COOKER CLAM CHOWDER

Clam chowder is especially tasty when it's served with a sprinkle of fresh thyme, bacon crumbles and crispy oyster crackers on top. If you like your chowder on the thick side, add another tablespoon of flour after it is done in the pressure cooker.
—*Taste of Home* Test Kitchen

PREP: 20 MIN. • **COOK:** 25 MIN.
MAKES: 8 SERVINGS (2 QT.)

- 4 medium potatoes, peeled and cut into ½-in. cubes (about 5 cups)
- 1 medium onion, chopped
- 2 celery ribs, chopped
- 2 medium carrots, chopped
- 4 garlic cloves, minced
- 1 bottle (8 oz.) clam juice
- 1 cup chicken broth
- 1 tsp. dried thyme
- 1 tsp. salt
- ½ tsp. pepper
- 2 cans (6½ oz. each) minced clams, undrained
- 2 Tbsp. all-purpose flour
- 1 cup heavy whipping cream
- 4 bacon strips, cooked and crumbled
  Optional: Oyster crackers and fresh thyme

1. Place first 10 ingredients in a 6-qt. electric pressure cooker. Drain and reserve the liquid from clams; add the liquid to pressure cooker and set clams aside. Lock lid; close pressure-release valve. Adjust to pressure-cook on high for 15 minutes. Quick-release pressure.
2. Select saute setting and adjust for low heat. Mix flour and cream until smooth; stir into soup. Cook and stir until slightly thickened, 6-8 minutes. Stir in clams; heat through. Serve with bacon and, if desired, crackers and fresh thyme.

1 cup: 227 cal., 13g fat (7g sat. fat), 56mg chol., 673mg sod., 21g carb. (4g sugars, 2g fiber), 8g pro.

IRISH SODA BREAD MUFFINS

Irish soda bread is traditionally prepared in a loaf shape, but these muffins have the same terrific flavor.
—Lorraine Ballsieper, Deep River, CT

TAKES: 30 MIN. • **MAKES:** 1 DOZEN

- 2¼ cups all-purpose flour
- ½ cup plus 1 Tbsp. sugar, divided
- 2 tsp. baking powder
- ½ tsp. salt
- ¼ tsp. baking soda
- 1 tsp. caraway seeds
- 1 large egg, room temperature
- 1 cup buttermilk
- ¼ cup butter, melted
- ¼ cup canola oil
- ¾ cup dried currants or raisins

1. In a large bowl, combine the flour, ½ cup sugar, baking powder, salt, baking soda and caraway seeds. In another bowl, beat the egg, buttermilk, butter and oil. Stir into dry ingredients just until moistened. Fold in currants.
2. Fill greased muffin cups three-fourths full. Sprinkle with remaining sugar. Bake at 400° for 15 minutes or until a toothpick inserted in the center comes out clean. Cool for 5 minutes before removing from pan to wire rack. Serve warm.
1 serving: 235 cal., 9g fat (3g sat. fat), 28mg chol., 247mg sod., 35g carb. (17g sugars, 1g fiber), 4g pro.

LUCKY TABLE DECOR

Small details set the scene without going overboard. Hints of green and subtle nods to Irish culture will keep your celebration classy.

AIR-FRYER POTATO CHIPS

For Christmas last year, I received an air fryer. Potato chips are simple to make in it and are an essential, crispy side for lunch.
—Melissa Obernesser, Oriskany, NY

PREP: 30 MIN. • **COOK:** 15 MIN./BATCH
MAKES: 6 SERVINGS

- 2 large potatoes
  Olive oil-flavored cooking spray
- ½ tsp. sea salt
  Minced fresh parsley, optional

1. Preheat air fryer to 360°. Using a mandoline or vegetable peeler, cut potatoes into very thin slices. Transfer to a large bowl; add enough ice water to cover. Soak for 15 minutes; drain. Add more ice water and soak another 15 minutes.
2. Drain the potatoes; place on towels and pat dry. Spritz with cooking spray; sprinkle with salt. In batches, place potato slices in a single layer on tray in greased air-fryer basket. Cook until crisp and golden brown, 15-17 minutes, stirring and turning every 5-7 minutes. If desired, sprinkle with parsley.
1 cup: 148 cal., 1g fat (0 sat. fat), 0 chol., 252mg sod., 32g carb. (2g sugars, 4g fiber), 4g pro. **Diabetic exchanges:** 2 starch.

MINT CHOCOLATE CHEESECAKE

I created this mint chocolate cheesecake for our high school's annual fundraiser. We were told that it brought a hefty price and was one of the first desserts to go! If desired, the cookie pieces may be stirred into the batter instead of being added in a layer. Keep the pieces fairly small or they have a tendency to rise to the top.
—Sue Gronholz, Beaver Dam, WI

PREP: 20 MIN. • **BAKE:** 1¼ HOURS + CHILLING
MAKES: 16 SERVINGS

- 1 cup Oreo cookie crumbs
- 3 Tbsp. sugar
- 2 Tbsp. butter, melted

FILLING
- 4 pkg. (8 oz. each) cream cheese, softened
- 1 cup sugar
- 1 cup white baking chips, melted and cooled
- 6 Tbsp. creme de menthe
- ¼ cup all-purpose flour
- 2 Tbsp. creme de cacao
- ½ tsp. peppermint extract
- 4 large eggs, lightly beaten
- 1 cup coarsely crushed Oreo cookies (about 10 cookies)

GANACHE
- ¾ cup semisweet chocolate chips
- 6 Tbsp. heavy whipping cream

1. Preheat the oven to 325°. Place a greased 9-in. springform pan on a double thickness of heavy-duty foil (about 18 in. square). Wrap foil securely around pan. In a small bowl, mix cookie crumbs and sugar; stir in butter. Press onto bottom of prepared pan.
2. In a large bowl, beat cream cheese and sugar until smooth. Beat in cooled chips, creme de menthe, flour, creme de cacao and extract. Add eggs; beat on low speed just until blended. Pour half the batter over crust; sprinkle with crushed Oreos. Carefully spoon the remaining batter over top. Place the springform pan in a larger baking pan; add 1 in. hot water to larger pan.
3. Bake until center is just set and top appears dull, 75-80 minutes. Remove springform pan from water bath. Cool cheesecake on a wire rack 10 minutes. Loosen sides from pan with a knife; remove the foil. Cool 1 hour longer. Refrigerate overnight, covering when completely cooled.
4. Remove the rim from the pan. Place the chocolate chips in a small bowl. In a small saucepan, bring cream just to a boil. Pour over chocolate; stir with a whisk until smooth. Carefully spread over the cheesecake.
1 slice: 518 cal., 33g fat (18g sat. fat), 116mg chol., 296mg sod., 46g carb. (38g sugars, 1g fiber), 7g pro.

SPEAK LIKE A CELT

Celebrate as if you just came across the pond. Try these Irish Gaelic phrases at the table.

HAPPY ST. PATRICK'S DAY TO YOU.
Lá Fhéile Pádraig sona dhuit.
(Law ale-yeh pah-drig sunna gwitch.)

CHEERS!
Sláinte!
(SLAWN-cha!)

KISS ME; I'M IRISH.
Tabhair póg dom; taím Éireannach.
(Tower pahg dum; toyme AYE-ron-okh.)

A PINT OF GUINNESS, PLEASE.
Píonta Guinness, le do thoil.
(Pyun-tah Guinness, leh duh hul.)

3. Add cabbage to pot; return to a boil. Reduce heat; simmer, covered, until cabbage is tender, about 15 minutes. Remove vegetables and corned beef; keep warm.

4. For horseradish sauce, strain and reserve 1½ cups cooking juices; skim fat from reserved juices. Discard the remaining juices. In a small saucepan, melt the butter over medium heat; stir in flour until smooth. Gradually whisk in 1 cup reserved juices. Stir in sugar, vinegar and horseradish; bring to a boil, stirring constantly. Cook and stir until thickened. If desired, thin with additional juices and season to taste with additional sugar, vinegar or horseradish.

5. Cut beef across the grain into slices. Serve with vegetables and sauce.

1 serving with 2 Tbsp. horseradish sauce: 564 cal., 28g fat (10g sat. fat), 134mg chol., 1616mg sod., 50g carb. (11g sugars, 8g fiber), 29g pro.

FAVORITE CORNED BEEF & CABBAGE

It may be the most famous dish to eat on St. Patrick's Day, but this Irish-American classic is a favorite at our table all year long.
—Evelyn Kenney, Trenton, NJ

PREP: 10 MIN. • **COOK:** 2¾ HOURS
MAKES: 10 SERVINGS

- 1 corned beef brisket (about 4 lbs.) with spice packet
- 2 Tbsp. brown sugar
- 2 bay leaves
- 3½ lbs. small potatoes (10-15), peeled
- 8 medium carrots, halved crosswise
- 1 medium head cabbage, cut into wedges

HORSERADISH SAUCE

- 3 Tbsp. butter
- 2 Tbsp. all-purpose flour
- 1 Tbsp. sugar
- 1 Tbsp. cider vinegar
- ¼ cup horseradish

1. Place brisket, contents of seasoning packet, brown sugar and bay leaves in a large Dutch oven or stockpot; cover with water. Bring to a boil. Reduce heat; simmer, covered, 2 hours.

2. Add potatoes and carrots; return to a boil. Reduce heat; simmer, covered, just until the beef and vegetables are tender, 30-40 minutes. (If pot is full, remove potatoes and carrots before adding cabbage; reheat before serving.)

CORNED BEEF AND CABBAGE 101

WHAT'S THE BEST CUT OF CORNED BEEF TO BUY?
It depends on your personal preference. There are two cuts of brisket for corned beef: flat cut and point cut. The flat cut is square, has less fat, slices easily and is found in grocery stores more commonly. The point cut is pointed, has more fat and is better for shredding. Another option would be to purchase an entire brisket, which has the point and flat cuts, or a beef round, although that is a much less common cut for corned beef.

COLCANNON IRISH POTATOES

My mother came from Ireland as a teen and brought this homey recipe with her. I find that it's a fantastic way to get my family to eat cooked cabbage—it is hidden in Grandma's potatoes!
—Marie Pagel, Lena, WI

TAKES: 30 MIN. • **MAKES:** 10 SERVINGS

2½ lbs. potatoes (about 6 medium), peeled and cut into 1-in. pieces
2 cups chopped cabbage
1 large onion, chopped
1 tsp. salt
¼ tsp. pepper
¼ cup butter, softened
1 cup 2% milk

1. Place potatoes in a 6-qt. stockpot; add water to cover. Bring to a boil. Reduce heat to medium; cook, covered, until potatoes are almost tender, about 8-10 minutes.
2. Add the cabbage and onion; cook, covered, until cabbage is tender, about 5-7 minutes. Drain; return to pot. Add the salt and pepper; mash to desired consistency, gradually adding butter and milk.

¾ cup: 129 cal., 5g fat (3g sat. fat), 14mg chol., 290mg sod., 19g carb. (4g sugars, 2g fiber), 3g pro. **Diabetic exchanges:** 1 starch, 1 fat.

IRISH STEW PIE

The only thing more comforting than a hearty bowl of Irish stew is when it's baked into a pie! The flavors blend well with lamb, but you can use cuts of beef instead if you wish.
—Nicolas Hortense, Perth, AA

PREP: 1 HOUR • **BAKE:** 35 MIN. + STANDING
MAKES: 6 SERVINGS

½ cup plus 1 Tbsp. all-purpose flour, divided
¾ tsp. salt, divided
¾ tsp. pepper, divided
1 lb. boneless lamb shoulder roast, cubed
2 Tbsp. canola oil
2 medium carrots, finely chopped
1 medium onion, halved and sliced
1¼ cups beef stock
2 medium Yukon Gold potatoes, peeled and cubed
1 fresh thyme sprig
1 bay leaf
1 tsp. Worcestershire sauce
1 tsp. tomato paste
3 Tbsp. chopped fresh mint
1 large egg yolk
2 Tbsp. heavy whipping cream
1 pkg. (17.3 oz.) frozen puff pastry, thawed

1. Preheat oven to 350°. In a shallow bowl, mix ½ cup flour, ½ tsp. salt and ½ tsp. pepper. Add lamb, a few pieces at a time, and toss to coat; shake off excess. In a Dutch oven, heat oil over medium-high heat. Brown the lamb in batches. Remove from pan. Add carrots and onion to same pan; cook and stir until crisp-tender, 6-8 minutes. Stir in remaining 1 Tbsp. flour until blended; gradually whisk in stock. Bring to a boil, stirring to loosen the browned bits from the pan.
2. Add the potatoes, thyme, bay leaf, Worcestershire sauce, tomato paste, the remaining ¼ tsp. salt and ¼ tsp. pepper, and the lamb; return to a boil. Reduce heat. Simmer, uncovered, until sauce is thickened and lamb is tender, 25-30 minutes. Discard thyme sprig and bay leaf. Stir in mint. Transfer to a greased 9-in. deep-dish pie plate. Whisk egg yolk and cream; brush around edge of pie plate to help pastry adhere.
3. On a lightly floured surface, unfold 1 sheet puff pastry; top with remaining sheet. Roll to fit over pie plate. Carefully place over the filling; trim to fit. Using a fork, press the crust firmly onto rim of pie plate to seal edge. Brush with the remaining egg mixture; cut slits in top. Place on a rimmed baking sheet. Bake until golden brown, 35-40 minutes. Let stand 10 minutes before serving.

1 serving: 731 cal., 40g fat (11g sat. fat), 75mg chol., 608mg sod., 71g carb. (4g sugars, 8g fiber), 24g pro.

March Madness

Turn the man cave into the most delicious spot in your house by serving up these b-ball greats. You'll make everyone's hoop dreams come true when you turn on the games and they can settle in with savory favorites. In fact, these full-flavored dishes are so satisfying that you'll crave them all year long! Turn here any time you want to surprise the gang with a few finger-licking bites.

CHILI-CHOCOLATE CARAMEL CORN

Warning: It's really hard to walk away from this sweet, salty, spicy, crunchy snack. If you're taking it to a party, consider making a double batch because you won't come home with leftovers.
—*Taste of Home* Test Kitchen

TAKES: 10 MIN. • **MAKES:** 3½ QT.

2⅓ cups chocolate chips
2 Tbsp. shortening
  Dash ground ancho chili pepper
  Dash ground cinnamon
3½ qt. caramel popcorn with peanuts
1 cup dried cranberries, optional

In a microwave, melt chocolate chips and shortening; stir until smooth. Stir in chili pepper and cinnamon. Drizzle over caramel popcorn with peanuts; toss to coat. Arrange on a waxed paper-lined baking sheet. Refrigerate until set; break into pieces. If desired, add dried cranberries. Store caramel corn in an airtight container.

1 cup: 336 cal., 13g fat (6g sat. fat), 6mg chol., 97mg sod., 51g carb. (34g sugars, 3g fiber), 5g pro.

MUSTARD PRETZEL DIP

This flavorful dip is addictive, so be careful! It's also delicious served with pita chips, crackers and fresh veggies.
—Iola Egle, Bella Vista, AR

PREP: 10 MIN. + CHILLING
MAKES: 3½ CUPS

1 cup sour cream
1 cup mayonnaise
1 cup prepared mustard
½ cup sugar
¼ cup dried minced onion
1 envelope ranch salad dressing mix
1 Tbsp. prepared horseradish
  Sourdough pretzel nuggets

In a large bowl, combine the first 7 ingredients. Cover and refrigerate for at least 30 minutes. Serve with pretzels. Refrigerate leftovers.

2 Tbsp.: 101 cal., 8g fat (2g sat. fat), 8mg chol., 347mg sod., 6g carb. (4g sugars, 0 fiber), 1g pro.

REUBEN PUFF PASTRY STROMBOLI

I love this quick-to-fix, layered Reuben Stromboli. I used another sandwich recipe as a guide but made it with Reuben fixings instead. Switch things up by using sliced turkey and coleslaw instead of corned beef and sauerkraut.
—Joan Hallford, North Richland Hills, TX

PREP: 25 MIN. • **BAKE:** 40 MIN.
MAKES: 6 SERVINGS

1 sheet frozen puff pastry, thawed
⅔ cup Thousand Island salad dressing, divided
3 Tbsp. dill pickle relish
½ lb. thinly sliced deli corned beef
½ lb. thinly sliced deli pastrami
4 Tbsp. spicy brown mustard
8 slices Swiss or fontina cheese
1½ cups sauerkraut, rinsed and well drained
1 large egg white, lightly beaten
2 tsp. caraway seeds or sesame seeds

1. Preheat oven to 400°. On a lightly floured surface, unfold the puff pastry. Roll into a 14x11-in. rectangle. Spread ⅓ cup dressing to within ½ in. of edges. Sprinkle with relish. Layer with corned beef, pastrami, mustard, cheese and sauerkraut. Roll up jelly-roll style, starting with a long side. Place on a parchment-lined baking sheet, seam side down; tuck the ends under and press to seal.
2. Brush with egg white and sprinkle with caraway seeds; cut small slits in top. Bake until golden brown and pastry is cooked through, 40-45 minutes. Let stand 10 minutes before slicing. Serve with remaining dressing.

1 serving: 491 cal., 32g fat (10g sat. fat), 50mg chol., 1566mg sod., 32g carb. (4g sugars, 4g fiber), 18g pro.

HOISIN CHICKEN PIZZA

Use leftover or rotisserie chicken if you have it on hand. During the summer months, it's worth taking the time to grill fresh chicken to add a smokier flavor to the pizza.
—Jessie Apfel, Berkeley, CA

TAKES: 30 MIN.
MAKES: 2 PIZZAS (6 SERVINGS EACH)

- ¾ cup hoisin sauce, divided
- 1 Tbsp. rice vinegar
- 1 Tbsp. sesame oil
- 1½ tsp. minced fresh gingerroot
- 1 garlic cloves, minced
- 2 pkg. (6 oz. each) ready-to-use grilled chicken breast strips
- 16 large fresh mushrooms, thinly sliced
- 2 prebaked 12-in. pizza crusts
- 4 green onions, chopped
- 1 can (8 oz.) sliced water chestnuts, drained
- 4 cups (16 oz.) shredded part-skim mozzarella cheese

1. Preheat oven to 350°. In a small bowl, combine ½ cup hoisin, the vinegar, oil, gingerroot and garlic. In a large bowl, combine the chicken, mushrooms and remaining hoisin; toss to coat.
2. Place crusts on 2 ungreased 12-in. pizza pans. Spread hoisin mixture over crusts. Top with the chicken mixture, onions, water chestnuts and cheese.
3. Bake until heated through and the cheese is melted, 10-15 minutes.

1 piece: 380 cal., 13g fat (5g sat. fat), 41mg chol., 877mg sod., 44g carb. (8g sugars, 2g fiber), 23g pro.

MAPLE-BARBECUE PORK SANDWICHES

If you're serving this pork at a party, keep it warm in a slow cooker. Stir in water, a little at a time, if the mixture gets too thick.
—Sharlene Heatwole, McDowell, VA

PREP: 30 MIN. • **BAKE:** 2½ HOURS
MAKES: 10 SERVINGS

- 1 boneless pork shoulder butt roast (3 to 4 lbs.)
- 1 Tbsp. cider vinegar
- 1 cup ketchup
- 1 cup barbecue sauce
- ½ cup maple syrup
- 2 Tbsp. Dijon mustard
- 1 tsp. liquid smoke, optional
- ½ tsp. pepper
- ¼ tsp. salt
- 10 hamburger buns, split

1. Preheat oven to 350°. Place pork in a large roasting pan; brush with vinegar. Add ½ in. water to pan. Cover and bake until tender, 2½-3 hours. Remove roast; when cool enough to handle, shred meat with 2 forks.
2. In a large saucepan, combine the ketchup, barbecue sauce, maple syrup, Dijon mustard, liquid smoke if desired, pepper and salt. Bring to a boil over medium heat. Reduce heat; simmer, uncovered, for 2 minutes. Add pork; heat through. Serve on buns.

1 sandwich: 460 cal., 16g fat (5g sat. fat), 81mg chol., 1018mg sod., 50g carb. (28g sugars, 1g fiber), 28g pro.

TEST KITCHEN TIP

If you'd like your sandwiches to look like basketballs, draw lines on top of the buns using a black food-safe marker. Visit *Wilton.com* to find FoodWriter edible markers sold in a variety of colors.

MARCH MADNESS PARTY IDEAS

Kick off the "Big Dance" with a bash for sports lovers!

SEND GAME BRACKETS AS PARTY INVITATIONS
Have guests fill out the brackets before they arrive at the party so you will be able to start the fun with a basketball pool.

DECORATIONS
Orange and black are neutral basketball colors to use when decorating a March Madness party. If guests will all be cheering for the same team, by all means decorate accordingly.

USE A COOLER TO STORE DRINKS AT YOUR PARTY
In addition to serving soda, bottled water and beer, throw a couple of sports drinks like Gatorade in your cooler to create a game-time atmosphere.

DRESS THE PART
As the host, mix things up a bit by wearing a referee jersey and carrying a whistle.

WORLD'S GREATEST FAN
Create a basketball trivia game with questions about the teams playing in the games.

CRANK THE TUNES
Try something from the ESPN "Jock Jams" collection. These songs are designed to pump up fans during games.

PICKUP GAME
Guests won't mind helping pick up when you put a basketball hoop over your trash can.

ROASTED RED PEPPER, SPINACH & ARTICHOKE SPREAD

I found a simple spinach and artichoke spread in a cookbook and added my own touches—roasted red peppers, pesto, lemon zest and wine. You'll be surprised at how much your guests enjoy it.
—Be Jones, Brunswick, MO

PREP: 20 MIN. • **BAKE:** 30 MIN.
MAKES: 5 CUPS

- ½ cup white wine or chicken broth
- 2 shallots, minced
- 1 garlic clove, minced
- 1 can (10¾ oz.) reduced-fat reduced-sodium condensed cream of mushroom soup, undiluted
- 1 cup (8 oz.) reduced-fat sour cream
- ½ cup prepared pesto
- 2 Tbsp. all-purpose flour
- 1 Tbsp. reduced-sodium soy sauce
- 1 tsp. grated lemon zest
- ½ tsp. hot pepper sauce
- 2 pkg. (10 oz. each) frozen chopped spinach, thawed and squeezed dry
- 1 can (14 oz.) water-packed artichoke hearts, rinsed, drained and chopped
- ¾ cup roasted sweet red peppers, drained and chopped
- 2 cups shredded part-skim mozzarella cheese, divided Assorted crackers and/or breads

1. In a large skillet, combine the wine, shallots and garlic. Bring to a boil; cook until liquid is reduced to about 2 Tbsp. Stir in the soup, sour cream, pesto, flour, soy sauce, lemon zest and pepper sauce. Fold in the spinach, artichokes, red peppers and half the cheese.

2. Transfer to a greased 11x7-in. baking dish; sprinkle with remaining cheese. Bake at 400° until set, 30-35 minutes. Serve with crackers and/or breads.
¼ cup: 104 cal., 6g fat (2g sat. fat), 9mg chol., 341mg sod., 8g carb. (2g sugars, 1g fiber), 6g pro.

TEST KITCHEN TIP
This recipe makes a lot! Use up any leftovers as a sandwich spread or as a change-of-pace filling for meat-free quesadillas. It's also excellent over grilled chicken breasts or tossed with hot pasta.

STICKY HONEY CHICKEN WINGS

This chicken wings recipe was given to me by a special lady who was like a grandmother to me.
—Marisa Raponi, Vaughan, ON

PREP: 15 MIN. + MARINATING
BAKE: 30 MIN. **MAKES:** 3 DOZEN

- ½ cup orange blossom honey
- ⅓ cup white vinegar
- 2 Tbsp. paprika
- 2 tsp. salt
- 1 tsp. pepper
- 4 lbs. chicken wings

1. Combine honey, vinegar, paprika, salt and pepper in a small bowl.
2. Cut through the 2 wing joints with a sharp knife, discarding wing tips. Add the remaining wing pieces and honey mixture to a large bowl; stir to coat. Cover and refrigerate at least 4 hours or overnight.
3. Preheat oven to 375°. Remove wings; reserve honey mixture. Place wings on greased 15x10x1-in. baking pans. Bake until juices run clear, about 30 minutes, turning halfway through.
4. Meanwhile, place reserved honey mixture in a small saucepan. Bring to a boil; cook 1 minute.
5. Remove wings from oven; preheat broiler. Place wings on a greased rack in a broiler pan; brush with the honey mixture. Broil 4-5 in. from heat until crispy, about 3-5 minutes. Serve with the remaining honey mixture.
1 piece: 71 cal., 4g fat (1g sat. fat), 16mg chol., 147mg sod., 4g carb. (4g sugars, 0 fiber), 5g pro.

BEER & SMOKED SAUSAGE STEW

Cold weather means it's time for hearty, comforting meals. This slow-cooker stew is perfect for keeping warm on even the coldest nights, and the meal is ready when you are. Feel free to add corn, peas, green beans, etc.
—Jesi Allen, Gastonia, NC

PREP: 10 MIN. • **COOK:** 8 HOURS
MAKES: 12 SERVINGS

- 4 large potatoes, cubed
- 2 lbs. smoked sausage, cut into ¾-in. pieces
- 2 bottles (12 oz. each) beer
- 2 cups reduced-sodium chicken broth
- 2 ribs celery, sliced
- 1 medium onion, chopped
- 2 garlic cloves, minced
- 2 bay leaves
- ½ tsp. minced fresh thyme
- ¼ tsp. minced fresh rosemary
- 2 Tbsp. butter, cubed

In a 6-qt. slow cooker, combine the first 10 ingredients. Dot with butter. Cook, covered, on low until vegetables are tender, 8-10 hours. Discard bay leaves before serving.
1 cup: 357 cal., 22g fat (10g sat. fat), 56mg chol., 979mg sod., 25g carb. (4g sugars, 3g fiber), 14g pro.

CHOCOLATE-PEANUT BUTTER CUP COOKIES

If you want to still enjoy one of these soft, fully loaded treats the day after you make them, you'd better find a good hiding spot.
—Jennifer Krey, Clarence, NY

PREP: 25 MIN. • **BAKE:** 10 MIN./BATCH
MAKES: 4 DOZEN

- 1 cup butter, softened
- ¾ cup creamy peanut butter
- 1 cup packed brown sugar
- ½ cup sugar
- 2 large egg yolks, room temperature
- ¼ cup 2% milk
- 2 tsp. vanilla extract
- 2⅓ cups all-purpose flour
- ⅓ cup baking cocoa
- 1 tsp. baking soda
- 1 cup milk chocolate chips
- 1 cup peanut butter chips
- 6 pkg. (1½ oz. each) peanut butter cups, chopped

1. Preheat oven to 350°. In a large bowl, cream butter, peanut butter and sugars until light and fluffy, 5-7 minutes. Beat in egg yolks, milk and vanilla. Combine flour, cocoa and baking soda; gradually add to creamed mixture and mix well. Stir in chips and peanut butter cups.
2. Drop heaping tablespoonfuls 2 in. apart onto ungreased baking sheets. Bake 8-10 minutes or until set (do not overbake). Cool 2 minutes before removing from pans to wire racks. Store in an airtight container.
1 cookie: 170 cal., 10g fat (4g sat. fat), 20mg chol., 100mg sod., 18g carb. (12g sugars, 1g fiber), 3g pro.

SOUR CREAM SUGAR COOKIE CAKE

My husband requested a giant sugar cookie for his birthday. I wanted to do something a bit more exciting than big birthday cookies, so I came up with this sugar cookie cake. The secret to a dense yet cakelike texture is to make sure that you don't overbake the cake.
—Carmell Childs, Orangeville, UT

PREP: 20 MIN. • **BAKE:** 20 MIN. + COOLING
MAKES: 20 SERVINGS

- ½ cup butter, softened
- 1½ cups sugar
- 2 large eggs, room temperature
- 1 tsp. vanilla extract
- 3 cups all-purpose flour
- ¾ tsp. salt
- ½ tsp. baking powder
- ½ tsp. baking soda
- 1 cup sour cream
- 1 can (16 oz.) vanilla frosting
  Optional: Coarse sugar, sprinkles and additional frosting

1. Preheat oven to 350°. In a large bowl, cream butter and sugar until light and fluffy, 5-7 minutes. Beat in eggs and vanilla. In another bowl, whisk flour, salt, baking powder and baking soda; add to the creamed mixture alternately with sour cream, beating after each addition just until combined. Spread into a greased 13x9-in. baking pan.
2. Bake until a toothpick inserted in the center comes out clean, 20-25 minutes. Cool completely on a wire rack. Spread frosting over top. Decorate with optional toppings as desired.
1 piece: 295 cal., 11g fat (6g sat. fat), 34mg chol., 228mg sod., 46g carb. (29g sugars, 1g fiber), 3g pro.

Easter Egg Decorating Party

Invite friends and little ones over for an Easter egg decorating party! Here you'll find fun new ways to decorate eggs, some family-friendly recipes perfect for a springtime gathering and cute-as-can-be sweet treats. Let's decorate!

DIY EASTER EGG DYE

In a glass cup, mix ½ cup boiling water, 1 tsp. white vinegar and drops of food coloring to reach your desired color.

HAM & CHEESE LOAF

This golden loaf starts with convenient refrigerated dough and is stuffed with deli ham and three types of cheese. I created the recipe by experimenting with ingredients my family loves. It makes a delicious hot sandwich in hardly any time.
—Gloria Lindell, Welcome, MN

PREP: 15 MIN. • **BAKE:** 30 MIN.
MAKES: 6 SERVINGS

1   tube (13.8 oz.) refrigerated pizza crust
10 slices deli ham
¼   cup sliced green onions
1   cup shredded part-skim mozzarella cheese
1   cup shredded cheddar cheese
4   slices provolone cheese
1   Tbsp. butter, melted

1. Preheat oven to 350°. Unroll dough onto a greased baking sheet; top with the ham, onions and cheeses. Roll up tightly jelly-roll style, starting with a long side; pinch the seam to seal and tuck the ends under. Brush with butter.
2. Bake 30-35 minutes or until golden brown. Let stand for 5 minutes; cut into 1-in. slices.
Freeze option: Cool unsliced loaf on a wire rack. Spray a large piece of foil with cooking spray. Wrap the loaf in prepared foil and freeze up to 3 months. To use, thaw at room temperature for 2 hours. Unwrap and place on a greased baking sheet. Bake at 350° for 15-20 minutes or until heated through. Let stand for 5 minutes; cut into 1-in. slices.
2 slices: 406 cal., 18g fat (10g sat. fat), 65mg chol., 1151mg sod., 34g carb. (5g sugars, 1g fiber), 26g pro.

CUPCAKE EASTER BASKETS

These cute cupcakes with their mild orange flavor are fun to dress up for Easter. As we raised four sons and a daughter, I prepared many, many school lunches and often added these springtime treats.
—Julie Johnston, Shaunavon, SK

PREP: 20 MIN. • **BAKE:** 20 MIN. + COOLING
MAKES: 1½ DOZEN

½   cup butter, softened
1   cup sugar
1   large egg, room temperature
1   tsp. grated orange zest
2   cups cake flour
¾   tsp. baking soda
½   tsp. baking powder
¼   tsp. salt
⅔   cup buttermilk

FROSTING
¾   cup butter, softened
6   oz. cream cheese, softened
1   tsp. vanilla extract
3   cups confectioners' sugar
1   tsp. water
4   drops green food coloring
1½ cups sweetened shredded coconut
    Chocolate licorice twists
    Chocolate egg candy

1. Preheat oven to 350°. In a large bowl, cream the butter and sugar until light and fluffy, 5-7 minutes. Beat in the egg and orange zest. Combine flour, baking soda, baking powder and salt; add to the creamed mixture alternately with the buttermilk.
2. Fill 18 paper-lined muffin cups two-thirds full. Bake until a toothpick comes out clean, 20-25 minutes. Cool for 10 minutes before removing from pans to wire racks to cool completely.
3. For the frosting, in a small bowl, beat butter, cream cheese and vanilla until smooth. Gradually beat in confectioners' sugar; spread over cupcakes. Combine the water and food coloring in a large bowl; add coconut. Stir to coat. Sprinkle over the cupcakes.
4. Using a metal or wooden skewer, poke 2 holes in the top of each cupcake, 1 hole on each side. Cut licorice into 6-in. strips for handles; insert each end of a licorice piece into a hole. Decorate with candy eggs.
1 cupcake: 351 cal., 18g fat (11g sat. fat), 51mg chol., 273mg sod., 47g carb. (33g sugars, 1g fiber), 3g pro.

AUNT FRANCES' LEMONADE

My sister and I spent a week each summer with our Aunt Frances, who always had this lemonade in a stoneware crock in her refrigerator. It makes a refreshing drink after a hot day of running around.
—Debbie Reinhart, New Cumberland, PA

TAKES: 15 MIN.
MAKES: 16 SERVINGS (1 GALLON)

- 5 lemons
- 5 limes
- 5 oranges
- 3 qt. water
- 1½ to 2 cups sugar

1. Squeeze the juice from 4 each of the lemons, limes and oranges; pour into a gallon container.
2. Thinly slice the remaining fruit and set aside for garnish. Add water and sugar to the juice mixture; mix well. Store in the refrigerator. Serve over ice with fruit slices.

1 cup: 92 cal., 0 fat (0 sat. fat), 0 chol., 1mg sod., 24g carb. (21g sugars, 1g fiber), 0 pro.

EDAMAME HUMMUS

We love hummus at our house. This recipe is a scrumptious and refreshing twist on an old favorite, and it's a wonderful way to incorporate healthy soy into our diets.
—Marla Clark, Albuquerque, NM

TAKES: 15 MIN. • **MAKES:** 3 CUPS

- 1 pkg. (16 oz.) frozen shelled edamame, thawed
- ½ cup tahini
- ½ cup water
- ⅓ to ½ cup lemon juice
- 2 garlic cloves, minced
- 1 tsp. sea salt
- ¼ cup olive oil
- ¼ cup minced fresh mint
- 2 jalapeno peppers, seeded and chopped
  Assorted fresh vegetables
  Rice crackers

Microwave the edamame, covered, on high until tender, 2-3 minutes. Transfer to a food processor; add the next 8 ingredients. Process until smooth, 1-2 minutes. Serve with assorted fresh vegetables and rice crackers.

¼ cup: 167 cal., 13g fat (2g sat. fat), 0 chol., 167mg sod., 7g carb. (1g sugars, 2g fiber), 7g pro.

STRAWBERRY RICOTTA BRUSCHETTA

Here's an interesting spin on bruschetta. The creamy ricotta cheese spread is an ideal complement to the sweet, minty strawberry topping.
—Laura Stricklin, Jackson, MS

TAKES: 25 MIN. • **MAKES:** 2 DOZEN

- 24 slices French bread baguette (½ in. thick)
- 3 Tbsp. butter, melted
- 3 cups fresh strawberries, chopped
- 3 Tbsp. minced fresh mint
- 3 Tbsp. honey
- ½ cup ricotta cheese
- 2 Tbsp. seedless strawberry jam
- 1½ tsp. grated lemon zest

1. Preheat oven to 375°. Brush the bread slices with butter; place on an ungreased baking sheet. Bake for 8-10 minutes or until lightly browned.
2. Meanwhile, in a small bowl, combine the strawberries, mint and honey; set aside. In another bowl, combine the ricotta, jam and lemon zest. Spread ricotta mixture over toast; top with strawberry mixture.

1 piece: 89 cal., 3g fat (1g sat. fat), 6mg chol., 88mg sod.,14g carb. (4g sugars, 1g fiber), 2g pro. **Diabetic exchanges:** 1 starch, ½ fat.

READER REVIEW

"A fab way to use up small strawberries! We cut up the berries, added the honey and mint, and let them sit for a little while to help the flavors meld. You can substitute flavored kinds of honey for the regular honey if you want a slightly different flavor."
—NH-RESCUE, TASTEOFHOME.COM

EASY EGG DESIGNS

Embrace your inner artist with one of these easy techniques to decorate eggs.

MARBLE

For a marbled effect, add a few drops of food coloring to a bowl of whipped cream and swirl it using a toothpick. Roll eggs in the rainbow mixture and let sit for 45 minutes to an hour before rinsing in water.

MESSAGE

To add a message, dip eggs in your choice of homemade or store-bought egg dyes. Let dry, then write words, draw pictures or add patterns on the eggs using an opaque white food-safe marker.

STAMP

To stamp a pattern, use mini rubber stamps—like the flower varieties shown here—dipped in food dye poured onto a paper towel or napkin. Make sure you choose tiny stamps so you can see the entire shape.

MARSHMALLOW EASTER EGGS

I've been making this delightful Easter candy for years. These eggs are a big hit with everyone who loves marshmallows.
—Betty Claycomb, Alverton, PA

PREP: 45 MIN. + STANDING • **COOK:** 15 MIN.
MAKES: ABOUT 3 DOZEN

- 25 cups all-purpose flour (about 8 lbs.)
- 1 large egg
- 2 Tbsp. unflavored gelatin
- ½ cup cold water
- 2 cups sugar
- 1 cup light corn syrup, divided
- ¾ cup hot water
- 2 tsp. vanilla extract
- 1 lb. dark chocolate candy coating, melted
  Candy coating disks, multiple colors

1. Spread 7 cups flour in each of three 13x9-in. pans and 4 cups flour in a 9-in. square pan. Carefully wash egg in a mild bleach solution (1 tsp. chlorine bleach to 1 qt. warm water); dry. Press egg halfway into the flour to form an impression. Repeat 35 times, making impressions 2 in. apart; set aside.
2. In a small bowl, sprinkle the gelatin over cold water; set aside.
3. In a large saucepan, combine sugar, ½ cup corn syrup and hot water. Bring to a boil over medium heat, stirring constantly, until a candy thermometer reads 238° (soft-ball stage). Remove from heat; stir in remaining corn syrup.
4. Pour into a large bowl. Add reserved gelatin, 1 Tbsp. at a time, beating on high speed until candy is thick and has cooled to lukewarm, about 10 minutes. Beat in vanilla.
5. Spoon lukewarm gelatin mixture into the egg depressions; dust with flour. Let stand for 3-4 hours or until set.
6. Brush excess flour off marshmallow eggs. Dip each egg in chocolate candy coating. Place flat side down on waxed paper. Let stand until set. Drizzle each colored candy coating over eggs.
1 piece: 147 cal., 4g fat (4g sat. fat), 0 chol., 7mg sod., 28g carb. (28g sugars, 0 fiber), 1g pro.

TEST KITCHEN TIP
Instead of using a real egg, you can use a plastic egg to make the impressions in the flour. When your marshmallows are set, sift the flour to remove any stray pieces of marshmallow; you can save any pieces for a future use.

EASTER BUNNY TREATS

Our whole family has fun making these bunny-riffic treats together. They are just so cute!
—Holly Jost, Manitowoc, WI

TAKES: 15 MIN. • **MAKES:** 1 DOZEN

⅓ cup vanilla frosting
36 large marshmallows
36 miniature marshmallows
  Red and pink heart-shaped decorating sprinkles
  Small black nonpareils
  White jimmies
  Pink colored sugar

Place frosting in piping bag. For each bunny, cut 2 mini marshmallows in half and use frosting to attach them to a large marshmallow to form arms and legs. For the face, attach 2 mini marshmallow halves for cheeks. Use white jimmies, black nonpareils and heart-shaped sprinkles to form the whiskers, eyes and nose. For the ears, cut a large marshmallow in half diagonally. Dip each sticky side in colored sugar and use frosting to attach the ears to the top of the large marshmallow. Use frosting to connect the 2 large marshmallows; let stand until dry.

1 treat: 128 cal., 2g fat (1g sat. fat), 0 chol., 48mg sod., 27g carb. (20g sugars, 0 fiber), 0 pro.

SPECIAL STUFFED STRAWBERRIES

These sweet bites can be made ahead of time, and they look really colorful on a tray. I sometimes sprinkle the piped filling with finely chopped pistachio nuts.
—Marcia Orlando, Boyertown, PA

TAKES: 20 MIN. • **MAKES:** 2 DOZEN

- 24 **large fresh strawberries**
- ½ **cup spreadable strawberry cream cheese**
- 3 **Tbsp. sour cream**
  Graham cracker crumbs

1. Place strawberries on a cutting board and cut off tops; remove bottom tips so they sit flat. Using a small paring knife, hull out the center of each berry.

2. In a small bowl, beat cream cheese and sour cream until smooth. Pipe or spoon filling into each berry. Top with crushed graham crackers. Refrigerate until serving.

1 strawberry: 18 cal., 1g fat (1g sat. fat), 4mg chol., 22mg sod., 1g carb. (1g sugars, 0 fiber), 1g pro.

READER REVIEW

"These were so easy to make and tasted so good. I need to find other ways to use this filling—maybe spread it on top of a shortcake and cover it with glazed strawberries. Mmmmm, sounds good!"
—IMPAGANMISS, TASTEOFHOME.COM

EASTER SUGAR COOKIES

Cream cheese contributes to the rich taste of these melt-in-your-mouth cookies. They have such nice flavor, you can even skip the frosting and sprinkle them with colored sugar for a change.
—Julie Brunette, Green Bay, WI

PREP: 15 MIN. + CHILLING
BAKE: 10 MIN./BATCH • **MAKES:** 4 DOZEN

- 1 **cup butter, softened**
- 3 **oz. cream cheese, softened**
- 1 **cup sugar**
- 1 **large egg yolk, room temperature**
- ½ **tsp. vanilla extract**
- ¼ **tsp. almond extract**
- 2¼ **cups all-purpose flour**
- ½ **tsp. salt**
- ¼ **tsp. baking soda**
  Tinted frosting or colored sugar

1. In a bowl, cream the butter, cream cheese and sugar. Beat in the egg yolk and extracts. Combine the flour, salt and baking soda; gradually add to the creamed mixture. Cover and refrigerate for 3 hours or until easy to handle.

2. Preheat oven to 375°. On a lightly floured surface, roll out the dough to ⅛-in. thickness. Cut with a 2½-in. cookie cutter dipped in flour. Place the cutouts 1 in. apart on ungreased baking sheets. Bake until the edges begin to brown, 8-10 minutes. Cool for 2 minutes before removing from the pans to wire racks. Decorate as desired.

1 cookie: 79 cal., 5g fat (3g sat. fat), 16mg chol., 67mg sod., 9g carb. (4g sugars, 0 fiber), 1g pro.

PBJ ON A STICK

Take the classic peanut butter and jelly sandwich on the go with these skewers. They also make easy snacks.
—Sara Martin, Brookfield, WI

TAKES: 10 MIN. • **MAKES:** 4 SKEWERS

- 2 **peanut butter and jelly sandwiches**
- 1 **cup seedless red or green grapes**
- 1 **small banana, sliced**
- 4 **wooden skewers (5 to 6 in.)**

Cut sandwiches into 1-in. squares. Alternately thread grapes, sandwich squares and banana slices onto each skewer. Serve immediately.

2 skewers: 415 cal., 14g fat (3g sat. fat), 0 chol., 368mg sod., 63g carb. (30g sugars, 7g fiber), 13g pro.

Easter Dinner

After months of cold weather and cabin fever, the sun is shining, the birds are chirping and spring plans are in the making. Gather the family to feast on the season's favorites with a modern and chic Easter dinner. Get ready for compliments when you set a California-inspired roast lamb on the table alongside a fresh, colorful array of accompaniments and desserts.

Easter Day Countdown

Refer to this handy cooking timeline to help you create a modern, elegant Easter gathering that's celebratory and delicious!

A FEW WEEKS BEFORE

☐ Bake the Whole Wheat Dinner Rolls, but do not brush with butter. Wrap securely in an airtight container and store in the freezer.

☐ Prepare the dough for the Gougeres, but do not bake. Freeze unbaked puffs on parchment-lined sheets until firm; transfer puffs to freezer bags and return to freezer.

THE DAY BEFORE

☐ Bake Easy Scottish Shortbread. Store in an airtight container.

☐ If you don't have hard-boiled Easter eggs, prepare eggs for Smoked Deviled Eggs. Cover and store in the refrigerator.

☐ Bake the cake layers for the Pineapple Carrot Cake, but do not assemble. Store unfrosted layers in an airtight container.

☐ Make the Poppy Seed Snack Crisps & Vegetable Spread. Store crisps in an airtight container. Store spread in the refrigerator.

☐ Prepare the Rhubarb Relish. Let cool and store in the refrigerator until ready to serve.

EASTER DAY

☐ In the morning, remove dinner rolls from the freezer to thaw. Assemble and frost carrot cake; refrigerate until ready to serve.

☐ Make the Lemon Polenta-Topped Berry Cobbler; cover and set aside until ready to serve. Mix together the Raspberry Lemonade ingredients, minus the club soda and ice; refrigerate.

☐ About 4-5 hours before dinner, grill deviled eggs (use prepared hard-boiled eggs or leftover Easter eggs). Pipe filling into eggs and top with paprika and parsley if desired. Cover and refrigerate until ready to serve.

☐ About 4 hours before dinner, bake the California Roast Lamb and/or the Apricot-Glazed Ham. Keep meats warm until serving.

☐ Prepare Roasted Asparagus immediately after removing the lamb or ham from oven. Roast for 12-15 minutes; keep warm until ready to serve.

☐ About 45 minutes before dinner, assemble the Three-Green Salad and make the Italian dressing. Chill, separately, in the fridge for at least 30 minutes.

☐ About 30 minutes before dinner, removed frozen dough for the Gougeres from the freezer. Top and bake as directed.

☐ About 30 minutes before dinner, prepare the Creamed Garden Potatoes & Peas and Buttery Carrots.

☐ About 10 minutes before dinner, reheat the rolls in the oven. Brush with melted butter and serve warm.

☐ Just before dinner, remove salad and dressing from the refrigerator. Shake dressing and toss with salad to coat.

☐ Just before dinner, add club soda and ice to the Raspberry Lemonade. Serve immediately.

☐ After dinner, reheat the cobbler in the oven; serve warm. Serve with carrot cake and shortbread.

WHOLE WHEAT DINNER ROLLS

It always does my heart good to see everyone at our table reach for one of my hearty whole wheat rolls. They're rich with old-fashioned goodness and bake to a beautiful golden brown.
—Ruby Williams, Bogalusa, LA

PREP: 30 MIN. + RISING • **BAKE:** 15 MIN.
MAKES: 4 DOZEN

  2 pkg. (¼ oz. each) active dry yeast
2¼ cups warm water (110° to 115°)
  ½ cup plus 1 Tbsp. sugar
  ¼ cup shortening
  2 tsp. salt
  2 large eggs, room temperature
  3 cups whole wheat flour
3½ to 4 cups all-purpose flour
  ¼ cup butter, melted

1. In a large bowl, dissolve yeast in warm water. Add the sugar, shortening, salt, eggs and whole wheat flour. Beat until smooth. Stir in enough all-purpose flour to form a soft dough.

2. Turn onto a floured surface; knead until smooth and elastic, 6-8 minutes. Place in a greased bowl, turning once to grease top. Cover and let rise in a warm place until doubled, about 1 hour.

3. Punch dough down. Turn onto a lightly floured surface; divide into 4 pieces. Shape each into 12 balls. Place 1 in. apart on greased baking sheets. Cover and let dough rise until doubled, about 25 minutes.

4. Bake at 375° for 11-15 minutes or until browned. Remove from pans to wire racks. Brush with melted butter. Serve warm.

1 roll: 89 cal., 2g fat (1g sat. fat), 11mg chol., 111mg sod., 15g carb. (3g sugars, 1g fiber), 2g pro.

2. Shake dressing before serving; pour desired amount over salad and toss to coat.

1 cup: 136 cal., 12g fat (2g sat. fat), 1mg chol., 51mg sod., 5g carb. (2g sugars, 2g fiber), 2g pro. **Diabetic exchanges:** 2 fat, 1 vegetable.

SMOKED DEVILED EGGS

Give all those leftover Easter eggs a flavor upgrade. Grilling these smoked deviled eggs gives them a distinctive taste that will have everyone talking.
—Catherine Woods, Lexington, MO

PREP: 20 MIN. • **GRILL:** 10 MIN. + CHILLING
MAKES: 2 DOZEN

½ cup soaked hickory wood chips
12 hard-cooked large eggs, peeled
½ cup Miracle Whip
1 tsp. prepared mustard
¼ tsp. salt
⅛ tsp. pepper
⅛ tsp. paprika
Minced fresh parsley, optional

1. Add wood chips to grill according to manufacturer's directions. Place eggs on grill rack. Grill, covered, over indirect medium heat for 7-10 minutes or until golden brown. Cool slightly.
2. Cut eggs lengthwise in half. Remove yolks, reserving whites. In a small bowl, mash yolks. Stir in the Miracle Whip, mustard, salt, pepper and paprika. Spoon or pipe into egg whites. Top with additional paprika and chopped parsley if desired. Refrigerate eggs, covered, until serving.

1 stuffed egg half: 52 cal., 4g fat (1g sat. fat), 94mg chol., 91mg sod., 1g carb. (1g sugars, 0 fiber), 3g pro.

THREE-GREEN SALAD

This bright, beautiful vegetable salad is a fine addition to any celebration—and it's good for you, too. The homemade Italian dressing can't be beat.
—Gina Squires, Salem, OR

PREP: 15 MIN. + CHILLING
MAKES: 12 SERVINGS (ABOUT ¾ CUP DRESSING)

4 cups torn iceberg lettuce
4 cups torn leaf lettuce
4 cups torn fresh spinach
1 medium cucumber, sliced
2 carrots, sliced
2 celery ribs, sliced
6 fresh broccoli florets, sliced
3 fresh cauliflowerets, sliced
6 radishes, sliced
4 green onions, sliced
5 fresh mushrooms, sliced
ITALIAN DRESSING
⅓ cup olive oil
¼ cup plus 2 Tbsp. red wine vinegar
2 Tbsp. grated Parmesan cheese
1 tsp. sugar
1 to 2 garlic cloves, minced
¼ tsp. dried oregano
¼ tsp. dried basil
Pinch salt and pepper

1. In a large salad bowl, toss the greens and vegetables. Cover and chill. In a blender, combine all of the dressing ingredients; cover and process until blended. Pour into a jar with tight-fitting lid; chill for at least 30 minutes.

POPPY SEED SNACK CRISPS & VEGETABLE SPREAD

I developed these crunchy crisps as a fun and healthy snack for a wedding shower. They're delicious with the homemade vegetable spread, or try them with preserves or jam.

—Awynne Thurstenson, Siloam Springs, AR

PREP: 1½ HOURS + RISING • **BAKE:** 15 MIN.
MAKES: 34 DOZEN CRISPS (1 CUP SPREAD)

- 1 pkg. (¼ oz.) active dry yeast
- 1½ cups warm water (110° to 115°)
- ¼ cup canola oil
- 2 Tbsp. sugar
- 2 Tbsp. poppy seeds
- 2 tsp. salt
- 3 to 4 cups bread flour

VEGETABLE SPREAD
- 1 medium cucumber, peeled, seeded and grated
- 1 tsp. salt
- 1 pkg. (8 oz.) cream cheese, softened
- ¼ tsp. garlic powder
- 1 small carrot, grated

1. In a large bowl, dissolve yeast in warm water. Add the oil, sugar, poppy seeds, salt and 2 cups flour. Beat on medium speed for 3 minutes. Stir in enough remaining flour to form a soft dough (dough will be sticky).
2. Turn onto a floured surface; knead until smooth and elastic, 6-8 minutes. Place in a greased bowl, turning once to grease the top. Cover and let rise in a warm place until doubled, about 1 hour.
3. Punch dough down. Divide into fourths. Shape each into a 13-in. log. Place on baking sheets. Cover and let rise in a warm place until doubled, about 30 minutes.
4. Bake at 350° for 15-20 minutes or until golden brown. Cool completely.
5. Cut into ⅛-in. slices; place slices on ungreased baking sheets. Bake at 350° for 15-20 minutes or until golden brown and crisp.
6. Meanwhile, place cucumber in a colander over a plate; sprinkle with salt and toss. Let stand 30 minutes. Drain and pat dry. In a small bowl, beat the cream cheese and garlic powder until smooth. Beat in carrot and cucumber. Serve with crisps. Store leftover crisps in an airtight container.

1 cracker with 1 tsp. spread: 24 cal., 2g fat (1g sat. fat), 5mg chol., 76mg sod., 1g carb. (0 sugars, 0 fiber), 1g pro.

RASPBERRY LEMONADE

Sweet and tangy raspberry lemonade makes the perfect spring drink. Pretty enough to serve at a formal dinners and picnics alike, it's a fun change from iced tea or regular lemonade.

—Dorothy Jennings, Waterloo, IA

TAKES: 15 MIN. • **MAKES:** 3½ QT.

- 2 cans (12 oz. each) frozen lemonade concentrate, thawed
- 2 pkg. (10 oz. each) frozen sweetened raspberries, partially thawed
- 2 to 4 Tbsp. sugar
- 2 liters club soda, chilled
  Ice cubes

In a blender, combine the lemonade concentrate, raspberries and sugar. Cover and process until blended. Strain to remove seeds. In a 4½-qt. container, combine raspberry mixture, club soda and ice cubes. Serve immediately.

1 cup: 144 cal., 0 fat (0 sat. fat), 0 chol., 34mg sod., 37g carb. (32g sugars, 2g fiber), 0 pro.

CREAMED GARDEN POTATOES & PEAS

New potatoes and peas are treated to a creamy sauce in this special side.
—Jane Uphoff, Cunningham, KS

TAKES: 25 MIN. • **MAKES:** 12 SERVINGS

- 2 lbs. small red potatoes, quartered
- 3 cups fresh or frozen peas
- 1 cup water
- 2 Tbsp. chopped onion
- 2 Tbsp. butter
- 3 Tbsp. plus 1 tsp. all-purpose flour
- 1½ tsp. salt
- ¼ tsp. pepper
- 2 cups 2% milk
- 1 cup half-and-half cream

1. Place potatoes in a large saucepan and cover with water. Bring to a boil. Reduce heat; cover and simmer until tender, 8-12 minutes. Drain.
2. Meanwhile, place peas and water in a small saucepan. Bring to a boil. Reduce heat; cover and simmer until tender, 3-5 minutes. Drain.
3. In a large saucepan, saute onion in butter until tender. Stir in the flour, salt and pepper until blended; gradually add milk and cream. Bring to a boil; cook and stir until sauce is thickened, about 2 minutes. Stir in potatoes and peas; heat through.
⅔ cup: 156 cal., 5g fat (3g sat. fat), 18mg chol., 345mg sod., 22g carb. (6g sugars, 3g fiber), 6g pro. **Diabetic exchanges:** 1½ starch, 1 fat.

APRICOT-GLAZED HAM

(PICTURED ON BACK COVER)

I glaze a bone-in ham with apricot jam to give it an attractive look and delicious flavor. It's the star of any special dinner, and yields lots of extra ham for meals you can put together in minutes later in the week.
—Galelah Dowell, Fairland, OK

PREP: 15 MIN. • **BAKE:** 1¼ HOURS
MAKES: 20 SERVINGS

 1   **fully cooked bone-in ham (6 to 8 lbs.)**
 ½   **cup packed brown sugar**
 2   **to 3 Tbsp. ground mustard**
     Whole cloves
 ½   **cup apricot preserves**

1. Place ham on a rack in a shallow roasting pan. Score the surface of the ham, making diamond shapes ½ in. deep. Combine brown sugar and mustard; rub over surface of ham. Insert a whole clove in the center of each diamond.
2. Place ham on a rack in a shallow roasting pan. Bake, uncovered, at 325° for 1 hour. Spoon preserves over ham. Bake 15-30 minutes longer or until a thermometer reads 140° and ham is heated through.

3 oz. cooked ham: 233 cal., 13g fat (5g sat. fat), 48mg chol., 926mg sod., 11g carb. (8g sugars, 0 fiber), 17g pro.

HOW TO CARVE PERFECT HAM SLICES

Carving a ham is easy! You're just four steps away from beautiful slices worthy of your best Easter serving platter.

STEP 1
Begin by cutting off the cushion (boneless) portion of the meat.

STEP 2
Holding the cushion portion steady with a meat fork, cut it into even slices from the top down.

STEP 3
Cut the remaining (bone-in) portion of the ham horizontally above the bone.

STEP 4
Carve into even vertical slices. Save the remaining bone-in slab for soup.

GOUGERES

I brought this recipe back from a trip to Nice, France. The original called for Gruyere cheese, but I found that Gouda is a more budget-friendly alternative. These puffs are a wonderful bite-sized treat. If you have leftovers, float a few of these gems on a bowl of soup in place of croutons.
—Lily Julow, Lawrenceville, GA

PREP: 40 MIN. • **BAKE:** 20 MIN.
MAKES: ABOUT 3 DOZEN

- 1   cup water
- 6   Tbsp. unsalted butter, cubed
- ½   tsp. sea salt
- ¼   tsp. pepper
- ¾   cup all-purpose flour
- 4   large eggs
- 1   cup (4 oz.) shredded regular or smoked Gouda cheese
- ⅓   cup minced fresh chives
- ⅛   tsp. ground nutmeg
TOPPING
- 1   large egg
- 1   tsp. water
- ⅓   cup shredded regular or smoked Gouda cheese

1. Preheat oven to 425°. In a large heavy saucepan, bring first 4 ingredients to a rolling boil. Remove from the heat; add flour all at once and beat until blended. Cook over medium-low heat, stirring vigorously until mixture pulls away from sides of pan and forms a ball, about 3 minutes.
2. Transfer to a large bowl; beat for 1 minute to cool slightly. Add the eggs, 1 at a time, beating well after each addition until smooth. Continue beating until shiny. Beat in the shredded cheese, minced chives and nutmeg. Drop the dough by tablespoonfuls 2 in. apart onto parchment-lined baking sheets. For topping, whisk together egg and water; brush lightly over tops. Sprinkle with cheese. Bake until gougeres are puffed, firm and golden brown, 20-25 minutes. Serve warm.
Freeze option: Freeze unbaked puffs on parchment-lined baking sheets until firm; transfer to resealable freezer bags and return to freezer. To use, place frozen puffs on parchment-lined baking sheets. Top and bake as directed, increasing time by 2-3 minutes.
1 appetizer: 52 cal., 4g fat (2g sat. fat), 36mg chol., 71mg sod., 2g carb. (0 sugars, 0 fiber), 2g pro.

ROASTED ASPARAGUS

Since asparagus is so abundant here come spring, I like to put it to great use with this recipe. We all look forward to this side dish each year.
—Vikki Rebholz, West Chester, OH

TAKES: 25 MIN. • **MAKES:** 12 SERVINGS

- 4   lbs. fresh asparagus, trimmed
- ¼   cup olive oil
- ½   tsp. salt
- ¼   tsp. pepper
- ¼   cup sesame seeds, toasted

Preheat the oven to 400°. Arrange the asparagus in a single layer in 2 foil-lined 15x10x1-in. baking pans. Drizzle with oil. Sprinkle with salt and pepper. Bake, uncovered, until crisp-tender, 12-15 minutes, turning once. Sprinkle with sesame seeds.
1 serving: 73 cal., 6g fat (1g sat. fat), 0 chol., 122mg sod., 4g carb. (1g sugars, 2g fiber), 2g pro. **Diabetic exchanges:** 1 vegetable, 1 fat.

BUTTERY CARROTS

My mother received this recipe from a friend who was a chef at a local restaurant. The onions bring out the carrots' sweetness. When I have carrots fresh from the garden, I don't even peel them—I just scrub them well before cutting. I often double or triple the recipe for holiday buffets.
—Mary Ellen Chambers, Lakewood, OH

TAKES: 20 MIN. • **MAKES:** 12 SERVINGS

- 3   lbs. medium carrots, halved crosswise and cut into strips
- 2   medium onions, halved and thinly sliced
- ½   cup butter, melted
- ½   cup chopped fresh parsley
- ½   tsp. salt
       Coarsely ground pepper, optional

1. Place 2 in. water in a 6-qt. stockpot. Add carrots and onions; bring to a boil. Reduce heat; simmer, covered, until carrots are crisp-tender, 10-12 minutes.
2. Drain vegetables. Toss with the remaining ingredients.
¾ cup: 123 cal., 8g fat (5g sat. fat), 20mg chol., 240mg sod., 13g carb. (6g sugars, 4g fiber), 1g pro.

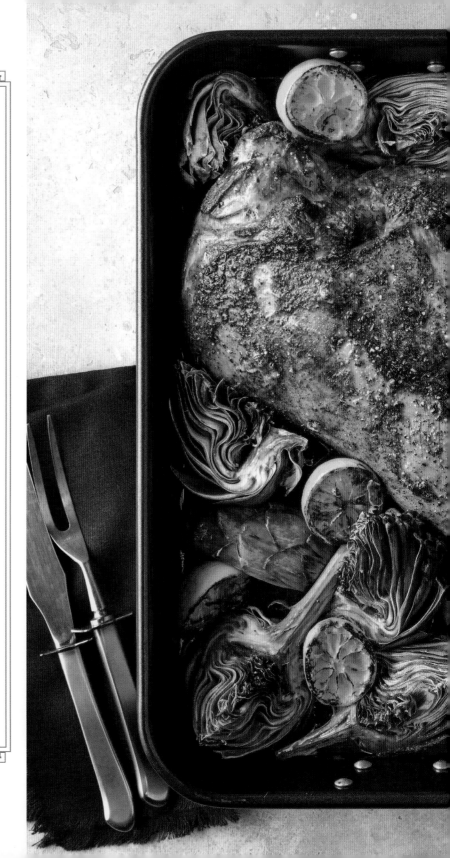

LAMB 101

Tender and moist, lamb is a delightful change-of-pace entree.

WHEN BUYING LAMB, LOOK FOR:

A pinkish red color and a package with no holes, tears or excessive liquid.

A sell-by date on the package that is later than the day of your purchase. Same date? Use it that day or freeze it for later.

WHEN ROASTING LAMB, FOLLOW THESE GUIDELINES:

Place lamb, fat side up, on a rack in a shallow roasting pan. Roast, uncovered, according to your recipe. Roasting is a dry-heat method; no liquid should be added to the pan. Insert an oven-safe thermometer in the thickest part of the roast, not touching bone or fat. Or, use an instant-read thermometer to test meat for doneness.

Roasts continue cooking after they are removed from the oven. Remove at 5^0-10^0 below desired doneness. Allow to stand at room temperature, tented with foil, for 10-15 minutes before serving.

WHEN CARVING A LEG OF LAMB, FOLLOW THESE TIPS:

Cut a few ¼-in. slices on the thin side of the leg and remove to a platter. Turn the roast over so it rests on the cut surface.

Hold roast steady by using paper towels around bone with one hand. With a carving knife, make a series of ¼-in. slices along leg down to bone. Then cut along the bone to free slices.

CALIFORNIA ROAST LAMB

Lamb makes any occasion special. Our California artichokes star alongside lemons and fresh herbs, making this entree even more impressive. This recipe is easy and requires little attention once it's in the oven.
—Ann Eastman, Santa Monica, CA

PREP: 10 MIN.
BAKE: 2½ HOURS + STANDING
MAKES: 12 SERVINGS

- 1 leg of lamb (4 to 5 lbs.)
- 2 to 3 garlic cloves, halved
- 1 tsp. seasoned salt
- 1 tsp. pepper
- 1 tsp. dried oregano
- 2 cans (8 oz. each) tomato sauce
- 1 cup water
  Juice of 1 lemon
- 3 to 5 large fresh artichokes, quartered
- 3 small lemons, halved, optional
  Optional: Fresh oregano and thyme sprigs

1. Cut slits in lamb; insert garlic. Rub meat with salt, pepper and oregano. Roast at 400° for 30 minutes. Reduce heat to 350°; roast 1 hour more.
2. Skim off any fat in pan; pour tomato sauce, water and lemon juice over lamb. Place artichokes and, if desired, lemons around meat. Roast 1 hour longer or until meat reaches desired doneness (for medium-rare, a thermometer should read 135°; medium, 140°; medium-well, 145°). Let lamb stand for 15 minutes before slicing. If desired, garnish with fresh herbs.
3 oz. cooked lamb with 1 artichoke wedge: 152 cal., 5g fat (2g sat. fat), 68mg chol., 365mg sod., 6g carb. (1g sugars, 3g fiber), 21g pro. **Diabetic exchanges:** 3 lean meat.

RHUBARB RELISH

Use this savory relish to complement lamb, ham or any meat of your choosing. It's good on cold roast beef, too.
—Mina Dyck, Boissevain, MB

PREP: 10 MIN. • **COOK:** 30 MIN.
MAKES: 3 CUPS

- 2 cups finely chopped fresh or frozen rhubarb
- 2 cups finely chopped onion
- 2½ cups packed brown sugar
- 1 cup vinegar
- 1 tsp. salt
- ½ tsp. ground cinnamon
- ½ tsp. ground allspice
- ¼ tsp. ground cloves
- ¼ tsp. pepper

In a saucepan, combine all ingredients. Cook over medium heat for 30 minutes or until thickened, stirring occasionally. Cool; store in the refrigerator.
¼ cup: 191 cal., 0 fat (0 sat. fat), 0 chol., 212mg sod., 49g carb. (46g sugars, 1g fiber), 1g pro.

TEST KITCHEN TIP

Rhubarb is a perennial plant that grows well in cool climates. The stalks are edible, but it's sometimes used as an ornamental plant because of its beautiful, vibrant red stalks and wide green leaves. Rhubarb grows best in cool weather below 75°, so it's widely available during the springtime. You'll find it in most areas beginning in April or May, although some regions tolerate rhubarb growth throughout the summer months.

LEMON POLENTA-TOPPED BERRY COBBLER

I love polenta, so I was excited when I came up with this way to use it in a dessert.
—Andrea Bollinger, Carmichael, CA

PREP: 20 MIN. • **BAKE:** 35 MIN.
MAKES: 12 SERVINGS

- 3½ cups fresh blueberries
- 3½ cups fresh blackberries
- 3 Tbsp. cornstarch
- 2 Tbsp. plus ⅓ cup sugar, divided
- ½ cup butter, softened
- 2 tsp. grated lemon zest
- ¾ cup all-purpose flour
- ½ cup cornmeal
- 2 tsp. baking powder
- ½ tsp. salt
- ¾ cup reduced-fat sour cream
- 2 Tbsp. coarse sugar
- 2 Tbsp. lemon juice
- 1 Tbsp. honey

1. In a large bowl, combine blueberries, blackberries, cornstarch and 2 Tbsp. sugar. Transfer to a 13x9-in. baking dish coated with cooking spray.
2. In a large bowl, cream butter and remaining ⅓ cup sugar until light and fluffy, 5-7 minutes. Beat in lemon zest. Combine the flour, cornmeal, baking powder and salt; add to the creamed mixture alternately with sour cream. Beat just until combined. Drop by tablespoonfuls onto berry mixture.
3. In a small bowl, combine the coarse sugar, lemon juice and honey; brush over dough. Bake at 350° until filling is bubbly and a toothpick inserted in the topping comes out clean, 35-40 minutes. Serve warm.
1 serving: 230 cal., 9g fat (6g sat. fat), 25mg chol., 230mg sod., 35g carb. (19g sugars, 4g fiber), 3g pro.

EASY SCOTTISH SHORTBREAD

These traditional butter cookies require only three ingredients. They're so yummy, you won't be able to stop at just one!
—Peggy Goodrich, Enid, OK

PREP: 20 MIN.
BAKE: 10 MIN./BATCH + COOLING
MAKES: ABOUT 3½ DOZEN

- ¾ cup plus 2 Tbsp. butter, softened
- ¼ cup sugar
- 2 cups all-purpose flour

1. In a small mixing bowl, cream butter and sugar. Gradually add flour and mix well. (Dough will be crumbly). Shape into a ball.
2. On a lightly floured surface, press dough to ½-in. thickness. Cut out with a floured 1-in. diamond-shaped cookie cutter; place 1 in. apart on ungreased baking sheets. Prick each cookie with a fork. Reroll scraps if desired. Bake at 350° for 12-15 minutes or until firm. Cool for 2 minutes before carefully removing to wire racks to cool completely.

1 cookie: 55 cal., 3g fat (2g sat. fat), 9mg chol., 26mg sod., 6g carb. (1g sugars, 0 fiber), 1g pro.

PINEAPPLE CARROT CAKE

This moist carrot cake with cream cheese frosting is the best I've ever eaten. It's easy, too, because it uses two jars of baby food instead of fresh carrots that require grating.
—Jeanette McKenna, Vero Beach, FL

PREP: 20 MIN.
BAKE: 35 MIN. + COOLING
MAKES: 12 SERVINGS

- 2 cups all-purpose flour
- 2 cups sugar
- 2 tsp. baking soda
- 2 tsp. ground cinnamon
- 1 tsp. salt
- 1½ cups canola oil
- 4 large eggs, room temperature
- 3 jars (4 oz. each) carrot baby food
- 1 can (8 oz.) crushed pineapple, drained
- ½ cup chopped walnuts

FROSTING
- 1 pkg. (8 oz.) cream cheese, softened
- ½ cup butter, softened
- 1 tsp. vanilla extract
- 3¾ cups confectioners' sugar
  Additional chopped walnuts and edible blossoms, optional

1. In a bowl, combine dry ingredients. Add the oil, eggs and baby food; mix on low speed until well blended. Stir in the pineapple and nuts. Pour into 2 greased and floured 9-in. round baking pans. Bake at 350° until a toothpick inserted in the center comes out clean, 35-40 minutes. Cool for 10 minutes before removing from pans to wire racks to cool completely.
2. For frosting, in a bowl, beat cream cheese and butter until smooth. Beat in vanilla and confectioners' sugar until mixture reaches spreading consistency. Spread between layers and over top and sides of cake. Garnish with nuts and blossoms if desired. Store cake in the refrigerator.
1 slice: 798 cal., 46g fat (13g sat. fat), 112mg chol., 569mg sod., 92g carb. (70g sugars, 1g fiber), 7g pro.

Cinco de Mayo

On May 5th, say *hola* to a lineup of authentic Mexican flavors that are guaranteed to steal the show. Make your Cinco de Mayo fiesta unforgettable with traditional tamales, refreshing sangria, homemade guac, tres leche cake and other zesty, spicy, cheesy favorites. *Deliciosa*!

CHILES RELLENOS SQUARES

A friend from work gave me the recipe for this simple variation of chiles rellenos many years ago, and it quickly became a standby at our house. My family requests it often. Serve these squares to complement any Mexican-style meal, or as a tasty appetizer for parties and gatherings.
—Fran Carll, Long Beach, CA

PREP: 10 MIN. • **BAKE:** 25 MIN.
MAKES: 16 SERVINGS

- 3 cups shredded Monterey Jack cheese
- 1½ cups shredded cheddar cheese
- 2 cans (4 oz. each) chopped green chiles, drained
- 2 large eggs
- 2 Tbsp. 2% milk
- 1 Tbsp. all-purpose flour

1. Preheat oven to 375°. Sprinkle half of each cheese onto bottom of a greased 8-in. square baking dish. Layer with chiles and remaining cheeses.
2. Whisk together eggs, milk and flour; pour over top. Bake, uncovered, until set, 25-30 minutes. Cool 15 minutes before cutting.

1 piece: 130 cal., 10g fat (7g sat. fat), 57mg chol., 214mg sod., 1g carb. (0 sugars, 0 fiber), 8g pro.

CANTINA PINTO BEANS

Cumin, cilantro and red pepper flakes lend southwestern flair to tender pinto beans in this dish, which was inspired by one we had at a restaurant in Dallas. The chef added chunks of ham, but my version is meatless. It makes a great Tex-Mex side or a filling lunch when served with cornbread.
—L.R. Larson, Sioux Falls, SD

PREP: 15 MIN. + STANDING
COOK: 1½ HOURS
MAKES: 10 SERVINGS

- 2 cups dried pinto beans (about ¾ lb.)
- 2 cans (14½ oz. each) reduced-sodium chicken broth
- 2 celery ribs, diced
- ¼ cup diced onion
- ¼ cup diced green pepper
- 1 garlic clove, minced
- 2 bay leaves
- 1 tsp. ground cumin
- ½ tsp. rubbed sage
- ¼ tsp. crushed red pepper flakes
- 2 cans (14½ oz. each) Mexican diced tomatoes, undrained
- ½ tsp. salt
  Chopped fresh cilantro

1. Sort beans and rinse with cold water. Place beans in a Dutch oven; add water to cover by 2 in. Bring to a boil; boil for 2 minutes. Remove from heat; let stand, covered, 1 hour.
2. Drain and rinse beans, discarding the liquid. Return beans to pan. Stir in broth, celery, onion, green pepper, garlic and seasonings; bring to a boil. Reduce heat; simmer, uncovered, until beans are very tender, about 1 hour.
3. Discard bay leaves. Stir in tomatoes and salt. Simmer, uncovered, until heated through, 25-30 minutes, stirring occasionally. Serve with cilantro.

¾ cup: 162 cal., 1g fat (0 sat. fat), 0 chol., 536mg sod., 29g carb. (4g sugars, 7g fiber), 10g pro. **Diabetic exchanges:** 2 starch.

TEST KITCHEN TIP
Pinto beans are medium-sized, mottled pinkish tan, and kidney-shaped. Common in Mexican and Latin American cooking, they're perfect for adding a little southwestern flair to your meal. Incorporate pintos into salads, casseroles or soups.

SIMPLE GUACAMOLE

Because avocados can brown quickly, it's best to make this guacamole just before serving. If you do have to make it a little in advance, place the avocado pit in the guacamole until it's time to dig in.

—Heidi Main, Anchorage, AK

TAKES: 10 MIN. • **MAKES:** 1½ CUPS

- 2 medium ripe avocados
- 1 Tbsp. lemon juice
- ¼ cup chunky salsa
- ⅛ to ¼ tsp. salt

Peel and chop avocados; place in a small bowl. Sprinkle with lemon juice. Add salsa and salt; mash coarsely with a fork. Refrigerate until serving.
2 Tbsp.: 53 cal., 5g fat (1g sat. fat), 0 chol., 51mg sod., 3g carb. (0 sugars, 2g fiber), 1g pro.

SALSA PINTO BEANS

Want an alternative to refried beans? Try this side dish. Sometimes I top it off with a sprinkling of shredded cheese or a dollop of sour cream.

—Lorna Nault, Chesterton, IN

TAKES: 15 MIN. • **MAKES:** 6 SERVINGS

- 1 small onion, chopped
- 2 tsp. minced fresh cilantro
- 1 Tbsp. canola oil
- 1 garlic clove, minced
- 2 cans (15 oz. each) pinto beans, rinsed and drained
- ⅔ cup salsa

In a large skillet or saucepan, saute onion and cilantro in oil until tender. Add garlic; cook 1 minute longer. Stir in the beans and salsa; heat through.
½ cup: 159 cal., 3g fat (0 sat. fat), 0 chol., 296mg sod., 26g carb. (4g sugars, 6g fiber), 7g pro. **Diabetic exchanges:** 2 starch, ½ fat.

HOW TO MAKE GUACAMOLE

Do you put guac on just about everything, from burritos to burgers? (We sure do!) To keep up with those cravings, learn how to make this basic guacamole at home—it's super simple and so tasty.

STEP 1
Cut avocados into quarters, peel, and place in a bowl. Mash chunks with a fork.

STEP 2
Add salt and minced garlic.

STEP 3
Stir in onions, tomatoes, lime juice and cilantro. Refrigerate until serving.

MEXICAN STUFFED PEPPERS

My stuffed peppers make a nutritious and economical meal. I top them with sour cream and serve tortilla chips and salsa on the side. Replace the ground beef with lean ground turkey if you want to cut fat.
—Kim Coleman, Columbia, SC

PREP: 25 MIN. • **BAKE:** 30 MIN.
MAKES: 8 SERVINGS

- 1   lb. lean ground beef (90% lean)
- 1   can (14½ oz.) diced tomatoes and green chiles, undrained
- 1   envelope (5.4 oz.) Mexican-style rice and pasta mix
- 1½ cups water
- 8   medium sweet peppers
- 2   cups shredded Mexican cheese blend, divided

1. Preheat oven to 375°. In a large skillet, cook and crumble ground beef over medium heat until no longer pink, 5-7 minutes; drain. Stir in tomatoes, rice mix and water; bring to a boil. Reduce heat; simmer, covered, until liquid is absorbed, 6-8 minutes.

2. Cut and discard tops from peppers; remove seeds. Place peppers in a greased 13x9-in. baking dish. Place ⅓ cup beef mixture in each pepper; sprinkle each with 2 Tbsp. cheese. Top with the remaining rice mixture. Bake, covered, 25 minutes.

3. Sprinkle with the remaining cheese. Bake, uncovered, until the cheese is melted and peppers are crisp-tender, 5-10 minutes.

1 stuffed pepper: 301 cal., 14g fat (8g sat. fat), 61mg chol., 797mg sod., 23g carb. (4g sugars, 3g fiber), 20g pro.

CHICKEN TAMALES

I love making tamales from scratch for my husband and our four children.
—Cindy Pruitt, Grove, OK

PREP: 2½ HOURS + SOAKING
COOK: 50 MIN. • **MAKES:** 20 TAMALES

- 24 **dried corn husks**
- 1 **broiler/fryer chicken (3 to 4 lbs.), cut up**
- 1 **medium onion, quartered**
- 2 **tsp. salt**
- 1 **garlic clove, crushed**
- 3 **qt. water**

DOUGH
- 1 **cup shortening**
- 3 **cups masa harina**

FILLING
- 6 **Tbsp. canola oil**
- 6 **Tbsp. all-purpose flour**
- ¾ **cup chili powder**
- ½ **tsp. salt**
- ¼ **tsp. garlic powder**
- ¼ **tsp. pepper**
- 2 **cans (2¼ oz. each) sliced ripe olives, drained**
  Hot water

1. Cover corn husks with cold water; soak until softened, at least 2 hours.
2. Place chicken, onion, salt and garlic in a 6-qt. stockpot. Pour in 3 qt. water; bring to a boil. Reduce heat; simmer, covered, until chicken is tender, 45-60 minutes. Remove chicken. When cool enough to handle, remove bones and skin; discard. Shred chicken. Strain juices; skim fat. Reserve 6 cups stock.
3. For dough, beat shortening until light and fluffy, about 1 minute. Beat in small amounts of masa harina alternately with small amounts of reserved stock, using no more than 2 cups stock. Drop a small amount of dough into a cup of cold water; dough should float. If dough does not float, continue beating, rechecking every 1-2 minutes.
4. For filling, heat oil in a Dutch oven; stir in flour until blended. Cook and stir over medium heat until lightly browned, 7-9 minutes. Stir in seasonings, chicken and remaining stock; bring to a boil. Reduce heat; simmer, uncovered, stirring occasionally, until thickened, about 45 minutes.
5. Drain the corn husks and pat dry; tear 4 husks to make 20 strips for tying tamales. (To prevent the husks from drying out, cover with a damp towel until ready to use.) On wide end of each remaining husk, spread 3 Tbsp. dough to within ½ in. of side edges; top each with 2 Tbsp. chicken filling and 2 tsp. olives. Fold long sides of husk over filling, overlapping slightly. Fold over narrow end of husk; tie with a strip of husk to secure.
6. Place a large steamer basket in the stockpot over water; place tamales upright in steamer. Bring to a boil; steam, covered, adding hot water as needed, until dough peels away from husk, about 45 minutes.

2 tamales: 564 cal., 35g fat (7g sat. fat), 44mg chol., 835mg sod., 43g carb. (2g sugars, 7g fiber), 20g pro.

HOW TO MAKE TAMALES

Refer to these photos when following the steps for prepping, wrapping and steaming tamales. Feel free to mix up the filling ingredients to appeal to various palates.

TOPSY-TURVY SANGRIA

I got this recipe from a friend a few years ago. It's perfect for relaxed get-togethers. It tastes best when you make it the night before and let the flavors steep. But be careful —it goes down easy!
—Tracy Field, Bremerton, WA

TAKES: 10 MIN.
MAKES: 10 SERVINGS (ABOUT 2 QT.)

- 1 bottle (750 ml) merlot
- 1 cup sugar
- 1 cup orange liqueur
- ½ to 1 cup brandy
- 3 cups cold lemon-lime soda
- 1 cup sliced fresh strawberries
- 1 medium orange, sliced
- 1 medium lemon, sliced
- 1 medium peach, sliced
  Ice cubes

In a pitcher, stir the first 4 ingredients until sugar is dissolved. Stir in soda and fruit. Serve over ice.
¾ cup: 292 cal., 0 fat (0 sat. fat), 0 chol., 11mg sod., 42g carb. (39g sugars, 0 fiber), 0 pro.

GRILLED STEAK TACOS

Spicy aioli brings a zesty kick to steak tacos, and the ribeye is a nice upgrade from typical ground beef. Grab one and enjoy the burst of flavor in each bite!

—Michael Compean, Los Angeles, CA

PREP: 25 MIN. • **GRILL:** 15 MIN.
MAKES: 4 SERVINGS

SPICY AIOLI
- ¼ cup mayonnaise
- 2 tsp. Sriracha chili sauce or 1 tsp. hot pepper sauce
- ⅛ tsp. sesame oil

AVOCADO-CORN SALSA
- 1 medium ripe avocado, peeled and finely chopped
- ½ medium tomato, seeded and chopped
- 3 Tbsp. sliced ripe olives
- 2 Tbsp. canned whole kernel corn
- 2 Tbsp. chopped sweet red pepper
- 2 Tbsp. lime juice
- 4 tsp. minced fresh cilantro
- 1 tsp. kosher salt
- 1 tsp. finely chopped onion
- 1 garlic clove, minced
- ¼ tsp. ground cumin

STEAKS
- 2 tsp. pepper
- 2 tsp. olive oil
- 1 tsp. kosher salt
- 1 tsp. seafood seasoning
- 1 beef ribeye steak (1 lb.), trimmed
- 8 flour tortillas (6 in.)
- Optional toppings: Shredded lettuce, cheddar cheese and Cotija cheese

1. In a small bowl, combine the aioli ingredients. In another bowl, combine the salsa ingredients. Refrigerate until serving.

2. Combine the pepper, oil, salt and seafood seasoning; rub over both sides of steak.

3. Grill, covered, over medium heat until meat reaches desired doneness (for medium-rare, a thermometer should read 135°; medium, 140°; medium-well, 145°), 6-8 minutes on each side. Let stand for 5 minutes.

4. Meanwhile, grill flour tortillas until warm, about 45 seconds on each side. Thinly slice steak; place on tortillas. Serve with aioli, salsa and toppings of your choice.

2 tacos: 650 cal., 45g fat (10g sat. fat), 72mg chol., 1843mg sod., 35g carb. (2g sugars, 4g fiber), 28g pro.

SOUTHWESTERN RICE

I created this zippy rice dish after trying something similar at a restaurant. It's a colorful addition to meals when you want to bring the Southwest to your table. Add cubes of grilled chicken to make it a meal.

—Michelle Dennis, Clarks Hill, IN

TAKES: 30 MIN. • **MAKES:** 8 SERVINGS

- 1 Tbsp. olive oil
- 1 medium green pepper, diced
- 1 medium onion, chopped
- 2 garlic cloves, minced
- 1 cup uncooked long grain rice
- ½ tsp. ground cumin
- ⅛ tsp. ground turmeric
- 1 can (14½ oz.) reduced-sodium chicken broth
- 2 cups frozen corn (about 10 oz.), thawed
- 1 can (15 oz.) black beans, rinsed and drained
- 1 can (10 oz.) diced tomatoes and green chiles, undrained

1. In a large nonstick skillet, heat oil over medium-high heat; saute pepper and onion 3 minutes. Add garlic; cook and stir 1 minute.

2. Stir in rice, spices and broth; bring to a boil. Reduce heat; simmer, covered, until rice is tender, about 15 minutes. Stir in remaining ingredients; cook, covered, until heated through.

¾ cup: 198 cal., 3g fat (1g sat. fat), 1mg chol., 339mg sod., 37g carb. (0 sugars, 5g fiber), 7g pro.

READER REVIEW

"I made this recipe for a campout covered dish, reheated it in my 9x13 casserole slow cooker, sprinkled it with cheddar cheese upon reheating, and it was a hit! Planning to include it in our family Mexican night buffet. Great side dish!"

—AMY, TASTEOFHOME.COM

FRIED ICE CREAM

Refrigerated pie crust sprinkled with cinnamon sugar makes short work of this popular Mexican restaurant-style treat. Top scoops with honey, caramel ice cream topping or sweetened whipped cream.
—*Taste of Home* Test Kitchen

PREP: 30 MIN. + FREEZING
MAKES: 8 SERVINGS

1	sheet refrigerated pie pastry
1½	tsp. sugar
1	tsp. ground cinnamon
1	qt. vanilla ice cream
	Oil for deep-fat frying
½	cup honey

1. Preheat oven to 400°. Unroll pastry onto an ungreased baking sheet. Mix sugar and cinnamon; sprinkle over pastry. Prick pastry thoroughly with a fork. Bake until golden brown, 10-12 minutes. Cool crust completely on a wire rack.

2. Place crust in a large resealable plastic bag; crush to form coarse crumbs. Transfer to a shallow bowl. Using a ½-cup ice cream scoop, drop a scoop of ice cream into crumbs; roll quickly to coat and shape into a ball. Transfer to a waxed paper-lined baking sheet; place in freezer. Repeat 7 times; freeze until firm, 1-2 hours.

3. To serve, heat oil to 375° in an electric skillet or deep-fat fryer. Fry ice cream balls until golden, 8-10 seconds. Drain on paper towels. Serve immediately in chilled dishes. Drizzle with honey.

1 serving: 423 cal., 25g fat (8g sat. fat), 34mg chol., 154mg sod., 47g carb. (33g sugars, 1g fiber), 3g pro.

CLASSIC TRES LECHES CAKE

A classic dessert in Mexican kitchens for generations, this fluffy cake gets its name from the three milk products —evaporated, sweetened condensed and heavy whipping cream —used to create a super moist and tender texture.

—*Taste of Home* Test Kitchen

PREP: 45 MIN. • **BAKE:** 20 MIN. + CHILLING
MAKES: 10 SERVINGS

- 4 large eggs, separated, room temperature
- ⅔ cup sugar, divided
- ⅔ cup cake flour
  Dash salt
- ¾ cup heavy whipping cream
- ¾ cup evaporated milk
- ¾ cup sweetened condensed milk
- 2 tsp. vanilla extract
- ¼ tsp. rum extract

TOPPING

- 1¼ cups heavy whipping cream
- 3 Tbsp. sugar
  Optional: Dulce de leche or sliced fresh strawberries

1. Place egg whites in a large bowl. Line bottom of a 9-in. springform pan with parchment; grease the paper.
2. Meanwhile, preheat oven to 350°. In another large bowl, beat egg yolks until slightly thickened. Gradually add ⅓ cup sugar, beating on high speed until thick and lemon-colored. Fold in flour, a third at a time.
3. Add salt to egg whites; with clean beaters, beat on medium until soft peaks form. Gradually add remaining sugar, 1 Tbsp. at a time, beating on high after each addition until the sugar is dissolved. Continue beating until soft glossy peaks form. Fold a third of the whites into batter, then fold in remaining whites. Gently spread batter into the prepared pan.

4. Bake until top springs back when lightly touched, 20-25 minutes. Cool 10 minutes before removing from pan to a wire rack to cool completely.
5. Place cake on a rimmed serving plate. Poke holes in top with a skewer. In a small bowl, mix cream, evaporated milk, sweetened condensed milk and extracts; brush slowly over the cake. Refrigerate, covered, 2 hours.
6. For topping, beat cream until it begins to thicken. Add sugar; beat until peaks form. Spread over the top of cake. If desired, top cake with dulce de leche or strawberries just before serving.
1 slice: 392 cal., 23g fat (14g sat. fat), 142mg chol., 104mg sod., 40g carb. (33g sugars, 0 fiber), 8g pro.

WATERMELON SPRITZER

Watermelon blended with limeade is cool and refreshing. It's a great served with any Mexican-themed meal.

—Geraldine Saucier, Albuquerque, NM

PREP: 5 MIN. + CHILLING
MAKES: 5 SERVINGS

- 4 cups cubed seedless watermelon
- ¾ cup frozen limeade concentrate, thawed
- 2½ cups carbonated water
  Lime slices

1. Place watermelon in a blender. Cover and process until blended. Strain and discard pulp; transfer juice to a pitcher. Stir in limeade concentrate. Refrigerate for 6 hours or overnight.
2. Just before serving, stir in the carbonated water. Garnish servings with lime slices.
1 cup: 140 cal., 0 fat (0 sat. fat), 0 chol., 4mg sod., 38g carb. (36g sugars, 1g fiber), 0 pro.

Mother's Day Brunch

This year, celebrate Mom with an assortment of homemade sweet and savory brunch dishes. Whether you're serving her a leisurely breakfast in bed or hosting the entire family, you're sure to impress with a sunny cheese-filled frittata, crab cake lettuce wraps and strawberry bruschetta. Top off these Sunday bites with a fitting finale of deep-dish lime-raspberry pie or chocolaty scones.

Cheers to Mom!

RHUBARB MINT TEA

A bumper crop of rhubarb and mint from my garden inspired me to create this lovely thirst-quenching pick-me-up. Raspberries deepen the tea's vibrant red color, making the tea a pretty addition to your table.
—Laurie Bock, Lynden, WA

PREP: 15 MIN. • **COOK:** 45 MIN. + CHILLING
MAKES: 12 SERVINGS

- 4 cups chopped fresh or frozen rhubarb
- 2 cups fresh or frozen raspberries
- 2 pkg. (¾ oz. each) fresh mint leaves
- 3 qt. water
- 4 black tea bags
- 2 cups sugar
- 12 mint sprigs

In a 6-qt. stockpot, combine rhubarb, raspberries, mint and water; bring to a boil. Reduce heat; simmer, uncovered, 30 minutes. Remove from heat. Add tea bags; steep, covered, 3-5 minutes according to taste. Using a fine mesh strainer, strain tea, discarding tea bags and pulp. Stir in sugar until dissolved; cool slightly. Transfer to a pitcher; refrigerate until cooled completely. Serve over ice with mint sprigs.
1 cup: 151 cal., 0 fat (0 sat. fat), 0 chol., 3mg sod., 38g carb. (35g sugars, 2g fiber), 1g pro.

STRAWBERRY SPINACH SALAD WITH CANDIED WALNUTS

This classic salad goes with just about anything you're serving. The juicy berries add a pop of color to the greens, and the sweet, crunchy nuts are good enough to eat all on their own!
—Susan Howell, Royal Oak, MI

TAKES: 20 MIN.
MAKES: 10 SERVINGS

- ½ cup sugar
- ¼ cup water
- ½ tsp. ground cinnamon
- ½ tsp. chili powder
- ¼ tsp. curry powder
- 2 cups walnut halves

SALAD
- 1 pkg. (9 oz.) fresh baby spinach
- 2 cups sliced fresh strawberries (about 1 lb.)
- 1 medium cucumber, halved and sliced

VINAIGRETTE
- ¼ cup olive oil
- 2 Tbsp. balsamic vinegar
- 2 Tbsp. seedless raspberry jam
- 1 tsp. lemon juice
- ¼ tsp. salt
- ⅛ tsp. pepper
- ⅓ cup grated Parmesan cheese

1. In a small heavy saucepan, combine the first 5 ingredients; stir to moisten all the sugar. Cook over medium-low heat, gently swirling pan occasionally, until sugar is dissolved. Cover; bring to a boil over medium heat. Cook 1 minute. Uncover pan; continue to boil and gently swirl the pan until the syrup turns a deep amber color, about 2-3 minutes. Immediately remove from heat and carefully stir in walnuts until evenly coated. Spread onto foil to cool completely. Break into pieces.

2. In a large bowl, combine the spinach, strawberry slices and cucumber. In a small bowl, whisk the first 6 vinaigrette ingredients. Drizzle over salad; toss to coat. Sprinkle with cheese and walnuts. Serve immediately.
1 cup: 262 cal., 19g fat (2g sat. fat), 2mg chol., 132mg sod., 21g carb. (16g sugars, 3g fiber), 5g pro.

DID YOU KNOW?
Curry powder is a combination of ground cumin, ground ginger, ground coriander, chili powder and turmeric. Due to its strong, earthy flavor, a little goes a long way. If you don't have any curry powder on hand, try replacing it with ground cumin or coriander.

CRAB CAKE LETTUCE WRAPS

I love dishes you can put together and eat with your hands. These little crab cakes are healthy, fast and flavorful.

—Joyce Huang, New York, NY

TAKES: 10 MIN. • **MAKES:** 1 DOZEN

- 2 cans (6 oz. each) lump crabmeat, drained
- ¼ cup finely chopped celery
- ¼ cup seasoned stuffing cubes, coarsely crushed
- ¼ cup plain Greek yogurt
- ⅛ tsp. salt
- ⅛ tsp. pepper
- 12 Bibb or Boston lettuce leaves
  Finely chopped tomatoes, optional

In a large bowl, mix the crab, celery, stuffing cubes, yogurt, salt and pepper. To serve, spoon 2 Tbsp. crab mixture into each lettuce leaf. If desired, sprinkle with tomatoes. Fold lettuce over filling.

1 filled lettuce wrap: 37 cal., 0 fat (0 sat. fat), 25mg chol., 139mg sod., 1g carb. (0 sugars, 0 fiber), 7g pro.

ONION-GARLIC HASH BROWNS

Quick to assemble, these slow-cooked hash browns are one of my go-to sides. Stir in hot sauce if you like a bit of heat. I top off my finished dish with a sprinkling of shredded cheddar cheese.

—Cindi Boger, Ardmore, AL

PREP: 20 MIN. • **COOK:** 3 HOURS
MAKES: 12 SERVINGS

- ¼ cup butter, cubed
- 1 Tbsp. olive oil
- 1 large red onion, chopped
- 1 small sweet red pepper, chopped
- 1 small green pepper, chopped
- 4 garlic cloves, minced
- 1 pkg. (30 oz.) frozen shredded hash brown potatoes
- ½ tsp. salt
- ½ tsp. pepper
- 3 drops hot pepper sauce, optional
- 2 tsp. minced fresh parsley

1. In a large skillet, heat the butter and oil over medium heat. Add the onion and peppers. Cook and stir until crisp-tender. Add garlic; cook 1 minute longer. Stir in hash browns, salt, pepper and, if desired, pepper sauce.

2. Transfer to a 5-qt. slow cooker coated with cooking spray. Cook, covered, 3-4 hours or until heated through. Sprinkle with parsley just before serving.

½ cup: 110 cal., 5g fat (3g sat. fat), 10mg chol., 136mg sod., 15g carb. (1g sugars, 1g fiber), 2g pro. **Diabetic exchanges:** 1 starch, 1 fat.

STRAWBERRY & CREAM BRUSCHETTA

This is a dessert take on bruschetta. Sweet, cinnamony toast slices are topped with a cream cheese mixture, strawberries and almonds. These treats remind me of mini cheesecakes. They're so yummy!
—Christi Meixner, Aurora, IL

TAKES: 25 MIN. • **MAKES:** 2 DOZEN

- 1 French bread baguette (8 oz.), cut into 24 slices
- ¼ cup butter, melted
- 3 Tbsp. sugar
- ½ tsp. ground cinnamon
- 1 pkg. (8 oz.) cream cheese, softened
- ¼ cup confectioners' sugar
- 2 tsp. lemon juice
- 1 tsp. grated lemon zest
- 2½ cups fresh strawberries, chopped
- ⅓ cup slivered almonds, toasted

1. Preheat oven to 375°. Place bread on an ungreased baking sheet; brush with butter. Combine sugar and cinnamon; sprinkle over bread. Bake 4-5 minutes on each side or until lightly crisp.

2. In a small bowl, beat cream cheese, confectioners' sugar, and lemon juice and zest until blended; spread over toast. Top with strawberries; sprinkle with almonds.

1 appetizer: 94 cal., 6g fat (3g sat. fat), 15mg chol., 70mg sod., 8g carb. (4g sugars, 1g fiber), 2g pro.

TURKEY TEA SANDWICHES WITH BASIL MAYONNAISE

Basil mayonnaise is the secret to these tasty little sandwiches. Keep any extra mayo in the fridge to spread on other sandwiches, stir into egg salad or layer on pizza crust before topping it with other ingredients.
—Lara Pennell, Mauldin, SC

TAKES: 15 MIN.
MAKES: 20 TEA SANDWICHES

- ½ cup mayonnaise
- ⅓ cup loosely packed basil leaves
- 10 slices white bread, crusts removed
- 10 oz. thinly sliced deli turkey
- 5 slices provolone cheese

Place mayonnaise and basil in a food processor; process until basil is finely chopped, scraping down the sides as needed. Spread mayonnaise mixture over each bread slice. Layer 5 bread slices with turkey and cheese; top with remaining bread slices. Cut each into 4 long pieces.

1 tea sandwich: 90 cal., 6g fat (2g sat. fat), 9mg chol., 230mg sod., 4g carb. (0 sugars, 0 fiber), 5g pro.

MOTHER'S DAY SPA BASKET

Celebrated on the second Sunday in May, Mother's Day is the time to honor and thank the moms in our lives. While we may not be able to repay them for all the homemade meals, words of wisdom, and thousands of hugs and kisses, we can treat them to a homemade gift from the heart.

To surprise a special mom in your life, try this thoughtful gift idea. Fill a decorative basket with items she can use for a relaxing spa day at home. A few fun, simple and inexpensive gifts like these make the day last longer.

GIFT BASKET ITEMS
Bath soaks

Scented candle

Tea tins filled with Mom's favorite tea

Clear tea cup with infuser

Sleep mask

Journal

Stationery pens

"Best Mom Ever" knick-knacks

DOUBLE CHEESE ARTICHOKE FRITTATA

Fresh flavors make this pretty egg bake a delightful entree for a special occasion brunch or light luncheon.

—Joyce Moynihan, Lakeville, MN

PREP: 15 MIN. • **BAKE:** 40 MIN.
MAKES: 8 SERVINGS

1	pkg. (8 oz.) frozen artichoke hearts
1	Tbsp. butter
1	Tbsp. olive oil
1	medium onion, chopped
1	garlic clove, minced
¼	tsp. dried oregano
¾	cup shredded Parmesan cheese, divided
6	large eggs
½	cup 2% milk
¼	tsp. salt
⅛	tsp. white pepper
⅛	tsp. ground nutmeg
1	cup shredded Monterey Jack cheese
	Minced chives, optional

1. Cook artichokes according to package directions; drain. Cool slightly; coarsely chop. Preheat oven to 350°.
2. In a large skillet, heat butter and oil over medium-high heat. Add the onion; cook and stir until tender. Add garlic; cook 1 minute longer. Stir in oregano and artichokes; remove from heat.
3. Sprinkle ¼ cup Parmesan cheese in a greased 11x7-in. baking dish. Top with artichoke mixture.
4. In a large bowl, whisk eggs, milk, salt, pepper and nutmeg. Stir in Monterey Jack cheese and ¼ cup Parmesan cheese. Pour over artichoke mixture.
5. Bake, uncovered, 30 minutes. Sprinkle with remaining Parmesan cheese. Bake until a knife inserted in center comes out clean, 6-8 minutes longer. If desired, sprinkle with the minced chives.
1 piece: 192 cal., 13g fat (7g sat. fat), 163mg chol., 373mg sod., 5g carb. (2g sugars, 2g fiber), 13g pro.

HOMEMADE SAGE SAUSAGE PATTIES

Oregano, garlic and sage add zippy flavor to these quick-to-fix ground pork patties. I've had this Pennsylvania Dutch recipe for years, and it always brings compliments.

—Diane Hixon, Niceville, FL

PREP: 10 MIN. + CHILLING • **COOK:** 15 MIN.
MAKES: 8 SERVINGS

1	lb. ground pork
¾	cup shredded cheddar cheese
¼	cup buttermilk
1	Tbsp. finely chopped onion
2	tsp. rubbed sage
¾	tsp. salt
¾	tsp. pepper
⅛	tsp. garlic powder
⅛	tsp. dried oregano

1. In a bowl, combine all the ingredients, mixing lightly but thoroughly. Shape into eight ½-in.-thick patties. Refrigerate for 1 hour.
2. In a large cast-iron or other heavy skillet, cook the patties over medium heat until a thermometer reads 160°, 6-8 minutes on each side.
1 patty: 162 cal., 11g fat (5g sat. fat), 49mg chol., 323mg sod., 1g carb. (0 sugars, 0 fiber), 13g pro.

DOUBLE CHOCOLATE SCONES

Chocolate lovers will adore these moist, decadent scones that won me a blue ribbon in a baking competition. They're perfect for a tea or brunch, and the mix of cocoa and chocolate chips makes them sweet enough for dessert.
—Stephanie Sorbie, Peoria, AZ

PREP: 15 MIN. • **BAKE:** 20 MIN.
MAKES: 8 SCONES

1¾ cups all-purpose flour
½ cup baking cocoa
⅓ cup sugar
1½ tsp. baking powder
½ tsp. salt
4 oz. cream cheese, cubed
¼ cup cold butter, cubed
2 large eggs
¾ cup heavy whipping cream
2 tsp. vanilla extract
⅔ cup semisweet chocolate chips

1. Preheat oven to 375°. In a large bowl, whisk the first 5 ingredients. Cut in the cream cheese and butter until mixture resembles coarse crumbs. In another bowl, whisk 1 egg, cream and vanilla; stir into the crumb mixture just until moistened. Stir in chocolate chips.
2. Turn onto a floured surface; knead gently 10 times. Pat dough into a 6-in. circle. Cut into 8 wedges. Place the wedges on a greased baking sheet. In a small bowl, whisk remaining egg; brush over scones. Bake 18-20 minutes or until a toothpick inserted in center comes out clean. Serve warm.
1 scone: 412 cal., 25g fat (15g sat. fat), 114mg chol., 334mg sod., 42g carb. (17g sugars, 3g fiber), 8g pro.

CHAMPAGNE SIPPER

This is a terrific cocktail for any celebration. And because you make it by the pitcher, feel free to mingle with your guests instead of tending bar.

—Moffat Frazier, New York, NY

TAKES: 10 MIN. • **MAKES:** 12 SERVINGS

- 1½ cups sugar
- 1 cup lemon juice
- 3 cups cold water
- 1½ cups sweet white wine, chilled
- 1 bottle (750 milliliters) champagne, chilled
  Sliced fresh strawberries, optional

In a 3-qt. pitcher, dissolve sugar in lemon juice. Add cold water and wine. Stir in champagne. If desired, serve with fresh strawberries.

¾ cup: 168 cal., 0 fat (0 sat. fat), 0 chol., 2mg sod., 28g carb. (26g sugars, 0 fiber), 0 pro.

> ### TEST KITCHEN TIP
> While this refreshing sipper is perfect for spring, try it for any holiday. Swap the strawberries for orange slices and a few whole cranberries to enjoy a lovely Christmas beverage.

LIME-RASPBERRY PIE WITH COCONUT CREAM

During my family trips to Florida, I've had Key lime pie from many restaurants, and each one is different. I wanted to create my own spin on the pie to make it my signature dessert. Whipped egg whites in the filling make it light and mousselike, sweet raspberries balance the tartness, and coconut and cashews amp up the tropical flavor. Garnish with fresh raspberries and toasted shredded coconut if you like.

—Elise Easterling, Chapel Hill, NC

PREP: 50 MIN. • **BAKE:** 25 MIN. + CHILLING
MAKES: 12 SERVINGS

- 3 large egg whites
- 18 whole graham crackers, crushed (about 2½ cups)
- ½ cup packed brown sugar
- ½ cup unsalted cashews, finely chopped
- ¾ cup butter, melted
- 2 cans (14 oz. each) sweetened condensed milk
- ¾ cup Key lime juice
- 6 large egg yolks
- ¼ cup sugar

TOPPINGS
- 1 can (13.66 oz.) coconut milk
- 1 cup heavy whipping cream
- ½ cup confectioners' sugar
- ½ cup seedless raspberry jam
  Optional: Fresh raspberries and toasted flaked coconut

1. Place egg whites in a small bowl; let stand at room temperature 30 minutes. Preheat oven to 350°.
2. In a large bowl, mix the crushed crackers, brown sugar and cashews; stir in melted butter. Press onto the bottom and 2 in. up sides of a greased 9-in. springform pan.
3. In a large bowl, mix condensed milk, lime juice and egg yolks until blended. With clean beaters, beat egg whites on medium speed until soft peaks form. Gradually add sugar, 1 Tbsp. at a time, beating on high after each addition until sugar is dissolved. Continue beating until stiff peaks form. Fold into milk mixture; pour into crust.
4. Bake 25-30 minutes or until filling is set. Cool 4 hours on a wire rack. Refrigerate 6 hours or overnight, covering when cold.
5. Spoon the cream layer from top of coconut milk into a large bowl (discard remaining liquid). Add whipping cream and confectioners' sugar to bowl; beat until stiff peaks form.
6. Spread the jam over pie. Dollop coconut cream over pie or serve on the side. If desired, top with raspberries and coconut.

1 piece: 678 cal., 34g fat (20g sat. fat), 168mg chol., 349mg sod., 86g carb. (69g sugars, 1g fiber), 11g pro.

Slumber Party

Don't even try to tire out a group of giggling girls. Keep their little hands busy with party-friendly food so adorable and delicious that they'll be craving it for years to come. Let them decorate their own Sleeping Bag Blondies or prepare for movie time by stirring up a batch of White Chocolate Party Mix, which can also double as a take-home treat. Let the sleepover fun begin!

WHITE CHOCOLATE PARTY MIX

I get rave reviews every time I prepare this crispy combination of cereal, popcorn, pretzels, nuts and candies. Coated in white chocolate, this mix is spectacular for parties and for gift giving.
—Rose Wentzel, St. Louis, MO

PREP: 10 MIN. + STANDING
COOK: 5 MIN. • **MAKES:** 9½ QT.

- 16 cups popped popcorn
- 3 cups Frosted Cheerios
- 1 pkg. (10 oz.) fat-free pretzel sticks
- 2 cups milk chocolate M&M's (about 12 oz.)
- 1½ cups pecan halves
- 1 pkg. (8 oz.) milk chocolate English toffee bits or brickle toffee bits
- 2 pkg. (10 to 12 oz. each) white baking chips
- 2 Tbsp. canola oil

1. In a large bowl, combine the first 6 ingredients. In a microwave or heavy saucepan over low heat, melt baking chips with oil; stir until smooth.
2. Pour over popcorn mixture; toss to coat. Immediately spread onto 2 baking sheets and let stand until set, about 2 hours. Store in airtight containers.
1 cup: 279 cal., 16g fat (6g sat. fat), 7mg chol., 221mg sod., 33g carb. (22g sugars, 2g fiber), 3g pro.

SLEEPING BAG BLONDIES

Here's the only golden brownie recipe you'll ever need. These tasty pecan bars can be dressed up for slumber parties, camping trips and Girl Scout events.
—Sharon Bickett, Chester, SC

PREP: 20 MIN. • **BAKE:** 35 MIN. + COOLING
MAKES: 16 BLONDIE BROWNIES

- 1 cup butter, softened
- 1 cup sugar
- 1 cup packed brown sugar
- 2 large eggs, room temperature
- 2 tsp. vanilla extract
- 2 cups self-rising flour
- 2 cups chopped pecans, optional
- 1½ cups white frosting
  Brown, yellow, green, orange, pink and blue gel food coloring
- 8 large marshmallows
- 16 miniature vanilla wafers
  Optional: Assorted sprinkles and mini honey bear-shaped crackers

1. Preheat oven to 325°. Line a 13x9-in. baking pan with foil, letting ends extend up sides; grease the foil. In a large bowl, cream the butter and sugars until light and fluffy, 5-7 minutes. Beat in the eggs and vanilla. Gradually beat in flour. If desired, stir in pecans.
2. Spread mixture into prepared pan. Bake 35-40 minutes or until a toothpick inserted in the center comes out clean. Cool on a wire rack.
3. Lifting with foil, remove the brownie from pan. Trim ½ in. off edges. Cut the remaining brownie lengthwise in half; cut each half crosswise into 8 bars to make 16 sleeping bags.
4. Tint ¼ cup frosting brown and 2 Tbsp. yellow; transfer each color to a resealable plastic bag. Cut a small hole in a corner of each bag and set aside. Divide the remaining frosting among 4 bowls; tint green, orange, pink and blue. Spread each of the 4 frostings over 4 brownies, reserving a small amount of each frosting to attach wafers.
5. For pillows, cut marshmallows vertically in half; place on 1 end of brownies, cut side down. Attach vanilla wafers to pillows. Pipe faces and hair on wafers using brown and yellow frostings. If desired, decorate with sprinkles and bear crackers.
1 brownie: 392 cal., 16g fat (9g sat. fat), 54mg chol., 352mg sod., 59g carb. (43g sugars, 0 fiber), 3g pro.

QUESO BAKED NACHOS

I modified a nachos recipe I found, and my family loves it! It's now a regular at all of our parties or any time we're craving nachos.

—Denise Wheeler, Newaygo, MI

PREP: 25 MIN. • **BAKE:** 10 MIN.
MAKES: 12 SERVINGS

- 1 lb. ground beef
- 1 envelope taco seasoning
- ¾ cup water
- 1 pkg. (13 oz.) tortilla chips
- 1 cup refried beans
- 1 jar (15½ oz.) salsa con queso dip
- 2 plum tomatoes, chopped
- ¼ cup minced fresh chives, optional
- ½ cup sour cream

1. Preheat oven to 350°. In a large skillet, cook and crumble beef over medium heat until no longer pink, 5-7 minutes; drain. Stir in the taco seasoning and water; bring to a boil. Reduce heat; simmer, uncovered, until thickened, about 5 minutes, stirring occasionally.
2. In an ungreased 13x9-in. baking pan, layer a third each of the following: chips, beans, beef mixture and queso dip. Repeat layers twice.
3. Bake, uncovered, until heated through, 10-15 minutes. Top with the tomatoes and, if desired, chives; serve immediately with sour cream on the side.

1 serving: 313 cal., 16g fat (5g sat. fat), 29mg chol., 786mg sod., 32g carb. (2g sugars, 2g fiber), 11g pro.

STRAWBERRY-PEACH MILK SHAKES

You'll either need thick drinking straws or spoons to enjoy this refreshing shake that combines two favorite fruits—strawberries and peaches—for a thirst-quenching treat.

—Karen Edwards, Sanford, ME

TAKES: 15 MIN. • **MAKES:** 4 SERVINGS

- ¼ cup milk
- 3 Tbsp. sugar
- 2 cups halved fresh strawberries
- 1¾ cups sliced peeled peaches (about 3 medium) or frozen unsweetened sliced peaches, thawed
- 2 cups vanilla ice cream

Place the milk, sugar, strawberries and peaches in a blender; cover and process until fruit is pureed. Add the ice cream; cover and process until blended. Serve immediately.

¾ cup: 230 cal., 8g fat (5g sat. fat), 31mg chol., 60mg sod., 38g carb. (31g sugars, 3g fiber), 4g pro.

TEST KITCHEN TIP

For an ultra-rich shake, use whole milk or milk with a little half-and-half cream, but never use heavy cream. If you send that through the blender, it'll create little bits of butter.

HOW TO MAKE HEART-SHAPED STRAWBERRY GARNISHES

STEP 1
Wash and gently dry the berries.

STEP 2
Use a paring knife to cut a V-shaped notch in the top of each strawberry.

STEP 3
Slice each berry into ¼-inch hearts.

STEP 4
To use as a drink garnish, cut a short vertical slit at the bottom of each slice and arrange on each glass as desired.

MINI PB&J CHEESECAKES

I got hooked on these mini peanut butter and jelly cheesecakes when a friend made them. She let me steal her recipe, and now I'm sharing this tasty treat with you!
—Elizabeth King, Duluth, MN

PREP: 35 MIN. • **BAKE:** 15 MIN. + COOLING
MAKES: ABOUT 2½ DOZEN

- 1 cup creamy peanut butter
- ½ cup sugar
- 1 large egg
  CHEESECAKE LAYER
- 1 pkg. (8 oz.) cream cheese, softened
- ½ cup sugar
- 1 large egg, lightly beaten
- 1 tsp. vanilla extract
- ¼ cup strawberry jelly, warmed
  OPTIONAL DRIZZLE
- ½ cup confectioners' sugar
- 2 to 3 Tbsp. heavy whipping cream

1. Preheat the oven to 350°. In a small bowl, beat the peanut butter and sugar until blended. Beat in egg. Press 2 tsp. mixture into each of 32 paper-lined mini-muffin cups.
2. For the cheesecake layer, in another bowl, beat the cream cheese and sugar until smooth. Beat in egg and vanilla. Spoon a scant 2 tsp. cream cheese mixture into each cup. Drop the jelly by ¼ teaspoonfuls over the tops. Cut through batter with toothpick to swirl.
3. Bake 12-14 minutes or until centers are set. Cool completely on a wire rack.
4. If desired, mix confectioners' sugar and enough cream to reach desired consistency; drizzle over cheesecakes. Refrigerate until serving.
1 mini cheesecake: 119 cal., 7g fat (3g sat. fat), 20mg chol., 61mg sod., 12g carb. (11g sugars, 0 fiber), 3g pro.

BEAN & SALSA STUFFED PIZZA

Get the party started with this out-of-the box appetizer pizza. It has all the Mexican flavors you love packed into convenient slices!
—Elizabeth Wright, Las Vegas, NV

TAKES: 30 MIN. • **MAKES:** 6 SERVINGS

- 2 sheets refrigerated pie crust
- 1 envelope taco seasoning, divided
- 1 cup refried beans
- ⅓ cup chopped onion
- 1 can (15 oz.) black beans, rinsed and drained
- 1 can (4 oz.) chopped green chiles, drained
- 1 cup chunky salsa
- 1 cup shredded Mexican cheese blend, divided
- 1 tsp. canola oil
  Optional: Sour cream and additional salsa

1. Preheat oven to 400°. On a work surface, unroll 1 pie crust sheet. Roll into a 12-in. circle. Transfer to an ungreased 12-in. pizza pan.
2. Reserve 1 Tbsp. taco seasoning for topping. In a small bowl, mix refried beans and remaining taco seasoning; spread over crust to within 1 in. of edge. Top with onion, black beans, chiles and salsa. Sprinkle with ¾ cup cheese.
3. Unroll remaining pie crust sheet; roll into a 13-in. circle. Place over cheese. Trim, seal and flute edge. Cut slits in top. Brush the top crust with oil; sprinkle with the reserved taco seasoning.
4. Bake 15-17 minutes or until golden brown. Sprinkle with remaining cheese. Bake 3-5 minutes longer or until cheese is melted. If desired, serve pizza with sour cream and additional salsa.
1 piece: 527 cal., 26g fat (11g sat. fat), 30mg chol., 1427mg sod., 59g carb. (5g sugars, 5g fiber), 12g pro.

TEST KITCHEN TIP

A fluted edge is one of the most common finishes for pie crusts, and it's simple to do. Flute the crust by positioning your index finger on the edge pointing outward. Then place your thumb and index finger of your other hand on the outside of the edge and pinch the pastry around your finger to form a V. Continue around the entire edge of the pie.

TACO PUFF PASTRIES

You won't be able to put these tasty taco appetizers down! And the recipe makes 80 servings, so you'll definitely be ready for guests to come over and chow down.

—Ruth Coffland, Fair Oaks, CA

PREP: 45 MIN. + COOLING
BAKE: 10 MIN./BATCH
MAKES: 80 APPETIZERS

- 2 lbs. ground beef
- 1 large onion, chopped
- 4 garlic cloves, minced
- 2 envelopes taco seasoning
- ½ tsp. pepper
- 2 cans (8 oz. each) tomato sauce
- 2 cans (4 oz. each) chopped green chiles
- 2 pkg. (17.3 oz. each) frozen puff pastry, thawed
- 1 Tbsp. water
- 2 large egg whites
- ½ cup grated Parmesan cheese

1. Preheat the oven to 400°. In a large skillet, cook beef, onion and garlic over medium heat 8-10 minutes or until beef is no longer pink, breaking the beef into crumbles; drain. Stir in taco seasoning, pepper, tomato sauce and chiles. Cool completely.
2. On a lightly floured surface, unfold 1 puff pastry sheet. Roll into a 15x12-in. rectangle; cut into twenty 3-in. squares. Spoon 1 rounded Tbsp. beef mixture in the center of each square. Brush edges of pastry with a bit of water; fold pastry over filling, forming a triangle. Press the edges with a fork to seal. Place on ungreased baking sheets. Repeat with remaining pastry and filling.
3. In a small bowl, whisk 1 Tbsp. water and egg whites; brush over the tops. Sprinkle with the Parmesan cheese. Bake until golden brown, 10-14 minutes. Serve warm.

1 appetizer: 86 cal., 4g fat (1g sat. fat), 6mg chol., 174mg sod., 8g carb. (0 sugars, 1g fiber), 3g pro.

BAKED MOZZARELLA STICKS

This is a fantastic, healthier substitute for deep-fried mozzarella sticks. I like to serve the sticks with spaghetti.

—Julie Puderbaugh, Berwick, PA

TAKES: 20 MIN. • **MAKES:** 16 APPETIZERS

- 2 tubes (8 oz. each) refrigerated crescent rolls
- 8 pieces string cheese, cut crosswise in half
- 1 cup marinara or spaghetti sauce, warmed

1. Preheat oven to 375°. Unroll crescent dough and separate each tube of dough into 8 triangles. Place 1 halved string cheese at the wide end of each triangle; roll up and seal edges.
2. Place 2 in. apart on a foil-lined baking sheet, point side down. Bake 10-12 minutes or until golden brown. Serve with marinara sauce.

1 appetizer with 1 Tbsp. sauce: 160 cal., 9g fat (4g sat. fat), 10mg chol., 370mg sod., 13g carb. (3g sugars, 0 fiber), 6g pro.

S'MORE POPS

My daughters and I came up with this treat when planning a candy-making party. The pops also make adorable hostess gifts, are perfect for potlucks and would sell out quickly at a bake sale.

—Lisa Haboush, Geneva, IL

TAKES: 20 MIN. • **MAKES:** 2 DOZEN

- 4 whole graham crackers, coarsely crushed
- 24 lollipop sticks
- 24 large marshmallows
- 4 oz. milk chocolate candy coating, melted

1. Place crushed crackers in a shallow bowl. Insert 1 lollipop stick into each marshmallow. Dip two-thirds of each marshmallow in the melted candy coating; allow excess to drip off. Dip in cracker crumbs, covering about half the chocolate.
2. Place on waxed paper; let stand until set. Store in an airtight container.

1 pop: 42 cal., 1g fat (0 sat. fat), 0 chol., 15mg sod., 8g carb. (6g sugars, 0 fiber), 0 pro.

S'MORE SPRINKLES

Kids will have fun creating their own marshmallow pops when various toppings are available. In addition to graham cracker crumbs, try crushed cookies or candy coatings such as sprinkles or nonpareils.

Baby Shark Birthday Party

Get ready for some under-the-sea fun! Baby sharks—and Mommy, Daddy, Grandma and Grandpa sharks, too!—won't be able to wait to take a big bite out of these yummy party foods. There are so many fun and creative things you can do (do do do) to make this a birthday that everyone will remember!

CHICKEN BITES WITH APRICOT SAUCE

Satisfying a hungry crowd is simple with these oven-baked morsels. The bite-sized chicken pieces are served with an incredibly easy sauce that combines apricot preserves and mustard.

—Michelle Krzmarzick, Redondo Beach, CA

PREP: 25 MIN. • **BAKE:** 15 MIN.
MAKES: 2 DOZEN (1 CUP SAUCE)

- ¾ cup all-purpose flour
- ½ cup buttermilk, divided
- 2 large eggs
- 2 cups crushed cornflakes
- ½ tsp. onion powder
- ½ tsp. garlic salt
- ¼ tsp. salt
- ¼ tsp. dried oregano
- ⅛ tsp. pepper
- 1 lb. boneless skinless chicken breasts, cut into 1-in. cubes
- 1 cup apricot preserves
- 2 Tbsp. prepared mustard

1. Preheat oven to 350°. Place flour and ¼ cup buttermilk in separate shallow bowls. In another shallow bowl, whisk eggs and remaining ¼ cup buttermilk. In a fourth shallow bowl, combine the cornflakes, onion powder, garlic salt, salt, oregano and pepper. Dip chicken in buttermilk, then dip in flour to coat all sides; shake off excess. Dip in egg mixture and then the cornflake mixture, patting to help coating adhere. Arrange the chicken in a greased 15x10x1-in. baking pan.
2. Bake 15-18 minutes or until juices run clear. In a small bowl, combine the apricot preserves and mustard. Serve with chicken.
1 piece with 2 tsp. sauce: 102 cal., 1g fat (0 sat. fat), 26mg chol., 163mg sod., 18g carb. (7g sugars, 0 fiber), 6g pro.

PEANUT BUTTER & JELLY FINGER SANDWICHES

Peanut butter and jelly sandwiches were my favorite food when I was a kid. My dad and I used to make PB&J crackers for an evening snack. And we usually had cinnamon-raisin bread in the house, so this version was a natural favorite.

—Erica Allen, Tuckerton, NJ

TAKES: 20 MIN. • **MAKES:** 2 DOZEN

- 6 Tbsp. creamy peanut butter
- 12 slices cinnamon-raisin bread, lightly toasted
- 6 Tbsp. whipped cream cheese
- 6 Tbsp. strawberry jelly

Spread the peanut butter over each of 6 bread slices. Spread cream cheese, then jelly, over remaining 6 bread slices. Top with the peanut butter bread slices. Cut each sandwich into 4 triangles.
1 triangle: 80 cal., 3g fat (1g sat. fat), 3mg chol., 60mg sod., 12g carb. (5g sugars, 1g fiber), 3g pro.

OCEAN PUNCH

This berry punch is refreshing and not overly sweet. Use your favorite Kool-Aid mix to switch up the flavor for every season and occasion.

—Elizabeth LeBlanc, Bourg, LA

PREP: 10 MIN. + CHILLING
MAKES: 18 SERVINGS (ABOUT 4½ QT.)

- 1 envelope unsweetened mixed berry Kool-Aid mix
- 2 qt. water
- ¾ cup sugar
  Swedish Fish candies, optional
- 1 can (46 oz.) pineapple juice, chilled
- 1 liter ginger ale, chilled

In a large pitcher, combine Kool-Aid mix, water and sugar. Stir until mix is dissolved; refrigerate. If desired, dip Swedish Fish in water and adhere to the sides of an empty punch bowl; let stand until set. Just before serving, pour mixture into punch bowl; add pineapple juice and ginger ale.
1 cup: 94 cal., 0 fat (0 sat. fat), 0 chol., 7mg sod., 24g carb. (21g sugars, 0 fiber), 0 pro.

BEACH BALL COOKIES

These cookies are as colorful as beach balls and just as fun. They're delightful for kids parties, school bake sales or when you just want a playful treat. Use bright, bold colors or soft pastels for springtime.
—Darlene Brenden, Salem, OR

PREP: 45 MIN. • **BAKE:** 10 MIN./BATCH
MAKES: 2 DOZEN

- ½ cup butter, softened
- ½ cup sugar
- ½ cup confectioners' sugar
- 1 large egg, room temperature
- ½ cup canola oil
- 1 tsp. vanilla extract
- 2½ cups all-purpose flour
- ½ tsp. baking soda
- ½ tsp. cream of tartar
- ¼ tsp. salt
  Assorted food coloring

1. Preheat oven to 350°. In a large bowl, cream butter and sugars until light and fluffy. Beat in egg, oil and vanilla. In another bowl, whisk flour, baking soda, cream of tartar and salt; gradually beat into creamed mixture.
2. Divide dough into 5 equal portions. Tint each portion a different color with food coloring. Divide each portion into 24 equal pieces; roll each piece into a ball. Gently press together 1 ball of each color to form a larger ball; place 1 in. apart on greased baking sheets. Flatten slightly with bottom of a glass.
3. Bake until the bottoms are lightly browned, 10-12 minutes. Remove from pans to wire racks to cool.

1 cookie: 152 cal., 9g fat (3g sat. fat), 18mg chol., 85mg sod., 17g carb. (7g sugars, 0 fiber), 2g pro.

SOUTHWESTERN SEASHELL SALAD

Serve up southwestern flavor with this quick and lovely pasta salad. It is an excellent dish for picnics since no ingredients will sour. Mix it ahead for convenience, then toss with dressing just before serving.
—Marguerite Shaeffer, Sewell, NJ

TAKES: 25 MIN. • **MAKES:** 10 SERVINGS

- 8 oz. uncooked small pasta shells
- 1 cup frozen corn, thawed
- 1 can (15 to 16 oz.) kidney or black beans, rinsed and drained
- 1 medium sweet yellow pepper, chopped
- 1 medium tomato, chopped
- ½ cup chopped red onion
- ¼ cup sliced pimiento-stuffed olives
- 3 Tbsp. lemon juice
- 2 Tbsp. minced fresh cilantro
- 2 tsp. ground cumin
- 2 tsp. olive oil
- ½ tsp. salt
- ½ tsp. pepper

1. Cook pasta according to the package directions, adding corn during the last 2 minutes. Drain and rinse in cold water.
2. Place the pasta and corn in a large bowl; add beans, yellow pepper, tomato, onion and olives. In a small bowl, whisk the lemon juice, cilantro, cumin, oil, salt and pepper. Pour over salad and toss to coat. Serve immediately.
¾ cup: 164 cal., 2g fat (0 sat. fat), 0 chol., 263mg sod., 30g carb. (3g sugars, 4g fiber), 7g pro.

SEASONED FISH CRACKERS

These zesty, easy-to-fix little bites are irresistible. Once you start snacking on them, you'll have a difficult time stopping. For parties, I double the recipe. Even then, I never have enough!
—Deanne Causey, Midland, TX

PREP: 10 MIN. • **BAKE:** 15 MIN. + COOLING
MAKES: ABOUT 2½ QT.

- 3 pkg. (6.6 oz. each) Goldfish cheddar crackers
- 1 envelope ranch salad dressing mix
- 3 tsp. dill weed
- ½ tsp. garlic powder
- ½ tsp. lemon-pepper seasoning
- ¼ tsp. cayenne pepper
- ⅔ cup canola oil

1. Preheat oven to 250°. Place crackers in a large bowl. Combine remaining ingredients; drizzle over the crackers and toss to coat evenly. Transfer to 2 ungreased 15x10x1-in. baking pans.
2. Bake 15-20 minutes, stirring the crackers occasionally. Cool completely in pans. Store in an airtight container.
¼ cup: 117 cal., 7g fat (1g sat. fat), 2mg chol., 197mg sod., 10g carb. (0 sugars, 0 fiber), 2g pro.

PIZZA STROMBOLI

I used to own a bakery, and this bread was one of our customers' favorites. Once they smelled the aroma of pizza and sampled these tempting spiral slices, they just couldn't resist taking some home.
—John Morcom, Oxford, MI

PREP: 25 MIN. + RISING • **BAKE:** 25 MIN.
MAKES: 1 LOAF

- 1   pkg. (¼ oz.) active dry yeast
- ¾   cup warm water (110° to 115°)
- 4½ tsp. honey
- 1   Tbsp. nonfat dry milk powder
- 2   cups bread flour
- ½   cup whole wheat flour
- 2   tsp. Italian seasoning
- 1   tsp. salt
- 4½ tsp. pizza sauce
- ¾   cup chopped pepperoni
- ½   cup shredded cheddar cheese, divided
- ¼   cup shredded Parmesan cheese
- ¼   cup shredded part-skim mozzarella cheese, divided
- 2   Tbsp. finely chopped onion
- 1   Tbsp. each chopped ripe olives, chopped pimiento-stuffed olives and chopped canned mushrooms

1. In a large bowl, dissolve the yeast in warm water. Stir in the honey and milk powder until well blended. In a small bowl, combine 1 cup bread flour, whole wheat flour, seasoning and salt. Add to the yeast mixture; beat until smooth. Stir in the pizza sauce. Stir in enough remaining bread flour to form a soft dough.
2. Turn onto a floured surface; knead until smooth and elastic, 6-8 minutes. Place in a greased bowl, turning once to grease top. Cover; let rise in a warm place until doubled, about 1 hour.
3. Preheat oven to 350°. Punch the dough down. Turn onto a lightly floured surface; roll into a 14x12-in. rectangle. Sprinkle pepperoni, ¼ cup cheddar cheese, Parmesan cheese, 2 Tbsp. mozzarella cheese, onion, olives and mushrooms to within ½ in. of edges.
4. Roll up jelly-roll style, starting with a long side; pinch seam to seal and tuck ends under. Place seam side down on a greased baking sheet. Cover and let rise for 45 minutes.
5. Sprinkle with the remaining cheddar and mozzarella cheeses. Bake until golden brown, 25-30 minutes. Remove from pan to a wire rack. Serve warm. Refrigerate leftovers.
1 slice: 192 cal., 7g fat (3g sat. fat), 15mg chol., 478mg sod., 24g carb. (3g sugars, 1g fiber), 8g pro.

HOMEMADE SLOPPY JOES

I simmer a big batch of this hot and tangy sandwich filling, then freeze the extras. Just thaw and reheat it for a quick dinner.
—Sandra Castillo, Janesville, WI

PREP: 10 MIN. • **COOK:** 30 MIN.
MAKES: 12 SERVINGS

- 2   lbs. ground beef
- 2   medium onions, chopped
- 2   to 3 garlic cloves, minced
- 2   cups ketchup
- 1   cup barbecue sauce
- ¼   cup packed brown sugar
- ¼   cup cider vinegar
- 2   Tbsp. prepared mustard
- 1   tsp. Italian seasoning
- 1   tsp. onion powder
- ½   tsp. pepper
- 12 hamburger buns, split

In a large skillet, cook beef, onions and garlic over medium heat until the meat is no longer pink, breaking meat into crumbles; drain. Stir in ketchup, barbecue sauce, brown sugar, vinegar, mustard, Italian seasoning, onion powder and pepper. Bring to a boil. Reduce heat; simmer, uncovered, for 20 minutes. Serve on buns.
Freeze option: Freeze cooled meat mixture in freezer containers. To use, partially thaw in refrigerator overnight. Heat through in a saucepan, stirring occasionally; add water if necessary.
1 sandwich: 368 cal., 11g fat (4g sat. fat), 47mg chol., 1029mg sod., 49g carb. (27g sugars, 1g fiber), 18g pro.

READER REVIEW
"This is delicious. I made it for a large group of friends, and it was all gone! Definitely a keeper!"
—COOKINAMA, TASTEOFHOME.COM

BABY SHARK BIRTHDAY CAKE

It doesn't take much to add a fun theme to a birthday party. This simply decorated cake, plus a few adorable frills, will bring a baby shark theme to life.
—*Taste of Home* Test Kitchen

PREP: 1 HOUR • **BAKE:** 25 MIN. + COOLING
MAKES: 16 SERVINGS

1 cup butter, softened
2½ cups sugar
4 large eggs, room temperature
4 cups all-purpose flour
3 tsp. baking powder
1 tsp. salt
½ tsp. baking soda
1½ cups sour cream

FROSTING

6 oz. white baking chips
¼ cup heavy whipping cream
2 tsp. vanilla extract
6 large egg whites, room temperature
1½ cups sugar
½ tsp. cream of tartar
½ tsp. salt
2 cups unsalted butter, cubed

Blue, red and green liquid food coloring
4 oz. prepared fondant
2 candy eyes
Optional: Sea creature candies and graham cracker crumbs

1. Preheat oven to 350°. Line bottoms of 3 greased and floured 9-in. round baking pans with parchment; grease paper. In a large bowl, cream butter and sugar until light and fluffy, 5-7 minutes. Add eggs, 1 at a time, beating well after each addition. Combine flour, baking powder, salt and baking soda; add to creamed mixture alternately with sour cream, beating well after each addition.
2. Transfer to prepared pans. Bake until edges begin to brown, 25-30 minutes. Cool the cakes for 10 minutes before removing from pans to wire racks to cool completely.
3. In a microwave, melt the baking chips with cream until smooth, stirring every 30 seconds. Stir in vanilla. Set aside to cool slightly. Meanwhile, in heatproof bowl of stand mixer, whisk egg whites, sugar, cream of tartar and salt until blended. Place over simmering water in a large saucepan over medium heat. Whisking constantly, heat mixture until thermometer reads 160°, 8-10 minutes.
4. Remove from the heat. With whisk attachment of stand mixer, beat mixture on high speed until cooled to 90°, about 7 minutes. Gradually beat in the butter, a few tablespoons at a time, on medium speed until smooth. Beat in the cooled baking chip mixture until blended.
5. Set aside ¼ cup frosting. Tint the remaining frosting desired shades of blue; spread blue frosting between layers and over top and sides of cake. Tint ½ oz. fondant red. Divide remaining fondant in half. Tint 1 portion blue. Leave the other half white. On a work surface dusted with confectioners' sugar, roll out the blue fondant to ⅛-in.-thick. Using a 3-in. round cutter, cut out 1 circle; repeat with the white fondant. Using a sharp knife, cut mouth opening, teeth and body shape on lower portion of white circle. Place the white fondant cutout onto blue circle. Roll red fondant to ⅛-in thick; cut a small triangle and place in mouth opening, under white fondant and on top of blue fondant. If needed, brush fondant lightly with water to help layers adhere. With the remaining rolled blue fondant, cut a crescent moon shape for the tail and a triangle for the fin. Secure fin and tail to shark body, brushing edges lightly with water, if needed, to help pieces adhere. Secure candy eyes to shark body with small amount of reserved frosting. Place fondant shark on side of cake by pressing gently into frosting. Tint remaining reserved frosting green. Using a leaf tip, pipe seaweed on sides of cake. If desired, decorate cake with the sea creature candies and graham cracker crumbs for sand. Refrigerate until serving. Remove from refrigerator 30 minutes before serving. Refrigerate any leftovers.

1 piece: 777 cal., 46g fat (28g sat. fat), 150mg chol., 503mg sod., 86g carb. (62g sugars, 1g fiber), 8g pro.

DID YOU KNOW?

A mixture of sugar, water and cream of tartar that has been cooked to the soft-ball stage, fondant is often used for decorative purposes or as a candy center. It is commonly rolled into a sheet and draped over cakes or molded into shapes. Food coloring and flavoring are often added.

SANDY BEACH TRIFLE

My husband doesn't like chocolate, so I created this dessert using vanilla pudding and cookies. It is simple to put together and can be made ahead. Everyone loves it!
—JoAnn Wegrzyn, Kingsley, MI

PREP: 25 MIN. + CHILLING
MAKES: 10 SERVINGS

- 2 cups cold 2% milk
- 1 pkg. (3.4 oz.) instant vanilla pudding mix
- 1 pkg. (8 oz.) cream cheese, softened
- ¼ cup butter, softened
- ¾ cup confectioners' sugar
- 1 carton (8 oz.) frozen whipped topping, thawed
- 1 pkg. (19.1 oz.) Golden Oreo cookies, finely crushed

1. In a small bowl, whisk the milk and pudding mix for 2 minutes. In a large bowl, beat cream cheese and butter until smooth. Beat in confectioners' sugar until light and fluffy. Gradually beat in prepared pudding. Fold in the whipped topping.
2. Place 1⅔ cups crushed cookies in a 3-qt. trifle or glass bowl. Top with half the pudding mixture. Repeat layers. Top with remaining crushed cookies. Cover and refrigerate at least 4 hours or overnight.

1 cup: 550 cal., 28g fat (14g sat. fat), 39mg chol., 383mg sod., 66g carb. (44g sugars, 0 fiber), 5g pro.

HOMEMADE SANDCASTLES

Here's the perfect centerpiece for a beach-themed party. Kids can help make this easy project.
—*Taste of Home* Test Kitchen

TAKES: 20 MIN.
MAKES: VARIOUS SANDCASTLE MOLDS

- ⅓ cup all-purpose flour
- 2 Tbsp. sugar
- 1 cup cold water
- 6 cups moist sand
  Sandcastle molds of various shapes and sizes
  Nautical rope, rocks and seashells

1. In a saucepan, combine the flour and sugar. Gradually add cold water; mix well. Cook and stir over low heat until the mixture thickens to pudding consistency.
2. Place sand in a large pail; stir in flour mixture. When cool to the touch, mix together with your hands, adding more water if needed so that the sand holds its shape. Firmly pack into molds. Invert on a flat surface; remove molds.
3. Let dry completely before handling. Depending on the humidity, this may take a few days.
4. To create a centerpiece, weave rope between the sandcastles; fill in with sand, rocks and seashells. The sand mixture will keep for weeks when stored in an airtight container.

Summer Bashes

Gender Reveal Party

Chubby cheeks, teeny-tiny toes, precious coos and that first big gummy smile—talk about love at first sight. Mama-to-be is aglow with happiness, and everyone's sharing in the excitement and anticipation. Then there's the big question: Is it a handsome lad or a pretty little lady? Get inspired to share the exciting news with these culinary creations and turn to page 147 for more fun ideas for the big reveal.

STRAWBERRY MIMOSAS

Here's a terrific twist on the classic mimosa. To make this refreshing drink friendly for kids or mamas-to-be, substitute lemon-lime soda or ginger ale for the champagne.
—Kelly Maxwell, Plainfield, Il

TAKES: 15 MIN. • **MAKES:** 12 SERVINGS

- 7 **cups sliced fresh strawberries (about 2 qt.)**
- 3 **cups orange juice**
- 4 **cups champagne, chilled**
GARNISHES
   Optional: Fresh strawberries and orange slices

1. Place half each of the strawberries and orange juice in a blender; cover and process until smooth. Press the mixture through a fine mesh strainer. Repeat with remaining strawberries and orange juice.
2. Pour a scant ⅔ cup strawberry mixture into each champagne flute or wine glass. Top each with about ⅓ cup champagne. If desired, serve each with a fresh strawberry and an orange slice.

1 cup: 112 cal., 0 fat (0 sat. fat), 0 chol., 1mg sod., 15g carb. (10g sugars, 2g fiber), 1g pro.

LIME-CILANTRO SHRIMP SKEWERS

My friend gave me this recipe. The combo of the lime, cilantro and soy sauce gives these shrimp skewers a memorable taste reminiscent of tropical cuisine. To make it a main dish, serve with rice or couscous.
—Theresa Dibert, Cynthiana, KY

PREP: 10 MIN. + MARINATING
GRILL: 10 MIN. • **MAKES:** 1 DOZEN

- ⅓ **cup lime juice**
- 3 **Tbsp. minced fresh cilantro**
- 2 **Tbsp. soy sauce**
- 3 **garlic cloves, minced**
- 2 **tsp. olive oil**
- 1¼ **lbs. uncooked shrimp (26-30 per lb.), peeled and deveined**
- 1 **cup soaked mesquite wood chips, optional**

1. In a large bowl, whisk the first 5 ingredients until blended. Add shrimp; toss to coat. Refrigerate, covered, 30 minutes.
2. If desired, add wood chips to grill according to the manufacturer's directions. Drain shrimp, discarding marinade. On each of 12 soaked wooden appetizer skewers, thread the shrimp.
3. Grill on an oiled rack, covered, over medium heat until shrimp turn pink, 3-4 minutes per side.

1 skewer: 43 cal., 1g fat (0 sat. fat), 57mg chol., 94mg sod., 1g carb. (0 sugars, 0 fiber), 8g pro.

LAYERED HUMMUS DIP

My love for Greece inspired this fast, easy Mediterranean dip. It is fabulous for parties and a delicious way to include garden-fresh veggies on your menu.
—Cheryl Snavely, Hagerstown, MD

TAKES: 15 MIN. • **MAKES:** 12 SERVINGS

- 1 **carton (10 oz.) hummus**
- ¼ **cup finely chopped red onion**
- ½ **cup Greek olives, chopped**
- 2 **medium tomatoes, seeded and chopped**
- 1 **large English cucumber, chopped**
- 1 **cup crumbled feta cheese**
   Baked pita chips

Spread the hummus into a shallow 10-in. round dish. Layer with onion, olives, tomatoes, cucumber and feta cheese. Refrigerate until serving. Serve with pita chips.

1 serving: 88 cal., 5g fat (2g sat. fat), 5mg chol., 275mg sod., 6g carb. (1g sugars, 2g fiber), 4g pro. **Diabetic exchanges:** 1 fat, ½ starch.

CRUNCHY CHICKEN SALAD CROISSANTS

Folks have come to expect these quick and satisfying sandwiches when I host showers or parties. Feel free to add pineapple or grapes to the sandwich filling.
—Angela Lively, Conroe, TX

TAKES: 20 MIN. • **MAKES:** 1 DOZEN

- 2½ cups cubed cooked chicken
- 2 celery ribs, finely chopped
- ½ cup sliced almonds, toasted
- ¾ cup mayonnaise
- ½ tsp. salt
- ¼ tsp. coarsely ground pepper
- ¼ cup heavy whipping cream
- 1 Tbsp. sugar
- 12 miniature croissants, split
  Bibb lettuce leaves, optional

1. In a large bowl, combine chicken, celery and almonds. In a small bowl, mix mayonnaise, salt and pepper. In another bowl, beat cream until it begins to thicken. Add sugar; beat until stiff peaks form. Fold into mayonnaise mixture. Pour over chicken mixture; toss to coat.

2. If desired, line croissant bottoms with lettuce leaves; top each with ⅓ cup chicken salad. Replace tops.

1 sandwich: 457 cal., 33g fat (10g sat. fat), 77mg chol., 617mg sod., 23g carb. (4g sugars, 2g fiber), 18g pro.

GRILLED FRUIT PHYLLO TART

This tart was a hit at my friend's baby shower. It reminds me of a fruit salad that my mother used to make with cream cheese and whipped topping. Everyone loved the flaky crust, and the bright colors make it a pretty addition to any spread.
—Laura McAllister, Morganton, NC

PREP: 30 MIN. • **GRILL:** 10 MIN.
MAKES: 12 SERVINGS

- 3 **Tbsp. butter, melted**
- 4 **tsp. canola oil**
- 8 **sheets phyllo dough (14x9-in. size)**
- 1 **large lemon**
- 3 **medium peaches, peeled and halved**
- 2 **cups large fresh strawberries, stems removed**
- 4 **slices fresh pineapple (½ in. thick)**
- ⅓ **cup packed brown sugar**
- ½ **tsp. salt**
- ½ **cup heavy whipping cream**
- 1 **pkg. (8 oz.) cream cheese, softened**
- ⅓ **cup confectioners' sugar**
- 2 **Tbsp. chopped fresh mint**

1. Preheat oven to 400°. In a small bowl, mix butter and oil. Brush a 15x10x1-in. baking pan with some of the butter mixture. Place 1 sheet of phyllo dough into prepared pan; brush with butter mixture. Layer with the 7 additional phyllo sheets, brushing each layer. (Keep remaining phyllo covered with a damp towel to prevent it from drying out.) Bake 5-7 minutes or until golden brown (the phyllo will puff up during baking). Cool completely.

2. Finely grate enough zest from the lemon to measure 1 Tbsp. Cut lemon crosswise in half; squeeze juice into a bowl. In a large bowl, toss peaches, strawberries, pineapple, brown sugar, salt, and lemon zest and juice. Remove strawberries; thread fruit onto 3 metal or soaked wooden skewers.

3. Place fruit on oiled grill rack. Grill, covered, over medium heat until fruit is tender, turning once, 8-10 minutes for pineapple and peaches, 4-5 minutes for strawberries. Remove and set aside.

4. In a small bowl, beat the cream until soft peaks form. In another bowl, beat cream cheese and confectioners' sugar until smooth. Fold in whipped cream. Spread over phyllo crust. Slice grilled fruit; arrange over filling. Sprinkle with mint; cut into pieces.

1 piece: 233 cal., 15g fat (8g sat. fat), 38mg chol., 216mg sod., 24g carb. (18g sugars, 2g fiber), 3g pro.

PHYLLO FACTS

Phyllo (pronounced *FEE-lo*) is a tissue-thin pastry that's made by gently stretching dough into thin, fragile sheets. It can be layered, shaped and baked in a variety of sweet and savory ways. Because phyllo is thin and tears easily, working on a smooth, dry surface and handling it quickly is key. Follow the manufacturer's instructions for thawing phyllo in the unopened package. Count the number of phyllo sheets required for your recipe, place them on a smooth, dry surface and immediately cover them with a damp towel. Gently pull sheets from the stack, keeping the rest covered until needed.

ARTICHOKE CRESCENT APPETIZERS

This colorful appetizer is sure to please guests at any affair. My family loves it served both warmed up and chilled.

—Mary Ann Dell, Phoenixville, PA

PREP: 20 MIN. • **BAKE:** 15 MIN.
MAKES: 2 DOZEN

1 tube (8 oz.) refrigerated crescent rolls
2 Tbsp. grated Parmesan cheese
6 oz. cream cheese, softened
½ cup sour cream
1 large egg
½ tsp. dill weed
¼ tsp. seasoned salt
1 can (14 oz.) water-packed artichoke hearts, rinsed, drained and chopped
⅓ cup thinly chopped green onions
1 jar (2 oz.) diced pimientos, drained

1. Unroll crescent dough and press onto the bottom and ½ in. up the sides of an ungreased 13x9-in. baking dish; seal seams and perforations. Sprinkle with Parmesan cheese. Bake at 375° until lightly browned, 8-10 minutes.
2. Meanwhile, in a small bowl, beat cream cheese, sour cream and egg until smooth. Stir in dill and seasoned salt. Spread over crust. Sprinkle with artichokes, green onions and pimientos.
3. Bake until edges are golden brown, 15-20 minutes. Cut into 24 pieces.
1 piece: 81 cal., 5g fat (2g sat. fat), 16mg chol., 163mg sod., 6g carb. (2g sugars, 0 fiber), 2g pro.

GENDER REVEAL GUESSING GAME

Frame a poem and decorate wood clothespins with ribbon to create a fun "Is It a Boy or a Girl?" guessing game. Guests will select either a pink or blue clothespin and then clip it to their collar or sleeve to reveal their prediction.

MATERIALS
☐ Standard-size wood spring clothespins (estimate at least two clothespins per guest)

☐ Grosgrain ribbon of the same width as clothespins—pastel blue and pastel pink

☐ 8½x11-in. sheet of white card stock

☐ White 8x10 photo frame

☐ Craft glue

☐ Small basket to hold clothespins

STEP 1
Cut one approximately 4½-in. length of pink ribbon for each of half the clothespins. Repeat with blue ribbon for each of the remaining clothespins.

STEP 2
Glue a piece of ribbon to one outer side of each clothespin, wrapping the excess ribbon over the ends of the clothespin. Let dry.

STEP 3
Use a computer and printer to type and print the poem shown in photo onto white card stock, centering the poem on the page. Trim card stock as needed so it will fit inside the photo frame, keeping the poem centered.

STEP 4
Cut two pieces of pink ribbon so that the length matches the width of card stock. Repeat with blue ribbon.

STEP 5
Glue one blue and one pink ribbon across the card stock, positioning them just above the poem. In the same way, glue remaining two ribbons just below the poem. Let dry.

STEP 6
Place poem in frame. Place clothespins in basket.

Note: To make sure ribbon is secure, use glue to attach it to clothespins even if ribbon has adhesive backing.

SNOWBALL SURPRISE COOKIES

Keep the guests guessing until the big cake reveal! Use candy coating disks to tint the insides of these tender cookies pink and blue. Since these disks come in a variety of colors, you can also make the cookies to match any holiday or theme.
—Jan Whitworth, Roebuck, SC

PREP: 25 MIN. + CHILLING
BAKE: 15 MIN./BATCH
MAKES: ABOUT 3 DOZEN

- 1   cup butter, softened
- 1½   cups confectioners' sugar, divided
- 2   tsp. vanilla extract
- 2   cups all-purpose flour
- ¼   tsp. salt
- ⅓   cup each finely chopped pecans, walnuts and almonds, toasted
- 39   pink or blue candy coating disks

1. In a large bowl, cream butter, ½ cup confectioners' sugar and vanilla until light and fluffy. In another bowl, whisk the flour and salt; gradually beat into the creamed mixture. Stir in the nuts. Refrigerate 1 hour or until firm.

2. Preheat oven to 350°. Shape the dough into 1-in. balls; place 1 in. apart on ungreased baking sheets. Insert a candy disk into center of each cookie, reshaping the dough into a ball and covering the disk completely.

3. Bake 12-15 minutes or until bottoms are light brown. Cool on pans 2 minutes. Place remaining confectioners' sugar in a shallow bowl. Roll warm cookies in confectioners' sugar. Cool on wire racks. Re-roll cookies if needed.

1 cookie: 119 cal., 8g fat (4g sat. fat), 13mg chol., 56mg sod., 12g carb. (7g sugars, 0 fiber), 1g pro.

BACON-WRAPPED GRILLED ASPARAGUS

I tried this at a friend's house and modified the recipe to appeal to my family's tastes. I recommend cooking the asparagus outside on the grill. It's excellent for any celebration.
—Karyl Tobel, Helena, MT

PREP: 15 MIN. • **GRILL:** 20 MIN.
MAKES: 16 APPETIZERS

- 2   Tbsp. soy sauce
- 2   Tbsp. olive oil
- 1   garlic clove, minced
- 1   lb. bacon strips
- 16   fresh asparagus spears, trimmed

In a small bowl, mix soy sauce, oil and garlic. Wrap a bacon strip around each asparagus spear. Thread 8 asparagus spears onto 2 parallel soaked wooden skewers. Repeat with the remaining asparagus. Grill, covered, over medium-low heat 18-20 minutes or until bacon is crisp, turning occasionally. Brush with soy sauce mixture.

1 wrapped asparagus spear: 138 cal., 13g fat (4g sat. fat), 19mg chol., 304mg sod., 1g carb. (1g sugars, 0 fiber), 4g pro.

CREATIVE GENDER REVEAL IDEAS

Try these ideas to share the exciting news of the baby's gender with friends and family. It's even more fun if the parents-to-be are finding out for the first time, too!

THE SECRET'S IN THE CUPCAKE

Gender reveal cakes are all the rage, so why not try the same concept with cupcakes?

BALLOON LAUNCH

Place several pink or blue balloons in a large box. When the parents-to-be open the box, the balloons will float out, revealing a boy or a girl.

CONFETTI POPPERS

Make homemade confetti poppers using toilet paper tubes and a few other simple supplies. Fill the insides of the poppers with gender-hued confetti. When it's time to find out, have guests shoot the poppers into the air. Google "DIY Confetti Popper" to find easy tutorials.

SILLY STRING

Cover the outsides of cans filled with pink or blue silly string with white or yellow non-transparent paper. When it's time for the big reveal, have guests shake and spray to see baby's gender.

PINATA

Fill a pinata with pink or blue candies. When it's broken open and the loot spills out, baby's sex is a secret no more!

BUBBLY CITRUS PUNCH

Puckery lemonade and limeade combined with sweet pineapple juice give this fruity drink its bubbly goodness. It's easy to make and wonderful for large get-togethers.
—Jackie Flood, Geneseo, NY

TAKES: 15 MIN.
MAKES: 30 SERVINGS

- 1 **can (46 oz.) unsweetened pineapple juice, chilled**
- 2 **cans (12 oz. each) frozen lemonade concentrate, thawed**
- 1 **can (12 oz.) frozen limeade concentrate, thawed**
- 4½ **cups cold water**
- 2 **liters lemon-lime soda, chilled**

In a punch bowl, mix the juice, the concentrates and the water. Stir in soda. Serve immediately.
¾ cup: 120 cal., 0 fat (0 sat. fat), 0 chol., 10mg sod., 30g carb. (26g sugars, 0 fiber), 0 pro.

GENDER REVEAL CAKE

Is it a boy or a girl? Create the perfect reveal by displaying this scrumptious cake tinted with pink or blue frosting on the inside.
—Heather Chambers, Largo, FL

PREP: 45 MIN. • **BAKE:** 20 MIN. + COOLING
MAKES: 12 SERVINGS

- ½ **cup butter, softened**
- 1¼ **cups sugar**
- 3 **large eggs, room temperature**
- 1 **tsp. vanilla extract**
- 2 **cups all-purpose flour**
- 2 **tsp. baking powder**
- 1 **tsp. salt**
- 1 **cup 2% milk**
- FROSTING
- 1 **pkg. (8 oz.) cream cheese, softened**
- 1 **cup confectioners' sugar**
- 2 **tsp. vanilla extract**
- 2 **cups heavy whipping cream**
  Blue and pink paste food coloring

1. Preheat oven to 350°. Line bottoms of 2 greased 8-in. round baking pans with parchment; grease and flour paper.
2. In a large bowl, cream the butter and sugar until light and fluffy, 5-7 minutes. Add eggs, 1 at a time, beating well after each addition. Beat in vanilla. In another bowl, whisk the flour, baking powder and salt; add to the creamed mixture alternately with milk, beating well after each addition.
3. Transfer to prepared pans. Bake 20-25 minutes or until a toothpick inserted in each center comes out clean. Cool in pans 10 minutes before removing to wire racks; remove the parchment. Cool completely.
4. Place a large bowl and beaters in freezer until cold, about 15 minutes. In the chilled bowl, beat cream cheese, confectioners' sugar and vanilla until smooth. Gradually beat in cream until firm peaks form. Tint 1¼ cups blue and ¼ cup pink (switch measurements if it's a girl), and leave the remaining frosting white.
5. Place 1 cake layer on a serving plate. Pipe a circle of white frosting around top edge of layer. Spread 1 cup blue (or pink if it's a girl) frosting inside white frosting. Top with remaining cake layer. Frost top and sides with white frosting. Using a #8 tip and white frosting, pipe pearls around top and bottom edges of cake. Using a #12 tip, pipe blue and pink dots over the cake. With a #4 tip and pink frosting, add "It's a ... " to top of cake. Refrigerate until serving.
1 piece: 431 cal., 24g fat (15g sat. fat), 114mg chol., 377mg sod., 49g carb. (33g sugars, 1g fiber), 6g pro.

HOW TO MAKE A GENDER REVEAL CAKE

STEP 1: CREATE A BORDER
Place the first cake layer on a serving plate or cake pedestal. Pipe a thick circle of white frosting around top edge. This circle will be the barrier that conceals the colored frosting inside.

STEP 2: FILL WITH BLUE OR PINK FROSTING
Carefully spread a single cup of the blue or pink frosting inside the white circle. It's important to be precise so there are no leaky giveaways.

STEP 3: FINISH IT OFF
Place the second cake layer on top of the first. Cover the top and sides of the cake with a generous layer of white frosting. Pipe blue and pink dots over cake and inscribe a cute message on top.

Juneteenth

June 19, also known as Freedom Day or Emancipation Day, is an annual holiday generally commemorating the end of slavery in the United States. Celebrated since the late 1800s, Juneteenth is an exploration of black culture, lifestyle values and traditions. The day is often filled with fun community events and barbecue-style feasts with soul food dishes, one of the nation's most identifiable culinary traditions.

STRAWBERRY COOLER

This refreshing beverage is easy to double for a crowd. Just make two batches ahead of time, and add ginger ale and ice when you're ready for more!

—Judy Robertson, Southington, CT

TAKES: 10 MIN. • **MAKES:** 8 SERVINGS

- 3 cups water
- 5 cups sliced fresh strawberries
- ¾ to 1 cup sugar
- ¼ cup lemon juice
- 2 tsp. grated lemon zest
- 1 cup ginger ale
  Crushed ice
  Additional strawberries, optional

In a blender, process the water, sliced strawberries, sugar, and lemon juice and zest in batches until smooth. Strain the berry seeds if desired. Pour mixture into a pitcher; stir in ginger ale. Serve in chilled glasses over ice. If desired, garnish with strawberries.

1 cup: 116 cal., 0 fat (0 sat. fat), 0 chol., 3mg sod., 29g carb. (26g sugars, 2g fiber), 1g pro.

MARINATED SWEET POTATO SALAD

My dad has been growing sweet potatoes for more than two decades. My brother and I have been partners in the operation for the last several years. This recipe, from our mom and our wives, is a delicious way to serve our favorite vegetable.

—Tim Jack Edmondson, Vardaman, MS

PREP: 40 MIN. + CHILLING
MAKES: 12 SERVINGS

- 8 medium sweet potatoes (about 4 lbs.)
- 1 cup tarragon vinegar
- ½ cup vegetable oil
- 1 Tbsp. honey
- 2 garlic cloves, minced
- 2 bay leaves
- ½ tsp. salt
- ¼ tsp. pepper
- ¼ tsp. dried oregano
- ¼ tsp. dried thyme
- 1 medium onion, quartered and thinly sliced
- 1 medium green pepper, julienned and cut into 1-in. pieces.

1. Place sweet potatoes in a large saucepan or Dutch oven; cover with water. Bring to a boil. Reduce heat; cover and cook for 20-23 minutes or just until tender. Drain; cool slightly and peel.
2. Meanwhile, in a jar with a tight-fitting lid, combine the next 9 ingredients; shake well.
3. Cut potatoes in half lengthwise. In a large bowl, slice potato halves into ¼-in. slices. Add the onion and green pepper. Shake dressing; drizzle over the potato mixture and gently toss to coat. Cover and refrigerate for at least 3 hours. Discard bay leaves.

¾ cup: 222 cal., 9g fat (1g sat. fat), 0 chol., 112mg sod., 33g carb. (15g sugars, 4g fiber), 2g pro. **Diabetic exchanges:** 2 starch, 2 fat.

DID YOU KNOW?
Sweet potatoes are a low-calorie, high-fiber food that's packed full of vitamins and minerals. Every cup of baked sweet potato (with the skin on) contains a whopping 769% of the recommended daily value of vitamin A, along with vitamins C and B6, manganese and potassium.

WHAT IS JUNETEENTH?

Celebrated on June 19, the holiday remembers the emancipation of enslaved people in the United States. In 1872, Black ministers and leaders in Houston, Texas, purchased 10 acres of land and created Emancipation Park for the annual celebration.

This holiday is also called Juneteenth Independence Day, Freedom Day or Emancipation Day. It has long been celebrated in Texas and throughout the South but is becoming increasingly popular across the country with more than 200 official events.

HOW IS JUNETEENTH CELEBRATED?

To commemorate Emancipation Day, people gather to celebrate the legacy of resilience and to acknowledge the ongoing struggle through marches, prayers and other remembrances.

WHAT KIND OF FOOD IS SERVED?

The red trinity—barbecue, watermelon and a red beverage—is at the heart of the meal. But no Juneteenth menu is complete without traditional side dishes and desserts like collard greens, potato salad, cornbread pudding, peach cobbler and banana pudding.

This traditional cooking is an ode to history and heritage. Perhaps no region has had more impact on America's culinary history than the South.

BOURBON CANDIED BACON DEVILED EGGS

It doesn't get any better than deviled eggs with bacon—bourbon candied bacon, that is. See if you can resist them. We can't!
—Colleen Delawder, Herndon, VA

PREP: 20 MIN. • **BAKE:** 25 MIN.
MAKES: 2 DOZEN

- 2 Tbsp. brown sugar
- ¾ tsp. Dijon mustard
- ½ tsp. maple syrup
- ⅛ tsp. salt
- 2 tsp. bourbon, optional
- 4 thick-sliced bacon strips

EGGS
- 12 hard-boiled large eggs
- ¾ cup mayonnaise
- 1 Tbsp. maple syrup
- 1 Tbsp. Dijon mustard
- ¼ tsp. pepper
- ¼ tsp. ground chipotle pepper
  Minced fresh chives

1. Preheat oven to 350°. In a small bowl, mix the brown sugar, ¾ tsp. mustard, ½ tsp. syrup and salt. If desired, stir in bourbon. Coat bacon with brown sugar mixture. Place on a rack in a foil-lined 15x10x1-in. baking pan. Bake until crisp, 25-30 minutes. Cool completely.
2. Cut eggs in half lengthwise. Remove yolks, reserving whites. In a small bowl, mash yolks. Add mayonnaise, 1 Tbsp. syrup, 1 Tbsp. mustard and both types of pepper; stir until smooth. Chop bacon finely; fold half into egg yolk mixture. Spoon or pipe into egg whites. Sprinkle with remaining bacon and the chives. Refrigerate, covered, until serving.

1 stuffed egg half: 107 cal., 9g fat (2g sat. fat), 97mg chol., 142mg sod., 2g carb. (2g sugars, 0 fiber), 4g pro.

WATERMELON SALAD WITH CINNAMON PRETZEL CRUNCH

This is an excellent side dish during the hot summer, especially here in Texas. The pretzel crunch gives the salad a little bite.
—Joan Hallford, North Richland Hills, TX

PREP: 20 MIN. + CHILLING
BAKE: 5 MIN. + COOLING
MAKES: 10 SERVINGS

- 2 cups chopped seedless watermelon
- 2 cups fresh blueberries
- 1 medium peach, chopped
- 1 medium nectarine, chopped
- 1 large kiwifruit, peeled and chopped
- ½ cup sweet white wine or grape juice
- 3 Tbsp. sugar

CRUNCH
- 1 cup chopped miniature pretzels
- ½ cup packed brown sugar
- ½ cup butter, melted
- ½ cup chopped pecans
- ¼ tsp. ground cinnamon

1. Preheat oven to 425° In a large bowl, combine the watermelon, blueberries, peach, nectarine and kiwi. Drizzle with wine and sugar. Toss to coat. Cover and refrigerate 1 hour.
2. Meanwhile, in a small bowl, combine pretzels, brown sugar, butter, pecans and cinnamon; toss to coat. Spread the mixture evenly onto a parchment-lined 15x10x1-in. baking pan. Bake 5-7 minutes or until mixture is bubbly and sugar is dissolved. Cool mixture completely. Break into small chunks.
3. Just before serving, gently stir half the pretzel mixture into the fruit. Top with remaining pretzel mixture to serve.
¾ cup: 244 cal., 14g fat (6g sat. fat), 24mg chol., 146mg sod., 30g carb. (23g sugars, 2g fiber), 2g pro.

155

PECAN PIE COBBLER

I couldn't find a recipe, so I took it upon myself to devise this amazing dessert that combines the ease of a cobbler and the rich taste of pecan pie. It tastes even better with ice cream or whipped topping.
—Willa Kelley, Edmond, OK

PREP: 20 MIN. • **BAKE:** 30 MIN. + COOLING
MAKES: 12 SERVINGS

- ½ cup butter, cubed
- 1 cup plus 2 Tbsp. all-purpose flour
- ¾ cup sugar
- 3 tsp. baking powder
- ¼ tsp. salt
- ⅔ cup 2% milk
- 1 tsp. vanilla extract
- 1½ cups coarsely chopped pecans
- 1 cup packed brown sugar
- ¾ cup brickle toffee bits
- 1½ cups boiling water
  Vanilla ice cream, optional

1. Preheat oven to 350°. Place butter in a 13x9-in. baking pan; heat pan in oven 3-5 minutes or until butter is melted. Meanwhile, combine the flour, sugar, baking powder and salt. Stir in milk and vanilla until combined.

2. Remove baking pan from oven; add batter. Sprinkle with pecans, brown sugar and toffee bits. Slowly pour the boiling water over the top (do not stir). Bake, uncovered, until golden brown, 30-35 minutes. Cool on a wire rack for 30 minutes (cobbler will thicken upon cooling). Serve warm, with ice cream if desired.

1 serving: 411 cal., 23g fat (8g sat. fat), 26mg chol., 327mg sod., 51g carb. (41g sugars, 2g fiber), 3g pro.

SMOKED BRISKET

This is always a crowd favorite— it really melts in your mouth!
—Jodi Abel, La Jolla, CA

PREP: 20 MIN. + MARINATING
GRILL: 8 HOURS • **MAKES:** 20 SERVINGS

- 2 Tbsp. olive oil
- 1 fresh beef brisket (7 to 8 lbs.), flat cut

RUB
- 2 Tbsp. garlic powder
- 2 Tbsp. onion powder
- 2 Tbsp. chili powder
- 1 Tbsp. ground mustard
- 1 Tbsp. ground cumin
- 1 Tbsp. paprika
- 1 Tbsp. smoked sea salt

MOP SAUCE
- 2 cups beef broth
- ¼ cup olive oil
- 2 Tbsp. Worcestershire sauce
- 2 Tbsp. hickory-flavored liquid smoke

1. Brush olive oil over brisket. Combine the rub ingredients; rub over both sides of beef. Place the brisket on a rimmed baking sheet. Cover and refrigerate overnight or up to 2 days. Meanwhile, in a saucepan, combine mop sauce ingredients. Simmer for 15 minutes, stirring occasionally. Refrigerate until ready to grill.

2. Soak hickory and mesquite chips or pellets; add to smoker according to manufacturer's directions. Heat to 225°. Uncover the brisket. Place brisket in the smoker fat side up; smoke 2 hours. Brush generously with mop sauce; turn the meat. Smoke 2 more hours; brush generously with the mop sauce again. Wrap the brisket securely in heavy-duty aluminum foil; smoke until a thermometer inserted in beef reads 190°, 4-5 more hours.

3. Let beef stand 20-30 minutes before slicing; cut diagonally across the grain into thin slices.

4 oz. cooked beef: 252 cal., 11g fat (3g sat. fat), 68mg chol., 472mg sod., 2g carb. (0 sugars, 1g fiber), 33g pro.
Diabetic exchanges: 4 lean meat.

TEST KITCHEN TIP

When picking a brisket, it's all about the marbling—long streaks of white fat within the lean sections of the meat. As the brisket cooks, this intramuscular fat will melt and keep the lean meat juicy. So always look for marbling—the more marbling, the more flavorful and tender the brisket.

PEACH UPSIDE-DOWN CHEESECAKE

I make this recipe every summer when peaches are ripe. Each year I improve the dessert with slight changes, and this version is the best one yet.
—Kristin Renee Olbert, Richmond, VA

PREP: 30 MIN. • **BAKE:** 65 MIN. + CHILLING
MAKES: 16 SERVINGS

- ¼ cup butter, melted
- ½ cup packed brown sugar
- 3 medium peaches, divided
- 3 pkg. (8 oz. each) cream cheese, softened
- 1 cup sugar
- 1 cup sour cream
- 1 tsp. vanilla extract
- 4 large eggs, room temperature, lightly beaten

1. Preheat oven to 350°. Line the bottom and sides of a 9-in. round baking pan with parchment. Pour butter into the prepared pan; sprinkle with the brown sugar. Slice 2 peaches and arrange in a single layer over brown sugar.

2. In a large bowl, beat cream cheese and sugar until smooth. Beat in sour cream and vanilla. Add eggs; beat on low speed just until blended. Chop the remaining peach; fold into batter. Spoon over peach slices. Place the cake pan in a larger baking pan; add 1 in. of hot water to larger pan.

3. Bake until center is just set and top appears dull, 65-75 minutes. Remove the cake pan from water bath. Cool the cheesecake on a wire rack 10 minutes. Loosen the sides from the pan with a knife. Cool 1 hour longer. Refrigerate overnight, covering when completely cooled. Invert onto a serving plate.

1 piece: 309 cal., 22g fat (13g sat. fat), 101mg chol., 181mg sod., 25g carb. (24g sugars, 0 fiber), 5g pro.

LISA'S ALL-DAY SUGAR & SALT PORK ROAST

My family loves this tender and juicy roast. The salty crust is so tasty.
—Lisa Allen, Joppa, AL

PREP: 15 MIN. + MARINATING
COOK: 6¼ HOURS • **MAKES:** 12 SERVINGS

- 1 cup plus 1 Tbsp. sea salt, divided
- 1 cup sugar
- 1 bone-in pork shoulder butt roast (6 to 8 lbs.)
- ¼ cup barbecue seasoning
- ½ tsp. pepper
- ½ cup packed brown sugar
- 12 hamburger buns or kaiser rolls, split

1. Combine 1 cup sea salt and white granulated sugar; rub onto all sides of roast. Place in a shallow dish; cover and refrigerate overnight.
2. Preheat oven to 300°. Using a kitchen knife, scrape the salt and sugar coating from roast; discard any accumulated juices. Transfer pork to a large shallow roasting pan. Rub roast with barbecue seasoning; sprinkle with pepper. Roast until tender, 6-8 hours.
3. Increase oven temperature to 500°. Combine brown sugar and 1 Tbsp. sea salt; sprinkle over cooked pork. Return the pork to oven and roast until a crisp crust forms, 12-15 minutes. Remove; when cool enough to handle, shred meat with 2 forks. Serve warm on fresh buns or rolls.
Freeze option: Freeze cooled meat with some of the juices in freezer containers. To use, partially thaw in refrigerator overnight. Heat through in a saucepan, stirring occasionally; add water if necessary.
1 sandwich: 534 cal., 24g fat (9g sat. fat), 135mg chol., 2240mg sod., 33g carb. (14g sugars, 1g fiber), 43g pro.

BACON COLLARD GREENS

Collard greens are a staple vegetable of southern cuisine. This side dish is often eaten alongside smoked or salt-cured meats, such as ham hocks, pork or fatback.
—Marsha Ankeney, Niceville, FL

PREP: 25 MIN. • **COOK:** 55 MIN.
MAKES: 9 SERVINGS

- 2 lbs. collard greens
- 4 thick-sliced bacon strips, chopped
- 1 cup chopped sweet onion
- 5 cups reduced-sodium chicken broth
- 1 cup sun-dried tomatoes (not packed in oil), chopped
- ½ tsp. garlic powder
- ¼ tsp. salt
- ¼ tsp. crushed red pepper flakes

1. Trim thick stems from collard greens; coarsely chop leaves. In a Dutch oven, saute bacon for 3 minutes. Add onion; cook 8-9 minutes longer or until onion is tender and bacon is crisp. Add the greens; cook just until wilted.
2. Stir in remaining ingredients. Bring to a boil. Reduce the heat; cover and simmer for 45-50 minutes or until greens are tender.
¾ cup: 157 cal., 10g fat (4g sat. fat), 12mg chol., 651mg sod., 11g carb. (4g sugars, 5g fiber), 7g pro.

TEST KITCHEN TIP
Don't throw out the pot liquor—the liquid left behind after boiling greens. It's rich with flavor and nutrients. Dunking a big slice of warm cornbread in it is a wonderful way to sop up all the tasty goodness.

Father's Day BBQ

Honor Dad with a backyard barbecue featuring the savory favorites he likes best. From grilled chicken and burgers to baked beans and potato salad, the finger-licking greats found here make it a snap to create a memorable menu. You'll even find desserts so full of summer flavor that they're sure to get thumbs-up approval from Pops himself. In addition, these delicious recipes make fantastic go-tos for picnics, block parties, family reunions and other get-togethers all season long!

GRILLED LEMON CHICKEN

My chicken gets its subtle bit of pucker from lemonade concentrate. So simple, so sweet!
—Linda Nilsen, Anoka, MN

PREP: 5 MIN. • **GRILL:** 40 MIN.
MAKES: 12 SERVINGS

- ¾ cup thawed lemonade concentrate
- ⅓ cup soy sauce
- 1 garlic clove, minced
- 1 tsp. seasoned salt
- ½ tsp. celery salt
- ⅛ tsp. garlic powder
- 2 broiler/fryer chickens (3 to 3½ lbs. each), cut up

1. In a bowl, whisk the first 6 ingredients until combined. Pour half into a shallow glass dish. Cover and refrigerate the remaining lemonade mixture.
2. Dip chicken into lemonade mixture, turning to coat; discard lemonade mixture. Grill chicken, covered, over medium heat for 30 minutes, turning occasionally. Brush with the reserved lemonade mixture. Grill 10-20 minutes longer, brushing frequently, until a thermometer reads 165°.

5 oz. cooked chicken: 320 cal., 17g fat (5g sat. fat), 104mg chol., 504mg sod., 6g carb. (5g sugars, 0 fiber), 34g pro.

GRILLED BURGERS

Sour cream makes these burgers delightfully moist, and thyme and black pepper give them zip. They're a terrific taste of summer.
—Jesse and Anne Foust, Bluefield, WV

TAKES: 20 MIN. • **MAKES:** 10 SERVINGS

- ¼ cup sour cream
- 2 tsp. dried parsley flakes
- 1 tsp. dried thyme
- 1 tsp. salt
- ½ tsp. pepper
- 2½ lbs. ground beef
- 10 hamburger buns, split
   Optional: Lettuce leaves, sliced tomato and onion

1. In a large bowl, combine the first 5 ingredients; add the beef and mix gently. Shape into 10 patties.
2. Grill, uncovered, over medium heat for 4-5 minutes on each side or until meat is no longer pink. Serve on buns with lettuce leaves, tomato and onion if desired.

1 serving: 358 cal., 17g fat (7g sat. fat), 79mg chol., 534mg sod., 22g carb. (3g sugars, 1g fiber), 26g pro.

GOLDEN PEACH PIE

Years ago, I entered this pie in the Park County Fair in Livingston. It won a first-place blue ribbon plus a purple ribbon for best all-around! Family and friends agree with the judges—it's a perfectly peachy pie.
—Shirley Olson, Polson, MT

PREP: 20 MIN. • **BAKE:** 50 MIN. + COOLING
MAKES: 8 SERVINGS

- 2 sheets refrigerated pie crust
- 5 cups sliced peeled fresh peaches (about 5 medium)
- 2 tsp. lemon juice
- ½ tsp. grated orange zest
- ⅛ tsp. almond extract
- 1 cup sugar
- ¼ cup cornstarch
- ¼ tsp. ground nutmeg
- ⅛ tsp. salt
- 2 Tbsp. butter

1. Line a 9-in. pie plate with 1 crust; trim, leaving a 1-in. overhang around the edge. Set aside. In a large bowl, combine the peaches, lemon juice, orange zest and extract. Combine the sugar, cornstarch, nutmeg and salt. Add to peach mixture; toss gently to coat. Pour into crust; dot with butter.
2. Roll out the remaining crust to a ⅛-in.-thick circle; cut into strips. Arrange over filling in a lattice pattern. Trim and seal strips to bottom crust; fold overhang over. Lightly press or flute edge. Cover the edge loosely with foil.
3. Bake at 400° for 40 minutes. Remove foil; bake until the crust is golden brown and the filling is bubbly, 10-15 minutes longer. Cool on a wire rack. Store in the refrigerator.

1 piece: 425 cal., 17g fat (8g sat. fat), 18mg chol., 267mg sod., 67g carb. (36g sugars, 2g fiber), 3g pro.

LEMONY PINEAPPLE ICED TEA

I like to garnish this iced tea with some of our sweet Hawaiian pineapple.
—Beverly Toomey, Honolulu, HI

PREP: 20 MIN. + CHILLING • **COOK:** 10 MIN.
MAKES: 20 SERVINGS

- 16 cups water
- 24 tea bags
- 6 fresh mint sprigs
- 3⅓ cups sugar
- 3 cups unsweetened pineapple juice
- 1 cup lemon juice

1. In a stockpot, bring water to a boil; remove from heat. Add tea bags; steep, covered, 10 minutes. Discard tea bags. Add mint; steep 5 minutes. Discard mint. Add the remaining ingredients, stirring to dissolve sugar.
2. Transfer to pitchers or to a large covered container. Refrigerate, covered, until cold. If desired, serve with ice.
1 cup: 154 cal., 0 fat (0 sat. fat), 0 chol., 7mg sod., 40g carb. (38g sugars, 0 fiber), 0 pro.

TEST KITCHEN TIP

This delightful tea is a fun take on an Arnold Palmer—a beverage that's half lemonade and half iced tea. You can easily make it an adult drink by adding a little vodka.

PULLED BBQ PORK

After years of vacationing on the North Carolina coast, I became hooked on their pork barbecue. The version I developed is a must-have at potluck dinners.
—Joseph Sarnoski, West Chester, PA

PREP: 15 MIN. • **COOK:** 10 HOURS
MAKES: 8 SERVINGS

- 2 medium onions, finely chopped
- 1 Tbsp. canola oil
- 6 garlic cloves, minced
- 1 tsp. crushed red pepper flakes
- 1 tsp. pepper
- 1 can (14½ oz.) diced tomatoes, undrained
- ¼ cup packed brown sugar
- ¼ cup cider vinegar
- 2 Tbsp. hot pepper sauce
- 1 Tbsp. Worcestershire sauce
- 1 tsp. ground cumin
- 1 boneless pork shoulder butt roast (3 to 4 lbs.)
- 8 kaiser rolls, split

1. In a large skillet, saute onions in oil until tender. Add the garlic, red pepper flakes and pepper; cook 1 minute longer. Stir in the tomatoes, brown sugar, vinegar, hot pepper sauce, Worcestershire and cumin. Cook over medium heat until heated through and sugar is dissolved.
2. Cut roast in half. Place in a 5-qt. slow cooker; pour sauce over the top. Cover and cook on low for 10-12 hours or until the meat is tender. Remove roast; cool slightly. Skim fat from cooking juices. Shred meat with 2 forks and return to slow cooker. Heat through. With a slotted spoon, place ¾ cup meat mixture on each roll.
1 sandwich: 518 cal., 21g fat (7g sat. fat), 101mg chol., 528mg sod., 44g carb. (12g sugars, 3g fiber), 36g pro.

CHUNKY KETCHUP

I created this chunky homemade ketchup to help jazz up chopped steak sandwiches and hot sausage sandwiches for my family. It's so scrumptious and fresh-tasting. I gave some to our friends, too, and they enjoyed it on hamburgers and even stuffed peppers.
—Susan Stahr, Driftwood, PA

PREP: 20 MIN. • **COOK:** 1½ HOURS
MAKES: 3½ CUPS

- 4 cups chopped seeded peeled tomatoes
- 1 medium onion, chopped
- 1 medium green pepper, chopped
- 1 cup sugar
- 1 can (6 oz.) tomato paste
- 1 Tbsp. salt
- ¼ cup white vinegar

1. In a large saucepan, combine the tomatoes, onion, green pepper, sugar, tomato paste and salt; bring to a boil. Reduce heat; simmer, uncovered, until slightly thickened, about 1½ hours.
2. Stir in vinegar; heat through. Cool to room temperature; store up to 2 weeks in the refrigerator.
2 Tbsp.: 40 cal., 0 fat (0 sat. fat), 0 chol., 258mg sod., 10g carb. (9g sugars, 1g fiber), 0 pro.

BLT MACARONI SALAD

A friend served this salad, and I just had to get the recipe. My husband loves BLT sandwiches, so this has become a favorite of his. It's nice to serve on hot and humid days, which we frequently get during summer here in Virginia.

—Hamilton Myers Jr., Charlottesville, VA

TAKES: 30 MIN. • **MAKES:** 6 SERVINGS

- ½ cup mayonnaise
- 3 Tbsp. chili sauce
- 2 Tbsp. lemon juice
- 1 tsp. sugar
- 3 cups cooked elbow macaroni
- ½ cup chopped seeded tomato
- 2 Tbsp. chopped green onions
- 3 cups shredded lettuce
- 4 bacon strips, cooked and crumbled

In a large bowl, combine the first 4 ingredients. Add the macaroni, tomato and onions; toss to coat. Cover and refrigerate. Just before serving, add lettuce and bacon; toss to coat.

¾ cup: 259 cal., 17g fat (3g sat. fat), 10mg chol., 287mg sod., 21g carb. (4g sugars, 2g fiber), 5g pro.

SWEET & SPICY BAKED BEANS

This recipe is a hit with guests and family. It is sweet, simple and delicious, and someone always asks for the recipe.

—Elliot Wesen, Arlington, TX

PREP: 15 MIN. • **BAKE:** 50 MIN.
MAKES: 14 SERVINGS

- 2 cans (28 oz. each) baked beans
- 1 can (20 oz.) unsweetened crushed pineapple, drained
- 1 cup spicy barbecue sauce
- ½ cup molasses
- 2 Tbsp. prepared mustard
- ½ tsp. pepper
- ¼ tsp. salt
- 1 can (6 oz.) french-fried onions, crushed, divided
- 5 bacon strips, cooked and crumbled, divided

1. In a large bowl, combine the first 7 ingredients. Stir in half the onions and bacon. Transfer to a greased 13x9-in. baking dish.
2. Cover; bake at 350° for 45 minutes. Sprinkle with remaining onions and bacon. Bake, uncovered, 5-10 minutes longer or until bubbly.

¾ cup: 285 cal., 9g fat (3g sat. fat), 10mg chol., 860mg sod., 46g carb. (14g sugars, 7g fiber), 7g pro.

SOUTHERN POTATO SALAD

This potato salad with a southern twist is perfect for a church supper or potluck. The pickles add extra sweetness.
—Gene Pitts, Wilsonville, AL

PREP: 30 MIN. + CHILLING
MAKES: 8 SERVINGS

- 5   medium potatoes, peeled and cubed
- 6   hard-boiled large eggs, chopped
- ½   cup thinly sliced green onions
- ¼   cup chopped sweet pickles
- 1   tsp. prepared mustard
- 1   tsp. celery seed
- 1   cup mayonnaise
     Salt and pepper to taste

Place potatoes in a large saucepan; add water to cover. Bring to a boil. Reduce heat; cook, uncovered, until tender, 10-15 minutes. Drain; refrigerate until cold. Add eggs, onions and pickles; toss well. Stir in mustard, celery seed and mayonnaise. Season with salt and pepper; mix well. Refrigerate until serving.
¾ cup: 377 cal., 26g fat (4g sat. fat), 169mg chol., 275mg sod., 28g carb. (5g sugars, 2g fiber), 8g pro.

SUMMER IN THE CITY
Give your hot dog hometown flair with these fun frank flavors from across America.

PHILADELPHIA
Cheez Whiz • Sauteed peppers, onions and mushrooms

Served on a hoagie roll

DETROIT
Beanless chili • Mustard • Diced raw onion • Shredded cheddar

Placed in a poppy seed bun

NASHVILLE
Chicken hot dog • Hot sauce • Cayenne • Mayo • Sliced pickles

Tucked into a plain bun

TUCSON
Wrapped in bacon • Pinto beans • Chopped tomatoes • Diced raw onion • Avocado • Mayo • Jalapenos

Piled on a bolillo roll

KANSAS CITY
Melted Swiss cheese •Sauerkraut • Thousand Island dressing

Served on a sesame seed bun

CRISP ONION RELISH

I take this relish to picnics for people to use as a condiment on hamburgers and hot dogs. It adds a special zip!
—Marie Patkau, Hanley, SK

PREP: 10 MIN. + CHILLING
MAKES: ABOUT 6 CUPS

- 4   medium sweet onions, halved and thinly sliced
- ½   cup sugar
- ⅓   cup water
- ⅓   cup cider vinegar
- 1   cup mayonnaise
- 1   tsp. celery seed

1. Place onions in a large bowl. In a small bowl, combine the sugar, water and vinegar; stir until sugar is dissolved. Pour over onions. Cover and refrigerate for at least 3 hours.
2. Drain the onions, discarding liquid. Combine mayonnaise and celery seed; add to onions and mix well. Store in the refrigerator.
2 Tbsp.: 47 cal., 3g fat (1g sat. fat), 0 chol., 26mg sod., 4g carb. (3g sugars, 0 fiber), 0 pro.

ROASTED STRAWBERRY SHEET CAKE

My Grandma Gigi loved summer berry cakes. Almost any time I'd call her during the warmer months, she'd invite me over to taste her latest masterpiece. This cake is an ode to her.

—Kristin Bowers, Rancho Palos Verdes, CA

PREP: 1 HOUR • **BAKE:** 30 MIN. + COOLING
MAKES: 24 SERVINGS

4	lbs. halved fresh strawberries
½	cup sugar

CAKE

1	cup butter, softened
1½	cups sugar
2	large eggs, room temperature
2	tsp. almond extract
3	cups all-purpose flour
3	tsp. baking powder
2	tsp. salt
1	cup 2% milk
¼	cup turbinado (washed raw) sugar

1. Preheat oven to 350°. Place the strawberries on a parchment-lined rimmed baking sheet. Sprinkle with sugar and toss to coat. Bake until just tender, 35-40 minutes. Cool slightly.

2. Meanwhile, grease a 15x10x1-in. baking pan. In a large bowl, cream butter and sugar until light and fluffy, 5-7 minutes. Add eggs, 1 at a time, beating well after each addition. Beat in extract. In another bowl, whisk flour, baking powder and salt; add to creamed mixture alternately with milk, beating well after each addition (batter may appear curdled).

3. Transfer to prepared pan. Top with 3 cups roasted strawberries; sprinkle with turbinado sugar. Reserve the remaining strawberries for serving. Bake until a toothpick inserted in center comes out clean, 30-35 minutes. Cool completely in pan on a wire rack. Serve with reserved roasted strawberries.

1 piece: 235 cal., 9g fat (5g sat. fat), 37mg chol., 329mg sod., 37g carb. (23g sugars, 2g fiber), 3g pro.

DID YOU KNOW?

Fresh strawberries spoil within a few days. Roasting them is an excellent way to salvage a surplus on the brink of becoming moldy or shriveled. As the berries roast, their juice thickens into a sweet sauce. Bake the berries into this sheet cake for a delicious dessert; use them to top pancakes, crepes, waffles, biscuits or toast; or scoop them over ice cream or vanilla yogurt.

RAINBOW FRUIT SALAD

When my children were young, I would often dress up fresh fruit in this easy-to-fix salad. Decades later, my grandchildren and great-grandchildren still love digging into the fruity layers. The salad goes well with barbecued meats and cold sandwiches.
—Jonnie Adams Sisler, Stevensville, MT

PREP: 20 MIN. + CHILLING
MAKES: 20 SERVINGS

- 2 large firm bananas, sliced
- 2 Tbsp. lemon juice
- 2 cups seeded cubed watermelon
- 2 cups fresh or canned pineapple chunks
- 1 pint fresh blueberries
- 3 kiwifruit, peeled and sliced
- 1 pint fresh strawberries, halved
- 6 oz. cream cheese, softened
- ⅓ cup confectioners' sugar
- 2 Tbsp. fresh lime juice
- ½ tsp. grated lime zest
- 1 cup heavy whipping cream, whipped

1. Toss the bananas in lemon juice; place in a 4-qt. glass serving bowl. Add remaining fruit in layers.
2. In a bowl, beat cream cheese until smooth. Gradually add the sugar and the lime juice and zest. Stir in a small amount of whipped cream; mix well. Fold in remaining whipped cream. Spread over fruit. Chill until serving.
¾ cup: 123 cal., 7g fat (5g sat. fat), 22mg chol., 31mg sod., 14g carb. (10g sugars, 2g fiber), 1g pro.

Fourth of July Sundae Funday

Host a good old-fashioned ice cream social right in your kitchen with homemade recipes that will take you back to the simple pleasures of childhood. Whether you're partial to sundaes, parfaits, shakes, pops or other novelties, this frosty recipe collection will keep you chill when the weather's hot.

BLUEBERRY CREAM POPS

Blueberry and cream pops are a wonderful snack. And they're simple to make!
—Cindy Reams, Philipsburg, PA

PREP: 15 MIN. + FREEZING
MAKES: 8 POPS

- ⅔ **cup sugar**
- ⅔ **cup water**
- 2 **cups fresh or frozen blueberries, thawed**
- ¼ **cup heavy whipping cream**
- 8 **freezer pop molds or 8 paper cups (3 oz. each) and wooden pop sticks**

1. For the sugar syrup, in a small saucepan, combine sugar and water; bring to a boil, stirring to dissolve the sugar. Cool completely.
2. Meanwhile, in a bowl, coarsely mash the blueberries; stir in cream and sugar syrup. Spoon into molds or paper cups. Top molds with holders. If using cups, top with foil and insert sticks through foil. Freeze until firm. To serve, let the pops stand at room temperature 10 minutes before unmolding.

1 pop: 112 cal., 3g fat (2g sat. fat), 10mg chol., 3mg sod., 22g carb. (21g sugars, 1g fiber), 0 pro.

CHOCOLATE FRAMBOISE PARFAITS

Expecting company? Have these quick, delicious parfaits ready to pull out of the freezer for a welcoming treat.
—Charlene Chambers, Ormond Beach, FL

PREP: 15 MIN. + FREEZING
MAKES: 6 SERVINGS

- 6 **Tbsp. raspberry liqueur**
- 1½ **pints vanilla ice cream**
- 1½ **pints fresh raspberries**
- 2¼ **cups chocolate wafer crumbs**
  Sweetened whipped cream

Layer each of 6 parfait glasses with 1 tsp. raspberry liqueur, 2½ Tbsp. ice cream, 4 or 5 raspberries and 2 Tbsp. chocolate wafer crumbs. Repeat the layers twice. Freeze. To serve, top parfaits with whipped cream and the remaining raspberries.

1 parfait: 402 cal., 14g fat (6g sat. fat), 30mg chol., 297mg sod., 59g carb. (38g sugars, 6g fiber), 6g pro.

WATERMELON BOMBE DESSERT

When cut, this sherbet dessert looks like actual watermelon slices—complete with seeds. It is fun to eat and refreshing, too.
—Renae Moncur, Burley, ID

PREP: 20 MIN. + FREEZING
MAKES: 8 SERVINGS

- **About 1 pint lime sherbet**
- **About 1 pint pineapple sherbet**
- **About 1½ pints raspberry sherbet**
- ¼ **cup miniature semisweet chocolate chips**

Line a 1½-qt. bowl with plastic wrap. Press slightly softened lime sherbet against the bottom and sides of bowl. Freeze, uncovered, until firm. Spread pineapple sherbet evenly over lime sherbet layer. Freeze, uncovered, until firm. (The lime and pineapple sherbet layers should be thin.) Pack raspberry sherbet in center of sherbet-lined bowl. Smooth the top to resemble a cut watermelon. Cover and freeze until firm, about 8 hours. Just before serving, uncover bowl of molded sherbet. Place a serving plate on the bowl and invert. Remove bowl and peel off plastic wrap. Cut the bombe into wedges; press a few chocolate chips into the raspberry section of each wedge to resemble watermelon seeds.

1 piece: 205 cal., 4g fat (2g sat. fat), 8mg chol., 60mg sod., 43g carb. (35g sugars, 0 fiber), 2g pro.

DID YOU KNOW?
Sherbet originated in the Middle East as a popular drink made by adding sweetened fruit juice to water. The frosty version we know now gets its creamy texture from milk, egg whites and/or gelatin.

BUTTER PECAN SAUCE

Buttery, smooth and full of pecans, this sauce is just sensational over ice cream. It's hard to beat this homemade goodness.
—Kim Gilliland, Simi Valley, CA

TAKES: 15 MIN. • **MAKES:** 1½ CUPS

- ½ cup plus 2 Tbsp. packed brown sugar
- 2 Tbsp. sugar
- 4 tsp. cornstarch
- ¾ cup heavy whipping cream
- 1 Tbsp. butter
- ½ cup chopped pecans, toasted
  Vanilla ice cream or flavor of your choice

1. In a heavy saucepan, combine the sugars and cornstarch. Gradually stir in cream until smooth. Bring to a boil over medium heat, stirring constantly; cook and stir until slightly thickened, 2-3 minutes.
2. Remove from the heat; stir in butter until melted. Add the pecans. Serve warm over ice cream.
2 Tbsp.: 148 cal., 10g fat (4g sat. fat), 23mg chol., 20mg sod., 15g carb. (14g sugars, 0 fiber), 1g pro.

> **READER REVIEW**
> *"Excellent over French vanilla ice cream."*
> —KATLAYDEE, TASTEOFHOME.COM

BROWNIE WAFFLE ICE CREAM SUNDAES

I adore working with my four young daughters in the kitchen. My girls bake brownies from scratch, completely on their own, on a weekly basis. One summer we experimented by putting our famous brownie batter in the waffle iron! We then served the brownie waffles with ice cream.
—Juliana Evans, Wesley Chapel, FL

PREP: 15 MIN. • **COOK:** 5 MIN./BATCH
MAKES: 8 SERVINGS

- ½ cup unsalted butter
- 1 cup sugar
- ⅓ cup baking cocoa
- 1 tsp. vanilla extract
- 2 large eggs, room temperature
- ½ cup all-purpose flour
- ½ tsp. salt
- 4 cups vanilla ice cream
  Optional: Chocolate or hot fudge ice cream topping and sprinkles

1. Preheat a round Belgian waffle maker. In a microwave, melt butter on high, stirring every 30 seconds. Stir in sugar, cocoa and vanilla. Add eggs, 1 at a time, whisking after each addition. Add flour and salt; stir just until combined.
2. Bake the waffles according to the manufacturer's directions until cooked through, 4-5 minutes. Let stand on open waffle maker for 30-60 seconds to crisp up before carefully removing. Cut the waffles into fourths. Top each wedge with a scoop of ice cream. If desired, top with ice cream topping and sprinkles.
¼ waffle with ½ cup ice cream: 394 cal., 20g fat (12g sat. fat), 106mg chol., 220mg sod., 49g carb. (39g sugars, 1g fiber), 5g pro.

SCOOP DREAMS

Vanilla ice cream provides the coolest canvas for these tricked-out topping ideas that are making us all scream.

RITZ CRACKERS & CHOCOLATE SAUCE
Hershey's chocolate sauce and Ritz crackers!
—Brooklyn Reynolds, Anderson, IN

BACON & MAPLE SYRUP
I top mine with maple syrup and crispy thick-cut bacon.
—Carol Feldmann, Sheboygan Falls, WI

CORNFLAKES & CINNAMON
From my sister's brain: cornflakes and cinnamon. It tastes like apple pie.
—Sabrina Eileen Stebbins Brown, Saratoga Springs, UT

JAM & CHOCOLATE
I load mine up with strawberry jam, mini chocolate chips and chopped pecans.
—Donna Paprocki, Des Plaines, IL

COOLED ESPRESSO
Pour on some cooled Cuban coffee or espresso. It's just plain awesome.
—Cathy Killinger Lopez, Charlotte, NC

FRENCH FRIES & FUDGE
Fresh-baked french fries and hot fudge sauce. So good.
—Tracy Strickland, Shipshewana, IN

MELTED PEANUT BUTTER
I drizzle mine with melted peanut butter.
—Rd Stendel-Freels, Albuquerque, NM

CRUSHED POTATO CHIPS
The flavor combo gives you both sweet and salty. Yum!
—Pam Slack, Freeburg, IL

EASY RHUBARB SAUCE

Celebrate summer with the sweet-tart taste of rhubarb in this easy sauce. I enjoy it on toast, English muffins and pancakes, but it's equally decadent drizzled over pound cake or ice cream.
—Jackie Hutshing, Sonoma, CA

TAKES: 20 MIN. • MAKES: 1¼ CUPS

- ⅓ cup sugar
- ¼ cup water
- 2¼ cups sliced fresh or frozen rhubarb
- 1 tsp. grated lemon zest
- ⅛ tsp. ground nutmeg
  Pound cake or vanilla ice cream

1. In a small saucepan, bring sugar and water to a boil. Add the rhubarb; cook and stir until rhubarb is tender and the mixture is slightly thickened, 5-10 minutes. Remove from heat; stir in lemon zest and nutmeg.
2. Serve warm or chilled over pound cake or ice cream. Refrigerate leftovers.
¼ cup: 64 cal., 0 fat (0 sat. fat), 0 chol., 2mg sod., 16g carb. (14g sugars, 1g fiber), 1g pro.

TEST KITCHEN TIP

A sprinkle of lemon zest can go a long way toward making a dish pop. The zest packs so much punch because it's filled with the fruit's potent natural oils. Our Test Kitchen's preferred method for getting superfine lemon zest is with a microplane. To use, simply rub a washed and dried lemon over the plane, applying light pressure and turning as you work. This tool produces the finest zest possible. A box grater works well, too.

CHOCOLATE CHIP STRAWBERRY ICE CREAM

My husband and I have a favorite DQ Blizzard treat that we order every time we visit the restaurant, so I came up with my own version. Make sure ice cream mixture is cooled for several hours or overnight.
—Sandy Martin, Elizabethtown, PA

PREP: 25 MIN.
PROCESS: 15 MIN. + FREEZING
MAKES: 1½ QT.

- 1⅔ cups sugar
- 5 Tbsp. cornstarch, divided
- 4 cups 2% milk
- 2 large egg yolks
- 1⅓ cups heavy whipping cream
- ⅔ cup half-and-half cream
- 3 tsp. vanilla extract
- ¼ cup light corn syrup
- 3 cups fresh strawberries, hulled
- 1 dark chocolate candy bar (8 oz.), finely chopped
  Optional: Whipped cream and maraschino cherries

1. In a large heavy saucepan, whisk the sugar and 4 Tbsp. cornstarch until blended; whisk in the milk until smooth. Bring to a boil, stirring constantly; cook and stir until thickened, 1-2 minutes. Reduce heat to low. In a small bowl, whisk a small amount of hot mixture into egg yolks; return all to the pan, whisking constantly. Cook 2-3 minutes over low heat or until the mixture thickens and a thermometer reads 160°, stirring constantly. Remove from heat immediately.
2. Quickly transfer to a large bowl; place bowl in a pan of ice water. Stir gently and occasionally for 2 minutes. Stir in cream, half-and-half and vanilla. Press plastic wrap onto surface of custard. Refrigerate several hours or overnight.
3. Fill cylinder of ice cream freezer two-thirds full; freeze according to manufacturer's directions.
4. Meanwhile, place remaining 1 Tbsp. cornstarch in a large skillet. Whisk in the corn syrup until smooth; add the strawberries. Bring to a boil over medium heat; cook and stir 2 minutes or until thickened. Mash strawberries; let cool.
5. During last 5 minutes of processing, add strawberry mixture and chopped chocolate. Transfer the ice cream to freezer containers, allowing headspace for expansion. Freeze at least 4 hours or until firm. If desired, serve with whipped cream and cherries.
½ cup: 397 cal., 19g fat (12g sat. fat), 76mg chol., 59mg sod., 56g carb. (50g sugars, 2g fiber), 6g pro.

PEACHY BUTTERMILK SHAKES

My husband and grandkids sure enjoy the tang of buttermilk blended with sweet peaches in these delightful shakes.
—Anna Mayer, Fort Branch, IN

TAKES: 10 MIN. • **MAKES:** 3 SERVINGS

- 1 cup buttermilk
- 3 cups fresh or frozen unsweetened sliced peaches, thawed
- 1 cup vanilla ice cream, softened
- ¼ cup sugar
- ¾ tsp. ground cinnamon
  Optional: Whipped cream and additional sliced peaches

Place the first 5 ingredients in a blender; cover and process until smooth. Pour into chilled glasses; serve immediately. If desired, top with whipped cream and sliced peaches.

1 cup: 250 cal., 6g fat (3g sat. fat), 23mg chol., 191mg sod., 46g carb. (42g sugars, 3g fiber), 6g pro.

READER REVIEW

"Fantastic flavor. I just got back from a peach festival loaded down with peaches that were on the tree an hour ago and threw this together. What a terrific taste!"
—JWESTCLARK, TASTEOFHOME.COM

CHOCOLATE DESSERT DELIGHT

Some of my friends refer to this rich ice cream dessert as death by chocolate— before they ask for seconds! It's a yummy, festive, do-ahead treat.
—Lee Ann Stidman, Spirit Lake, ID

PREP: 25 MIN. + FREEZING
MAKES: 20 SERVINGS

- 2 cups chocolate graham cracker crumbs (about 32 squares)
- ½ cup butter, melted
- ½ cup chopped walnuts
- 1 Tbsp. sugar
FILLING
- ½ gallon chocolate ice cream, softened
- 1 jar (12¼ oz.) caramel ice cream topping
- 1 jar (11¾ oz.) hot fudge ice cream topping
- ½ cup miniature semisweet chocolate chips
- ½ cup chopped walnuts
TOPPING
- 2 cups heavy whipping cream
- 3 Tbsp. sugar
- 1 Tbsp. baking cocoa
- 1 tsp. vanilla extract
- ½ tsp. instant coffee granules
  Additional miniature chocolate chips and chopped walnuts

1. For the crust, combine the crumbs, butter, walnuts and sugar; press into an ungreased 13x9-in. baking pan. Bake at 350° for 10 minutes; cool completely.
2. Spread half the ice cream over crust; spoon caramel and hot fudge toppings over ice cream. Sprinkle with chocolate chips and walnuts; freeze until firm. Spread with remaining ice cream over the top. Cover and freeze for at least 2 hours.

3. In a large bowl, beat cream until stiff peaks form. Fold in sugar, cocoa, vanilla and coffee granules. Pipe or spoon onto dessert. Sprinkle with the additional chocolate chips and walnuts. Return to freezer until 10 minutes before serving.
1 piece: 443 cal., 26g fat (13g sat. fat), 63mg chol., 230mg sod., 50g carb. (39g sugars, 2g fiber), 6g pro.

RUM BANANA SAUCE

Plain vanilla ice cream becomes amazing thanks to this delectable sauce.
—Katherine Desrosiers, Trail, BC

TAKES: 15 MIN. • **MAKES:** 4 SERVINGS

- ¾ cup packed brown sugar
- ¼ cup butter, cubed
- ¼ cup heavy whipping cream
- 2 Tbsp. maple syrup
- 2 large bananas, cut into ½-in. slices
- ½ tsp. rum extract
  Vanilla ice cream

In a small saucepan, combine the brown sugar, butter, cream and maple syrup. Cook and stir over medium heat until sauce is smooth, 4-5 minutes. Stir in bananas; heat through. Remove from the heat; stir in extract. Serve with ice cream.
½ cup: 397 cal., 17g fat (11g sat. fat), 50mg chol., 104mg sod., 63g carb. (54g sugars, 2g fiber), 1g pro.

Fireworks Party

Are you ready for a bang-up Fourth of July? No need to apply the sunscreen or worry about melting away in the heat—this year's party is an evening affair, complete with fireworks and a rooftop view. Your ultimate patriotic shindig starts with summertime cocktails followed by an array of tempting appetizers, sliders, pizza and more. Grab your city-dwelling crew and head upstairs for cool breezes, an unparalleled panoramic view, and the best food and libations. This Fourth of July, your summer bash is the place to be!

FRESH HERB VEGETABLE DIP

I entertain a lot and am always looking for an easy crowd pleaser. If it's a dish in which I can use fresh ingredients from my herb and vegetable garden, it's even better. I serve this dip in individual servings for large parties so each person has their own cup.
—Isabel Minunni, Poughkeepsie, NY

TAKES: 15 MIN. • **MAKES:** 3 CUPS

- ¼ cup olive oil
- 3 Tbsp. lemon juice
- 1½ cups fat-free sour cream
- 2 medium ripe avocados, peeled and cubed
- 2 Tbsp. chopped chives
- 2 Tbsp. chopped fresh parsley
- 2 Tbsp. chopped fresh basil
- 1 Tbsp. chopped fresh tarragon
- 1 Tbsp. chopped fresh thyme
- 1 garlic clove, halved
- ½ tsp. salt
- ¼ tsp. pepper
- Assorted fresh vegetables

Place the first 12 ingredients in a food processor; process until smooth. Refrigerate until serving. Serve with vegetables.

¼ cup: 110 cal., 8g fat (1g sat. fat), 1mg chol., 126mg sod., 4g carb. (2g sugars, 2g fiber), 3g pro. **Diabetic exchanges:** 1½ fat.

TURKEY SLIDERS WITH SESAME SLAW

I'm a fan of sliders, especially if they are Asian inspired. Sweet Hawaiian rolls make these especially amazing.
—Gloria Bradley, Naperville, IL

TAKES: 30 MIN.
MAKES: 12 SERVINGS

- ⅔ cup mayonnaise
- 2 Tbsp. hoisin sauce
- 2 tsp. Sriracha chili sauce
- 1½ lbs. ground turkey
- ½ cup panko bread crumbs
- 2 green onions, finely chopped
- 2 Tbsp. reduced-sodium soy sauce, divided
- 2 tsp. minced fresh gingerroot
- 2 Tbsp. rice vinegar
- 2 tsp. sugar
- 2 tsp. sesame oil
- 6 small carrots, grated (about 1½ cups)
- ⅓ cup thinly sliced red onion
- 3 Tbsp. chopped fresh cilantro
- 1 tsp. sesame seeds, toasted
- 12 slider buns or dinner rolls, split and toasted

1. In a small bowl, mix the mayonnaise, hoisin sauce and chili sauce. Refrigerate until serving.
2. In a large bowl, combine the turkey, bread crumbs, green onions, 1 Tbsp. soy sauce and ginger, mixing lightly but thoroughly. Shape mixture into twelve ½-in.-thick patties.
3. In a small bowl, whisk the vinegar, sugar, oil and remaining soy sauce. Add the carrots, onion, cilantro and sesame seeds; toss to combine.
4. Grill sliders, covered, on a greased rack over medium heat or broil 4 in. from heat until a thermometer reads 165°, about 3 minutes on each side. Spread the cut sides of buns with mayonnaise mixture. Layer each bottom with a burger and 2 Tbsp. slaw. Replace tops.

1 burger with 2 Tbsp. slaw: 314 cal., 16g fat (3g sat. fat), 56mg chol., 522mg sod., 26g carb. (6g sugars, 2g fiber), 15g pro.

TEST KITCHEN TIP
Cut the carbs by skipping the buns. Set the grilled patties in lettuce leaves (you may have to cut the patties in half), and serve the mayo mixture and slaw on the side.

FETA-CUCUMBER CHEESE BALLS

The light and refreshing flavor of this recipe has made it one of my favorites. I've made variations of it for three different holidays — this Fourth of July version with tomato and basil was gone by the end of the day!
—Shelly Bevington, Hermiston, OR

PREP: 20 MIN. + CHILLING • **MAKES:** 2 DOZEN

- 1 pkg. (8 oz.) reduced-fat cream cheese
- 1 pkg. (4 oz.) crumbled tomato and basil feta cheese
- ⅛ tsp. salt
- ½ cup peeled, seeded and finely chopped cucumber
- 1 cup finely chopped walnuts
- 24 fresh basil leaves
- 24 toothpicks

1. In a small bowl, mix cream cheese, feta cheese and salt until blended. Stir in the cucumber. Refrigerate, covered, 30 minutes.
2. Shape tablespoonfuls of the cheese mixture into balls. Roll in the walnuts. Thread a folded basil leaf and cheese ball on each toothpick. Refrigerate until serving.

1 appetizer: 67 cal., 6g fat (2g sat. fat), 9mg chol., 98mg sod., 1g carb. (1g sugars, 1g fiber), 3g pro.

GRILLED TOMATO-PEACH PIZZA

This scrumptious pizza is unique, healthy and easy to make. The fresh flavors make it a perfect appetizer for a summer party.
—Scarlett Elrod, Newnan, GA

PREP: 20 MIN. + STANDING • **GRILL:** 5 MIN.
MAKES: 16 PIECES

- 4 medium tomatoes, thinly sliced
- ¼ tsp. salt
- 2 medium peaches, halved
  Cooking spray
- 1 Tbsp. cornmeal
- 1 tube (13½ oz.) refrigerated pizza crust
- 4 oz. fresh mozzarella cheese, sliced
- 6 fresh basil leaves, thinly sliced
- ⅛ tsp. coarsely ground pepper

1. Sprinkle the tomatoes with salt; let stand 15 minutes. Drain tomatoes on paper towels and pat dry.
2. Grill peaches on an oiled grill rack, covered, over medium heat or broil 4 in. from heat until the peaches have grill marks and are tender, 2-3 minutes on each side, turning once. Remove peaches; cool slightly. Cut into slices.
3. Coat a 15x10x1-in. baking pan with cooking spray; sprinkle with cornmeal. Unroll crust into pan, pressing into a 12x10-in. rectangle. Spritz with cooking spray. Carefully invert the crust onto grill. Grill, covered, over medium heat until the bottom is lightly browned, 2-3 minutes. Remove from the grill, inverting onto baking pan.
4. Layer the grilled side of pizza with tomatoes, peaches and cheese. Return pizza to grill. Cook, covered, until crust is lightly browned and cheese is melted, 3-4 minutes, rotating halfway through cooking to ensure an evenly browned crust. Sprinkle with basil and pepper.

1 piece: 98 cal., 3g fat (1g sat. fat), 6mg chol., 208mg sod., 15g carb. (3g sugars, 1g fiber), 4g pro. **Diabetic exchanges:** 1 starch.

MINTY PINEAPPLE RUM

This delicious drink is a fabulous way to use fresh mint and celebrate summer. If the pineapple isn't overly ripe, add a bit more sugar. Save any leftover pineapple-mint syrup in an airtight glass container, or freeze the mixture in ice cube trays to use later.
—Colleen Delawder, Herndon, VA

TAKES: 10 MIN.
MAKES: 14 SERVINGS

- 6 Tbsp. fresh lime juice (about 3 limes)
- 4 cups cubed fresh pineapple (1 in.)
- 40 fresh mint leaves
- ⅔ cup superfine sugar
- ⅛ tsp. kosher salt
- 1½ cups light rum
  Ice cubes
- 7 cups club soda, chilled
  GARNISH
  Fresh pineapple slices and additional fresh mint leaves

Place the first 5 ingredients in a blender; cover and process until pureed. Transfer to a 1½-qt. pitcher; stir in rum. Pour ⅓ cup mixture into each glass. Add ice; pour ½ cup soda over the ice. Garnish with pineapple slices and additional mint leaves.
¾ cup: 118 cal., 0 fat (0 sat. fat), 0 chol., 44mg sod., 17g carb. (14g sugars, 1g fiber), 0 pro.

WATERMELON MARGARITAS

Summer's best flavors get frosty in the cocktail we serve during all our backyard shindigs. We mix sun-ripened watermelon and our favorite tequila with just the right amount of ice for a thick and boozy sipper that's perfect when we're grilling and chilling with friends.

—Alicia Cummings, Marshalltown, IA

TAKES: 20 MIN. • **MAKES:** 12 SERVINGS

- 2 medium limes
- ⅓ cup sugar
- 8 cups cubed seedless watermelon (1 in.)
- 2 cups ice cubes
- 2 cups tequila
- 1 cup Triple Sec
- ¼ cup lime juice

1. Cut 1 lime into 12 wedges; reserve for garnishes. If desired, coat the rim of each glass with sugar: Cut remaining lime into wedges. Using these wedges, moisten the rims of 12 margarita or cocktail glasses. Sprinkle sugar on a plate; hold each glass upside down and dip the rim into the sugar. Discard remaining sugar.
2. Place half the watermelon in a blender; cover and process until pureed (this should yield 3 cups). Add half each of the following: ice cubes, tequila, Triple Sec and lime juice. If desired, add sugar to taste. Cover and process until blended.
3. Serve in prepared glasses. Repeat with remaining ingredients. Garnish with reserved lime wedges.

¾ cup: 188 cal., 0 fat (0 sat. fat), 0 chol., 5mg sod., 19g carb. (17g sugars, 1g fiber), 0 pro.

LEMON BASIL MOJITO MOCKTAILS

In this tasty twist on the classic summer beverage, lemon basil takes the place of mint. For a grown-up version, just add your favorite rum or vodka.

—Cheryl Perry, Hertford, NC

PREP: 15 MIN. + CHILLING
MAKES: 12 SERVINGS

- 1½ cups sugar
- 4 cups water
- 6 cups fresh basil leaves, divided
  Crushed ice, divided
- 2 bottles (1 liter each) club soda

GARNISH
  Fresh lemon wedges

1. In a small saucepan, bring the sugar and water to a boil. Cook and stir until sugar is dissolved. Place half the basil in a small bowl. With a pestle or wooden spoon, crush the basil until its aroma is released. Stir into the sugar mixture. Remove from heat; cool completely. Strain; refrigerate until cold.
2. Place 2 cups crushed ice and the remaining basil in a 4-qt. pitcher. Using a muddler or wooden spoon, press basil leaves against ice until their aroma is released. Stir in basil syrup and soda. Serve over crushed ice in tall glasses; squeeze lemon wedges into drink.

1 serving: 101 cal., 0 fat (0 sat. fat), 0 chol., 36mg sod., 26g carb. (25g sugars, 0 fiber), 0 pro.

EASY STRAWBERRY SALSA

My salsa is sweet and colorful, with just a little bite from jalapeno peppers. I love to use fresh strawberries and my own homegrown vegetables, but you can also use produce that is available year-round. It's perfect with tortilla chips or even as a topping for grilled chicken or pork.
—Dianna Wara, Washington, IL

PREP: 20 MIN. + CHILLING
MAKES: 16 SERVINGS

- 3 cups chopped seeded tomatoes (about 4 large)
- 1⅓ cups chopped fresh strawberries
- ½ cup finely chopped onion (about 1 small)
- ½ cup minced fresh cilantro
- 1 to 2 jalapeno peppers, seeded and finely chopped
- ⅓ cup chopped sweet yellow or orange pepper
- ¼ cup lime juice
- ¼ cup honey
- 4 garlic cloves, minced
- 1 tsp. chili powder
  Baked tortilla chip scoops

In a large bowl, combine the first 10 ingredients. Refrigerate, covered, at least 2 hours. Serve with chips.
¼ cup: 33 cal., 0 fat (0 sat. fat), 0 chol., 4mg sod., 8g carb. (6g sugars, 1g fiber), 1g pro. **Diabetic exchanges:** ½ starch.

CHOCOLATE-COVERED STRAWBERRY SNACK MIX

I crave chocolate-covered strawberries, but that's a treat you want to make only on special occasions. With just a little experimenting, I've captured the same incredible flavor in a snack I can take anywhere. Everyone is always in awe when I pull this out at a picnic or tailgate, or on a car trip.
—TerryAnn Moore, Vineland, NJ

PREP: 15 MIN. + STANDING • **MAKES:** 2 QT.

- 6 cups Rice Chex
- 2 cups Chocolate Chex
- 1 cup semisweet chocolate chips
- ½ cup seedless strawberry jam
- 3 Tbsp. butter
- 1 tsp. almond extract
- 2 cups ground almonds
- 1 cup white baking chips
  Sprinkles, optional

1. In a large bowl, combine cereals. In a microwave, melt the chocolate chips, jam and butter; stir until smooth. Add the extract. Pour over cereal mixture and toss to coat. Sprinkle with almonds; toss to coat.
2. Immediately spread cereal mixture onto waxed paper. In a microwave, melt white chips; stir until smooth. Drizzle over the cereal mixture. If desired, add sprinkles. Let stand until set. Break into pieces. Store in an airtight container.
¾ cup: 443 cal., 24g fat (9g sat. fat), 11mg chol., 231mg sod., 55g carb. (33g sugars, 3g fiber), 7g pro.

THE ESSENTIAL SUMMER BAR

Hosting a warm-weather bash? Start by making sure the bar is ready. An initial investment in a few key ingredients and items will pay you back for years to come. So create a well-stocked bar, then sit back and enjoy!

THE BASICS
Rum • Bourbon or whiskey • Gin • Vodka • Tequila

BUILD ON THE BASE
Bitters • Orange liqueur • Elderflower liqueur • Ginger liqueur

MIXERS
Club soda • Tonic water • Colas and ginger ale • Juice • Simple syrups

THE TOOL KIT
Cocktail shaker and strainer • Muddler (or the handle of a wooden spoon) • Ice cube trays • Paring knife • Peeler • Bottle/wine opener • Hand-held citrus press

SOUTH-OF-THE-BORDER BRUSCHETTA

I like to get creative in the kitchen, and this is one of the first dishes I threw together without using a recipe. It boats a zesty Mexican flavor everyone is sure to adore.
—Rebecca Spoolstra, Pilot Point, TX

PREP: 20 MIN. + CHILLING • **BROIL:** 5 MIN.
MAKES: 12 SERVINGS

- 2   medium ripe avocados, peeled and finely chopped
- 3   Tbsp. minced fresh cilantro
- 1   to 2 red chili peppers, finely chopped
- ¼   tsp. salt
- 2   small limes
- 12 slices French bread baguette (½ in. thick)
     Crumbled Cotija cheese, optional

1. In a small bowl, mix the avocados, cilantro, chili peppers and salt. Finely grate zest from limes. Cut the limes crosswise in half; squeeze juice from limes. Stir lime zest and juice into the avocado mixture. Refrigerate 30 minutes.

2. Preheat broiler. Place bread slices on an ungreased baking sheet. Broil 3-4 in. from heat 1-2 minutes on each side or until golden brown. Top with avocado mixture. If desired, sprinkle with cheese.
1 appetizer: 62 cal., 4g fat (0 sat. fat), 0 chol., 100mg sod., 7g carb. (0 sugars, 2g fiber), 2g pro.

SUMMER FRESH PASTA SALAD

While preparing lunch one day, I made this fast and easy salad for dinner. I served it with almond crackers and sharp cheddar slices. It's so tasty, especially when the fresh fruits and veggies are in season!
—Cathy Orban, Chandler, AZ

PREP: 20 MIN. + CHILLING
MAKES: 12 SERVINGS

- 4   cups uncooked campanelle or spiral pasta
- 2   medium carrots, finely chopped
- 2   medium peaches, chopped
- 1   pouch (11 oz.) light tuna in water
- ½   cup sliced celery
- ½   cup julienned cucumber
- ½   cup julienned zucchini
- ½   cup fresh broccoli florets, chopped
- ½   cup grated red cabbage
- ½   tsp. salt
- ½   tsp. pepper
- 2   cups Caesar salad dressing

Cook pasta according to the package directions for al dente. Drain; rinse with cold water and drain well. Transfer to a large bowl. Add carrots, peaches, tuna, celery, cucumber, zucchini, broccoli, cabbage, salt and pepper. Drizzle with the dressing; toss to coat. Refrigerate, covered, at least 3 hours before serving.
¾ cup: 357 cal., 23g fat (4g sat. fat), 25mg chol., 651mg sod., 26g carb. (5g sugars, 2g fiber), 10g pro.

GRILLED CHERRY-GLAZED CHICKEN WINGS

When I take these grilled wings to events, there are never any leftovers. Friends and family frequently request them.
—Ashley Gable, Atlanta, GA

PREP: 20 MIN. • **GRILL:** 15 MIN.
MAKES: 1 DOZEN

- 12 chicken wings (about 3 lbs.)
- 3 Tbsp. canola oil, divided
- 1 garlic clove, minced
- 1 cup ketchup
- ½ cup cider vinegar
- ½ cup cherry preserves
- 2 Tbsp. Louisiana-style hot sauce
- 1 Tbsp. Worcestershire sauce
- 3 tsp. coarse salt, divided
- 1 tsp. coarsely ground pepper, divided

1. Using a sharp knife, cut through the 2 wing joints; discard wing tips. In a small saucepan, heat 1 Tbsp. oil over medium heat. Add garlic; cook and stir 1 minute. Stir in the ketchup, vinegar, preserves, hot sauce, Worcestershire sauce, 1 tsp. salt and ½ tsp. pepper. Cook and stir until heated through. Brush the wings with the remaining oil; sprinkle with remaining salt and pepper.

2. Grill, covered, over medium heat 15-18 minutes or until juices run clear, turning occasionally and brushing with the glaze during the last 5 minutes of grilling. Serve with remaining glaze.

1 chicken wing: 214 cal., 12g fat (3g sat. fat), 36mg chol., 867mg sod., 15g carb. (14g sugars, 0g fiber), 12g pro.

Family Reunion

When loved ones gather, it's not just about the fellowship—it's also about fantastic food! With this lineup of unforgettable culinary creations, you no longer need to count on luck to find the perfect potluck recipe. From fun finger foods and comforting main courses to sensational sides and dreamy desserts, this selection makes it easy to find the ideal contribution.

ARTICHOKE SHRIMP PASTA SALAD

I have enjoyed this recipe for as long as I can remember. My mom made it famous, and she passed it down to me on my wedding day. It's one of those potluck staples that folks can't get enough of.
—Mary McCarley, Charlotte, NC

PREP: 20 MIN. • **COOK:** 10 MIN. + CHILLING
MAKES: 12 SERVINGS

- 1 pkg. (16 oz.) bow tie pasta
- 2 lbs. peeled and deveined cooked shrimp (31-40 per lb.)
- 2 cans (7½ oz. each) marinated quartered artichoke hearts, drained
- 2 cans (2¼ oz. each) sliced ripe olives, drained
- 2 cups crumbled feta cheese
- 8 green onions, sliced
- ½ cup chopped fresh parsley
- ¼ cup chopped fresh basil

DRESSING
- ½ cup white wine vinegar
- ½ cup olive oil
- ¼ cup lemon juice
- 2 Tbsp. chopped fresh basil
- 2 tsp. Dijon mustard
  Fresh ground pepper, optional

1. Cook pasta according to package directions for al dente. Drain pasta; rinse with cold water and drain well. In a large bowl, combine the pasta, shrimp, artichokes, olives, cheese, green onions, parsley and basil.
2. In a small bowl, whisk vinegar, oil, lemon juice, basil, mustard and, if desired, pepper. Pour dressing over pasta mixture; toss to coat. Refrigerate, covered, 2 hours before serving.
1⅓ cups: 453 cal., 23g fat (7g sat. fat), 135mg chol., 757mg sod., 34g carb. (2g sugars, 6g fiber), 28g pro.

TRIPLE CHEESE POTATO CAKE WITH HAM

This delicious and exquisite soufflelike side dish combines the classic flavors of ham, chives and three different cheeses. The crispy crust and fluffy interior make it over-the-top amazing.
—Rebekah Radewahn, Wauwatosa, WI

PREP: 35 MIN. • **BAKE:** 35 MIN.
MAKES: 12 SERVINGS

- ¼ cup plus 1 Tbsp. dry bread crumbs, divided
- 3 lbs. medium potatoes, peeled and cubed (about 8 cups)
- ½ cup heavy whipping cream
- ¼ cup butter, cubed
- 3 Tbsp. minced fresh chives
- 1 tsp. salt
- ¼ tsp. pepper
- 3 large eggs
- 4 slices Swiss cheese
- 4 slices part-skim mozzarella cheese
- 4 oz. thinly sliced deli ham, cut into ½-in. pieces
- ⅓ cup grated Parmesan cheese
- 1 Tbsp. butter, melted

1. Preheat oven to 350°. Grease a 9-in. springform pan; dust with ¼ cup bread crumbs.
2. Place potatoes in a Dutch oven; add water to cover. Bring to a boil. Reduce heat; cook, uncovered, 10-15 minutes or until tender. Drain; return to pan. Mash potatoes, gradually adding the cream, cubed butter, chives, salt and pepper. Cool slightly.
3. Add eggs, 1 at a time, stirring to blend after each addition. Spread half of the potato mixture into prepared pan. Layer with cheese slices, ham and the remaining potatoes. In a small bowl, mix Parmesan cheese and remaining bread crumbs; stir in butter. Sprinkle over potatoes.
4. Bake 35-40 minutes or until golden brown. Cool on a wire rack 10 minutes. Loosen sides from pan with a knife. Serve warm.
1 slice: 241 cal., 15g fat (8g sat. fat), 88mg chol., 520mg sod., 19g carb. (2g sugars, 1g fiber), 10g pro.

CHICKEN & SWISS CASSEROLE

It's nice to have an alternative to the traditional baked ham on Easter. This comforting casserole is always a reliable crowd-pleaser. Using rotisserie chicken from the deli makes prep simple.
—Christina Petri, Alexandria, MN

PREP: 30 MIN. • **BAKE:** 10 MIN.
MAKES: 8 SERVINGS

5½ cups uncooked egg noodles (about ½ lb.)
  3 Tbsp. olive oil
  3 shallots, chopped
  3 small garlic cloves, minced
  ⅓ cup all-purpose flour
  2 cups chicken broth
  ¾ cup 2% milk
1½ tsp. dried thyme
  ¾ tsp. grated lemon zest
  ½ tsp. salt
  ¼ tsp. ground nutmeg
  ¼ tsp. pepper
  5 cups cubed rotisserie chicken
1½ cups frozen peas
  2 cups shredded Swiss cheese
  ¾ cup dry bread crumbs
  2 Tbsp. butter, melted

1. Preheat oven to 350°. Cook noodles according to package directions; drain.
2. In a large skillet, heat oil over medium heat. Add shallots and garlic; cook and stir 45 seconds. Stir in flour; cook and stir 1 minute. Add broth, milk, thyme, lemon zest, salt, nutmeg and pepper. Stir in chicken and peas; heat through. Stir in noodles and cheese.
3. Transfer to a greased 13x9-in. baking dish. In a small bowl, mix bread crumbs and butter; sprinkle over top. Bake 8-10 minutes or until top is browned.
1¼ cups: 551 cal., 25g fat (10g sat. fat), 136mg chol., 661mg sod., 38g carb. (4g sugars, 3g fiber), 41g pro.

MAKE-AHEAD VEGGIE SALAD

Assemble this colorful mix of vegetables and let it soak up the sweet-and-sour dressing overnight. The next day, you'll be ready to go with a refreshing, delicious salad that tastes extraordinary!
—Shirley Glaab, Hattiesburg, MS

PREP: 35 MIN. + MARINATING
MAKES: 30 SERVINGS

- 1 pkg. (24 oz.) frozen shoepeg corn, thawed
- 1 pkg. (16 oz.) frozen peas, thawed
- 1 pkg. (16 oz.) frozen French-style green beans, thawed
- 1 large red onion, chopped
- 4 celery ribs, thinly sliced
- 2 medium carrots, thinly sliced
- 1 medium green pepper, chopped
- 1 medium sweet red pepper, chopped
- 1 jar (4½ oz.) sliced mushrooms, drained
- 1 jar (4 oz.) diced pimientos, drained

DRESSING
- ½ cup sugar
- ½ cup olive oil
- ½ cup red wine vinegar
- ¾ tsp. salt
- ¼ tsp. pepper

In a large bowl, combine the first 10 ingredients. Place the dressing ingredients in a jar with a tight-fitting lid; shake well. Pour over vegetable mixture; toss to coat. Refrigerate salad, covered, 8 hours or overnight, stirring occasionally.
½ cup: 91 cal., 4g fat (1g sat. fat), 0 chol., 116mg sod., 13g carb. (6g sugars, 2g fiber), 2g pro. **Diabetic exchanges:** 1 starch, 1 vegetable, 1 fat.

APRICOT-CHIPOTLE CHEESE SPREAD

Creamy cheese, sweet preserves and spicy chipotle are just the right combo for an easy cracker spread. If you want to experiment with some variations, try using cherry or raspberry preserves in place of the apricot.
—Barb Templin, Norwood, MN

PREP: 10 MIN. + CHILLING • **MAKES:** 2 CUPS

- 12 oz. cream cheese, softened
- 1 cup shredded cheddar cheese
- 2 garlic cloves, minced
- ½ tsp. onion powder
- ½ cup apricot preserves
- 3 tsp. minced fresh gingerroot
- 3 tsp. minced chipotle peppers in adobo sauce
  Assorted crackers and vegetables

1. In a large bowl, beat cream cheese, cheddar cheese, garlic and onion powder until blended. Shape cheese mixture into a log. Wrap and refrigerate at least 2 hours.
2. In a small bowl, mix preserves, ginger and chipotle peppers until blended. Spoon over cream cheese. Serve with crackers and vegetables.
2 Tbsp.: 129 cal., 10g fat (6g sat. fat), 28mg chol., 123mg sod., 8g carb. (5g sugars, 0 fiber), 3g pro.

TEST KITCHEN TIP
If you like, you can shape the cheese spread into a disk rather than a log to provide more surface area for the sauce. This spread goes best with plain crackers; you don't want the flavors to clash with those of a heavily spiced cracker!

GARLIC-DILL DEVILED EGGS

Fresh dill and garlic perk up the flavor of these irresistible appetizers you'll want to eat on every occasion.
—Kami Horch, Calais, ME

PREP: 20 MIN. + CHILLING • **MAKES:** 2 DOZEN

- 12 hard-boiled large eggs
- ⅔ cup mayonnaise
- 4 tsp. dill pickle relish
- 2 tsp. snipped fresh dill
- 2 tsp. Dijon mustard
- 1 tsp. coarsely ground pepper
- ¼ tsp. garlic powder
- ⅛ tsp. paprika or cayenne pepper

1. Cut eggs lengthwise in half. Remove yolks, reserving whites. In a bowl, mash yolks. Stir in all remaining ingredients except paprika. Spoon or pipe into egg whites.
2. Refrigerate, covered, for at least 30 minutes before serving. Sprinkle with paprika.

1 stuffed egg half: 81 cal., 7g fat (1g sat. fat), 94mg chol., 81mg sod., 1g carb. (0 sugars, 0 fiber), 3g pro.

FRUIT WITH POPPY SEED DRESSING

Cool, colorful and easy to prepare, this refreshing, good-for-you fruit salad is a summmertime favorite.
—Peggy Mills, Texarkana, AR

PREP: 20 MIN. + STANDING
MAKES: 12 SERVINGS

- 3 Tbsp. honey
- 1 Tbsp. white vinegar
- 1 tsp. ground mustard
- ¼ tsp. salt
- ¼ tsp. onion powder
- ⅓ cup canola oil
- 1 tsp. poppy seeds

- 1 fresh pineapple, cut into 1½-in. cubes
- 3 medium kiwifruit, halved and sliced
- 2 cups fresh strawberries, halved

1. In a small bowl, whisk the first 5 ingredients. Gradually whisk in oil until blended. Stir in poppy seeds; let stand 1 hour.
2. In a large bowl, combine the fruits. Drizzle with the dressing; toss gently to coat.
1 cup: 129 cal., 7g fat (0 sat. fat), 0 chol., 51mg sod., 19g carb. (14g sugars, 2g fiber), 1g pro. **Diabetic exchanges:** 1½ fat, 1 fruit.

HOW TO MAKE CLASSIC DEVILED EGGS

Egg aficionados, rejoice! There are endless variations on this fun finger food.
Begin by following these easy steps for basic deviled eggs, then season as desired.

STEP 1
Hard-cook the eggs. Arrange
in a single layer and add water to
cover by 1 inch. Bring to a rolling boil,
uncovered. Remove from the heat.
Cover and let stand 14-17 minutes.

STEP 2
Drain the hot water and cover the
eggs in cold water. Gently crack the
shells and return to the cold water.
Let stand 1 hour. After 1 hour,
the shells will peel off easily.

STEP 3
Trim white on both sides so eggs will
sit level. Halve eggs lengthwise and
gently squeeze the whites or use a
small spoon to remove the yolks.
Place the yolks in a bowl.

STEP 4
Mash the yolks with the back of
a fork until crumbly. Stir in the rest
of the filling ingredients.

STEP 5
Spoon or pipe filling into egg
whites until slightly mounded.

STEP 6
Garnish with paprika or your
favorite herbs or spices.

CHOCOLATE-COCONUT LAYER BARS

I'm a huge fan of Nanaimo bars, the no-bake dessert named for the city in British Columbia. For fun, I reinvented this treat with coconut lovers in mind.
—Shannon Dobos, Calgary, AB

PREP: 20 MIN. + CHILLING • **MAKES:** 3 DOZEN

- ¾ cup butter, cubed
- 3 cups Oreo cookie crumbs
- 2 cups sweetened shredded coconut
- ½ cup cream of coconut

FILLING
- ⅓ cup butter, softened
- 3 Tbsp. cream of coconut
- ¼ tsp. coconut extract
- 3 cups confectioners' sugar
- 1 to 2 Tbsp. 2% milk

TOPPING
- 1½ cups semisweet chocolate chips
- 4 tsp. canola oil
- 3 Mounds candy bars (1¾ oz. each), coarsely chopped, optional

1. Microwave butter on high until melted; stir until smooth. Stir in cookie crumbs, coconut and cream of coconut until blended (mixture will be wet). Spread onto bottom of an ungreased 13x9-in. baking pan. Refrigerate until set, about 30 minutes.

2. For filling, beat butter, cream of coconut and extract until smooth. Gradually beat in confectioners' sugar and enough milk to reach a spreading consistency. Spread over crust.

3. For topping, microwave chocolate chips and oil until melted; stir until smooth. Cool slightly; spread over the filling. If desired, sprinkle with chopped candy bars. Refrigerate.

1 bar: 229 cal., 13g fat (8g sat. fat), 15mg chol., 124mg sod., 28g carb. (23g sugars, 1g fiber), 1g pro.

FROSTED CARROT CAKE COOKIES

I took my favorite carrot cake recipe and slightly tweaked it to make cookies. Just like the cake, the yummy bites are filled with shredded carrot, pineapple and raisins—and topped with a homemade cream cheese frosting.
—Lawrence Earl, Sumner, MI

PREP: 30 MIN.
BAKE: 10 MIN./BATCH + COOLING
MAKES: ABOUT 4½ DOZEN

- 1 cup butter, softened
- 1 cup sugar
- 1 cup packed brown sugar
- 2 large eggs, room temperature
- 1 tsp. vanilla extract
- 3 cups all-purpose flour
- 1 tsp. baking soda
- ½ tsp. salt
- 1 medium carrot, shredded
- ½ cup crushed pineapple, drained and patted dry
- ½ cup golden raisins

FROSTING
- 6 oz. cream cheese, softened
- 3¾ cups confectioners' sugar
- 1½ tsp. vanilla extract
- 2 to 3 Tbsp. 2% milk
- Toasted chopped walnuts, optional

1. Preheat oven to 350°. In a large bowl, cream butter, sugar and brown sugar until light and fluffy, 5-7 minutes. Beat in eggs and vanilla. In another bowl, whisk the flour, baking soda and salt; gradually beat into creamed mixture. Stir in carrot, pineapple and raisins.

2. Drop dough by tablespoonfuls 2 in. apart onto ungreased baking sheets. Bake 10-12 minutes or until light brown. Remove from pans to wire racks to cool completely.

3. In a small bowl, beat cream cheese until smooth. Gradually beat in the confectioners' sugar, vanilla and enough milk to reach a spreading consistency. Frost cookies. If desired, sprinkle with walnuts. Store in an airtight container in the refrigerator.

Freeze option: Drop cookie dough by tablespoonfuls onto waxed paper-lined baking sheets; freeze until firm. Transfer to airtight freezer containers; return to freezer. To use, bake cookies as directed.

1 cookie: 129 cal., 4g fat (3g sat. fat), 18mg chol., 81mg sod., 22g carb. (16g sugars, 0 fiber), 1g pro.

Beach Party

Grab your beach towel, flip-flops and shades—it's time for a beach bash! Whether you live on the water or just want to bring a seaside vibe to your summer gathering, turn to these easy-to-eat recipes that are portable, refreshing, cooler-friendly and delicious.

PINEAPPLE & MINT INFUSED WATER

This pineapple and mint water is like a tropical cocktail but without the sticky-sweet taste.
—James Schend, Pleasant Prairie, WI

PREP: 5 MIN. + CHILLING
MAKES: 8 SERVINGS

- 2 qt. water
- ¼ fresh pineapple, sliced
- 3 fresh mint sprigs

Combine all ingredients in a large glass carafe or pitcher. Cover and refrigerate 12-24 hours. Strain before serving.
1 cup: 0 cal., 0 fat (0 sat. fat), 0 chol., 0 sod., 0 carb. (0 sugars, 0 fiber), 0 pro.

SUN-DRIED TOMATO MAYONNAISE

I admit it—I'm a mayo fanatic. And I'm always looking for ways to kick it up. This tomato-y sauce is fantastic slathered on burgers, brushed on grilled meats or as a dipping sauce for just about anything.
—Debbie Glasscock, Conway, AR

TAKES: 5 MINUTES • **MAKES:** ABOUT ½ CUP

- ½ cup mayonnaise
- 2 Tbsp. jarred sun-dried tomato pesto

Stir together the mayonnaise and the pesto until well blended. Spread on hamburgers, or serve as desired.
1 Tbsp.: 96 cal., 10g fat (2g sat. fat), 1mg chol., 109mg sod., 1g carb. (0 sugars, 0 fiber), 0 pro.

TEXAS TEA

Make a pitcher full of this tea for a get-together on a hot summer day. It's a potent drink, so enjoy responsibly!
—*Taste of Home* Test Kitchen

TAKES: 10 MIN. • **MAKES:** 8 SERVINGS

- 1 cup cola
- 1 cup sour mix
- ½ cup vodka
- ½ cup gin
- ½ cup Triple Sec
- ½ cup golden or light rum
- ½ cup tequila
  Lemon or lime slices

In a pitcher, combine first 7 ingredients; serve over ice. Garnish each individual serving with a slice of lemon or lime.
¾ cup: 246 cal., 0 fat (0 sat. fat), 0 chol., 2mg sod., 24g carb. (22g sugars, 0 fiber), 0 pro.

MOJITO-STYLE YELLOW TOMATO SALSA

With grilled tomatoes, crunchy peppers and a sprinkle of mint, this fresh salsa is excellent with fish tacos, on tortilla chips or by the spoonful!
—Patterson Watkins, Philadelphia, PA

PREP: 20 MIN. • **GRILL:** 10 MIN. + CHILLING
MAKES: 4 CUPS

- 2 lbs. large yellow tomatoes, halved
- 1 Tbsp. olive oil
- 2 garlic cloves, minced
- 1 tsp. chopped shallot
- ¾ tsp. salt, divided
- 3 medium limes
- 2 tsp. coarse sugar
- 12 fresh mint leaves
- ¼ cup chopped Cubanelle or banana peppers

1. Grill tomatoes, uncovered, on an oiled rack over high heat or broil 3-4 in. from the heat until skin is slightly charred, 3-4 minutes on each side. Cool to room temperature. Meanwhile, combine the oil, garlic, shallot and ¼ tsp. salt. When the tomatoes are cool enough to handle, finely chop; stir in garlic mixture until well combined.
2. Finely grate zest of each lime; set aside. Peel limes and discard the white membranes; section limes. In a food processor, pulse lime sections, sugar, mint and the remaining ½ tsp. salt until finely chopped. Combine with tomatoes; add peppers and lime zest. Mix well.
3. Refrigerate at least 1 hour. Serve with chips or grilled meats.
¼ cup: 23 cal., 1g fat (0 sat. fat), 0 chol., 161mg sod., 4g carb. (1g sugars, 1g fiber), 1g pro. **Diabetic exchanges:** 1 vegetable.

ALL-AMERICAN HAMBURGERS

We do a lot of camping and outdoor cooking. Hamburgers are on our menu more than any other food.
—Diane Hixon, Niceville, FL

TAKES: 20 MIN. • **MAKES:** 4 SERVINGS

- 1   lb. ground beef
- 2   Tbsp. finely chopped onion
- 2   Tbsp. chili sauce
- 2   tsp. Worcestershire sauce
- 2   tsp. prepared mustard
- 4   slices American cheese or cheddar cheese, halved diagonally
- 2   slices Swiss cheese, halved diagonally
- 4   hamburger buns, split and toasted
      Optional: Lettuce leaves, sliced tomato, sliced onion, cooked bacon strips, ketchup and mustard

1. Combine the first 5 ingredients, mixing lightly but thoroughly. Shape into 4 patties. Grill burgers, covered, on an oiled rack over medium direct heat until a thermometer reads 160° and juices run clear, about 6 minutes on each side.
2. During the last minute of cooking, top each patty with 2 triangles American cheese and 1 triangle Swiss cheese. Serve on buns. As desired, top with lettuce, tomato, onion, bacon, ketchup and mustard.

1 hamburger: 432 cal., 21g fat (9g sat. fat), 80mg chol., 681mg sod., 26g carb. (6g sugars, 1g fiber), 30g pro.

GARDEN PESTO PASTA SALAD

My family and I live on a homestead in the Missouri Ozarks and produce much of our own food. In the summer, when the garden is bursting with fresh vegetables and it's too hot to cook, I like to use the season's veggies for pasta salads and other cool meals.
—Sarah Mathews, Ava, MO

PREP: 15 MIN. + CHILLING
MAKES: 10 SERVINGS

- 3   cups uncooked spiral pasta (about 9 oz.)
- ½   cup prepared pesto
- 3   Tbsp. white wine vinegar
- 1   Tbsp. lemon juice
- ½   tsp. salt
- ¼   tsp. pepper
- ¼   cup olive oil
- 1   medium zucchini, halved and sliced
- 1   medium sweet red pepper, chopped
- 1   medium tomato, seeded and chopped
- 1   small red onion, halved and thinly sliced
- ½   cup grated Parmesan cheese

1. Cook the pasta according to package directions; drain. Rinse with cold water and drain well.
2. Meanwhile, whisk together pesto, vinegar, lemon juice, salt and pepper. Gradually whisk in oil until blended.
3. Combine the vegetables and pasta. Drizzle with pesto dressing; toss to coat. Refrigerate, covered, until cold, about 1 hour. Serve with Parmesan cheese.

1 serving: 217 cal., 11g fat (2g sat. fat), 3mg chol., 339mg sod., 23g carb. (3g sugars, 2g fiber), 6g pro. **Diabetic exchanges:** 2 fat, 1½ starch.

PACK LIKE A PRO
Transport food with confidence using these easy hacks.

BUILD A DIY MULTILEVEL TOTE
If you have more dishes than hands, use a cooling rack with folding legs to create sturdy, stable levels inside a carrying tote. You can also build layers by propping a sheet pan with ring molds or cans.

ENSURE A NO-SLIP TRIP
Grippy drawer liners or silicone baking mats will keep dishes from sliding around in your car and will contain any errant spills. A yoga mat works, too!

KEEP A LID ON IT
Use a bungee cord, painter's tape or a thick ribbon to secure the lid for your slow cooker, Dutch oven or other serving vessel. Wrap the cord around the handles and over the top. Now you're ready to transport without risk of a mess.

BRING A SALAD
Yes, you can serve a crisp, freshly tossed salad when you're far from home. Just bring the fixings in a serving bowl, along with the utensils. Toss the salad at your destination. Voila!

CHIPOTLE GUACAMOLE

My guacamole is so tasty because it has just a hint of smoke from the chipotle pepper. Stir in the chopped pepper or put a dollop in the center of the dip so people who aren't into the pepper can scoop around it.
—Gayle Sullivan, Salem, MA

PREP: 15 MIN. + CHILLING • **MAKES:** 3 CUPS

- 4 medium ripe avocados, peeled and pitted
- 1 small tomato, seeded and chopped
- ⅓ cup finely chopped red onion
- 3 garlic cloves, minced
- 2 Tbsp. lemon juice
- 2 Tbsp. olive oil
- ¼ tsp. salt
- 1 to 2 Tbsp. minced fresh cilantro, optional
- 1 finely chopped chipotle pepper in adobo sauce plus 1 tsp. adobo sauce
  Tortilla chips

Mash the avocados. Stir in the next 6 ingredients and, if desired, cilantro. Dollop chipotle pepper and adobo sauce over center of guacamole. Refrigerate 1 hour. Serve with chips.

¼ cup: 103 cal., 9g fat (1g sat. fat), 0 chol., 70mg sod., 5g carb. (1g sugars, 3g fiber), 1g pro.

ITALIAN HERO BRAID

My mother-in-law used to make these pastry pockets for my husband while he was growing up. After we got married, I changed her recipe a little to fit our family's tastes.
—Amanda Kohler, Redmond, WA

PREP: 20 MIN. • **BAKE:** 25 MIN.
MAKES: 8 SERVINGS

- ½ lb. bulk Italian sausage
- 1 pkg. (¼ oz.) active dry yeast
- 1 cup warm water (110° to 115°)
- 2¾ to 3¼ cups all-purpose flour
- 1 Tbsp. butter, melted
- ⅓ lb. sliced provolone cheese
- ⅓ lb. thinly sliced Genoa salami
- 1 cup shredded cheddar cheese
- 1 large egg white

1. Preheat oven to 400°. In a large skillet over medium heat, cook and crumble the Italian sausage until no longer pink, 4-6 minutes; drain.
2. Meanwhile, dissolve the yeast in the warm water. In another bowl, combine 1½ cups flour and butter; add yeast mixture. Beat on medium speed until smooth. Stir in enough remaining flour to form a soft dough.
3. Turn the dough onto a lightly floured surface; roll into a 13x10-in. rectangle. Transfer to a parchment-lined baking sheet. Layer the cheese and salami slices down center of rectangle; top with the crumbled sausage and the shredded cheddar. On each long side, cut 1-in.-wide strips about 2 in. into the center. Starting at 1 end, fold alternating strips at an angle across filling. Pinch both ends to seal.
4. Whisk the egg white; brush over the pastry. Bake until golden brown, 25-30 minutes.

1 slice: 436 cal., 23g fat (11g sat. fat), 64mg chol., 823mg sod., 35g carb. (0 sugars, 1g fiber), 21g pro.

FRESH CUCUMBER SALAD

Crisp, garden-fresh cukes are always in season when we hold our family reunion, and they really shine in this simple salad. The recipe can easily be expanded to make party-sized quantities, too.
—Betsy Carlson, Rockford, IL

PREP: 10 MIN. + CHILLING
MAKES: 10 SERVINGS

- 3 medium cucumbers, sliced
- 1 cup sugar
- ¾ cup water
- ½ cup white vinegar
- 3 Tbsp. minced fresh dill or parsley

Place cucumbers in a 1½- or 2-qt. glass container. In a jar with a tight-fitting lid, shake the remaining ingredients until combined. Pour over cucumbers. Cover and refrigerate overnight. Serve with a slotted spoon.

½ cup: 87 cal., 0 fat (0 sat. fat), 0 chol., 0 sod., 22g carb. (21g sugars, 1g fiber), 1g pro.

PEACH CRUMB BARS

I had the most beautiful peaches and really wanted to bake with them. I started with my blueberry crumb bar recipe, and after a couple of tries, I was so happy with the results. My co-worker taste testers were, too!
—Amy Burns, Newman, IL

PREP: 30 MIN. • **BAKE:** 40 MIN. + COOLING
MAKES: 2 DOZEN

3	cups all-purpose flour
1½	cups sugar, divided
1	tsp. baking powder
½	tsp. salt
	Dash ground cinnamon
1	cup shortening
1	large egg
1	tsp. vanilla extract
9	medium peaches, peeled and chopped
1	tsp. almond extract
4	tsp. cornstarch

1. Preheat oven to 375°. Whisk flour, 1 cup sugar, baking powder, salt and cinnamon; cut in the shortening until crumbly. In another bowl, whisk egg and vanilla until blended; add to the flour mixture, stirring with a fork until crumbly.
2. Reserve 2½ cups crumb mixture for topping. Press the remaining mixture onto bottom of a greased 13x9-in. baking pan.
3. Toss peaches with almond extract. In another bowl, mix cornstarch and remaining ½ cup sugar; add to peaches and toss to coat. Spread over crust; sprinkle with reserved topping.
4. Bake until lightly browned and the filling is bubbly, 40-45 minutes. Cool completely in the pan on a wire rack. Cut into bars.

1 bar: 207 cal., 9g fat (2g sat. fat), 8mg chol., 73mg sod., 30g carb. (17g sugars, 1g fiber), 2g pro.

BLUEBERRY PIE

During blueberry season, this pie always makes an appearance. It has a wonderful fresh berry flavor and a bit of tang from the lemon zest.

—Richard Case, Johnstown, PA

PREP: 30 MIN. • **BAKE:** 1 HOUR + COOLING
MAKES: 8 SERVINGS

- 4 cups fresh blueberries
- 1 Tbsp. lemon juice
- ½ tsp. grated lemon zest
- 1¼ to 1½ cups sugar
- ¼ cup quick-cooking tapioca
- 1 Tbsp. cornstarch
- ½ tsp. ground cinnamon
  Pastry for double-crust pie (9 in.)
- 1 Tbsp. butter, softened
- 1 large egg
- 1 Tbsp. 2% milk
  Coarse sugar, optional

1. Preheat oven to 350°. Combine the blueberries, lemon juice and lemon zest. In another bowl, combine sugar, tapioca, cornstarch and cinnamon. Add to berries; toss gently to coat.
2. On a lightly floured surface, roll half the pie dough to a ⅛-in.-thick circle; transfer to a 9-in. pie plate. Trim crust to ½ in. beyond rim of plate. Add the blueberry mixture. Dot with butter.
3. Roll remaining dough to a ⅛-in.-thick circle; cut into 1-in.-wide strips. Arrange over the filling in a lattice pattern. Trim and seal strips to edge of bottom crust; flute edge. Whisk egg and milk; brush over the crust. If desired, sprinkle with coarse sugar.
4. Bake for 30 minutes. Cover the edge loosely with foil. Bake until the crust is golden brown and berries have burst, about 30-35 minutes more. Cool on a wire rack.

1 piece: 553 cal., 25g fat (16g sat. fat), 87mg chol., 332mg sod., 78g carb. (40g sugars, 3g fiber), 6g pro.

Pastry for double-crust pie (9 in.): Combine 2½ cups all-purpose flour and ½ tsp. salt; cut in 1 cup cold butter until crumbly. Gradually add ⅓-⅔ cup ice water, tossing with a fork until dough holds together when pressed. Divide the dough in half. Shape each half into a disk; cover and refrigerate 1 hour or overnight.

RAINBOW FRUIT BOWL

I've discovered that mint gives melon a delicious zip. When mint is mixed with fruit juices and then served over melon, a pleasant blend is created that's both sweet and refreshing.

—Dorothy Pritchett, Wills Point, TX

PREP: 15 MIN. + CHILLING
MAKES: 8 SERVINGS

- 2 cups watermelon balls
- 2 cups honeydew balls
- 2 cups cantaloupe balls
- ½ cup orange juice
- ¼ cup lime juice
- 2 Tbsp. sugar
- 1 Tbsp. snipped fresh mint
- 1 Tbsp. grated orange zest
- 1 cup lemon-lime soda

1. Combine melon balls in a glass bowl. In a small bowl, whisk together juices, sugar, mint and orange zest; pour over melon and toss gently.
2. Cover and refrigerate for 2 hours. Just before serving, add soda and toss gently.

¾ cup: 77 cal., 0 fat (0 sat. fat), 0 chol., 13mg sod., 19g carb. (18g sugars, 1g fiber), 1g pro. **Diabetic exchanges:** 1 fruit, ½ starch.

Unicorn Birthday Party

Is your little one dreaming of a magical unicorn birthday party? Unleash your creativity and playfulness to create a mythically magnificent celebration that kids and adults won't soon forget. Frolic down the road of sweet surprises with these enchanted ideas for a whimsical menu, plenty of party fun and a unicorn cake that will be both a darling dessert and a sparkling centerpiece. Just follow the rainbows!

MAGIC WANDS

These fun and colorful wands don't need to be made by a magician to be magical. You can change the colors to fit any party theme.
—Renee Schwebach, Dumont, MN

PREP: 25 MIN. + STANDING
MAKES: 2 DOZEN

1½ cups white baking chips
1 pkg. (10 oz.) pretzel rods
  Colored candy stars or sprinkles
  Colored sugar or edible glitter

In a microwave, melt chips; stir until smooth. Dip each pretzel rod halfway into melted chips; allow excess to drip off. Sprinkle coatings with candy stars and colored sugar. Place the pretzels on waxed paper; let stand until dry. Store in an airtight container.
1 wand: 103 cal., 4g fat (2g sat. fat), 2mg chol., 164mg sod., 15g carb. (0 sugars, 0 fiber), 2g pro.

STAR SANDWICHES

These star-shaped sandwiches are my favorite way to enjoy savory egg salad. You can use whatever bread you like, but I prefer yellow egg bread.
—Pam Lancaster, Willis, VA

TAKES: 25 MIN. • **MAKES:** 8 SANDWICHES

4 hard-boiled large eggs, diced
½ cup mayonnaise
1 tsp. Dijon mustard
¼ tsp. dill weed
⅛ tsp. salt
⅛ tsp. pepper
16 slices egg bread or white bread

In a small bowl, combine the eggs, mayonnaise, mustard, dill, salt and pepper. Using a large star-shaped cookie cutter, cut out 16 stars from the bread slices. Spread half the bread cutouts with egg salad; top with remaining bread.
1 sandwich: 359 cal., 17g fat (4g sat. fat), 135mg chol., 457mg sod., 39g carb. (2g sugars, 2g fiber), 11g pro.

KIDDIE CRUNCH MIX

This no-bake snack mix is a delightful treat for kids, and you can easily increase the amount to fit your needs. Place in individual bags, or pour some into colored ice cream cones for a cute presentation.
—Kara de la Vega, Santa Rosa, CA

TAKES: 10 MIN. • **MAKES:** 6 CUPS

1 cup plain or frosted
  animal crackers
1 cup bear-shaped crackers
1 cup miniature pretzels
1 cup salted peanuts
1 cup M&M's
1 cup yogurt- or
  chocolate-covered raisins

In a bowl, combine all ingredients. Store in an airtight container.
½ cup: 266 cal., 14g fat (5g sat. fat), 4mg chol., 159mg sod., 33g carb. (23g sugars, 3g fiber), 6g pro.

LITTLE DIPPERS

Get ready for blue skies and sunny days with these rainbow-colored, candy-dunked strawberries. Sweet!

Dip berries in melted candy coating disks. Let dry on parchment. Add sprinkles or decorate as desired.

CRAZY-COLORED FRUIT POPS

Orange, pear, banana, raspberry, grape—the gang's all here! See if your pals can guess the flavors in one of these summery rainbow pops.
—Vikki Spengler, Ocala, FL

PREP: 20 MIN. + FREEZING • **MAKES:** 19 POPS

- 1 cup orange-tangerine juice
- 2 cans (15 oz. each) reduced-sugar sliced pears, drained and divided
- 1 medium banana, sliced and divided
- 2 to 3 drops yellow food coloring, optional
- 4 drops red food coloring, optional, divided
- 1 cup red raspberry juice
- 1 cup grape juice
- 19 freezer pop molds or 19 paper cups (3 oz. each) and wooden pop sticks

1. In a blender, combine the orange-tangerine juice, ¾ cup pears, a third of the banana and, if desired, the yellow food coloring and 1 drop red. Cover and process until smooth. Fill each mold or cup with 1 Tbsp. mixture. Top molds with holders. If using cups, top with foil and insert sticks through foil. Freeze 30 minutes or until firm.
2. In a blender, combine raspberry juice, ¾ cup pears, a third of the banana and 3 drops red food coloring if desired. Cover; process until smooth. If using pop molds, remove holders. If using cups, remove foil. Pour mixture over orange layer. Return holders or foil. Freeze 30 minutes or until firm.
3. In a blender, combine the grape juice and remaining pears and banana slices; cover and process until smooth. If using pop molds, remove the holders. If using cups, remove foil. Pour grape mixture over tops; return holders or foil. Freeze 30 minutes or until firm.

1 pop: 47 cal., 0 fat (0 sat. fat), 0 chol., 6mg sod., 11g carb. (10g sugars, 1g fiber), 0 pro. **Diabetic exchanges:** ½ starch.

TEST KITCHEN TIP
To avoid sticky fingers, skewer a cupcake liner through the end of the wooden pop stick. It'll help collect any drippings. Plus, colorful liners can help give your fruit pops extra flair.

CRANBERRY TURKEY WRAPS

Fruity and flavorful, these grab-and-go wraps are quick to assemble, easy to handle and low in calories.
—Bobbie Keefer, Byers, CO

TAKES: 15 MIN. • **MAKES:** 8 SERVINGS

- 1 can (11 oz.) mandarin oranges, drained
- 1 medium tart apple, peeled and diced
- 3 Tbsp. dried cranberries
- ¾ cup fat-free plain yogurt
- 2 Tbsp. fat-free mayonnaise
- 8 flour tortillas (8 in.)
- 8 lettuce leaves
- 1½ lbs. thinly sliced deli turkey
- 8 slices (1 oz. each) part-skim mozzarella cheese
- 2 Tbsp. chopped pecans, toasted

In a small bowl, combine the oranges, apple and cranberries. In another bowl, combine the yogurt and mayonnaise; spread over tortillas. Layer each with lettuce, turkey, cheese, fruit mixture and pecans. Roll up tightly.

1 wrap: 374 cal., 12g fat (4g sat. fat), 54mg chol., 1477mg sod., 40g carb. (9g sugars, 1g fiber), 27g pro.

APRICOT-RICOTTA STUFFED CELERY

The healthful protein filling can double as a dip for sliced apples. I often make this treat ahead so the kids can help themselves to an after-school snack.
—Dorothy Reinhold, Malibu, CA

TAKES: 15 MIN. • **MAKES:** ABOUT 2 DOZEN

- 3 dried apricots
- ½ cup part-skim ricotta cheese
- 2 tsp. brown sugar
- ¼ tsp. grated orange zest
- ⅛ tsp. salt
- 5 celery ribs, cut into 1½-in. pieces

Place the apricots in a food processor. Cover and process until finely chopped. Add the ricotta cheese, brown sugar, orange zest and salt; cover and process until blended. Stuff or pipe into celery. Chill until serving.

1 piece: 12 cal., 0 fat (0 sat. fat), 2mg chol., 25mg sod., 1g carb. (1g sugars, 0 fiber), 1g pro.

CARROT CABBAGE SLAW

This crunchy salad with a homemade honey dressing is light and could complement almost any main dish.
—Geordyth Sullivan, Cutler Bay, FL

TAKES: 20 MIN. • **MAKES:** 12 SERVINGS

- 4 cups shredded cabbage
- 2 cups shredded carrots
- 2 medium Golden Delicious apples, chopped
- 1 cup raisins
- ½ cup chopped walnuts
- ½ cup honey
- 1 Tbsp. lemon juice
- 1 cup sour cream
- ¼ tsp. salt
- ⅛ tsp. pepper
- ⅛ to ¼ tsp. ground nutmeg, optional

1. In a large serving bowl, combine the cabbage, carrots, apples, raisins and walnuts.
2. In a small bowl, combine the honey and lemon juice until smooth. Stir in the sour cream, salt, pepper and, if desired, nutmeg. Stir into cabbage mixture. Chill until serving.

⅔ cup: 176 cal., 6g fat (2g sat. fat), 13mg chol., 71mg sod., 29g carb. (24g sugars, 2g fiber), 3g pro.

RANCH BROCCOLI PASTA SALAD

Here's an easy summer salad for potlucks, luncheons and picnics. Tricolor spiral pasta and broccoli florets are coated with a mild dressing and bits of bacon.
—Margie Shaw, Americus, GA

PREP: 10 MIN. + CHILLING
MAKES: 12 SERVINGS

- 1 pkg. (16 oz.) tricolor spiral pasta, cooked, rinsed and drained
- 3 cups broccoli florets
- ⅓ cup finely chopped onion
- ½ cup reduced-fat mayonnaise
- 2 Tbsp. fat-free milk
- 1 envelope reduced-fat ranch salad dressing mix
- ½ tsp. salt
- 6 bacon strips, cooked and crumbled

In a large bowl, combine the pasta, broccoli and onion. In a small bowl, combine mayonnaise, milk, salad dressing mix and salt. Add to pasta mixture; toss to coat evenly. Cover and refrigerate for at least 1 hour. Just before serving, stir in bacon.

¾ cup: 215 cal., 6g fat (1g sat. fat), 8mg chol., 523mg sod., 33g carb. (2g sugars, 2g fiber), 7g pro. **Diabetic exchanges:** 2 starch, 1 fat.

MARSHMALLOW FRUIT DIP

You can whip up this sweet and creamy dip in just 10 minutes. For spring brunches or luncheons, I like to serve it in a bowl surrounded by fresh-picked strawberries.
—Cindy Steffen, Cedarburg, WI

TAKES: 10 MIN.
MAKES: 5 CUPS (40 SERVINGS)

- 1   pkg. (8 oz.) cream cheese, softened
- ¾   cup cherry yogurt
- 1   carton (8 oz.) frozen whipped topping, thawed
- 1   jar (7 oz.) marshmallow creme
  Assorted fresh fruit

In a large bowl, beat cream cheese and yogurt until blended. Fold in the whipped topping and marshmallow creme. Serve with fruit.
2 Tbsp.: 56 cal., 3g fat (2g sat. fat), 7mg chol., 24mg sod., 6g carb. (5g sugars, 0 fiber), 1g pro.

READER REVIEW
"This was easy and very tasty. It was wonderful with grapes, apples and strawberries."
—QUEENLALISA, TASTEOFHOME.COM

UNICORN CAKE

This magical unicorn cake tastes as good as it looks. Baking the layers in three small 6-in. pans creates impressive height, and a few simple decorating tricks turn it into a showstopping dessert everyone will love.
—Lauren McAnelly, Des Moines, IA

PREP: 1 HOUR • **BAKE:** 25 MIN. + COOLING
MAKES: 20 SERVINGS

2¼ cups cake flour
1½ cups sugar
3½ tsp. baking powder
½ tsp. salt
½ cup unsalted butter, cubed

4 large egg whites, room temperature
¾ cup 2% milk, divided
1 tsp. clear vanilla extract
½ tsp. almond extract
⅓ cup rainbow jimmies

BUTTERCREAM
6 oz. white baking chocolate, chopped
¼ cup heavy whipping cream
6 large egg whites
1½ cups sugar
½ tsp. cream of tartar
½ tsp. salt
2 cups unsalted butter, cubed
1½ tsp. vanilla extract
Paste food coloring

1. Preheat oven to 350°. Line bottoms of three 6-in. round baking pans with parchment; grease and flour pans.
2. In a large bowl, whisk flour, sugar, baking powder and salt. Beat in butter until crumbly. Add egg whites, 1 at a time, beating well after each addition. Gradually beat in ¼ cup milk and the extracts; beat on medium until light and fluffy, about 2 minutes. Gradually beat in remaining milk. Gently fold in rainbow jimmies.
3. Transfer the batter to prepared cake pans. Bake until a toothpick inserted in each center comes out clean, 25-30 minutes. Cool cake layers in pans for 10 minutes before removing to wire racks; remove the parchment. Cool completely.
4. For buttercream, in a microwave, melt the chocolate with the cream until smooth, stirring every 30 seconds. Set aside to cool slightly. In heatproof bowl of stand mixer, whisk egg whites, sugar, cream of tartar and salt until blended. Place over simmering water in a large saucepan over medium heat. Whisking constantly, heat the mixture until a thermometer reads 160°, 8-10 minutes.
5. Remove from the heat. With whisk attachment of stand mixer, beat on high speed until cooled to 90°, about 7 minutes. Gradually beat in butter, a few Tbsp. at a time, on medium speed until smooth; beat in vanilla and the white chocolate mixture.
6. Spread the frosting between layers and over top and sides of cake. Divide the remaining buttercream into smaller portions; stir in food coloring to achieve desired colors. Decorate as desired. Store in refrigerator.

1 piece: 460 cal., 28g fat (17g sat. fat), 65mg chol., 245mg sod., 51g carb. (38g sugars, 0 fiber), 4g pro.

HOW TO MAKE FANCY FINISHES

STEP 1: To make the ears, mix your favorite sugar cookie dough with jimmies; cut into 2-in. hearts and bake.

STEP 2: For eyes, pipe melted white candy coating disks onto parchment; chill until set. Make extra, just in case!

STEP 3: Spray the piped eyes with edible gold glitter spray. (Available from Wilton Brands, wilton.com.)

STEP 4: To make the horn, spray a sugar ice cream cone with gold glitter spray.

STEP 5: While the baked cookies are warm, mold them onto the curve of a large metal spoon; let stand until cooled.

STEP 6: Dip the straight edges of the cooled cookies into melted white chocolate; let set.

STEP 7: Gently push the horn and ears into place on the top of the cake.

STEP 8: To make the mane, gently press meringues (store-bought work terrific!) into the top and side of cake.

STEP 9: Using an open star nozzle tip, fill in between the meringues with your first color of frosting.

STEP 10: Add additional frosting in other colors around the outside of the meringues to fill in the mane.

STEP 11: Continue to add frosting to finish the mane, switching frosting colors and decorating tips as desired.

STEP 12: Use clean tweezers to set each eye in place on the front of the cake; press gently to adhere.

CHERRY PUNCH

Back in 1952, a co-worker gave me the recipe for this versatile rosy punch. It's not too sweet, so it really refreshes. Over the years, I've served it to my family and friends at countless gatherings, from picnics to holiday parties.
—Davlyn Jones, San Jose, CA

TAKES: 20 MIN. • **MAKES:** ABOUT 6 QT.

- ¾ cup thawed lemonade concentrate
- 1 can (6 oz.) frozen limeade concentrate, thawed
- 1 can (20 oz.) pineapple chunks, undrained
- 2 cups water
- 2 liters cherry soda, chilled
- 2 liters ginger ale, chilled
  Optional: Lemon slices and lime slices

In a blender, combine concentrates and the pineapple; cover and blend until smooth. Pour the mixture into a gallon-sized container; stir in water. Store in the refrigerator. To serve, pour the mixture into a punch bowl; add the cherry soda and ginger ale. Garnish with lemon and lime slices if desired.

1 cup: 120 cal., 0 fat (0 sat. fat), 0 chol., 20mg sod., 31g carb. (19g sugars, 0 fiber), 0 pro.

RAINBOW SHORTBREAD COOKIES

Everyone loves a classic shortbread cookie. Make each cookie magical with a quick dip into melted baking chips and rainbow-colored sprinkles. Your unicorns will love these rainbow bites.
—Angela Lemoine, Howell, NJ

PREP: 15 MIN. • **BAKE:** 10 MIN.
MAKES: 24 COOKIES

½   **cup butter, softened**
¾   **cup confectioners' sugar**
1   **large egg**
1½   **cups all-purpose flour**
¼   **cup sprinkles**
½   **cup white baking chips, melted**
    Additional sprinkles

1. In large bowl, cream butter and sugar until light and fluffy. Beat in egg. Gradually add flour until blended. Stir in sprinkles. Form dough into a disk; cover and refrigerate 1 hour.
2. Preheat oven to 375°. Line a baking sheet with parchment. Place dough on parchment; roll into a 12x8-in. rectangle. Score the dough into 24 rectangles. Bake until edges are golden brown, 10-15 minutes. Remove to a cooling rack; cool.
3. Break or cut along score marks. Dip 1 edge of each cookie into melted chips, then dip in additional sprinkles; place on waxed paper until set.
1 cookie: 97 cal., 5g fat (3g sat. fat), 18mg chol., 35mg sod., 12g carb. (6g sugars, 0 fiber), 1g pro.

Autumn Gatherings

Bonfire Party

It's officially autumn, but there's still a warm breeze kissing your cheek. After soaking up the final days of swimming, kayaking, hiking or laying in a hammock, gather with family and friends around a crackling bonfire. The cozy comfort and delicious food will turn any early fall evening into a memorable night.

PINEAPPLE STRAWBERRY PUNCH

For us, this drink has always been a must at holiday gatherings and other special occasions. It's fruity and fun.
—Heather Dollins, Poplar Bluff, MO

TAKES: 10 MIN. • **MAKES:** 12 SERVINGS (3 QT.)

- 2 pkg. (10 oz. each) frozen sweetened sliced strawberries, thawed
- 1 can (46 oz.) pineapple juice, chilled
- 4 cups lemon-lime soda, chilled

In a food processor, puree strawberries. Pour into a large punch bowl. Stir in the pineapple juice and soda. Serve immediately.

1 cup: 109 cal., 0 fat (0 sat. fat), 0 chol., 12mg sod., 28g carb. (23g sugars, 1g fiber), 1g pro.

VEGGIE BACON SLAW

This crunchy salad is nutrient-dense and tasty, too. Mix and match with your favorite dried fruit and nuts or whatever you have on hand.
—Jeanne Larson, Rancho Santa Margarita, CA

PREP: 20 MIN. + CHILLING
MAKES: 12 SERVINGS

- 4 cups shredded fresh Brussels sprouts
- 4 large carrots, peeled and shredded
- 1 lb. bacon strips, cooked and crumbled
- 8 green onions, chopped
- ⅔ cup dried cranberries
- 1 cup sliced almonds, toasted

DRESSING
- 1 cup plain Greek yogurt
- ½ cup reduced-fat mayonnaise
- ½ cup cider vinegar
- ⅓ cup honey
- ½ tsp. garlic powder
- ½ tsp. sea salt

In a large bowl, combine the first 6 ingredients. In another bowl, whisk the dressing ingredients until smooth; drizzle over the salad and toss to coat. Refrigerate, covered, at least 2 hours before serving.

¾ cup: 269 cal., 16g fat (4g sat. fat), 22mg chol., 423mg sod., 25g carb. (18g sugars, 4g fiber), 9g pro.

GRANDMA'S CLASSIC POTATO SALAD

When I asked my grandmother how old this classic potato salad recipe is, she told me that her mom used to make it when she was a little girl. It has definitely stood the test of time.
—Kimberly Wallace, Dennison, OH

PREP: 25 MIN. • **COOK:** 20 MIN. + CHILLING
MAKES: 10 SERVINGS

- 6 medium potatoes, peeled and cubed
- ¼ cup all-purpose flour
- 1 Tbsp. sugar
- 1½ tsp. salt
- 1 tsp. ground mustard
- 1 tsp. pepper
- ¾ cup water
- 2 large eggs, beaten
- ¼ cup white vinegar
- 4 hard-boiled large eggs
- 2 celery ribs, chopped
- 1 medium onion, chopped
  Sliced green onions, optional

1. Place potatoes in a large saucepan and cover with water. Bring to a boil. Reduce heat; cover and cook until tender, 15-20 minutes. Drain and cool to room temperature.
2. Meanwhile, in a small heavy saucepan, combine flour, sugar, salt, mustard and pepper. Gradually stir in water until smooth. Cook and stir over medium-high heat until thickened and bubbly. Reduce heat; cook and stir 2 minutes longer.
3. Remove from the heat. Stir a small amount of hot mixture into eggs; return all to the pan, stirring constantly. Bring to a gentle boil; cook and stir 2 minutes longer. Remove from the heat and cool completely. Gently stir in vinegar.
4. Chop and set aside 1 hard-boiled egg; chop the remaining hard-boiled eggs. In a large bowl, combine the potatoes, celery, onion and eggs; add dressing and stir until blended. Refrigerate the salad until chilled. Garnish with the reserved chopped egg and, if desired, sliced green onions.

¾ cup: 144 cal., 3g fat (1g sat. fat), 112mg chol., 402mg sod., 23g carb. (3g sugars, 2g fiber), 6g pro. **Diabetic exchanges:** 1½ starch, ½ fat.

VANILLA CHAI TEA

An aromatic chai is comfort in a cup. It is extra special with a dollop of fresh whipped cream and a sprinkling of ground allspice on top.
—*Taste of Home* Test Kitchen

TAKES: 25 MIN. • **MAKES:** 6 SERVINGS

- 8 whole peppercorns
- ½ tsp. whole allspice
- 2 cardamom pods
- 1 cinnamon stick (3 in.)
- 4 whole cloves
- 8 tea bags
- 1 Tbsp. honey
- 4 cups boiling water
- 2 cups 2% milk
- 1 Tbsp. vanilla extract
- ½ cup heavy whipping cream
- 1½ tsp. confectioners' sugar
- Ground allspice

1. Place the first 5 ingredients in a large bowl. With the end of a wooden spoon handle, crush the mixture until aromas are released. Add tea bags, honey and boiling water; steep, covered, 6 minutes.

2. In a small saucepan, heat milk. Strain tea into a heat-proof pitcher; stir in milk and vanilla.

3. In a small bowl, beat cream until it begins to thicken. Add confectioners' sugar; beat until soft peaks form. Top servings with whipped cream; sprinkle with allspice.

1 cup (with 2½ Tbsp. topping): 131 cal., 9g fat (6g sat. fat), 33mg chol., 48mg sod., 9g carb. (7g sugars, 0 fiber), 3g pro.

FAVORITE HOT CHOCOLATE

You need just a few basic ingredients to stir up this hot chocolate. It's smooth and not too sweet, making it just right for a cozy night around a campfire.
—Flo Snodderly, North Vernon, IN

TAKES: 15 MIN. • **MAKES:** 8 SERVINGS

- 1 can (14 oz.) sweetened condensed milk
- ½ cup baking cocoa
- 6½ cups water
- 2 tsp. vanilla extract
  Optional: Sweetened whipped cream, marshmallows, chocolate syrup and Pirouette cookies

1. Place the milk and cocoa in a large saucepan; cook and stir over medium heat until blended. Gradually stir in the water; heat through, stirring occasionally.

2. Remove from heat; stir in vanilla. Add toppings as desired.

1 cup: 177 cal., 5g fat (3g sat. fat), 17mg chol., 63mg sod., 30g carb. (27g sugars, 1g fiber), 5g pro.

READER REVIEW

"This is the hot chocolate recipe we took with us when we stayed at a log cabin in the mountains. Delicious and wonderful memories, too!"
—LATELYLISA, TASTEOFHOME.COM

TIN CAN LANTERN

Upcycle an empty tin can into a twinkling outdoor lantern. Using a drill or hammer and nails, drill or punch holes into the can. You can create a decorative design if you like. Place a votive on the inside for a warm glow. Be sure to place the can on a firesafe surface and do not leave a lit votive unattended.

SPARKLER STATION

Use a galvanized metal bucket to house sparklers that guests can grab at their convenience. Then get ready to light up the night!

MAC & CHEESE CUPS

I started making these for a close friend's daughter when she started eating solid food. She loves mac and cheese and could hold these in her tiny hands to feed herself. Now the adults like them more than the kids! They're always requested at potlucks.
—Karen Lambert, Weaverville, NC

PREP: 20 MIN. • **BAKE:** 25 MIN.
MAKES: 24 SERVINGS

- 1   lb. uncooked elbow macaroni
- 3   cups (12 oz.) sharp cheddar cheese, finely shredded
- 5   Tbsp. butter, softened
- 3   large eggs
- 1   cup half-and-half cream
- ½   cup (8 oz.) sour cream
- 1   tsp. salt
- ½   tsp. pepper

1. Preheat oven to 350°. Cook macaroni according to package directions, drain. Transfer to a large bowl. Stir in cheese and butter until melted.
2. In another bowl, whisk the eggs, cream, sour cream, salt and pepper until blended. Add to the macaroni mixture; stir until well blended. Spoon the macaroni into 24 well-greased muffin cups. Bake until golden brown, 25-30 minutes.

1 cup: 178 cal., 10g fat (6g sat. fat), 50mg chol., 226mg sod., 15g carb. (1g sugars, 1g fiber), 7g pro.

DID YOU KNOW?

It's better to grate your own cheese by hand than to buy the pre-shredded kind. Pre-grated bagged cheese contains preservatives like potato starch and natamycin, meant to keep the shreds from clumping together in the bag. That also means they don't melt together as well when cooking. Freshly grated cheese lacks those additives, so your mac and cheese cups will turn out less clumpy and much smoother.

WATERMELON & CUCUMBER SALSA

The combo of watermelon and cucumber may sound unusual, but it tastes anything but! Serve the salsa as a hot dog topper or eat it with chips or on chicken tacos for a refreshing change of pace.
—Suzanne Curletto, Walnut Creek, CA

TAKES: 15 MIN. • **MAKES:** 3 CUPS

- 1½ cups seeded chopped watermelon
- ¾   cup finely chopped cucumber
- ½   cup finely chopped sweet onion
- ¼   cup minced fresh cilantro
- 1   jalapeno pepper, seeded and minced
- 2   Tbsp. lime juice
- ¼   tsp. salt

In a small bowl, combine all ingredients; refrigerate until serving.

¼ cup: 10 cal., 0 fat (0 sat. fat), 0 chol., 50mg sod., 3g carb. (2g sugars, 0 fiber), 0 pro.

JALAPENO SLIDERS WITH CRISPY ONIONS

My husband and I love spicy foods, and this recipe was an excellent step up from a typical burger. It has just the right amount of flavor and spice for us, but it can be adjusted to suit your family's tastes.
—Christina Addison, Blanchester, OH

TAKES: 25 MIN. • **MAKES:** 8 SERVINGS

- 1   lb. ground beef
- ½   tsp. salt
- ¼   tsp. pepper
- 1   to 2 jalapeno peppers, seeded and thinly sliced
- 2   slices white American cheese, cut into 4 squares
- 8   slider buns, split and toasted
- 1   can (2.8 oz.) french-fried onions

1. Shape beef into eight ½-in.-thick patties; sprinkle with salt and pepper. In a large skillet, cook the sliders over medium heat 2-3 minutes. Turn and top with peppers and cheese. Continue cooking until a thermometer reads 160°, 2-3 minutes.
2. Serve on buns. Top with the french-fried onions.

1 slider: 292 cal., 15g fat (5g sat. fat), 54mg chol., 517mg sod., 23g carb. (2g sugars, 1g fiber), 14g pro.

SPICY SOUTHWESTERN FRUIT SALAD

This colorful fruit salad is special enough for company or to take to a potluck dinner. It's easy to double the recipe or swap in different fruits depending on what your family prefers.

—Paula Marchesi, Lenhartsville, PA

TAKES: 30 MIN. • **MAKES:** 8 SERVINGS

- 1 cup cubed peeled mango
- 1 cup cubed peeled papaya
- 1 cup cubed peeled fresh peaches
- 1 cup fresh blueberries
- 1 medium ripe avocado, peeled and cubed
- 1 cup frozen corn, thawed
- ⅓ cup chopped dried apricots
- ⅓ cup flaked coconut
- ¼ cup minced fresh cilantro
- 1 cup corn chips, lightly crushed

CHIPOTLE-COCONUT DRESSING
- ¼ cup coconut milk
- 2 Tbsp. lime juice
- 1 Tbsp. cider vinegar
- 1 chipotle pepper in adobo sauce, chopped
- 2 garlic cloves, minced
- ¼ tsp. cayenne pepper
- ¼ tsp. brown sugar
  Optional: Additional corn chips or flaked coconut

In a large bowl, combine the first 10 ingredients. In a small bowl, whisk the coconut milk, lime juice, vinegar, chipotle, garlic, cayenne and brown sugar. Drizzle over the fruit mixture; toss to coat. Sprinkle with additional corn chips or coconut if desired. Serve immediately.

¾ cup: 161 cal., 7g fat (3g sat. fat), 0 chol., 65mg sod., 24g carb. (13g sugars, 4g fiber), 2g pro. **Diabetic exchanges:** 1 starch, 1 fat, ½ fruit.

CAMPFIRE DESSERT CONES

Kids love to make these! Set out the ingredients so they can mix and match their own creations.

—Bonnie Hawkins, Elkhorn, WI

TAKES: 20 MIN. • **MAKES:** 8 SERVINGS

- 8 ice cream sugar cones
- ½ cup milk chocolate M&M's
- ½ cup miniature marshmallows
- ½ cup salted peanuts
- ½ cup white baking chips

1. Prepare a campfire or a grill for medium heat. Fill cones with M&M's, marshmallows, peanuts and white chips. Fully wrap each cone with foil, sealing tightly.
2. Place packets over campfire or grill; cook until heated through, 7-10 minutes. Open foil carefully.

1 cone: 217 cal., 11g fat (5g sat. fat), 4mg chol., 78mg sod., 26g carb. (18g sugars, 1g fiber), 5g pro.

CHEESE & PIMIENTO SPREAD

My mother made delicious pimiento cheese, but this is a spicy, modern version of her recipe. Serve it stuffed in celery, on crackers or spread on a sandwich.

—Elizabeth Hester, Elizabethtown, NC

TAKES: 15 MIN. • **MAKES:** 2¾ CUPS

- 12 oz. sharp white cheddar cheese
- 8 oz. reduced-fat cream cheese, softened
- 2 tsp. Worcestershire sauce
- 2 tsp. white vinegar
- ¼ tsp. white pepper
- ¼ tsp. garlic powder
- ¼ tsp. cayenne pepper
- 1 jar (4 oz.) diced pimientos, undrained
  Assorted crackers and vegetables

Shred cheese; transfer to a large bowl. Add cream cheese, Worcestershire sauce, vinegar, pepper, garlic powder and cayenne; beat on low speed until blended. Drain pimientos, reserving 2 Tbsp. juice. Stir in pimientos and reserved juice. Serve with crackers and vegetables.

2 Tbsp.: 90 cal., 7g fat (4g sat. fat), 23mg chol., 150mg sod., 1g carb. (1g sugars, 0 fiber), 5g pro.

> **READER REVIEW**
> *"I made this over the holidays to have on hand as a snack. What a crowd pleaser!"*
> —ALLYBILLHORN, TASTEOFHOME.COM

SUMMER NIGHT SNUGGLES

Pack blankets inside a basket to easily tote to the party. Spread the blankets on the grass or beach (keeping a safe distance from the fire), or snuggle up in one if the night air gets chilly.

S'MORE BAR

It's not summer without everyone's favorite treat—s'mores! Pack a tray with mason jars, a Thermos, cups and other accouterments to create an al fresco s'more or hot cocoa bar.

S'MORES CUPCAKES

Marshmallow frosting puts these cupcakes over the top. Pieces of chocolate bars and graham cracker crumbs on top make them extra indulgent and even more like the real thing—but better!
—Erin Rachwal, Hartland, WI

PREP: 30 MIN. • **BAKE:** 20 MIN. + COOLING
MAKES: 2 DOZEN

- ¾ cup water
- ¾ cup buttermilk
- 2 large eggs, room temperature
- 3 Tbsp. canola oil
- 1 tsp. vanilla extract
- 1½ cups all-purpose flour
- 1½ cups sugar
- ¾ cup baking cocoa
- 1½ tsp. baking soda
- ¾ tsp. salt
- ¾ tsp. baking powder

FROSTING

- 1½ cups butter, softened
- 2 cups confectioners' sugar
- ½ tsp. vanilla extract
- 2 jars (7 oz. each) marshmallow creme
- 2 Tbsp. graham cracker crumbs
- 2 milk chocolate candy bars (1.55 oz. each)
  Optional: Toasted marshmallows and graham cracker pieces

1. Preheat oven to 350°. In a large bowl, beat water, buttermilk, eggs, oil and vanilla until well blended. Combine flour, sugar, cocoa, baking soda, salt and baking powder; gradually beat into water mixture until blended.
2. Fill paper-lined muffin cups half full. Bake until a toothpick comes out clean, 16-20 minutes. Cool in pans 10 minutes before removing from pans to wire racks to cool completely.
3. For frosting, in a large bowl, beat butter until fluffy; beat in confectioners' sugar and vanilla until smooth. Add marshmallow creme; beat until light and fluffy. Spread or pipe frosting over the cupcakes. Sprinkle with cracker crumbs. Break each candy bar into 12 pieces; garnish cupcakes. If desired, top with toasted marshmallows and graham cracker pieces.
1 cupcake: 330 cal., 15g fat (8g sat. fat), 47mg chol., 298mg sod., 43g carb. (35g sugars, 1g fiber), 3g pro.

CAMPFIRE PINEAPPLE UPSIDE-DOWN CAKES

We make these fun cakes while camping or in the backyard around a fire. They're yummy for kids and adults alike. Be aware that the sandwich iron gets hot, so adults should handle and open it.
—Cheryl Grimes, Whiteland, IN

PREP: 10 MIN. • **COOK:** 5 MIN./CAKE
MAKES: 6 SERVINGS

- 6 tsp. butter
- 6 Tbsp. brown sugar
- 6 canned pineapple slices
- 6 maraschino cherries
- 6 individual round sponge cakes

1. Place 1 tsp. butter in 1 side of the sandwich iron. Hold over fire to melt; remove from fire. Carefully sprinkle 1 Tbsp. brown sugar over melted butter. Top with pineapple ring; add cherry to center of pineapple. Top with cake (flat side up); close iron.
2. Cook pineapple side down over a hot campfire until the brown sugar is melted and the cake is heated through, 5-8 minutes. Invert iron to open, and serve cake on an individual plate.
1 cake: 211 cal., 6g fat (3g sat. fat), 38mg chol., 214mg sod., 39g carb. (32g sugars, 1g fiber), 2g pro.

Back to School

Whether learning the alphabet or writing a history paper, kids will be making school-day memories to last a lifetime. To keep them fueled all day long, turn to these fun, kid-friendly ideas for quick and easy breakfasts, school lunches, cute snacks and delightful dinners that will get the entire family excited to start a brand new year.

FRENCH TOAST FINGERS

Kids love anything on a stick. Bite-sized French toast skewers make a fun breakfast for them to munch before heading out the door.
—Mavis Diment, Marcus, IA

TAKES: 20 MIN. • **MAKES:** 4 SERVINGS

- 2 large eggs
- ¼ cup 2% milk
- ¼ tsp. salt
- ½ cup strawberry preserves
- 8 slices day-old white or whole wheat bread
  Optional: Halved strawberries and confectioners' sugar

1. In a shallow bowl, whisk together eggs, milk and salt. Spread preserves on 4 slices of bread; top with remaining bread. Trim crusts; cut each sandwich into 3 strips.

2. Preheat a griddle over medium heat. Lightly grease griddle. Dip both sides of strips in egg mixture; place on griddle. Cook bread strips until golden brown, about 2 minutes per side. If desired, cut into squares and alternately thread onto skewers with halved strawberries. Dust with confectioners' sugar if desired.

3 strips: 298 cal., 5g fat (1g sat. fat), 94mg chol., 474mg sod., 56g carb. (28g sugars, 2g fiber), 9g pro.

MUFFIN-CUP CORN DOGS

Bring a little bit of summer back with a county fair favorite. Little ones are sure to enjoy this take on traditional corn dogs.
—Grace Bryant, Merritt Island, FL

PREP: 15 MIN. • **BAKE:** 20 MIN.
MAKES: 6 SERVINGS

- 1 cup all-purpose flour
- 1 cup yellow cornmeal
- 2 Tbsp. sugar
- 2 tsp. baking powder
- 2 tsp. ground mustard
- 1 tsp. salt
- 2 large eggs
- 1 cup 2% milk
- 3 Tbsp. canola oil
- 6 hot dogs, each cut into 4 pieces
  Optional: Ketchup or honey mustard

1. Preheat oven to 375°. Whisk together the first 6 ingredients. In another bowl, whisk together egg, milk and oil. Add to flour mixture; stir just until moistened.

2. Fill 12 greased muffin cups three-fourths full with batter. Add 2 hot dog pieces to each muffin.

3. Bake until a toothpick inserted in muffin comes out clean, 17-20 minutes. Cool 5 minutes before removing from the pan. Serve warm with ketchup or honey mustard if desired.

2 muffins: 399 cal., 19g fat (5g sat. fat), 82mg chol., 906mg sod., 44g carb. (7g sugars, 2g fiber), 11g pro.

GUAC CROCS & VEGGIES

I'm all grown-up, but I still love to play with my food. Garbanzo beans in the guacamole add taste, texture and nutrition. The croc part is just plain fun.
—Kallee Krong-McCreery, Escondido, CA

TAKES: 20 MIN. • **MAKES:** 2 CUPS DIP

- 1 can (15 oz.) garbanzo beans or chickpeas, rinsed and drained
- 3 Tbsp. mayonnaise
- 1 Tbsp. lemon juice
- ½ tsp. garlic salt
- 2 large ripe avocados
  Optional decorations: Red and yellow pepper pieces, radishes, ripe olives and sliced miniature cucumbers
  Assorted fresh vegetables

1. For dip, place the first 4 ingredients in a food processor; process until smooth. Cut avocados lengthwise in half around the seed; remove seeds. Reserving the skins, carefully scoop out the avocado and add to the bean mixture; process until blended.

2. For crocodile heads, fill avocado skins with dip. If desired, add pepper pieces for teeth, radish and olive slices for eyes, olives for noses, and cucumbers and peppers for bodies. Serve with assorted vegetables.

¼ cup dip: 140 cal., 10g fat (1g sat. fat), 0 chol., 220mg sod., 11g carb. (1g sugars, 4g fiber), 3g pro. **Diabetic exchanges:** 2 fat, ½ starch.

CRUNCHY ORANGE CHICKEN STRIPS

Take a first piece for the crunch. Take a second for the sweet, spicy orange flavor. Also, try substituting apricot nectar for the orange juice and apricot jam for the marmalade.

—Nicole Filizetti, Stevens Point, WI

PREP: 20 MIN. + MARINATING • **COOK:** 35 MIN.
MAKES: 6 SERVINGS

- 1½ lbs. boneless skinless chicken breasts, cut into 1-in.-thick strips
- ⅔ cup plus 1 Tbsp. orange juice, divided
- ½ cup all-purpose flour
- 1 tsp. salt
- ½ tsp. pepper
- ⅛ tsp. cayenne pepper
- 2 large eggs, lightly beaten
- 4 cups Rice Krispies, slightly crushed
- 3 Tbsp. olive oil
- ⅓ cup orange marmalade
- 2 Tbsp. honey

1. Toss the chicken with ⅔ cup orange juice; refrigerate, covered, 1-4 hours.
2. In a shallow bowl, mix flour and seasonings. Place the eggs and Rice Krispies in separate shallow bowls. Dip chicken in flour mixture to coat both sides; shake off excess. Dip in the eggs, then the cereal, patting to help coating adhere.
3. In a large skillet, heat the oil over medium-high heat. Add the chicken in batches; cook until golden brown and chicken is no longer pink, 5-6 minutes per side. Drain on paper towels.
4. Wipe skillet clean if necessary. In same pan, mix marmalade, honey and remaining orange juice; cook and stir over low heat until slightly thickened. Add chicken; heat through, turning to coat. Serve immediately.

1 serving: 357 cal., 11g fat (2g sat. fat), 125mg chol., 375mg sod., 37g carb. (19g sugars, 0 fiber), 27g pro.

GARLIC BREAD PIZZA SANDWICHES

I love inventing new ways to make grilled cheese sandwiches for my children. This version tastes like pizza. Using frozen garlic bread is a timesaver.

—Courtney Stultz, Weir, KS

TAKES: 20 MIN. • **MAKES:** 4 SERVINGS

- 1 pkg. (11¼ oz.) frozen garlic Texas toast
- ¼ cup pasta sauce
- 4 slices provolone cheese
- 16 slices pepperoni
- 8 slices thinly sliced hard salami
  Additional pasta sauce, warmed, optional

1. Preheat griddle over medium-low heat. Add garlic toast; cook until lightly browned, 3-4 minutes per side.
2. Spoon 1 Tbsp. sauce over each of 4 pieces of toast. Top with the cheese, pepperoni, salami and remaining toast. Cook until crisp and cheese is melted, 3-5 minutes, turning as necessary. If desired, serve with additional sauce.

1 sandwich: 456 cal., 28g fat (10g sat. fat), 50mg chol., 1177mg sod., 36g carb. (4g sugars, 2g fiber), 19g pro.

CLEAN CUTTING
To slice Garlic Bread Pizza Sandwiches easily and cleanly without making a mess of the gooey melted cheese, use a pizza cutter instead of a knife.

APPLE DIPPERS

Gather your apple dunkin' gang to try these easy-to-make, easy-to-eat chocolate apple treats.

TO MAKE:
Place chocolate chips in a microwave-safe bowl, then microwave in 30-second intervals, stirring in between, until melted. Slice apples into wedges, then dunk, sprinkle and devour!

FUN COMBOS:
chocolate + marshmallows + crushed graham crackers

chocolate + chopped peanuts

chocolate + popcorn

chocolate + sea salt

chocolate + flaked coconut

chocolate + toffee

chocolate + granola

MUFFIN-TIN CHICKEN POTPIES

I made these personalized chicken pot pies in muffin tins for my kids, and they gobbled them up. The grown-ups did, too!
—Melissa Haines, Valparaiso, IN

PREP: 30 MIN. • **BAKE:** 15 MIN.
MAKES: 10 SERVINGS

- 1   Tbsp. butter
- 2   celery ribs, sliced
- ½   cup chopped onion
- 3   cups frozen mixed vegetables (about 15 oz.)
- 1   can (10¾ oz.) condensed cream of chicken soup, undiluted
- ½   cup 2% milk
- ½   tsp. onion powder
- ¼   tsp. garlic salt
- ⅛   tsp. dried thyme
- ⅛   tsp. pepper
- 2   cups cubed cooked chicken breast
- 4   tubes (6 oz. each) small refrigerated flaky biscuits (5 count)

1. Preheat oven to 375°. In a large skillet, heat butter over medium heat; saute celery and onion until tender, 4-5 minutes. Stir in vegetables, soup, milk and seasonings; heat through, stirring occasionally. Stir in chicken; remove from heat.
2. On a lightly floured surface, roll each biscuit into a 5-in. circle. Press each circle onto the bottom and up the sides of a greased muffin cup, allowing the edges to extend above cup. Fill with about 3 Tbsp. chicken mixture. Pull up edges of dough and fold partway over filling, pleating as needed.
3. Bake until golden brown and filling is bubbly, 15-18 minutes. Cool 1 minute before serving.

2 mini potpies: 330 cal., 12g fat (4g sat. fat), 28mg chol., 1049mg sod., 39g carb. (7g sugars, 3g fiber), 15g pro.

CRESCENT MAC & CHEESE BITES

My kids love mac and cheese, and they love crescent rolls. With the help of my daughter Lula, I decided to put the two together in one yummy recipe. They are perfect either as an appetizer for adults (who love them, too) or as a main dish for the little ones.
—Suzanne Gerrety, Jacksonville, FL

TAKES: 30 MIN. • **MAKES:** 8 SERVINGS

- ½   cup shredded cheddar cheese
- 3   Tbsp. 2% milk
- 2   Tbsp. cream cheese
- 1   Tbsp. butter
      Dash salt
      Dash pepper
- ¾   cup cooked elbow macaroni
- ¼   cup bacon bits
- 1   tube (8 oz.) refrigerated crescent rolls

1. Preheat oven to 375°. Place the first 6 ingredients in a microwave-safe bowl; microwave on high until blended, about 1 minute, stirring every 30 seconds. Stir in macaroni and bacon bits. Refrigerate 5 minutes.
2. Unroll crescent dough and separate into 8 triangles. Place 2 Tbsp. macaroni mixture on wide end of each triangle. Roll into crescents; place on ungreased baking sheet.
3. Bake 10-13 minutes or until golden brown. Serve warm.

1 filled crescent roll: 188 cal., 11g fat (3g sat. fat), 16mg chol., 552mg sod., 16g carb. (4g sugars, 0 fiber), 6g pro.

DIY BUTTERFLIES

Instead of recycling your empty toilet paper rolls the traditional way, give them new life as this kid-friendly craft. Start by painting the rolls with acrylic paint. Then lay down something to protect your surface—it's about to get a little messy! Let kids dip their hands in finger paint and then place their prints on pieces of card stock. Once the paint is dry, cut out the hand stamps and attach them to either side of each painted roll as the butterfly's wings. Add final touches—like googly eyes, pipe cleaner antennae and sweet smiles—if desired.

CHEESEBURGER OMELET SLIDERS

A cheeseburger inside an omelet? Yes, please! This fun twist on two breakfast and dinner faves is easy to assemble and delicious any time of day.
—Denise LaRoche, Hudson, NH

PREP: 25 MIN. • **COOK:** 25 MIN.
MAKES: 6 SERVINGS

- 1 lb. lean ground beef (90% lean)
- 1 tsp. salt, divided
- ½ tsp. pepper, divided
- 8 large eggs
- ½ cup water
- 1 cup shredded Havarti cheese
- 12 dinner rolls, split
- 12 tomato slices
  Optional: Ketchup, sliced onion and pickle slices

1. Combine beef, ½ tsp. salt and ¼ tsp. pepper, mixing lightly but thoroughly. Shape into twelve 2-in. patties. In a large skillet, cook burgers over medium heat until cooked through, 2-3 minutes per side. Remove burgers from heat; keep warm.
2. Whisk together eggs, water and the remaining salt and pepper. Place a small nonstick skillet, lightly oiled, over medium-high heat; pour in ½ cup egg mixture. Mixture should set immediately at edges. As eggs set, push the cooked edges toward the center, letting the uncooked eggs flow underneath. When the eggs are thickened and no liquid egg remains, sprinkle ⅓ cup cheese on 1 side. Top cheese with 3 burgers, spacing them evenly; fold the omelet in half. Slide onto a cutting board; tent with foil to keep warm. Repeat to make 3 more omelets.

3. To serve, cut each omelet into 3 wedges; place each wedge on a roll. Add tomatoes and, if desired, ketchup, onion and pickles.
2 sliders: 507 cal., 23g fat (9g sat. fat), 348mg chol., 1032mg sod., 39g carb. (5g sugars, 3g fiber), 34g pro.

CHEWY GRANOLA BARS

These bars manage to be both soft and crispy at the same time. They make a nutritious portable treat.
—Virginia Krites, Cridersville, OH

PREP: 10 MIN. • **BAKE:** 25 MIN. + COOLING
MAKES: 2 DOZEN

- ½ cup butter, softened
- 1 cup packed brown sugar
- ¼ cup sugar
- 1 large egg, room temperature
- 2 Tbsp. honey
- ½ tsp. vanilla extract
- 1 cup all-purpose flour
- 1 tsp. ground cinnamon
- ½ tsp. baking powder
- ¼ tsp. salt
- 1½ cups quick-cooking oats
- 1¼ cups Rice Krispies
- 1 cup chopped nuts
  Optional: Raisins or semisweet chocolate chips (1 cup each)

1. Preheat oven to 350°. Cream the butter and sugars until light and fluffy, 5-7 minutes. Beat in the egg, honey and vanilla. Whisk together flour, cinnamon, baking powder and salt; gradually beat into the creamed mixture. Stir in the oats, Rice Krispies, nuts and, if desired, raisins or chocolate chips.
2. Press into a greased 13x9-in. pan. Bake until light brown, 25-30 minutes. Cool on a wire rack. Cut into bars.
1 bar: 160 cal., 7g fat (3g sat. fat), 19mg chol., 91mg sod., 22g carb. (13g sugars, 1g fiber), 3g pro.

BROWNIE BATTER OATMEAL

We all grew up eating bowls of lumpy oatmeal for breakfast, and everyone has favorite toppings to make porridge more palatable. My recipe transforms a ho-hum morning staple into something that will make the kids jump out of bed!
—Kristen Moyer, Bethlehem, PA

TAKES: 30 MIN. • **MAKES:** 2 SERVINGS

- 1 cup pitted dates, chopped
- 1 cup 2% milk
- ½ cup ground almonds
- ⅓ cup old-fashioned oats
- 2 Tbsp. baking cocoa
- 1 tsp. butter
- 1 tsp. vanilla extract
- Optional: Fresh raspberries and sliced almonds

1. Place dates in a heatproof bowl; cover with boiling water. Let stand until softened, about 10 minutes. Drain, reserving ⅓ cup liquid. Place dates and reserved liquid in a food processor; process until smooth.
2. In a small saucepan, whisk milk, almonds, oats, cocoa and ¼ cup date puree until blended. (Save remaining puree for another use.) Bring to a boil over medium heat, stirring occasionally. Remove from heat; stir in the butter and vanilla. If desired, garnish with raspberries and sliced almonds.
¾ cup: 338 cal., 18g fat (4g sat. fat), 15mg chol., 73mg sod., 37g carb. (19g sugars, 7g fiber), 12g pro.

BEEF TACO MUFFINS

Who doesn't love tacos? I decided to re-create the beefy classic as muffins. We love the baked sour cream and cheese on top. Just add your favorite toppings!
—Melissa Haines, Valparaiso, IN

PREP: 25 MIN. • **BAKE:** 15 MIN.
MAKES: 8 SERVINGS

- 2 tubes (8 oz. each) refrigerated crescent rolls
- 1 lb. lean ground beef (90% lean)
- 1 envelope taco seasoning
- ¾ cup water
- 3 Tbsp. sour cream
- 1 cup shredded Colby-Monterey Jack cheese
  Optional toppings: Shredded lettuce, chopped green onions, chopped tomatoes and sliced ripe olives

1. Preheat oven to 375°. Unroll both tubes of crescent dough; separate each into 8 triangles. Press each triangle onto the bottom and up the sides of an ungreased muffin cup. Prick bottoms with a fork. Bake until light golden, 4-6 minutes. Using a spoon, press gently to reshape cups.
2. In a large skillet, cook and crumble beef over medium heat until no longer pink, 5-7 minutes. Stir in taco seasoning and water; bring to a boil. Reduce heat; simmer, uncovered, until thickened, 3-4 minutes.
3. In each muffin cup, place 1½ Tbsp. beef mixture, about ½ tsp. sour cream and 1 Tbsp. cheese. Bake until cheese is melted and crust is golden brown, 10-12 minutes. Top as desired.
2 muffins: 388 cal., 22g fat (10g sat. fat), 49mg chol., 963mg sod., 27g carb. (4g sugars, 0 fiber), 18g pro.

CHOCOLATE CHIP, PB & BANANA SANDWICHES

I love finding new ways to combine peanut butter, chocolate and bananas. I was shocked when my nephews (who are very picky eaters) loved these sammies.
—Charlotte Gehle, Brownstown, MI

TAKES: 10 MIN. • **MAKES:** 2 SERVINGS

- ¼ cup creamy peanut butter
- 2 Tbsp. honey
- ¼ tsp. ground cinnamon
- 2 Tbsp. miniature semisweet chocolate chips
- 4 slices whole wheat bread
- 1 medium banana, thinly sliced

Mix peanut butter, honey and cinnamon; stir in the chocolate chips. Spread over bread. Layer 2 bread slices with the banana slices; top with the remaining bread. If desired, cut into shapes using cookie cutters.
1 sandwich: 502 cal., 22g fat (6g sat. fat), 0 chol., 394mg sod., 69g carb. (36g sugars, 7g fiber), 15g pro.

Rosh Hashana

To celebrate the Jewish new year, many families prepare festive meals that feature breads, such as challah, and apples—both of which are traditionally dipped in honey. Carrots, raisins and pomegranates are ingredients included in many other delicacies often eaten during this holiday. In this chapter, learn about kosher foods, how to braid bread dough and more.

GARLIC ARTICHOKE DIP

Not only is this chilled dip delicious and lower in fat, but it also offers easy make-ahead convenience.
—Lisa Varner, El Paso, TX

PREP: 25 MIN. + CHILLING
MAKES: 2½ CUPS

- 1 large onion, chopped
- ½ tsp. dried oregano
- ½ tsp. dried thyme
- 2 Tbsp. olive oil
- 5 garlic cloves, minced
- 1 can (15 oz.) cannellini beans, rinsed and drained
- 1 can (14 oz.) water-packed artichoke hearts, rinsed and drained
- 1 Tbsp. lemon juice
- ½ tsp. salt
- ⅛ tsp. cayenne pepper
  Assorted fresh vegetables and/or baked pita chips

1. In a small nonstick skillet, saute the onion, oregano and thyme in oil until onions are tender. Add the garlic; cook 1 minute longer. Remove from heat; cool slightly.

2. In a food processor, combine the beans, artichokes, lemon juice, salt, cayenne and onion mixture; cover and process until pureed.

3. Transfer dip to a small bowl. Cover and refrigerate at least 2 hours before serving. Serve with vegetables and/or pita chips.

¼ cup: 81 cal., 3g fat (0 sat. fat), 0 chol., 271mg sod., 11g carb. (1g sugars, 2g fiber), 3g pro. **Diabetic exchanges:** 1 vegetable, ½ starch, ½ fat.

TEST KITCHEN TIP

Before mincing a garlic clove, remove the paperlike layer around it. To easily peel it away, pop the clove in the microwave for 20 seconds. After it's been heated, the skin will peel right off. You'll want to trim the top of the bulb and peel away any bits of easy-to-remove skin first, but otherwise you're good to go.

VEGETABLE SAMOSAS

My family enjoys the wonderful flavors in a traditional samosa. Baked instead of fried, this version has fewer calories but keeps all the classic tastes and textures we love.
—Amy Siegel, Clifton, NJ

PREP: 45 MIN. • **BAKE:** 20 MIN.
MAKES: ABOUT 3 DOZEN

- 2 large potatoes, peeled and cubed
- 1 medium onion, chopped
- 2 Tbsp. olive oil
- 2 garlic cloves, minced
- 1 tsp. salt
- 1 tsp. curry powder
- ½ tsp. ground cumin
- ¼ tsp. pepper
- 1 cup canned garbanzo beans or chickpeas, rinsed, drained and mashed
- 1 cup frozen peas, thawed
- 2 Tbsp. minced fresh cilantro
- 1 pkg. (16 oz., 14x9-in. sheet size) frozen phyllo dough, thawed
  Cooking spray
  Mint chutney, optional

1. Place potatoes in a large saucepan and cover with water. Bring to a boil. Reduce the heat; cover and cook for 15-20 minutes or until tender. Drain. Mash potatoes; set aside.

2. In a large skillet, saute the onion in oil until tender. Add the garlic, salt, curry powder, cumin and pepper; cook 1 minute longer. Remove from the heat. Stir in the mashed potatoes, garbanzo beans, peas and cilantro.

3. Place 1 sheet of phyllo dough on a work surface with a short end facing you. (Keep remaining phyllo covered with a damp towel to prevent it from drying out.) Spray sheet with cooking spray; repeat with 1 more sheet of phyllo, spraying the sheet with cooking spray. Cut into two 14x4½-in. strips.

4. Place 2 Tbsp. of filling on the lower corner of each strip. Fold dough over filling, forming a triangle. Fold triangle up, then fold triangle over, forming another triangle. Continue folding, like a flag, to the end of the strip.

5. Spritz end of dough with spray and press onto triangle to seal. Turn triangle and spritz top with spray. Repeat with remaining phyllo and filling.

6. Place triangles on greased baking sheets. Bake at 375° for 20-25 minutes or until golden brown. If desired, serve with mint chutney.

1 appetizer: 79 cal., 2g fat (0 sat. fat), 0 chol., 136mg sod., 13g carb. (1g sugars, 1g fiber), 2g pro. **Diabetic exchanges:** 1 starch.

BRAIDED EGG BREAD

For Rosh Hashana, loaves of braided bread—also commonly called challah—are baked to symbolize continuity. Since I first made this bread some years ago, it has become a much-requested recipe.
—Marlene Jeffery, Holland, MB

PREP: 30 MIN. + RISING
BAKE: 25 MIN. + COOLING
MAKES: 1 LOAF (16 SLICES)

3¼ to 3¾ cups all-purpose flour
1 Tbsp. sugar
1 pkg. (¼ oz.) active dry yeast
¾ tsp. salt
¾ cup water
3 Tbsp. canola oil
2 large eggs, room temperature
TOPPING
1 large egg
1 tsp. water
½ tsp. poppy seeds

1. In a large bowl, combine 2½ cups flour, sugar, yeast and salt. In a small saucepan, heat the water and oil to 120°-130°. Add to dry ingredients along with eggs. Beat on medium speed for 3 minutes. Stir in enough remaining flour to form a soft dough.
2. Turn dough onto a lightly floured surface; knead until smooth and elastic, 6-8 minutes. Place in a greased bowl, turning once to grease top. Cover and let rise in a warm place until doubled, about 1½ hours.
3. Punch the dough down. Turn onto a lightly floured surface. Set a third of the dough aside. Divide the remaining dough into 3 pieces. Shape each into a 13-in. rope. Place ropes on a greased baking sheet and braid; pinch ends to seal and tuck under.
4. Divide reserved dough into 3 equal pieces; shape each into a 14-in. rope. Braid ropes. Center 14-in. braid on top of the shorter braid. Pinch ends to seal and tuck under. Cover and let rise until doubled, about 30 minutes.
5. Preheat oven to 375°. In a small bowl, beat egg and water; brush over dough. Sprinkle with poppy seeds. Bake until golden brown, 25-30 minutes. Cover with foil during the last 15 minutes of baking. Remove from pan to a wire rack to cool.
1 slice: 134 cal., 4g fat (1g sat. fat), 40mg chol.,123mg sod., 20g carb. (1g sugars, 1g fiber), 4g pro.

HOLLER FOR CHALLAH!

What is challah bread? Challah is a kosher loaf of braided bread that has long been a symbolic centerpiece for a Rosh Hashana spread. It's at the heart of many Jewish celebrations, including Shabbat and Purim.

The simple dough is made with eggs, water, flour, yeast and salt. The bread is typically pale yellow in color because so many eggs are used, and it has a rich flavor, too.

HERE ARE MORE FUN TIPS FOR MAKING CHALLAH BREAD.
Add a small handful of raisins to symbolize sweetness and happiness, particularly around joyous holidays.

Add chocolate chips, cinnamon, orange zest or almonds for a pop of color or flavor.

Brush loaves with egg whites and honey before baking for a shiny and golden crust.

Sprinkle poppy or sesame seeds on top of the bread to symbolize the manna that fell from heaven after the Exodus from Egypt.

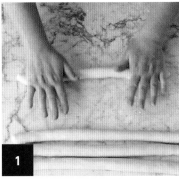

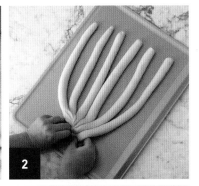

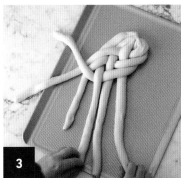

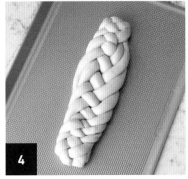

HOW TO BRAID BREAD DOUGH

Bake a gorgeous golden loaf of braided bread. These instructions are for our favorite way of braiding 6 equal strands of dough; see the Braided Egg Bread recipe and photo at left for detailed instructions on an easy way to braid 6 strands of 2 sizes.

STEP 1
On a lightly floured surface, divide dough into 6 even pieces. Roll each piece into a rope. Use even pressure when rolling so the ropes are the same width from end to end, as well as the same length.

STEP 2
Arrange the 6 ropes on a greased baking sheet. Pinch ropes together at one end and tuck under. Do not remove the ropes from the baking sheet. This way you won't have to transfer the braid just before baking and risk stretching the dough.

STEP 3
Rotate the baking sheet so the pinched end is at the top. Starting with the far right rope, weave toward the left following this pattern—over 2 strands, under 1 strand, over 2 strands. Start again at the (new) far right rope and weave toward the left in the same pattern—over 2 strands, under 1 strand, over 2 strands. Repeat until all the dough is braided.

STEP 4
At the end of the braided loaf, pinch the rope ends together and tuck under.

PARSNIP SWEET POTATO PANCAKES

Golden brown sweet potatoes make these pancakes pretty to look at and even better to eat. The green onions and thyme add an extra boost.
—Amy Short, Milton, WV

PREP: 20 MIN. • **COOK:** 30 MIN.
MAKES: 2 DOZEN

- 1 cup all-purpose flour
- 3 Tbsp. minced fresh thyme
- 2 tsp. salt
- ¼ tsp. pepper
- 4 large eggs, lightly beaten
- 2 lbs. sweet potatoes, peeled and grated
- 1 lb. parsnips, peeled and grated
- 12 green onions, sliced diagonally
- ½ cup canola oil

1. In a large bowl, combine the flour, thyme, salt and pepper. Stir in eggs until blended. Add the sweet potatoes, parsnips and onions; toss to coat.
2. In an electric skillet or a deep-fat fryer, heat the oil to 375°. Drop the batter by ¼ cupfuls, a few at a time, into hot oil; press lightly to flatten. Fry for 3-4 minutes on each side or until golden brown. Drain on paper towels. Serve warm.

2 pancakes: 280 cal., 14g fat (2g sat. fat), 62mg chol., 431mg sod., 34g carb. (10g sugars, 4g fiber), 5g pro.

MULLED POMEGRANATE SIPPER

This warm and festive drink fills the entire house with the delightful aroma of spices and simmering fruit juices. Kids and adults both love this spirit-warming sipper.
—Lisa Renshaw, Kansas City, MO

PREP: 10 MIN. • **COOK:** 1 HOUR
MAKES: 16 SERVINGS

- 1 bottle (64 oz.) cranberry-apple juice
- 2 cups unsweetened apple juice
- 1 cup pomegranate juice
- ⅔ cup honey
- ½ cup orange juice
- 3 cinnamon sticks (3 in. each)
- 10 whole cloves
- 2 Tbsp. grated orange zest

In a 5-qt. slow cooker, combine the first 5 ingredients. Place cinnamon sticks, cloves and orange zest on a double thickness of cheesecloth. Gather up corners of cloth to enclose seasonings; tie securely with string. Add to the slow cooker. Cook, covered, on low 1-2 hours or until heated through. Discard spice bag.

¾ cup: 131 cal., 0 fat (0 sat. fat), 0 chol., 21mg sod., 33g carb. (30g sugars, 0 fiber), 0 pro.

READER REVIEW

"I love this cozy, warm drink that bursts with flavor! I have been serving this to friends and family during the fall and winter months for the past several years, and I've never served it to anyone who hasn't loved it!"
—SIMARCIAL, TASTEOFHOME.COM

CARROT RAISIN COUSCOUS

Golden raisins add a slightly sweet flavor to this unique side dish featuring couscous and carrots. The recipe will brighten any holiday table.
—Jordan Sucher, Brooklyn, NY

PREP: 15 MIN. • **COOK:** 20 MIN.
MAKES: 10 SERVINGS

- ⅓ cup port wine or chicken broth
- ⅓ cup golden raisins
- 1 medium onion, chopped
- 3 Tbsp. olive oil, divided
- 1 pkg. (10 oz.) couscous
- 2 cups chicken broth
- ¼ tsp. salt, divided
- ¼ tsp. pepper, divided
- 4 medium carrots, julienned
- 1 Tbsp. sugar
- 1 tsp. molasses

1. In a small saucepan, heat the wine until hot. In a small bowl, soak raisins in wine for 5 minutes. Drain raisins, reserving wine.
2. In a large saucepan, saute onion in 1 Tbsp. oil until tender. Stir in couscous. Cook and stir until lightly browned. Stir in the broth, raisins and half each of the salt and pepper. Bring to a boil. Cover and remove from the heat. Let stand for 5 minutes; fluff with a fork.
3. In a small skillet, saute the carrots in the remaining oil until crisp-tender. Combine sugar, molasses, reserved wine, and the remaining salt and pepper. Stir into carrots; heat through.
4. In a large bowl, combine couscous mixture and carrots; toss to combine.

¾ cup: 188 cal., 5g fat (1g sat. fat), 1mg chol., 277mg sod., 32g carb. (8g sugars, 2g fiber), 5g pro. **Diabetic exchanges:** 1½ starch, 1 vegetable, 1 fat.

KEEP IT KOSHER

Kosher is a Hebrew word that means "fit," as in "fit to eat." It sounds simple, but the rules and spiritual laws that govern kosher cooking and eating are detailed. Truly keeping kosher requires rigorous adherence. Here are some basic guidelines.

WHICH FOODS ARE KOSHER?

You might know that keeping kosher means avoiding pork, since pigs don't qualify as kosher. But sea creatures without fins and scales are off-limits, too. This means no lobster, crab or beluga caviar (it comes from whales—no scales). Birds of prey also make the nonkosher list, as do any foods derived from animals that aren't considered kosher. Gelatin, for example, is not kosher if derived from pigs or horses.

PREPARATION IS KEY

It's not only about what foods are kosher but about how they're prepared. From the slaughterhouse to the kitchen, strict rules of preparation must be followed to make sure a food remains kosher. For example, meat and dairy must never be combined—or even touched by the same utensil.

A NOTE ABOUT "KOSHER" SALT

Some kosher salt, despite its name, may not be certified kosher at all. Instead, it may have gotten its name from originally being used in the process of koshering meats.

HOW TO CARVE A CHICKEN

STEP 1
Place the chicken on a cutting board with wings facing away from you. Lightly press a carving fork into the breastbone between the 2 breasts to stabilize the chicken. Using a sharp knife, cut the skin between the leg and the body.

STEP 2
Pull the leg away from the side of the chicken to expose the hip joint. Pierce the joint with the tip of the knife. (If you have trouble finding the joint, wiggle the leg back and forth, using your fingertip to find the moving joint.) Remove the leg.

STEP 3
Placing the carving fork in the thigh meat, cut straight down along the curve of the drumstick until you reach the joint. Gently pierce the joint between the drumstick and the thigh to separate the 2 pieces. Repeat steps 1, 2 and 3 to remove the second thigh and drumstick.

STEP 4
Place the cutting fork in the middle of the breastbone. Starting at the base of the left breast, position the knife right above the wing. Make a long, horizontal cut, starting from the top at the wing and continuing until you reach the point where the leg used to meet the breast.

STEP 5
With the cutting fork positioned in the right breast, make a deep vertical cut down along the breastbone of the left breast. Then, cut in an angled, downward motion underneath the breast and toward the horizontal cut to remove the breast meat from the rib cage.

STEP 6
Pull the wing away from the body of the chicken and cut through the joint. You may remove the wing tip, if desired, by piercing the joint between the wingette and the tip.

1. Place chicken breast side up on a rack in a shallow roasting pan. Stuff onion in chicken; tie the drumsticks together. Arrange garlic cloves around chicken. In a small bowl, combine the remaining ingredients. Drizzle over chicken and garlic.

2. Cover and bake at 350° for 1¾ hours. Uncover; bake 30-45 minutes longer or until a thermometer inserted in the thickest part of thigh reads 170°-175°, basting occasionally with pan drippings. (Cover loosely with foil if the chicken browns too quickly.) Cover and let stand for 10 minutes before slicing.

7 oz. cooked chicken: 556 cal., 36g fat (8g sat. fat), 149mg chol., 738mg sod., 8g carb. (1g sugars, 1g fiber), 49g pro.

POACHED ORANGE PEARS

Although these pears are simple to prepare, they are quite elegant. I love to serve them when fresh raspberries are in season. They make a beautiful presentation for special occasions and are always enjoyed by both young and old.
—Edna Lee, Greeley, CO

TAKES: 30 MIN. • **MAKES:** 8 SERVINGS

- 1½ cups orange juice
- ½ cup packed brown sugar
- 1 cinnamon stick (3 in.)
- 4 large pears, peeled and halved
- ½ cup fresh raspberries

1. In a large saucepan, bring the orange juice, brown sugar and cinnamon stick to a boil. Reduce heat; cook and stir over medium heat until sugar is dissolved. Add the pears; cover and simmer for 15-20 minutes or until tender but firm.

2. Using a slotted spoon, place each pear half in a dessert dish. Garnish with raspberries. Drizzle with poaching liquid.

1 serving: 138 cal., 0 fat (0 sat. fat), 0 chol., 5mg sod., 35g carb. (29g sugars, 3g fiber), 1g pro.

GARLIC CLOVE CHICKEN

My neighbors made this chicken frequently, and I couldn't get enough of it. If you like garlic, you'll love this recipe.
—Denise Hollebeke, Penhold, AB

PREP: 10 MIN.
BAKE: 2¼ HOURS + STANDING
MAKES: 6 SERVINGS

- 1 roasting chicken (5 to 6 lbs.)
- 1 small onion, quartered
- 40 garlic cloves, peeled
- ¼ cup canola oil
- 1½ tsp. salt
- 1 tsp. dried parsley flakes
- ½ tsp. dried celery flakes
- ½ tsp. each dried tarragon, thyme and rosemary, crushed
- ¼ tsp. pepper

MOM'S CELERY SEED BRISKET

Warning: Keep a close eye on this tangy pot of goodness. Because it's been fine-tuned to perfection, it tends to vanish at gatherings.

—Aysha Schurman, Ammon, ID

PREP: 20 MIN. • **COOK:** 8 HOURS
MAKES: 8 SERVINGS

- 1 fresh beef brisket (3 to 4 lbs.)
- 1 can (28 oz.) Italian crushed tomatoes
- 1 large red onion, chopped
- 2 Tbsp. red wine vinegar
- 2 Tbsp. Worcestershire sauce
- 4 garlic cloves, minced
- 1 Tbsp. brown sugar
- 1 tsp. celery seed
- 1 tsp. pepper
- ½ tsp. salt
- ½ tsp. ground cumin
- ½ tsp. liquid smoke
- 4 tsp. cornstarch
- 3 Tbsp. cold water

1. Cut brisket in half; place in a 5-qt. slow cooker. In a large bowl, combine the tomatoes, onion, red wine vinegar, Worcestershire sauce, garlic, brown sugar, celery seed, pepper, salt, cumin and liquid smoke. Pour over beef. Cover and cook on low for 8-10 hours or until meat is tender.

2. Remove meat to a serving platter; keep warm. In a large saucepan, combine cornstarch and water until smooth. Gradually stir in 4 cups cooking liquid. Bring to a boil; cook and stir for 2 minutes or until thickened. Slice the brisket across the grain; serve with the gravy.

5 oz. cooked meat with ½ cup gravy: 262 cal., 7g fat (3g sat. fat), 72mg chol., 425mg sod., 10g carb. (5g sugars, 1g fiber), 36g pro. **Diabetic exchanges:** 5 lean meat, 1 vegetable.

CITRUS SPINACH SALAD

Grapefruit and orange segments add zest to this lovely salad that's tossed with a pleasant honey-lime dressing. It's perfect for a luncheon or shower.

—Pauline Taylor, Spokane, WA

TAKES: 15 MIN. • **MAKES:** 12 SERVINGS

- 3 Tbsp. honey
- 2 Tbsp. lime juice
- 1 tsp. grated lime zest
- ⅛ to ¼ tsp. ground nutmeg
- ⅓ cup canola oil
- 10 cups torn fresh spinach
- 3 medium navel oranges, peeled and sectioned
- 2 medium pink grapefruit, peeled and sectioned
- 1 medium red onion, sliced and separated into rings

1. In a blender, combine the honey, lime juice, lime zest and nutmeg; cover and process until blended. While mixture is processing, gradually add oil in a steady stream until dressing is thickened.

2. In a large salad bowl, combine the spinach, oranges and grapefruit. Drizzle with the dressing; toss to coat. Top with onion. Serve immediately.

1 serving: 109 cal., 6g fat (1g sat. fat), 0 chol., 21mg sod., 14g carb. (11g sugars, 2g fiber), 1g pro.

GINGERED APRICOT-APPLE CRUMBLE

This crumble is tasty hot or cold, plain or topped with ice cream. If you're not fond of apricots, leave them out for a traditional apple crisp.

—Sylvia Rice, Didsbury, AB

PREP: 15 MIN. • **BAKE:** 50 MIN.
MAKES: 12 SERVINGS

- 1 cup apricot nectar
- ¾ cup finely chopped dried apricots
- ⅓ cup honey
- ¼ cup maple syrup
- 2 Tbsp. lemon juice
- 8 cups sliced peeled tart apples (about 8 large)
- 3 Tbsp. all-purpose flour
- 1 tsp. ground cinnamon
- ½ tsp. ground ginger
- ½ tsp. ground cardamom

TOPPING
- ¾ cup all-purpose flour
- ½ cup quick-cooking oats
- ¼ cup canola oil
- ¼ cup maple syrup
- ½ cup chopped pecans, optional

1. In a large bowl, combine the first 5 ingredients; set aside. Arrange the apples in an ungreased 13x9-in. baking dish.

2. Combine flour, cinnamon, ginger and cardamom; stir into the apricot mixture. Spoon over apples.

3. Combine the topping ingredients, adding pecans if desired; sprinkle over the fruit. Bake at 350° for 50-60 minutes or until the topping is golden brown and fruit is tender.

1 serving: 228 cal., 5g fat (1g sat. fat), 0 chol., 8mg sod., 46g carb. (32g sugars, 3g fiber), 2g pro.

Halloween Sips & Suspense

Halloween isn't just for kids. Adults relish the opportunity for spooky fall fun, too. This year, bewitch your party-loving crowd with devilishly delicious drinks and serve finger foods that are all treats, no tricks! Whether your guests come in costume or not, no one will be able to disguise their delight at your ghostly grown-up cocktail party!

GRILLED TERIYAKI BEEF SKEWERS

These beef skewers are easy to make and even easier to eat—perfect for any party! The horseradish cream sauce pairs well with the flavorful beef.
—Linda Flaherty, Lake Worth, FL

PREP: 15 MIN. + MARINATING • **GRILL:** 10 MIN.
MAKES: 16 KABOBS (1 CUP SAUCE)

- 2 cans (8 oz. each) pineapple chunks
- 1 bottle (10 oz.) teriyaki baste and glaze
- 3 Tbsp. minced fresh gingerroot
- 1 lb. beef tenderloin steaks, cut into 1-in. pieces

HORSERADISH CREAM SAUCE
- 1 cup (8 oz.) sour cream
- 1 Tbsp. prepared horseradish

1. Drain pineapple chunks, reserving juice. In a large bowl or shallow dish, combine teriyaki, ginger and pineapple juice. Add the beef and turn to coat. Refrigerate for up to 2 hours. Drain beef, discarding marinade.
2. On 16 soaked wooden appetizer skewers, alternately thread beef and pineapple. On a lightly greased grill rack, cook the kabobs, covered, over medium heat until beef reaches desired doneness, 6-8 minutes, turning once.
3. In a small bowl, combine sour cream and horseradish; serve with kabobs.
1 kabob with 1 Tbsp. sauce: 96 cal., 4g fat (2g sat. fat), 22mg chol., 233mg sod., 7g carb. (6 sugars, 0 fiber), 7g pro.

PUMPKIN PIE MARTINIS

My friends start requesting this cocktail in the fall and continue to ask for it throughout the holidays. Every delectable sip is like a taste of pumpkin pie!
—Cathleen Bushman, Geneva, IL

TAKES: 5 MIN. • **MAKES:** 2 SERVINGS

- 1 vanilla wafer, crushed, optional
  Ice cubes
- 2 oz. vanilla-flavored vodka
- 2 oz. 2% milk
- 2 oz. heavy whipping cream
- 1 oz. simple syrup
- 1 oz. hazelnut liqueur
- ⅛ tsp. pumpkin pie spice
  Dash ground cinnamon

1. If desired, for a cookie-crumb rim, moisten the rims of 2 chilled cocktail glasses with water. Place the cookie crumbs on a plate; dip rims in crumbs. Set aside.
2. Fill a mixing glass three-fourths full with ice. Add the remaining ingredients; stir until condensation forms on outside of mixing glass. Strain the mixture into 2 chilled cocktail glasses.
1 martini: 301 cal., 12g fat (7g sat. fat), 44mg chol., 25mg sod., 25g carb. (23g sugars, 0 fiber), 2g pro.

WITCHES' FINGERS

You don't need a cauldron to conjure these frightening fingers. They're a sweet-and-salty treat that's spooky easy to make.
—Beth Tomkiw, Milwaukee, WI

TAKES: 20 MIN. • **MAKES:** 1 DOZEN

- 1½ cups vibrant green candy coating disks
- 6 pretzel rods, broken in half
- 6 jelly beans, cut in half lengthwise

In a microwave, melt candy coating; stir until smooth. Dip broken ends of pretzel rods in coating; allow excess to drip off. Place on waxed paper; press a jelly bean half onto the dipped end of each pretzel to resemble a fingernail. Let stand until candy coating is almost set. Using a toothpick, make lines on each pretzel to resemble knuckles.
1 pretzel half: 155 cal., 7g fat (7g sat. fat), 1mg chol., 131mg sod., 21g carb. (18g sugars, 0 fiber), 1g pro.

TEST KITCHEN TIP
Candy coating—also known as almond bark or confectionery coating—usually comes in 1½- or 2-pound blocks or in bags of small flat disks.

HOT SPINACH SPREAD WITH PITA CHIPS

This warm, cheesy spread is absolutely scrumptious served on toasted pita wedges. And its colorful appearance makes it stand out on the buffet table.
—Teresa Emanuel, Smithville, MO

PREP: 30 MIN. • **BAKE:** 20 MIN.
MAKES: 16 SERVINGS (4 CUPS SPREAD)

- 2 **cups shredded Monterey Jack cheese**
- 1 **pkg. (10 oz.) frozen chopped spinach, thawed and squeezed dry**
- 1 **pkg. (8 oz.) cream cheese, cubed**
- 2 **plum tomatoes, seeded and chopped**
- ¾ **cup chopped onion**
- ⅓ **cup half-and-half cream**
- 1 **Tbsp. finely chopped seeded jalapeno pepper**
- 6 **pita breads (6 in.)**
- ½ **cup butter, melted**
- 2 **tsp. lemon-pepper seasoning**
- 2 **tsp. ground cumin**
- ¼ **tsp. garlic salt**

1. In a large bowl, combine the first 7 ingredients. Transfer mixture to a greased 1½-qt. baking dish. Bake, uncovered, at 375° for 20-25 minutes or until bubbly.
2. Meanwhile, cut each pita bread into 8 wedges. Place in two 15x10x1-in. baking pans. Combine butter, lemon pepper, cumin and garlic salt; brush over pita wedges.
3. Bake for 7-9 minutes or until crisp. Serve with spinach spread.

¼ cup spread with 3 pita wedges:
231 cal., 16g fat (10g sat. fat), 46mg chol., 381mg sod., 15g carb. (1g sugars, 1g fiber), 8g pro.

ROASTED RED PEPPER HUMMUS

My son taught me how to make hummus, which is a tasty and healthy alternative to calorie-filled dips. Fresh roasted red bell peppers make it special.
—Nancy Watson-Pistole, Shawnee, KS

PREP: 30 MIN. + STANDING • **MAKES:** 3 CUPS

- 2 large sweet red peppers
- 2 cans (15 oz. each) garbanzo beans or chickpeas, rinsed and drained
- ⅓ cup lemon juice
- 3 Tbsp. tahini
- 1 Tbsp. olive oil
- 2 garlic cloves, peeled
- 1¼ tsp. salt
- 1 tsp. curry powder
- ½ tsp. ground coriander
- ½ tsp. ground cumin
- ½ tsp. pepper
  Optional: Fresh vegetables, pita bread or assorted crackers

1. Broil the red peppers 4 in. from the heat until skins blister, about 5 minutes. With tongs, rotate the peppers a quarter turn. Broil and rotate until all sides are blistered and blackened. Immediately place peppers in a bowl; cover and let stand for 15-20 minutes.
2. Peel off and discard charred skin. Remove stems and seeds. Place the peppers in a food processor. Add the beans, lemon juice, tahini, oil, garlic and seasonings; cover and process until blended.
3. Transfer to a serving bowl. Serve with vegetables, pita bread or crackers as desired.

¼ cup: 113 cal., 5g fat (1g sat. fat), 0 chol., 339mg sod.,14g carb. (3g sugars, 4g fiber), 4g pro. **Diabetic exchanges:** 1 starch, 1 fat.

WITCHES' BREW

Stir up some Halloween beverages that are as bewitching as the rest of your menu. Omit the vodka for a nonalcoholic version so the kids can have some, too!
—*Taste of Home* Test Kitchen

PREP: 20 MIN. + CHILLING
MAKES: 6 SERVINGS

- 1 cup sugar
- 1 cup water
- 8 medium kiwifruit, peeled and quartered
- ½ cup fresh mint leaves
- 1 cup vodka, optional
- 1 liter ginger ale, chilled
  Ice cubes

1. In a small saucepan, bring sugar and water to a boil. Cook and stir until sugar is dissolved; set aside to cool.
2. Place kiwi, mint and sugar syrup in a blender; cover and process until blended. Pour into a large pitcher; stir in vodka if desired. Refrigerate until chilled.
3. Just before serving, stir in ginger ale. Serve over ice.

1 cup: 253 cal., 1g fat (0 sat. fat), 0 chol., 17mg sod., 64g carb. (57g sugars, 4g fiber), 1g pro.

WITCHES' BROOMS

Pair these edible mini brooms with Witches' Brew (p. 263) for a spellbinding combination. The only ingredients you need here are pretzel rods and licorice.
—*Taste of Home* Test Kitchen

TAKES: 30 MIN. • **MAKES:** 6 BROOMS

- 6 **pieces green shoestring licorice**
- 6 **pretzel rods**
- 6 **pieces black shoestring licorice**

Cut 1 green shoestring licorice into 1-in. lengths. Arrange around end of 1 pretzel rod to form broom bristles; tightly wrap the bristles with 1 black shoestring licorice, tucking in end to secure. Repeat with the remaining ingredients.

1 broom: 106 cal., 0 fat (0 sat. fat), 0 chol., 142mg sod., 24g carb. (10g sugars, 0 fiber), 1g pro.

HOW TO MAKE FANTASTICALLY FRIGHTENING HALLOWEEN CANDLE HOLDERS

Save some money and help out the environment this Halloween with these amazingly easy upcycled candle holders.

WHAT YOU'LL NEED:
- ☐ Empty clear wine bottle
- ☐ Black, red and gray acrylic paint for glass
- ☐ Straw
- ☐ Knife
- ☐ Taper candle (make sure it isn't a dripless candle)

STEP 1: PREP THE BOTTLE
Thoroughly wash the inside and outside of the wine bottle. If the bottle's label isn't peeling off, let the bottle first soak in a sink full of warm water, a cup of white vinegar, ¼ cup of baking powder and a tablespoon of dish soap for about 30 minutes or so. The label should then come off cleanly, just rinse and let dry completely.

STEP 2: START DRIPPING
Alternating colors, squeeze paint down the inside neck of the bottle. To get the paint farther down and create some texture, insert a straw into the bottle and gently blow the paint down, or carefully shake the bottle. When you've achieved your desired coverage and texture, allow the paint to dry completely.

Tip: You can use any color of paint you'd like. If you're throwing a witch-themed party, consider using purple, black and green. Or have your bottle resemble candy corn with an orange, yellow and white paint scheme.

STEP 3: PREP THE CANDLE
Carefully trim the last inch and a half of the candle so that it will tightly fit in the wine bottle's opening. Be sure to keep the candle on your work surface as you cut away from your body.

STEP 4: GET MELTING
When the bottle is completely dry, insert the trimmed candle into the opening, light it and allow the wax to drip down the sides. If you would like to speed the dripping process or want a lot of wax on your bottle, hold another lit candle to the side of the bottle, letting the excess wax drip down the candle and bottle.

Use the candle holder to decorate your house this Halloween. Be sure to never leave a lit candle unattended.

Cool on pans 2 minutes. Remove to wire racks to cool completely.

3. Meanwhile for the filling, in a small saucepan, whisk the milk and flour until smooth. Bring mixture to a boil, stirring constantly; cook and stir until thickened, 1-2 minutes. Cool completely.

4. In a large bowl, beat the butter and shortening until blended. Gradually beat in cooled milk mixture. Beat in the confectioners' sugar and vanilla until smooth. Refrigerate until chilled. Spread filling on bottoms of half the cookies. Top with remaining cookies. Refrigerate leftovers.

1 whoopie pie: 249 cal., 9g fat (3g sat. fat), 29mg chol., 198mg sod., 40g carb. (26g sugars, 1g fiber), 3g pro.

NO TRICKS
Send each friend home with a clever gift bag filled with themed treats, such as black nail polish, herbal lip balm, a witchy pin, temporary tattoos, confetti and a mood ring.

DEVIL'S FOOD WHOOPIE PIES

These mini cookie cakes were one of my favorite treats while I was growing up in Pennsylvania. We called them gobs because they are gobs of fun to eat! The recipe can make fewer or more, depending on how large or small you make the cookies. Place the finished chocolate whoopie pies in large cupcake liners for a professional look.
—Pamela Esposito, Galloway, NJ

PREP: 30 MIN.
BAKE: 10 MIN./BATCH + COOLING
MAKES: 2 DOZEN

1 pkg. devil's food cake mix (regular size)
1¼ cups all-purpose flour
1 cup water
3 large eggs, room temperature
⅓ cup canola oil
2 Tbsp. baking cocoa
¼ tsp. baking powder
¼ tsp. baking soda
FILLING
1 cup 2% milk
⅓ cup all-purpose flour
¼ cup butter, softened
¼ cup shortening
3¾ cups confectioners' sugar
1 tsp. vanilla extract

1. Preheat oven to 350°. In a large bowl, combine the first 8 ingredients; beat on low speed 30 seconds. Beat on medium 2 minutes.

2. Drop batter by tablespoonfuls 2 in. apart onto parchment-lined baking sheets. Bake until firm, 10-12 minutes.

MIDNIGHT COCKTAILS

This variation on a mojito uses blackberry spreadable fruit, which gives it a deep purple color and adds a bit of sweetness to every sip. You can also use raspberry spreadable fruit if you'd like.
—*Taste of Home* Test Kitchen

PREP: 15 MIN. + CHILLING
MAKES: 2 SERVINGS

- ⅓ cup seedless blackberry spreadable fruit
- 2 Tbsp. water
- ¼ cup fresh mint leaves
- 3 Tbsp. lime juice
- ⅓ cup rum or brandy
- 1 cup club soda

GARNISH
- Mint sprigs

1. In a small saucepan, combine the spreadable fruit and water. Cook and stir over medium heat until smooth; transfer to a small bowl. Refrigerate until chilled.
2. In a small pitcher, muddle the mint leaves and lime juice. Add blackberry syrup and rum. Divide the mixture between 2 cocktail glasses. Stir in club soda; garnish with mint sprigs.

¾ cup: 203 cal., 0 fat (0 sat. fat), 0 chol., 29mg sod., 30g carb. (22g sugars, 1g fiber), 0 pro.

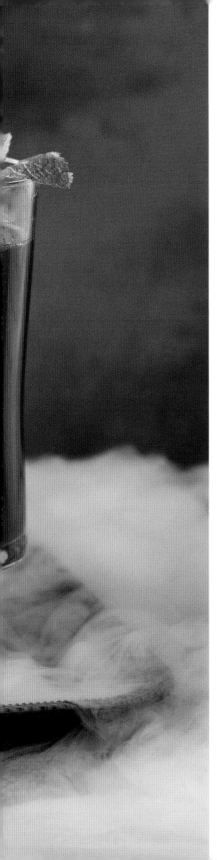

PECANS DIABLO

Spices showcase pecans in a new light. This recipe is a zesty snack for any party, but the heat of the pecans well suits the cool, crisp evenings that come with Halloween.
—*Taste of Home* Test Kitchen

TAKES: 25 MIN. • **MAKES:** 5 CUPS

- ¼ cup butter, melted
- ¾ tsp. dried rosemary, crushed
- ¼ to ½ tsp. cayenne pepper
- ¼ tsp. dried basil
- 5 cups pecan halves
- 2 tsp. kosher salt

1. In a large bowl, combine the butter, rosemary, cayenne and basil. Add the pecans and toss to coat. Spread in a single layer in a 15x10x1-in. baking pan. Sprinkle with salt.
2. Bake, uncovered, at 325° until the pecans are crisp, 17-20 minutes, stirring occasionally. Cool completely. Store in an airtight container.
⅓ cup: 276 cal., 29g fat (4g sat. fat), 8mg chol., 272mg sod., 5g carb. (1g sugars, 3g fiber), 3g pro.

READER REVIEW

"Add spice to suit your taste. We like it a little more spicy, so I added a dash more cayenne but kept the rest the same. Wonderful taste and easy to munch on!"
—SHERIELLEN, TASTEOFHOME.COM

CARAMEL HAVARTI

Havarti is a wonderful soft cheese made even better by pecans, apples and caramel topping. This recipe is elegant yet simple.
—Tia Thomas, Mountain City, TN

TAKES: 15 MIN. • **MAKES:** 10 SERVINGS

- 10 oz. Havarti cheese
- ¼ cup chopped pecans
- 1 Tbsp. butter
- ⅓ to ½ cup caramel ice cream topping, warmed
- 2 medium tart apples, cut into small wedges

1. Place cheese in an small ungreased cast-iron skillet or shallow 1-qt. baking dish. Bake at 375° until edges of cheese just begin to melt, 5-7 minutes.
2. Meanwhile, in a small skillet, saute pecans in butter until toasted. Drizzle caramel over cheese; sprinkle with pecans. Serve with apple wedges.
1 serving: 173 cal., 12g fat (6g sat. fat), 30mg chol., 205mg sod., 12g carb. (10g sugars, 1g fiber), 7g pro.

Day of the Dead Party

November 2 marks a beloved holiday throughout Latin America in which families celebrate the lives of all deceased loved ones. Today, people from coast to coast host these warm, upbeat Day of the Dead parties to honor their ancestors. This year, why not invite friends and family for a lively, colorful get-together? Set out a buffet of comforting Mini Chicken Empanadas, from-scratch guacamole and tres leches treats. For younger guests, you can't go wrong with cheesy quesadillas and Kiddie Sangria. And don't forget margaritas and assorted Mexican beers for the adults.

BLACK BEAN QUESADILLAS

Need a quick snack or appetizer? These bean and cheese quesadillas are the answer. I got the recipe at a Mexican festival that was held at our children's school and have served them regularly ever since.
—Dixie Terry, Goreville, IL

TAKES: 25 MIN. • **MAKES:** 4 SERVINGS

- 1 cup canned black beans, rinsed and drained
- 1 green onion, chopped
- 2 Tbsp. chopped red onion
- 2 Tbsp. finely chopped roasted sweet red pepper
- 1 Tbsp. minced fresh cilantro
- 1 Tbsp. lime juice
- 1 garlic clove, minced
- 4 flour tortillas (10 in.)
- 1 cup shredded Muenster or Monterey Jack cheese

1. In a small bowl, mash beans with a fork; stir in the green onion, red onion, pepper, cilantro, lime juice and garlic.
2. Spread ¼ cup bean mixture over half of each tortilla; top with ¼ cup cheese. Fold over.
3. Cook on a griddle coated with cooking spray over low heat, 1-2 minutes on each side or until cheese is melted. Cut into wedges.

1 quesadilla: 375 cal., 13g fat (6g sat. fat), 27mg chol., 720mg sod., 42g carb. (2g sugars, 9g fiber), 16g pro.

MINI CHICKEN EMPANADAS

Refrigerated pie crust makes quick work of assembling these bite-sized appetizers loaded with chicken and cheese. I've made them several times since receiving the recipe from a friend.
—Betty Fulks, Onia, AR

PREP: 30 MIN.
BAKE: 15 MIN./BATCH
MAKES: ABOUT 2½ DOZEN

- 1 cup finely chopped cooked chicken
- ⅔ cup shredded Colby-Monterey Jack cheese
- 3 Tbsp. cream cheese, softened
- 4 tsp. chopped sweet red pepper
- 2 tsp. chopped seeded jalapeno pepper
- 1 tsp. ground cumin
- ½ tsp. salt
- ⅛ tsp. pepper
- 2 sheets refrigerated pie crust

1. Preheat oven to 400°. In a small bowl, combine the first 8 ingredients. On a lightly floured surface, roll each pie crust into a 15-in. circle. Cut with a floured 3-in. round biscuit cutter.
2. Place about 1 tsp. filling on 1 half of each circle. Moisten edges with water. Fold pie crust over filling. Press edges with a fork to seal.
3. Transfer to greased baking sheets. Bake until golden brown, 12-15 minutes. Remove to wire racks. Serve warm.

1 empanada: 81 cal., 5g fat (2g sat. fat), 10mg chol., 108mg sod., 7g carb. (1g sugars, 0 fiber), 2g pro. **Diabetic exchanges:** 1 fat, ½ starch.

READER REVIEW
"Really good recipe. Not as spicy as I was expecting. I made this two nights in a row. The second night I added a few things like garlic and cayenne pepper to the mixture for a little extra flavor. I also used a bit of salsa for dipping."
—SANDYROSS, TASTEOFHOME.COM

HOW TO MAKE FLUFFY PAPER FLOWERS

For each flower, cut seven layers of brightly colored tissue paper into 5-in. to 9-in. squares, then fold each stack of tissue accordion style. (Each stack should consist of seven pieces of the same size squares.) Cinch at the center with wire or a pipe cleaner, then carefully separate and fluff each piece of tissue to form a pompom shape. For streamers, attach pompoms to fishing line or string. For tabletop floral displays, use pipe cleaners for flower stems.

TRES LECHES CUPCAKES

This cupcake version of tres leches cake actually uses four types of milk, including the cream, but "quatro leches cake" just doesn't have the same delicious ring to it. If you love dairy, you won't be disappointed with this special take on the classic.
—*Taste of Home* Test Kitchen

PREP: 45 MIN. + CHILLING
BAKE: 15 MIN. + COOLING
MAKES: 4 DOZEN

- 1 pkg. yellow cake mix (regular size)
- 1¼ cups water
- 4 large eggs, room temperature
- 1 can (14 oz.) sweetened condensed milk
- 1 cup coconut milk
- 1 can (5 oz.) evaporated milk
  Dash salt

WHIPPED CREAM
- 3 cups heavy whipping cream
- ⅓ cup confectioners' sugar
  Assorted fresh berries

1. Preheat oven to 350°. Line 48 muffin cups with paper liners.
2. In a large bowl, combine the cake mix, water and eggs; beat on low speed 30 seconds. Beat on medium 2 minutes.
3. Fill the prepared cups halfway, allowing room in liners for the milk mixture. Bake 11-13 minutes or until a toothpick inserted in center comes out clean. Cool 5 minutes before removing from pans to wire racks; cool slightly.
4. Place cupcakes in 15x10x1-in. pans. Poke holes in cupcakes with a skewer. In a small bowl, mix the milks and salt; spoon scant 1 Tbsp. mixture over each cupcake. Refrigerate, covered, overnight.
5. In a large bowl, beat the cream until it begins to thicken. Add confectioners' sugar; beat until soft peaks form. Spread over cupcakes; top with the berries. Store in the refrigerator.
1 cupcake: 143 cal., 9g fat (5g sat. fat), 40mg chol., 99mg sod., 15g carb. (11g sugars, 0 fiber), 2g pro.

FRESH LIME MARGARITAS

This basic and classic margarita recipe is easy to modify to your tastes. Try it frozen or with strawberries.
—*Taste of Home* Test Kitchen

TAKES: 15 MIN.
MAKES: 4 SERVINGS

- ½ cup tequila
- ¼ cup Triple Sec
- ¼ cup lime juice
- ¼ cup lemon juice
- 2 tablespoons superfine sugar
- 4 lime wedges
- 1 tablespoon kosher salt
- 1⅓ cups crushed ice

In a large pitcher, combine the first 5 ingredients; stir until the sugar is dissolved. Moisten rims of 4 margarita or cocktail glasses with lime wedges. Sprinkle salt on a plate; dip rims in the salt. Serve in prepared glasses over crushed ice.
⅓ cup (calculated without salt): 149 cal., 0 fat (0 sat. fat), 0 chol., 2mg sod., 15g carb. (13g sugars, 0 fiber), 0 pro.

MEXICAN CHOCOLATE CRINKLES COOKIES

I love to bake. In fact, my first time baking from scratch is still vivid in my memory. This recipe brings back memories, too, of when our girls often took these cinnamon-spiced cookies to their Scout outings.
—Pat Gregory, Tulsa, OK

TAKES: 30 MIN. • **MAKES:** 2½ DOZEN

- ¾ cup shortening
- 1 cup sugar
- 1 large egg, room temperature
- ¼ cup light corn syrup
- 1 oz. unsweetened chocolate, melted
- 1¾ cups all-purpose flour
- 2 tsp. baking soda
- ¼ tsp. salt
- 1 tsp. ground cinnamon
  Additional sugar

1. In a large bowl, cream shortening and sugar until light and fluffy, 5-7 minutes. Add the egg, corn syrup and melted chocolate. Combine the flour, baking soda, salt and cinnamon; gradually add to creamed mixture and mix well.
2. Roll dough into walnut-sized balls and roll in the additional sugar; place 3 in. apart on ungreased baking sheets. Bake at 350° for 10-12 minutes (cookies should be soft). Cool 2-3 minutes before removing to wire racks.

1 cookie: 112 cal., 6g fat (2g sat. fat), 7mg chol., 109mg sod., 15g carb. (8g sugars, 0 fiber), 1g pro.

HOMEMADE GUACAMOLE

Nothing is better than vibrant, freshly made guacamole when you're eating something spicy. It is easy to whip together in a matter of minutes and quickly tames anything that's too hot.
—Joan Hallford, North Richland Hills, TX

TAKES: 10 MIN. • **MAKES:** 2 CUPS

- 3 medium ripe avocados, peeled and cubed
- 1 garlic clove, minced
- ¼ to ½ tsp. salt
- 1 small onion, finely chopped
- 1 to 2 Tbsp. lime juice
- 1 Tbsp. minced fresh cilantro
- 2 medium tomatoes, seeded and chopped, optional
- ¼ cup mayonnaise, optional

Mash avocados with garlic and salt. Stir in remaining ingredients, adding tomatoes and mayonnaise if desired.
¼ cup: 90 cal., 8g fat (1g sat. fat), 0 chol., 78mg sod., 6g carb. (1g sugars, 4g fiber), 1g pro. **Diabetic exchanges:** 1½ fat.

KIDDIE SANGRIA

Everyone can join in the toast with this light and refreshing drink. It looks just like champagne complete with bubbles!
—Pam Ion, Gaithersburg, MD

PREP: 10 MIN. + FREEZING
MAKES: 8 SERVINGS

- 3 cups white grape juice, divided
- 2 cans (12 oz. each) ginger ale, chilled
- ½ cup chilled club soda
  Orange slices and sliced fresh strawberries

1. Pour 2 cups juice into ice cube trays; freeze until set.
2. Transfer ice cubes to a pitcher; add remaining juice. Slowly stir in the ginger ale and club soda. Garnish with oranges and strawberries. Serve immediately.
¾ cup: 86 cal., 0 fat (0 sat. fat), 0 chol., 15mg sod., 21g carb. (20g sugars, 0 fiber), 0 pro.

GET CRAFTY!

Do a DIY take on Day of the Dead with skull-and-coffin decor. Pick up paper masks, skulls and coffin boxes from a craft store. Spray-paint them white, then use bright paints to embellish with your own folk art designs.

DAY OF THE DEAD COOKIES

I use this basic butter cookie recipe to make shaped cutouts for a variety of holidays and occasions. In spring, I cut them into flowers and insert a lollipop stick in each to make a bouquet. Using candies, food coloring and a wild imagination, try your hand at this Day of the Dead version.

—Krissy Fossmeyer, Huntley, IL

PREP: 2 HOURS + CHILLING
BAKE: 10 MIN./BATCH + COOLING
MAKES: 1 DOZEN

1¼ cups butter, softened
1¾ cups confectioners' sugar
2 oz. almond paste
1 large egg
¼ cup 2% milk
1 tsp. vanilla extract
4 cups all-purpose flour
½ tsp. salt
2 pkg. (12 oz. each) white candy coating melts
Optional decorations: Jumbo sprinkles, peppermint candies, candy-coated sunflower kernels, Skittles, Twizzlers Rainbow Twists and Good & Plenty candies
Black paste food coloring

1. In a large bowl, cream butter and confectioners' sugar until light and fluffy; add almond paste. Beat in the egg, milk and vanilla. Combine flour and salt; gradually add to creamed mixture and mix well. Cover and refrigerate for 1 hour.
2. On a lightly floured surface, roll out the dough to ¼-in. thickness. Cut out with a floured 5-in. skull-shaped cookie cutter. Place 1 in. apart on ungreased baking sheets.
3. Bake at 375° for 7-9 minutes or until firm. Let stand for 2 minutes before removing to wire racks to cool completely.
4. In a large, shallow microwave-safe dish, melt the white candy coating melts according to package directions. Dip top side of each cookie into coating, allowing the excess to drip off; place on waxed paper.
5. Add decorations as desired. Tint remaining white candy coating black; pipe on mouth. Let stand until set.

½ cookie: 364 cal., 19g fat (14g sat. fat), 34mg chol., 164mg sod., 45g carb. (29g sugars, 1g fiber), 3g pro.

TIPS FOR ROLLING COOKIE DOUGH

To make the cookie dough easier to roll out, refrigerate it first. This is especially true if the dough was made with butter rather than shortening. Lightly dust the rolling pin and work surface with flour to prevent sticking. Working too much extra flour into the dough—as well as overhandling it—will result in tough cookies. So keep the extra flour to a minimum and use a light touch.

TAKE-HOME TREATS

These cookies make perfect parting gifts. Sugar skulls and chocolate coffins are also popular Day of the Dead confections. Look for them at specialty food shops and Mexican groceries in late fall. Tuck the treats in skull-festooned fabric bags.

Friendsgiving Dinner

Low-stress and low-key are the hallmarks of a casual Thanksgiving dinner spent with friends. Invite your favorite group of people together and make them part of the action with a bring-a-dish party. Delicious food, wine, laughter and conversation will make the occasion one to remember.

PARMESAN-PRETZEL CRISPS

I love this recipe because I usually have the ingredients on hand and it's so easy to prepare. It's one of those snacks that makes guests think you've gone the extra mile.
—Pauline Porterfield, Roxboro, NC

PREP: 10 MIN. • **BAKE:** 10 MIN./BATCH
MAKES: ABOUT 3 DOZEN

1½ cups shredded Parmesan cheese
¼ cup finely crushed pretzels
⅛ tsp. crushed red pepper flakes
Optional: Pizza sauce and sliced fresh basil

1. Preheat oven to 350°. Toss together cheese, pretzels and red pepper flakes. Place 2 tsp. mixture in each greased nonstick mini muffin cup.
2. Bake 10-15 minutes or until golden brown. If desired, serve with pizza sauce and basil.
1 crisp: 16 cal., 1g fat (1g sat. fat), 2mg chol., 66mg sod., 1g carb. (0 sugars, 0 fiber), 1g pro.

HARVEST BOW TIES

Spaghetti squash and bow ties make this meatless dish hearty and filling. Add a can of black beans if you'd like more protein, and switch up the tomatoes for variety. Try using Italian diced tomatoes or diced tomatoes with mild green chiles.
—Anne Lynch, Beacon, NY

PREP: 25 MIN. • **COOK:** 15 MIN.
MAKES: 8 SERVINGS

1 small spaghetti squash (about 1½ lbs.)
12 oz. uncooked bow tie pasta (about 4½ cups)
2 Tbsp. olive oil
1 lb. sliced fresh mushrooms
1 cup chopped sweet onion
2 garlic cloves, minced
1 can (14½ oz.) diced tomatoes, undrained
6 oz. fresh baby spinach (about 8 cups)
¾ tsp. salt
½ tsp. pepper
2 Tbsp. butter
2 Tbsp. sour cream

1. Halve squash lengthwise; discard seeds. Place squash on a microwave-safe plate, cut side down. Microwave, uncovered, on high 9-11 minutes or until tender. Cool slightly. Meanwhile, in a 6-qt. stockpot, cook pasta according to package directions. Drain; return to pot.
2. In a large skillet, heat the oil over medium-high heat; saute mushrooms and onion until tender. Add garlic; cook and stir 1 minute. Separate strands of squash with a fork; add to skillet. Stir in tomatoes, spinach, salt and pepper; cook until spinach is wilted, stirring occasionally. Stir in butter and sour cream until blended.
3. Add to the pasta. Heat through, tossing to coat.
1½ cups: 279 cal., 9g fat (3g sat. fat), 9mg chol., 364mg sod., 44g carb. (5g sugars, 5g fiber), 9g pro.

TEST KITCHEN TIP

To easily halve a spaghetti squash, use a rubber mallet and a large knife, such as a chef's knife. Start by covering the mallet with a food storage bag and securing the bag with a rubber band or twist tie. Then insert the knife lengthwise into the middle of the squash and carefully hit the top of the blade with the mallet. Continue until the squash is cut in half.

APPLE QUINOA SPOON BREAD

My cousin is a strict vegetarian, so creating satisfying vegetable dishes is my yearly challenge. This spoon bread can act as an amazing Thanksgiving side, but the addition of hearty, healthy quinoa and vegetables makes it a well-rounded casserole. Pair it with a seasonal salad to make a filling vegetarian meal.
—Christine Wendland, Browns Mills, NJ

PREP: 25 MIN. • **BAKE:** 25 MIN.
MAKES: 9 SERVINGS

- ⅔ **cup water**
- ⅓ **cup quinoa, rinsed**
- 1 **Tbsp. canola oil**
- 1 **small apple, peeled and diced**
- 1 **small onion, finely chopped**
- 1 **small parsnip, peeled and diced**
- ½ **tsp. celery seed**
- 1¼ **tsp. salt, divided**
- 1 **Tbsp. minced fresh sage**
- ¾ **cup yellow cornmeal**
- ¼ **cup all-purpose flour**
- 1 **Tbsp. sugar**
- 1 **tsp. baking powder**
- 1 **large egg, room temperature**
- 1½ **cups 2% milk, divided**

1. Preheat oven to 375°. In a small saucepan, bring water to a boil. Add quinoa. Reduce heat; simmer, covered, until liquid is absorbed, 12-15 minutes. Fluff with a fork; cool slightly.
2. Meanwhile, in a large skillet, heat oil over medium heat; saute the apple, onion and parsnip with celery seed and ½ tsp. salt until softened, 4-5 minutes. Remove from heat; stir in sage.
3. In a large bowl, whisk together the cornmeal, flour, sugar, baking powder and remaining ¾ tsp. salt. In another bowl, whisk together egg and 1 cup milk. Add to cornmeal mixture, stirring just until moistened. Fold in quinoa and apple mixture.
4. Transfer to a greased 8-in. square baking dish. Pour the remaining milk over top.
5. Bake, uncovered, until edges are golden brown, 25-30 minutes. Let stand 5 minutes before serving.

1 serving: 153 cal., 4g fat (1g sat. fat), 24mg chol., 412mg sod., 26g carb. (6g sugars, 2g fiber), 5g pro. **Diabetic exchanges:** 1½ starch, 1 fat.

WHITE GRAPE JUICE BRINED TURKEY BREAST

This year, brine your turkey in white grape juice. I found this recipe many years ago in a holiday menu magazine. The turkey has just the right amount of spices and seasonings.
—Edie DeSpain, Logan, UT

PREP: 25 MIN. + CHILLING
BAKE: 2 HOURS + STANDING
MAKES: 12 SERVINGS

- 4 **fresh rosemary sprigs**
- 1 **bottle (46 oz.) white grape juice**
- ¼ **cup kosher salt**
- 6 **bay leaves**
- 4 **garlic cloves, sliced**
- 2 **large oven roasting bags**
- 1 **bone-in turkey breast (5 to 6 lbs.)**
- 1 **Tbsp. butter, melted**
- 2 **garlic cloves, minced**
- 1 **tsp. paprika**
- 1 **tsp. dried thyme**
- ½ **tsp. rubbed sage**
- ½ **tsp. onion powder**
- ¼ **tsp. pepper**

1. In a large saucepan, combine the first 5 ingredients; bring to a boil. Cook and stir until salt is dissolved. Cool completely.
2. Place 1 oven roasting bag inside the other. Place the turkey inside both bags; pour in the cooled brine. Seal, pressing out as much air as possible; turn to coat turkey. Place in a large dish. Refrigerate for 8-24 hours, turning occasionally.
3. Preheat oven to 325°. Place a rack in a foil-lined roasting pan. Mix remaining ingredients. Remove the turkey from brine; rinse and pat dry. Discard brine. Place in prepared pan; rub with the butter mixture.
4. Roast turkey until a thermometer reads 170°, 2-2½ hours. (Cover loosely with foil if turkey browns too quickly.) Remove from oven; tent with foil. Let stand 15 minutes before carving.

5 oz. cooked turkey: 277 cal., 11g fat (4g sat. fat), 105mg chol., 257mg sod., 2g carb. (1g sugars, 0 fiber), 40g pro.

TEST KITCHEN TIP
Brining can be done with any cut of meat, but it's especially important with lean cuts like poultry. Brining uses salt to add flavor, tenderize and infuse meat with extra moisture. It can be done by submerging a cut of meat into a saltwater solution (a wet brine) or by sprinkling salt directly onto the meat (a dry brine). Either method will prevent a dry, flavorless bird.

GREEN BEANS WITH SMOKED TURKEY BACON

I really like cooking with curry, and this slow-cooker recipe is a wonderful way to enjoy it. Made with fresh green beans, turkey bacon and garbanzo beans, it has loads of flavor. It can be a main dish or a side dish. Eliminate the bacon for vegetarians.
—Nancy Heishman, Las Vegas, NV

PREP: 25 MIN. • **COOK:** 5 HOURS
MAKES: 10 SERVINGS

2 lbs. fresh green beans, trimmed
1 can (15 oz.) garbanzo beans or chickpeas, rinsed and drained
1 large red onion, chopped
1 large sweet red pepper, chopped
8 turkey bacon strips, chopped
1 can (15 oz.) crushed tomatoes
¼ cup lemon juice
2 Tbsp. minced fresh parsley
3 garlic cloves, minced
3 tsp. curry powder
1 tsp. freshly ground pepper
¾ tsp. salt
¼ cup minced fresh basil
1½ cups crumbled feta cheese

1. Place the first 4 ingredients in a 6-qt. slow cooker. In a large nonstick skillet, cook bacon over medium heat until crisp, stirring occasionally. Add to the slow cooker.
2. In a small bowl, mix tomatoes, lemon juice, parsley, garlic, curry, pepper and salt. Pour over bean mixture.
3. Cook, covered, on low 5-6 hours or until green beans are tender. Stir in basil. Top with cheese before serving.
¾ cup: 168 cal., 6g fat (3g sat. fat), 21mg chol., 633mg sod., 21g carb. (7g sugars, 7g fiber), 9g pro. **Diabetic exchanges:** 1 starch, 1 medium-fat meat, 1 vegetable.

SWEET POTATO PANZANELLA

Here is one of my favorite fall dishes. It is filled with flavor and texture but isn't too high in calories.
—Mary Leverette, Columbia, SC

TAKES: 30 MIN. • **MAKES:** 8 SERVINGS

2 cups cubed peeled sweet potatoes
4 cups cubed French bread
4 Tbsp. olive oil, divided
⅛ tsp. salt
⅛ tsp. pepper
4 cups fresh baby spinach
½ small red onion, thinly sliced
¼ cup minced fresh basil
¼ cup minced fresh cilantro
⅓ cup red wine vinegar

1. Preheat oven to 450°. Place the sweet potatoes and enough water to cover in a large saucepan; bring to a boil. Reduce heat; cook, covered, just until tender, 8-12 minutes. Drain; cool slightly.
2. Meanwhile, toss bread cubes with 2 Tbsp. oil, the salt and pepper. Spread evenly in an ungreased 15x10x1-in. pan. Bake 5 minutes or until golden brown. Transfer to a large bowl; cool slightly.
3. Add spinach, onion, herbs and sweet potatoes to toasted bread. In a small bowl, whisk together the vinegar and remaining oil. Drizzle over salad; toss gently to combine.
¾ cup: 142 cal., 7g fat (1g sat. fat), 0 chol., 150mg sod.,17g carb. (3g sugars, 2g fiber), 2g pro. **Diabetic exchanges:** 1 starch, 1½ fat.

MULLED WINE

This mulled wine is soothing and satisfying with a delightful blend of spices warmed to perfection. Refrigerating the wine mixture overnight allows the flavors to blend, so don't omit this essential step.
—*Taste of Home* Test Kitchen

PREP: 15 MIN. • **COOK:** 30 MIN. + CHILLING
MAKES: 5 SERVINGS

- 1 bottle (750 ml) fruity red wine
- 1 cup brandy
- 1 cup sugar
- 1 medium orange, sliced
- 1 medium lemon, sliced
- ⅛ tsp. ground nutmeg
- 2 cinnamon sticks (3 in.)
- ½ tsp. whole allspice
- ½ tsp. aniseed
- ½ tsp. whole peppercorns
- 3 whole cloves

Optional garnishes: Orange slices, star anise and additional cinnamon sticks

1. In a large saucepan, combine the first 6 ingredients. Place the remaining 5 spices on a double thickness of cheesecloth. Gather corners of cloth to enclose spices; tie securely with string. Place in pan.
2. Bring to a boil, stirring occasionally. Reduce heat; simmer gently, covered, 20 minutes. Transfer to a covered container; cool slightly. Refrigerate, covered, overnight.
3. Strain wine mixture into a large saucepan, discarding the fruit and the spice bag; reheat. Serve warm. Garnish as desired.

¾ cup: 379 cal., 0 fat (0 sat. fat), 0 chol., 10mg sod., 46g carb. (41g sugars, 0 fiber), 0 pro.

BOURBON SWEET POTATO PIE

There is nothing I don't love about this pie! I adore the flavors, and I like that I can sneak some whole grains into the crust. It belongs on every holiday dessert buffet.
—Mary Leverette, Columbia, SC

PREP: 25 MIN. • **BAKE:** 40 MIN.
MAKES: 8 SERVINGS

- 1 cup quick-cooking oats
- ¾ cup packed dark brown sugar
- ¾ cup self-rising flour
- ½ cup butter, melted
- ⅔ cup chopped walnuts

FILLING

- 2 medium sweet potatoes (about 8 oz. each)
- 2 large eggs, lightly beaten
- ½ cup packed dark brown sugar
- ½ cup butter, melted
- ¼ cup self-rising flour
- 2 Tbsp. bourbon
  Sweetened whipped cream

1. Preheat oven to 325°. Mix the first 4 ingredients. Firmly press 1⅔ cups mixture onto bottom and up sides of a well-greased 9-in. pie plate. Bake until light golden brown, 6-8 minutes. Cool on a wire rack.
2. Stir walnuts into the remaining oat mixture. Reserve for topping.
3. For filling, pierce potatoes with a fork; microwave on high until very tender, 10-13 minutes, turning once halfway. Cool slightly.
4. Peel the potatoes and place in a large bowl; mash until smooth. Beat in eggs, brown sugar, melted butter, flour and bourbon until well blended. Add to the crust.
5. Sprinkle with topping. Bake until golden brown and the filling is set, 30-35 minutes. Cool on a wire rack; serve or refrigerate within 2 hours. Serve with whipped cream.

1 piece: 570 cal., 31g fat (16g sat. fat), 108mg chol., 403mg sod., 67g carb. (40g sugars, 4g fiber), 7g pro.

TOP TIPS FOR A FABULOUS FRIENDSGIVING PARTY

A holiday potluck is the low-stress alternative to a fancy feast, so keep things simple and don't be afraid to ask for help. From setup to serving to cleanup, this party is about sharing—everyone has something to bring to the table.

The host makes the turkey and the gravy. The main course doesn't have to be turkey, but whatever it is, you should provide it.

Make a plan for general food categories and the number of dishes, and include it with your invitations. Ask guests to RSVP with what they're bringing.

Ask that dishes are ready to go or need only minimal reheating.

Music helps set the mood. Have a party playlist, or ask a friend to act as a DJ.

Wine and a nonalcoholic option are easy drink choices; a single specialty cocktail makes the occasion stand out.

Keep the decor simple, casual and pretty. This party is about relaxation, so you want people to feel at ease.

Let your guests help. Have a list of simple tasks they can do. Serving drinks, taking coats, stacking dishes—it all helps.

Stock up on takeout cartons, and send guests home with leftovers. They (and your refrigerator) will love it!

AUTUMN SURPRISE PIE

What better way to welcome fall than with a homemade pie? This one calls for apples, pears and raisins flavored with rum extract.
—Karen Gauvreau, Portage, MI

PREP: 40 MIN. + CHILLING • **BAKE:** 45 MIN.
MAKES: 8 SERVINGS

1½ cups all-purpose flour
3 Tbsp. sugar
¼ tsp. plus ⅛ tsp. salt
¼ tsp. plus ⅛ tsp. baking powder
6 Tbsp. cold butter, cubed
⅓ cup fat-free milk
1½ tsp. cider vinegar
FILLING
½ cup sugar
¼ cup all-purpose flour
1 tsp. ground cinnamon
¼ tsp. ground nutmeg
¼ tsp. ground cloves
5 cups sliced peeled apples
2 cups sliced peeled ripe pears
⅓ cup raisins
¾ tsp. rum extract
TOPPING
1 large egg, lightly beaten
1 tsp. coarse sugar

1. Mix the first 4 ingredients; cut in the butter until crumbly. Mix the milk and vinegar; add gradually to the crumb mixture, tossing with a fork until dough holds together when pressed. Divide dough into 2 portions, 1 slightly larger than the other. Shape each into a disk. Cover; refrigerate 1 hour or overnight.
2. Preheat oven to 425°. On a lightly floured surface, roll larger portion of dough to a ⅛-in.-thick circle; transfer to a greased 9-in. pie plate. Trim the crust even with rim. Refrigerate while preparing filling.
3. Mix first 5 filling ingredients. Place apples, pears and raisins in a large bowl. Add sugar mixture and extract; toss to combine. Spoon into crust.

4. Roll out the remaining dough to a ⅛-in.-thick circle; cut into ¾-in.-wide strips. Arrange over filling in a lattice pattern. Trim and seal strips to edge of bottom crust; flute edge. Brush lattice with beaten egg. Sprinkle with coarse sugar.
5. Bake pie on a lower oven rack for 15 minutes. Reduce oven setting to 350°. Bake until crust is golden brown and filling is bubbly, 30-35 minutes. Cool on a wire rack.
1 piece: 331 cal., 10g fat (6g sat. fat), 46mg chol., 217mg sod., 59g carb. (32g sugars, 3g fiber), 5g pro.

APRICOT-APPLE CIDER

Dried apricots give this comforting cider a delicious twist. Add cranberries, cinnamon, allspice and cloves, and you've got the perfect hot drink to sip on cool nights.
—Ginnie Busam, Pewee Valley, KY

PREP: 20 MIN. • **COOK:** 3 HOURS
MAKES: 13 SERVINGS (2½ QT.)

8 cups unsweetened apple juice
1 can (12 oz.) ginger ale
½ cup dried apricots, halved
½ cup dried cranberries
2 cinnamon sticks (3 in. each)
1 Tbsp. whole allspice
1 Tbsp. whole cloves

1. In a 5-qt. slow cooker, combine apple juice and ginger ale. Place the apricots, cranberries, cinnamon sticks, allspice and cloves on a double thickness of cheesecloth; bring up corners of cloth and tie with string to form a bag. Place in slow cooker; cover.
2. Cook on high until heated through, 3-4 hours. Discard spice bag.
¾ cup: 79 cal., 0 fat (0 sat. fat), 0 chol., 8mg sod., 20g carb. (17g sugars, 0 fiber), 0 pro. **Diabetic exchanges:** 2 fruit.

Thanksgiving Dinner

Few things warm hearts more than the comforting goodness found at a Thanksgiving table. Whether you're hosting at your house or taking a dish to share at someone else's, start here to create a holiday favorite, or two, that everyone will love. You'll find familiar staples—roasted turkey and stuffing—along with a few new ideas to spice things up.

Thanksgiving Day Countdown

It's among the most joyous holidays of the year, but Thanksgiving is also one of the busiest in the kitchen. Refer to this timeline to help plan the big feast. Many of the dishes in this menu are perfect for preparing ahead, leaving more time for those that need party-day attention.

A FEW WEEKS BEFORE
☐ Prepare two grocery lists—one for nonperishable items to buy now and one for perishable items to buy a few days before Thanksgiving.
☐ Prepare the Spicy Beet Relish. Store canning jars in a cool, dry place until ready to use.

TWO DAYS BEFORE
☐ Buy remaining grocery items.
☐ Bake the Sweet Milk Dinner Rolls. Store in an airtight container.
☐ Bake the Oatmeal-Chip Cranberry Bars. Store in an airtight container.

THE DAY BEFORE
☐ Mix ingredients for the brine for the Juicy Roast Turkey. Refrigerate turkey with brine overnight.
☐ Make filling for Rye Party Puffs. Cover and refrigerate.
☐ Prepare the Apple Ladyfinger Dessert, but do not sprinkle with cinnamon. Cover and refrigerate until serving.
☐ Bake Southern Sweet Potato Tart. Cover and refrigerate until serving.
☐ Prepare the Almond Broccoli Salad. Cover and refrigerate until serving.
☐ Set the table.

THANKSGIVING DAY
☐ About 4 hours before dinner, remove the turkey from the refrigerator. Roast the turkey and let stand 20 minutes before carving. If desired, prepare homemade gravy from the pan drippings. Keep turkey warm until ready to serve.
☐ About 3-4 hours before dinner, bake the Cranberry-Orange Meatballs. After baking, place meatballs in the slow cooker. Cover and cook on low for 3-4 hours.
☐ Bake the Rye Party Puffs. Allow to cool and fill with the prepared filling.
☐ About an hour before dinner, prepare Moist Turkey Sausage Stuffing and Hot Cider. Keep warm until serving.
☐ About 30-40 minutes before dinner, prepare the Rosemary Mashed Potatoes. Keep warm until serving.
☐ About 20 minutes before dinner, prepare the Herbed Corn. Keep warm until serving.
☐ Open one of the beet relish canning jars. Serve on baguettes for an appetizer or use relish to garnish turkey.
☐ Just before dinner, warm the dinner rolls in the oven.
☐ After dinner, remove the desserts from the refrigerator. Sprinkle the Apple Ladyfinger Dessert with cinnamon. If desired, slightly warm the Southern Sweet Potato Tart or serve cold. Serve alongside Oatmeal-Chip Cranberry Bars.

CRANBERRY-ORANGE MEATBALLS

I make these meatballs at Christmastime. It's a special request every year from my son, so I can't refuse!
—Delsia Lathrop, Westminster, CO

PREP: 45 MIN. • **COOK:** 3 HOURS
MAKES: ABOUT 6 DOZEN

- 2 large eggs, lightly beaten
- 1½ cups dry bread crumbs
- 1 cup chopped dried cranberries
- 1 small onion, finely chopped
- 1 small green pepper, finely chopped
- ¼ cup all-purpose flour
- 2 Tbsp. grated orange zest
- 2 tsp. onion powder
- ½ tsp. salt
- ½ tsp. rubbed sage
- ½ tsp. pepper
- 2 lbs. bulk pork sausage
- 1 lb. ground beef
- 2 cans (15 oz. each) tomato sauce
- 1 can (14 oz.) whole-berry cranberry sauce

1. Preheat oven to 400°. In a large bowl, combine the first 11 ingredients. Add the pork and beef; mix lightly but thoroughly. Shape into 1½-in. balls. Place meatballs on a greased rack in a 15x10x1-in. baking pan. Bake until browned, 18-22 minutes.
2. In a 6-qt. slow cooker, combine the tomato sauce and cranberry sauce. Add the meatballs; gently stir to coat. Cook, covered, on low 3-4 hours or until meatballs are cooked through.

1 meatball: 73 cal., 4g fat (1g sat. fat), 16mg chol., 172mg sod., 7g carb. (3g sugars, 1g fiber), 3g pro.

2. In a small bowl, mix mayonnaise, vinegar, sugar, salt and pepper. In a large bowl, combine broccoli, dried fruit and onion. Add the mayonnaise mixture; toss to coat. Refrigerate until serving.
3. Just before serving, sprinkle with almonds and bacon.

¾ cup: 236 cal., 17g fat (3g sat. fat), 1mg chol., 180mg sod., 21g carb. (15g sugars, 3g fiber), 3g pro.

ROSEMARY MASHED POTATOES

These special-occasion mashed potatoes call for whipping cream instead of milk. I admit I was a little shocked when a good friend suggested this, but I have to agree that it makes ordinary mashed potatoes taste exceptional.
—Sue Gronholz, Beaver Dam, WI

TAKES: 30 MIN. • **MAKES:** 12 SERVINGS

- 8 large potatoes (about 4 lbs.), peeled and quartered
- 1½ tsp. salt, divided
- ¾ cup heavy whipping cream
- ¼ cup butter, cubed
- ½ tsp. minced fresh rosemary
- ¼ tsp. ground nutmeg
- ¼ tsp. pepper

1. Place potatoes in a Dutch oven; add 1 tsp. salt. Cover with water. Bring to a boil. Reduce heat; cover and simmer for 15-20 minutes or until tender. Drain.
2. Place potatoes in a large bowl. Add the cream, butter, rosemary, nutmeg, pepper and remaining salt; mash until desired consistency.

¾ cup: 280 cal., 10g fat (6g sat. fat), 30mg chol., 342mg sod., 45g carb. (4g sugars, 4g fiber), 5g pro.

ALMOND BROCCOLI SALAD

This colorful salad is easy to make, and I like that it can be made ahead. Add the almonds and bacon just before serving so they stay nice and crunchy.
—Margaret Garbade, Tulsa, OK

TAKES: 25 MIN.
MAKES: 12 SERVINGS

- 1 bunch broccoli (about 1½ lbs.)
- 1 cup mayonnaise
- ¼ cup red wine vinegar
- 2 Tbsp. sugar
- ¼ tsp. salt
- ½ tsp. freshly ground pepper
- 1 pkg. (7 oz.) mixed dried fruit
- ¼ cup finely chopped red onion
- 1 pkg. (2¼ oz.) slivered almonds, toasted
- 4 bacon strips, cooked and crumbled

1. Cut florets from broccoli, reserving stalks; cut the florets into 1-in. pieces. Using a paring knife, remove peel from thick stalks; cut stalks into ½-in. pieces.

RYE PARTY PUFFS

I can't go anywhere without taking along my puffs. They're pretty enough for a wedding reception yet hearty enough to snack on while watching football on television. A platter of these will disappear even with a small group.
—Kelly Williams, Forked River, NJ

PREP: 30 MIN. • **BAKE:** 20 MIN. + COOLING
MAKES: 4½ DOZEN

- 1 cup water
- ½ cup butter, cubed
- ½ cup all-purpose flour
- ½ cup rye flour
- 2 tsp. dried parsley flakes
- ½ tsp. garlic powder
- ¼ tsp. salt
- 4 large eggs, room temperature
  Caraway seeds

CORNED BEEF FILLING

- 2 pkg. (8 oz. each) cream cheese, softened
- 2 pkg. (2 oz. each) thinly sliced deli corned beef, chopped
- ½ cup mayonnaise
- ¼ cup sour cream
- 2 Tbsp. minced chives
- 2 Tbsp. diced onion
- 1 tsp. spicy brown or horseradish mustard
- ⅛ tsp. garlic powder
- 10 small pimiento-stuffed olives, chopped

1. Preheat oven to 400°. In a large saucepan over medium heat, bring water and butter to a boil. Add flours, parsley, garlic powder and salt all at once; stir until a smooth ball forms. Remove from heat; let stand 5 minutes. Add the eggs, 1 at a time, beating well after each addition until smooth. Continue beating until the mixture is smooth and shiny.

2. Drop batter by rounded teaspoonfuls 2 in. apart onto greased baking sheets. Sprinkle with caraway seeds. Bake until golden brown, 18-20 minutes. Remove to wire racks. Immediately cut a slit in each puff to allow steam to escape; cool.

3. In a large bowl, combine the first 8 filling ingredients. Stir in olives. Split puffs; add filling.

1 appetizer: 78 cal., 7g fat (3g sat. fat), 29mg chol., 108mg sod., 2g carb. (0 sugars, 0 fiber), 2g pro.

HOT CIDER

I dress up traditional apple cider using lemonade, orange juice, honey and spices. It's a new version of a classic fall beverage.
—Glenna Tooman, Boise, ID

PREP: 5 MIN. • **COOK:** 45 MIN.
MAKES: 18 SERVINGS (4½ QT.)

- 4 cups water
- 2 tsp. ground allspice
- 1 cinnamon stick (3 in.)
  Dash ground cloves
- 1 gallon apple cider or unsweetened apple juice
- 1 can (12 oz.) frozen lemonade concentrate, thawed
- ¾ cup orange juice
- ⅓ cup honey
- 1 tea bag

1. In a large stockpot, combine the water, allspice, cinnamon stick and cloves. Bring to a boil. Reduce heat; simmer, uncovered, for 30 minutes.

2. Add the remaining ingredients. Return just to a boil. Discard the cinnamon stick and tea bag. Stir and serve warm.

1 cup: 168 cal., 0 fat (0 sat. fat), 0 chol., 24mg sod., 42g carb. (38g sugars, 0 fiber), 0 pro.

APPLE CIDER MIX-INS

Looking for a new way to enjoy apple cider? Try one of these fun add-ons or mix-ins for fall's most iconic drink.

CARAMEL

Caramel and apple is a match made in heaven. Next time you heat up your favorite apple cider recipe to enjoy by the fire, stir in some caramel sauce, sprinkle with cinnamon and top with whipped cream.

MAPLE SYRUP

Maple and apple go so well together. Have this combo cold—just add a teaspoon or so of syrup to cider and top with sparkling water. If you prefer warm cider, just stir in a bit of syrup while heating the cider.

GINGER BEER

A splash of ginger beer gives cider a bit of spice and some fizz. This combo is wonderful on its own as a mocktail. If you want to make an Apple Cider Mule (a take on a Moscow Mule), add a splash of vodka.

WINE

Turn apple cider into a fall sangria with just a few ingredients. Mix a favorite bottle of white wine with 2-3 cups of cider, a splash of brandy and a cinnamon stick. Stir together in a pitcher, and garnish with orange and apple slices.

MULLING SPICES

This one's a classic! Combine classic warming spices like clove, allspice and cinnamon in your cider for an especially autumnal treat.

SPICY BEET RELISH

We love the taste of this relish with any type of meat or bean dish. You can adjust the pepper and horseradish to taste.
—Norma Leatherwood, Sevierville, TN

PREP: 1 HOUR • **PROCESS:** 15 MIN.
MAKES: 3 PINTS

- 4 **lbs. fresh beets**
- 1 **cup sugar**
- 1 **cup cider vinegar**
- 2 **Tbsp. grated peeled horseradish**
- 2 **tsp. canning salt**
- ½ **tsp. cayenne pepper**
- ¼ **tsp. pepper**
  Optional: Sliced baguette and grated lemon zest

1. Scrub beets and trim tops to 1 in. Place in a Dutch oven; add water to cover. Bring to a boil. Reduce heat; simmer, covered, 45-60 minutes or until tender. Remove from the water; cool. Peel and shred beets.
2. In a Dutch oven, combine sugar and vinegar; cook and stir over medium heat until sugar is dissolved. Stir in the shredded beets, horseradish, salt, cayenne and pepper; bring to a boil.
3. Ladle hot mixture into hot 1-pint jars, leaving ½-in. headspace. Remove air bubbles and adjust the headspace, if necessary, by adding hot relish. Wipe rims. Center lids on jars; screw on bands until fingertip tight.
4. Place jars into canner, ensuring that they are completely covered with water. Bring to a boil; process for 15 minutes. Remove jars and cool. If desired, serve on baguette slices and sprinkle with lemon zest.
¼ cup: 70 cal., 0 fat (0 sat. fat), 0 chol., 256mg sod., 17g carb. (15g sugars, 2g fiber), 1g pro.

HOW TO REMOVE BEET SKIN

STEP 1
On a cutting board, cut the beet greens to 1 in. and cut off the tail (root end).

STEP 2
Place trimmed beets in a Dutch oven or baking dish; add enough water to cover. Cook according to the recipe's instructions.

STEP 3
With a slotted spoon, carefully remove beets to a bowl of cold water.

STEP 4
When beets are cool enough to handle, trim off what's left of the stem. Hold a piece of paper toweling in each hand. Pick up a beet with both hands, hold firmly and twist your hands in opposite directions. The skin will slide right off and your hands will stay clean.

⅔ cup: 176 cal., 3g fat (1g sat. fat), 13mg chol., 540mg sod., 30g carb. (8g sugars, 3g fiber), 7g pro. **Diabetic exchanges:** 2 starch, 1 lean meat.

OATMEAL-CHIP CRANBERRY BARS

These oat bars are a family favorite. The simple icing dresses them up and adds a touch more sweetness.
—Lee Roberts, Racine, WI

PREP: 15 MIN. • **BAKE:** 30 MIN. + COOLING
MAKES: 2 DOZEN

- 1   cup butter, softened
- 1   cup packed brown sugar
- ½   cup sugar
- 2   large eggs, room temperature
- 1   tsp. vanilla extract
- 3   cups old-fashioned oats
- 1½ cups all-purpose flour
- 1   tsp. baking soda
- 1   tsp. ground cinnamon
- ½   tsp. salt
- 1   cup dried cranberries
- 1   cup semisweet chocolate chips
- 1   cup confectioners' sugar
- 2   Tbsp. 2% milk

1. Preheat oven to 350°. In a large bowl, cream butter and sugars until light and fluffy, 5-7 minutes. Beat in the eggs and vanilla. Combine the oats, flour, baking soda, cinnamon and salt; gradually add to creamed mixture and mix well. Stir in cranberries and chocolate chips.
2. Press mixture into a greased 13x9-in. baking pan. Bake until golden brown, 30-35 minutes. Cool on a wire rack. Combine confectioners' sugar and milk; drizzle over bars.

1 bar: 266 cal., 11g fat (6g sat. fat), 36mg chol., 173mg sod., 41g carb. (27g sugars, 2g fiber), 3g pro.

MOIST TURKEY SAUSAGE STUFFING

With tangy apricots and turkey sausage, this stuffing is a terrific mix of sweet and savory.
—Priscilla Gilbert, Indian Harbour Beach, FL

PREP: 20 MIN. • **COOK:** 20 MIN.
MAKES: 16 SERVINGS

- 1   pkg. (19½ oz.) Italian turkey sausage links, casings removed
- 4   celery ribs, chopped
- 1   large onion, chopped
- 1½ cups chopped dried apricots
- ¼   cup minced fresh parsley
- 1   Tbsp. minced fresh sage or 1 tsp. dried sage
- 1   tsp. poultry seasoning
- ¼   tsp. pepper
- 3¼ cups chicken stock
- 1   pkg. (12 oz.) crushed cornbread stuffing
- 1   cup fresh or frozen cranberries, chopped

1. In a Dutch oven, cook turkey sausage, celery and onion over medium heat until meat is no longer pink and vegetables are tender, breaking the sausage into crumbles; drain. Stir in the apricots, parsley, sage, poultry seasoning and pepper; cook 3 minutes longer.
2. Add the stock; bring to a boil. Stir in cornbread stuffing; cook and stir until liquid is absorbed. Gently stir in the cranberries; heat through.

HERBED CORN

A pleasant blend of herbs dresses up this buttery, fresh-flavored corn dish that I often take to carry-in dinners. It's a must for my family's Thanksgiving meals.
—Edna Hoffman, Hebron, IN

TAKES: 20 MIN. • **MAKES:** 12 SERVINGS

- 12 cups frozen corn
- 1 cup water
- ½ cup butter, cubed
- 2 Tbsp. minced fresh parsley
- 2 tsp. salt
- 1 tsp. dill weed
- ½ tsp. garlic powder
- ½ tsp. Italian seasoning
- ¼ tsp. dried thyme

In a large saucepan, combine the corn and water. Bring to a boil. Reduce heat; cover and simmer until corn is tender, 3-4 minutes. Drain; stir in the remaining ingredients.

¾ cup: 212 cal., 9g fat (5g sat. fat), 20mg chol., 476mg sod., 34g carb. (3g sugars, 4g fiber), 5g pro.

SWEET MILK DINNER ROLLS

The hint of sweetness in these tender buns brings in many compliments. Served warm with butter or jam, they're a big hit at any meal. They reheat nicely, too.
—Merle Dyck, Elkford, BC

PREP: 20 MIN. + RISING • **BAKE:** 35 MIN.
MAKES: 16 ROLLS

- 1 pkg. (¼ oz.) active dry yeast
- 2 cups warm 2% milk (110° to 115°)
- ½ cup sugar
- 2 Tbsp. butter, melted
- 1 tsp. salt
- 4 to 5 cups all-purpose flour

1. In a large bowl, dissolve yeast in warm milk. Add the sugar, butter, salt and 3 cups flour. Beat until smooth. Add enough remaining flour to form a soft dough.
2. Turn onto a floured surface; knead until smooth and elastic, 6-8 minutes. Place in a greased bowl, turning once to grease the top. Cover and let rise in a warm place until doubled, about 1 hour.
3. Punch the dough down. Turn onto a floured surface; divide into 16 pieces. Shape each into a ball. Place 2 in. apart on greased baking sheets. Cover and let rise until doubled, about 30 minutes.
4. Bake at 350° until golden brown, 35-40 minutes. Remove from pans to wire racks. Serve warm.
1 roll: 168 cal., 2g fat (1g sat. fat), 6mg chol., 174mg sod., 32g carb. (8g sugars, 1g fiber), 4g pro.

JUICY ROAST TURKEY

I can't wait to serve this juicy turkey at Thanksgiving—so I make it several times throughout the year. The aroma that wafts through the house as it bakes is almost as mouthwatering as the bird itself.
—Terrie Herman, North Myrtle Beach, SC

PREP: 20 MIN. + CHILLING
BAKE: 3½ HOURS + STANDING
MAKES: 12 SERVINGS

- ¼ cup ground mustard
- 2 Tbsp. Worcestershire sauce
- 2 Tbsp. olive oil
- ½ tsp. white vinegar
- 1 tsp. salt
- ⅛ tsp. pepper
- 1 turkey (10 to 12 lbs.)
- 1 medium onion, quartered
- 2 celery ribs, quartered lengthwise
   Fresh parsley sprigs
- 2 bacon strips
- ¼ cup butter, softened
- 2 cups chicken broth
- 1 cup water

1. In a small bowl, combine the first 6 ingredients. Brush over the turkey. Place turkey on a platter. Cover and refrigerate for 1-24 hours.
2. Preheat oven to 325°. Place turkey on a rack in a shallow roasting pan, breast side up. Add the onion, celery and parsley to turkey cavity. Tuck wings under turkey; tie drumsticks together. Arrange bacon over the top of turkey breast. Spread butter over turkey. Pour broth and water into pan.
3. Bake, uncovered, until a thermometer inserted in the thickest part of thigh reads 170°-175°, 3½-4 hours, basting occasionally. Remove turkey from oven. If desired, remove and discard bacon. Tent with foil; let stand 20 minutes before carving. If desired, skim fat and thicken pan drippings for gravy. Serve with turkey.
8 oz. cooked turkey: 535 cal., 29g fat (9g sat. fat), 219mg chol., 594mg sod., 2g carb. (1g sugars, 0 fiber), 62g pro.

APPLE LADYFINGER DESSERT

I adapted this recipe from a German dessert that is unique to the region where I grew up. It's easy to assemble and perfect for making a day ahead. I use unsweetened applesauce because I love the combination of tart and creamy, but if you prefer your desserts a bit sweeter, use sweetened applesauce.
—Marly Chaland, Maple, ON

PREP: 40 MIN. + CHILLING
MAKES: 16 SERVINGS

- 1 carton (8 oz.) mascarpone cheese
- 1 pkg. (7 oz.) crisp ladyfinger cookies
- ¼ cup apple brandy
- 2 cups unsweetened applesauce
- ⅓ cup sugar
- 1 tsp. vanilla extract
- 1 cup heavy whipping cream
  Ground cinnamon

1. Stir mascarpone cheese; let stand at room temperature for 30 minutes. Meanwhile, arrange ladyfingers in a single layer in a 13x9-in. dish, breaking to fit as needed (save remaining for another use). Brush the ladyfingers generously with apple brandy; spread applesauce over ladyfingers.
2. Beat the mascarpone cheese, sugar and vanilla on low speed until blended. Gradually add heavy whipping cream, increasing speed to high. Beat until soft peaks form. Spread the cheese mixture over applesauce layer; refrigerate at least 2 hours. Before serving, sprinkle lightly with cinnamon.

1 piece: 187 cal., 12g fat (7g sat. fat), 45mg chol., 28mg sod., 16g carb. (12g sugars, 0 fiber), 2g pro.

DID YOU KNOW?
Mascarpone is a soft fresh cheese that is rich and buttery. It has a slightly sweet flavor and a smooth, thick, creamy texture, making it ideal for many desserts. It's also good paired with berries, shortbread and figs.

SOUTHERN SWEET POTATO TART

Our family loves sweet potatoes, so I try to incorporate them into as many dishes as I can. My secret ingredient is the bourbon—it's what makes this tart so delicious.
—Marie Bruno, Watkinsville, GA

PREP: 1 HOUR • **BAKE:** 25 MIN. + COOLING
MAKES: 8 SERVINGS

- 1 lb. sweet potatoes (about 2 small)
  Pastry for single-crust pie (see recipe on page 428)
- ¼ cup butter, softened
- ½ cup packed dark brown sugar
- 2 Tbsp. all-purpose flour
- 1 tsp. pumpkin pie spice
- ¼ tsp. salt
- 1 large egg
- ¼ cup heavy whipping cream
- 1 Tbsp. bourbon or 1 Tbsp. whipping cream plus ½ tsp. vanilla extract

TOPPING
- 2 Tbsp. butter, softened
- 2 Tbsp. dark brown sugar
- 2 Tbsp. dark corn syrup
- ½ cup chopped pecans

1. Preheat oven to 400°. Place potatoes on a foil-lined baking sheet. Bake until tender, 40-50 minutes.
2. On a lightly floured surface, roll the dough to a ⅛-in.-thick circle; transfer to a 9-in. tart pan with a removable bottom. Press onto bottom and sides of pan; trim edges to the edge of pan. Refrigerate while preparing filling.
3. Remove potatoes from oven; increase oven setting to 425°. When potatoes are cool enough to handle, remove peel and place the pulp in a large bowl; beat until smooth (you will need 1 cup mashed). Add butter, brown sugar, flour, pie spice and salt; beat until blended. Beat in egg, cream and bourbon. Pour into the crust. Bake on a lower oven rack 15 minutes.
4. Meanwhile, for topping, mix butter, brown sugar and corn syrup until blended. Stir in pecans.
5. Remove the pie; reduce oven setting to 350°. Spoon topping evenly over pie. Bake until a knife inserted in the center comes out clean, 8-10 minutes.
6. Cool on a wire rack. Serve the tart within 2 hours or refrigerate, covered, and serve cold.

1 piece: 477 cal., 29g fat (15g sat. fat), 85mg chol., 326mg sod., 52g carb. (27g sugars, 3g fiber), 5g pro.

Black Friday

On Black Friday, the day after Thanksgiving, early birds are up and at 'em scouting deals at their favorite stores. But serious shopping can work up a serious appetite. This year, plan a post-shopping potluck with a variety of slow-cooked sensations. Designate who is bringing what, and then flip the switch on the slow cooker before you hit the stores. Later, everyone can meet up with their dish to pass and feast on deliciously good eats! Please all tastes with a quick-prep dip, a delightful dessert, even a toasty fall beverage. This lineup might just inspire a new tradition!

SPICED CRANBERRY-APPLE PUNCH

This festive and fruity punch is made with five kinds of juice plus cinnamon and allspice for a well-balanced flavor that's a delightful change of pace.
—Jennifer Stout, Blandon, PA

PREP: 10 MIN. • **COOK:** 4 HOURS
MAKES: 16 SERVINGS

- 4 cups apple juice
- 4 cups orange juice
- 2 cups cranberry juice
- 1 can (11.3 oz.) pineapple nectar
- ½ cup sugar
- 2 tsp. lemon juice
- 3 to 4 cinnamon sticks (3 in.)
- 8 whole allspice
- 8 to 10 orange slices
  Optional: Apple slices and fresh cranberries

1. In a 5- or 6-qt. slow cooker, mix first 6 ingredients. Place cinnamon sticks and allspice on a double thickness of cheesecloth. Gather corners of cloth to enclose seasonings; tie securely with string. Place the spice bag and the orange slices in slow cooker. Cook, covered, on low for 4-5 hours to allow the flavors to blend.
2. Discard spice bag and orange slices. If desired, top punch with apple slices and cranberries. Serve warm.
¾ cup: 114 cal., 0 fat (0 sat. fat), 0 chol., 7mg sod., 28g carb. (26g sugars, 1g fiber), 1g pro.

GARDEN GREEN BEANS & POTATOES

Fresh green beans paired with red potatoes make for a simple and filling side dish. To make it even better, add crumbled bacon!
—Kelly Zinn, Cicero, IN

PREP: 10 MIN. • **COOK:** 6 HOURS
MAKES: 16 SERVINGS

- 2 lbs. fresh green beans, trimmed
- 1½ lbs. red potatoes, quartered
- 1 medium onion, chopped
- ½ cup beef broth
- 1½ tsp. salt
- 1 tsp. dried thyme
- ½ tsp. pepper
- ¼ cup butter, softened
- 1 Tbsp. lemon juice

In a 6-qt. slow cooker, combine first 7 ingredients. Cook, covered, on low until beans are tender, 6-8 hours. Stir in butter and lemon juice. Remove with a slotted spoon.
¾ cup: 77 cal., 3g fat (2g sat. fat), 8mg chol., 278mg sod., 12g carb. (2g sugars, 3g fiber), 2g pro. **Diabetic exchanges:** 1 vegetable, ½ starch, ½ fat.

SLOW-COOKER CRAB DIP

With just 10 minutes of prep time, this creamy and delicious crab dip couldn't be easier. The recipe comes from my hometown cookbook, and my co-workers rave about it at every work potluck!
—Julie Novotney, Rockwell, IA

PREP: 10 MIN. • **COOK:** 2 HOURS
MAKES: 2 CUPS

- 1 pkg. (8 oz.) cream cheese, softened
- ½ cup grated Parmesan cheese
- ½ cup mayonnaise
- 4 green onions, finely chopped
- ½ tsp. garlic powder
- 1 can (6 oz.) crabmeat, drained, flaked and cartilage removed
- ½ cup sliced almonds, toasted
  Assorted crackers

1. In a 1½-qt. slow cooker, combine the first 5 ingredients. Stir in the crab. Cook, covered, on low 2-3 hours or until the dip is heated through.
2. Just before serving, sprinkle with almonds. Serve with crackers.
2 Tbsp.: 132 cal., 12g fat (4g sat. fat), 27mg chol., 185mg sod., 2g carb. (1g sugars, 0 fiber), 4g pro.

SWEET ONION CREAMED CORN

A friend from church gave me this tasty, effortless recipe more than 40 years ago, and I still make it regularly. She was from the South, and whenever I cook it, I remember her fondly.

—Nancy Heishman, Las Vegas, NV

PREP: 25 MIN. • **COOK:** 3 HOURS 10 MIN.
MAKES: 8 SERVINGS

- 5 bacon strips, chopped
- 1 large sweet onion, chopped
- 1 medium sweet red pepper, chopped
- 5 cups frozen corn (about 24 oz.), thawed
- 2 cups cubed fully cooked ham
- ½ cup half-and-half cream
- 1 Tbsp. brown sugar
- 1 Tbsp. dried parsley flakes
- 1 tsp. smoked paprika
- ½ tsp. salt
- ½ tsp. pepper
- 1 pkg. (8 oz.) cream cheese, cubed and softened

1. In a large skillet, cook the bacon over medium heat until crisp, stirring occasionally. Remove with a slotted spoon, leaving drippings in pan; drain on paper towels.
2. Cook and stir the onion and sweet red pepper in the bacon drippings over medium-high heat until tender, 5-6 minutes.
3. In a greased 4-qt. slow cooker, combine corn, ham, cream, brown sugar, parsley, paprika, salt, pepper, bacon and the onion mixture. Cook, covered, on low until heated through, 3-4 hours. Stir in the cream cheese; cook, covered, 10 minutes longer. Stir before serving.

¾ cup: 336 cal., 20g fat (10g sat. fat), 68mg chol., 791mg sod., 26g carb. (8g sugars, 3g fiber), 15g pro.

A MESSAGE FOR EVERY POT

Use chalkboard paint and markers to add a fun message to your slow cooker.

WHAT YOU'LL NEED:

☐ Slow cooker

☐ Fine-grit sandpaper

☐ Painter's tape

☐ Spray paint primer

☐ Chalkboard spray paint

☐ Chalk or chalkboard markers

STEP 1:
Remove the slow-cooker lid, insert and knobs. Be sure to make note of the settings the knobs control—you may need to re-mark these when you're done painting!

STEP 2:
Thoroughly wipe the outer surface of slow cooker with a damp cloth, then lightly sand it with sandpaper.

STEP 3:
Use tape to cover the bottom edge, handles, electrical cord and any other areas that should not be painted.

Be careful when taping the curved areas, making sure the tape bonds to the surface so the spray paint cannot seep through.

STEP 4:
In a protected area, evenly spray the outer surface of the slow cooker with a thin coat of primer. Allow it to dry thoroughly.

STEP 5:
Evenly spray the outer surface with 2-3 coats of chalkboard paint, allowing the cooker to dry thoroughly between coats. To avoid drips, keep spray can level and use an even, steady motion.

STEP 6:
When the last coat is dry, carefully remove the tape. Reattach knobs; insert liner and lid. If desired, mark knob settings. Write a message or draw a picture on the slow cooker using chalk or chalkboard markers.

SLAW-TOPPED BEEF SLIDERS

When I was working full time, I would rely on these fantastic fast-to-fix beef sliders for simple meals. To speed prep time and avoid extra cleanup, I used bagged coleslaw mix and bottled slaw dressing.
—Jane Whittaker, Pensacola, FL

PREP: 20 MIN. • **COOK:** 6 HOURS
MAKES: 1 DOZEN

- 3 cups coleslaw mix
- ½ medium red onion, chopped (about ⅔ cup)
- ⅛ tsp. celery seed
- ¼ tsp. pepper
- ⅓ cup coleslaw salad dressing

SANDWICHES
- 1 boneless beef chuck roast (2 lbs.)
- 1 tsp. salt
- ½ tsp. pepper
- 1 can (6 oz.) tomato paste
- ¼ cup water
- 1 tsp. Worcestershire sauce
- 1 small onion, diced
- 1 cup barbecue sauce
- 12 slider buns or dinner rolls, split

1. Combine coleslaw, onion, celery seed and pepper. Add salad dressing; toss to coat. Refrigerate until serving.

2. Sprinkle roast with salt and pepper; transfer to a 5-qt. slow cooker. Mix the tomato paste, water and Worcestershire sauce; pour over roast. Top with onion. Cook, covered, on low 6-8 hours or until the meat is tender.

3. Shred meat with 2 forks; return to slow cooker. Stir in barbecue sauce; heat through. Serve beef on buns; top with coleslaw. Replace tops.

1 slider: 322 cal., 12g fat (4g sat. fat), 67mg chol., 726mg sod., 34g carb. (13g sugars, 3g fiber), 20g pro.

BLACK BEAN CHICKEN NACHOS

The best chicken nachos can be found at Zeppelins in Cedar Rapids, Iowa. Zeppelins' famous dish inspired me to make my own nachos—but with the added convenience of a slow cooker. I always use cilantro because it is economical and makes the dish pop with flavor.
—Natalie Hess, Pennsville, NJ

PREP: 10 MIN. • **COOK:** 4 HOURS
MAKES: 8 SERVINGS

- 1½ lbs. boneless skinless chicken breast
- 2 jars (16 oz. each) black bean and corn salsa
- 1 each medium green pepper and sweet red pepper, chopped
  Tortilla chips
- 2 cups shredded Mexican cheese blend
  Optional: Minced fresh cilantro, pickled jalapeno slices and sour cream

1. Place chicken, salsa and peppers in a 3- or 4-qt. slow cooker. Cook, covered, on low until meat is tender, 4-5 hours.
2. Remove chicken; shred with 2 forks. Return to slow cooker to heat through. Using a slotted spoon, serve chicken over chips; sprinkle with cheese and optional toppings.

½ cup chicken mixture: 280 cal., 11g fat (5g sat. fat), 72mg chol., 708mg sod., 20g carb. (5g sugars, 8g fiber), 27g pro.

BBQ TURKEY MEATBALLS

What's a party without meatballs? We have these at all our big gatherings, but they're also terrific as an easy weeknight meal. This recipe can also be made with ground beef or even store-bought meatballs.
—Lisa Harms, Moline, MI

PREP: 45 MIN. • **COOK:** 3 HOURS
MAKES: ABOUT 4 DOZEN

- 1 large egg, lightly beaten
- ⅔ cup soft bread crumbs
- ¼ cup finely chopped onion
- ½ tsp. pepper
- 2 lbs. ground turkey

SAUCE
- 1 bottle (20 oz.) ketchup
- ¼ cup packed brown sugar
- 2 Tbsp. Worcestershire sauce
- 1 tsp. garlic salt
- ½ to 1 tsp. hot pepper sauce

1. Preheat oven to 375°. Combine egg, bread crumbs, onion and pepper. Add turkey; mix lightly but thoroughly. Shape into 1-in. balls. Place on a greased rack in a 15x10x1-in. pan. Bake until lightly browned, 15-20 minutes.
2. Transfer meatballs to a 3-qt. slow cooker. Mix sauce ingredients; pour over top. Cook, covered, on low for 3-4 hours or until meatballs are cooked through.

Freeze option: Freeze cooled meatballs in sauce in freezer containers. To use, partially thaw in refrigerator overnight. Microwave, covered, on high in a microwave-safe dish until heated through, stirring occasionally; add a little water if necessary.

1 meatball: 44 cal., 1g fat (0 sat. fat), 16mg chol., 188mg sod., 4g carb. (4g sugars, 0 fiber), 4g pro.

WARM CINNAMON-APPLE TOPPING

You'll quickly warm up to the old-fashioned taste of this fruit topping! I like to spoon it over vanilla ice cream or slices of pound cake.
—Doris Heath, Franklin, NC

PREP: 10 MIN. • **COOK:** 3 HOURS
MAKES: ABOUT 6 CUPS

- 3 medium tart apples, peeled and sliced
- 3 medium pears, peeled and sliced
- 1 Tbsp. lemon juice
- ½ cup packed brown sugar
- ½ cup maple syrup
- ¼ cup butter, melted
- 2 Tbsp. cornstarch
- ½ cup chopped pecans
- ¼ cup raisins
- 2 cinnamon sticks (3 in. each)
  Pound cake or ice cream

1. In a 3-qt. slow cooker, toss apples and pears with lemon juice. Mix the brown sugar, maple syrup, butter and cornstarch; pour over the fruit. Stir in pecans, raisins and cinnamon sticks.
2. Cook, covered, on low until fruit is tender, 3-4 hours. Discard cinnamon sticks. Serve with cake or ice cream.
¼ cup: 95 cal., 4g fat (1g sat. fat), 5mg chol., 22mg sod., 16g carb. (14g sugars, 1g fiber), 0 pro.

PUMPKIN PIE PUDDING

My husband loves anything pumpkin, and this creamy, comforting dessert is one of his favorites. We make this super easy pudding year-round, but it's especially nice in fall.
—Andrea Schaak, Bloomington, MN

PREP: 10 MIN. • **COOK:** 6 HOURS
MAKES: 6 SERVINGS

- 1 can (15 oz.) pumpkin
- 1 can (12 oz.) evaporated milk
- ¾ cup sugar
- ½ cup biscuit/baking mix
- 2 large eggs, beaten
- 2 Tbsp. butter, melted
- 2½ tsp. pumpkin pie spice
- 2 tsp. vanilla extract
  Optional: Sweetened whipped cream or vanilla ice cream

Combine the first 8 ingredients. Transfer to a greased 3-qt. slow cooker. Cook, covered, on low until a thermometer reads 160°, 6-7 hours. If desired, serve with whipped cream or ice cream.
1 serving: 229 cal., 9g fat (5g sat. fat), 76mg chol., 187mg sod., 33g carb. (25g sugars, 2g fiber), 6g pro.

SIX-BEAN CHILI

When it's cold and frosty outside, this meatless chili is sure to keep you toasty. It's packed with fiber, protein and flavor. Serve it with sliced avocado, or add shredded cheese, corn tortilla chips or a side of your favorite cornbread.
—Liz Bellville, Tonasket, WA

PREP: 20 MIN. • **COOK:** 6 HOURS
MAKES: 14 SERVINGS (ABOUT 3½ QT.)

- 1 large white onion, chopped
- 2 large carrots, coarsely chopped
- ½ cup frozen corn
- 3 large garlic cloves, minced
- 1 can (16 oz.) chili beans, undrained
- 1 can (16 oz.) kidney beans, rinsed and drained
- 1 can (15½ oz.) navy beans, rinsed and drained
- 1 can (15½ oz.) great northern beans, rinsed and drained
- 1 can (15 oz.) pinto beans, rinsed and drained
- 1 can (15 oz.) black beans, rinsed and drained
- 2 cans (14½ oz. each) fire-roasted diced tomatoes, undrained
- 1 can (28 oz.) crushed tomatoes
- 1 can (4 oz.) chopped fire-roasted green chiles
- 1 Tbsp. chili powder
- 2 tsp. ground cumin
- 2 tsp. ground chipotle pepper
  Chopped avocado, optional

In a 6- or 7-qt. slow cooker, combine the first 16 ingredients. Cook, covered, on low until vegetables are tender, 6-8 hours. If desired, serve with chopped avocado.
1 cup: 196 cal., 1g fat (0 sat. fat), 0 chol., 658mg sod., 38g carb. (7g sugars, 10g fiber), 11g pro.

Star Wars Birthday Party

Jedis, Sith, droids, Wookiees and royalty—what's not to love? Make your child's birthday memorable by throwing an epic party based on the most popular sci-fi movie of all time. It will be the talk of the galaxy! Host a movie marathon, dress up like characters, take selfies and feast on a galactic smorgasbord of Star Wars-themed food. Party you will.

HOW TO HOST A SPECTACULAR STAR WARS-THEMED PARTY

Get ready for the most legendary Star Wars party from here to Tatooine. Use our guide and there is no try—you can DO!

PARTY INVITATIONS
Send special invites to every last Jedi! Craft your own or download printable sets from the internet. They can be personalized with the time and date of the party, and the name of the birthday boy or girl. Many printable sets can be downloaded instantly—which is excellent when you're short on time.

SET THE SCENE
Create the atmosphere of a galaxy far, far away by decorating with sci-fi party swag. Set a perfect table with a themed tablecloth, plates and cups, table decor and confetti.

WHEN THE FORCE ASSEMBLES...
Hand out character masks to the kids as they arrive. Use elastic and a stapler to complete the project. Then set everyone to work making simple (and safe) lightsabers using pool noodles—with electrical tape and duct tape for the handles.

PARTY GAMES
Play Star Wars-inspired party games. You can pin the lightsaber on Darth Vader, or create a plastic-wrap ball (ahem, Death Star) filled with party-perfect prizes. Use printable bingo cards for some cosmic birthday fun.

STAR WARS-INSPIRED FOOD
The most important part of any party is the food! Let the Force guide you—but we'll help out, too. Guests will dig the party favorites in this chapter.

SWEET TREATS
Any of the goodies in this chapter are sure winners! Or look on *tasteofhome.com* for a basic vanilla cupcake recipe and add adorable cupcake toppers. Or use Star Wars cookie cutters with your favorite sugar cookies and watch 'em all disappear into hyperspace.

DAZZLING DRINKS
You can't have your party at the Mos Eisley Cantina, but you can offer an out-of-this-world selection of drinks. Try the Yoda Soda (p. 319) or check *tasteofhome.com* for kiddie-friendly mocktails. And why not add some pizazz by labeling soda and other beverages with intergalactic names?

THE BEST CAKE
The cake is the crowning glory of every party, so make yours unforgettable! It's simple to use one of our best cake recipes from *tasteofhome.com* and then add a custom cake topper. Or make the BB-8 Cake on p. 317 to impress all the Jedi masters!

GOODY BAGS
When the guests return to their home planet, every space traveler will need treats for the road. To keep to the Star Wars theme, use colorful character bag covers and pack your bags with edible party favors that even Wookiees will love.

LIGHTSABER PRETZELS

Candy-coated pretzels take on an exciting Star Wars theme. These treats are wonderfully sweet and salty.
—*Taste of Home* Test Kitchen

PREP: 1 HOUR + STANDING
MAKES: 2½ DOZEN

- 8 oz. each blue, green and red candy coating disks
- 6 oz. each white and black candy coating disks
- 30 pretzel rods
  Blue, green and red colored sugar
- 30 M&M's minis

1. Place each color of candy melts into separate microwave-safe bowls. Working with 1 color at a time, heat in microwave, stirring every 30 seconds until smooth. Dip 10 pretzel rods in each blue, green and red melted candy coating, stopping 2 in. from end; allow excess to drip off. Immediately roll in matching colored sugar. Let stand on a parchment-lined pan until set. Reheat candy coating as needed.
2. Adding 1 tsp. at a time, stir melted black candy coating into the white until the desired shade of gray is achieved; reserve remaining melted black candy coating. Dip uncoated end of the pretzel rods into melted gray candy coating for handle; allow excess to drip off. Return to parchment-lined pan until set.
3. Place reserved melted black candy coating into a piping bag fitted with a small round tip; pipe 3 lines onto handle. For power buttons, secure M&M's minis to handles with melted black candy coating. Allow to set completely before serving. Store at room temperature in an airtight container between layers of waxed paper.
1 pretzel rod: 223 cal., 11g fat (9g sat. fat), 1mg chol., 244mg sod., 31g carb. (24g sugars, 0 fiber), 1g pro.

THE SKY'S THE LIMIT!

To Alderaan and beyond—make your decor fit your theme! White Christmas lights with paper planets and moons suspended from the ceiling create a sci-fi-worthy scene. Sachets filled with chocolate moon rocks make fantastic parting treats. Pair galaxy-themed serveware with a glowing letter board, and your space is set!

GALAXY BITES

These perky gelatin cubes are fun to serve, and to eat! I vary the colors to match the occasion—pink and blue for a baby shower, school colors for a graduation party, etc. Kids of all ages snap them up.
—Deanna Pietrowicz, Bridgeport, CT

PREP: 30 MIN. + CHILLING • **MAKES:** 9 DOZEN

- 4 pkg. (3 oz. each) assorted flavored gelatin
- 6 envelopes unflavored gelatin, divided
- 5¾ cups boiling water, divided
- 1 can (14 oz.) sweetened condensed milk
- ¼ cup cold water

1. In a small bowl, combine 1 package of flavored gelatin and 1 envelope of unflavored gelatin. Stir in 1 cup boiling water until dissolved. Pour into a 13x9-in. dish coated with cooking spray; refrigerate until set but not firm, about 20 minutes.
2. In small bowl, combine condensed milk and 1 cup boiling water. In another bowl, sprinkle 2 envelopes unflavored gelatin over cold water; let stand for 1 minute. Stir in ¾ cup boiling water. Add to milk mixture. Spoon 1 cup creamy gelatin mixture over the first flavored gelatin layer. Refrigerate until set but not firm, about 25 minutes.
3. Repeat from beginning of recipe twice, alternating flavored gelatin with creamy gelatin layers. Chill each layer until set but not firm before spooning next layer on top. Make final flavored gelatin layer; spoon on top. Refrigerate at least 1 hour after completing the last layer before cutting into 1-in. squares.
1 piece: 25 cal., 0 fat (0 sat. fat), 1mg chol., 13mg sod., 5g carb. (5g sugars, 0 fiber), 1g pro.

DEATH STAR CARAMEL TRUFFLES

Caramel truffles morph into Death Star candies for an adventurous sweet treat.
—*Taste of Home* Test Kitchen

PREP: 1 HOUR + CHILLING
MAKES: 2½ DOZEN

- 26 caramels
- 1 cup milk chocolate chips
- ¼ cup heavy whipping cream
- 2 cups white candy coating disks
- ½ cup black candy coating disks
- 30 lollipop sticks

1. Line an 8-in. square dish with plastic wrap; set aside. In a microwave-safe bowl, combine the caramels, milk chocolate chips and cream. Microwave, uncovered, on high for 1 minute; stir. Microwave 1 minute longer, stirring every 15 seconds or until caramels are melted and the mixture is smooth. Spread into prepared dish; refrigerate for 1 hour or until firm.
2. Using the plastic wrap, lift the candy out of the pan. Cut into 30 pieces; roll each piece into a 1-in. ball. Cover and refrigerate until firm, about 1 hour. Insert lollipop sticks into truffles. Press the end of a small wooden spoon into the upper portion of each truffle to create an indentation. Return to refrigerator until firm.
3. In separate microwave-safe bowls, melt the black and white candy disks; stir every 30 seconds until smooth. Tint white candy with black candy, adding 1 tsp. at a time until desired color of gray is achieved; reserve remaining melted black candy. Dip caramels in gray candy, allowing excess to drip off; let stand until set.
4. Tint remaining gray candy slightly darker with the reserved black candy. Place in piping bag fitted with small #1 round tip; pipe onto truffles to resemble Death Star. Refrigerate until firm.

1 truffle: 158 cal., 8g fat (6g sat. fat), 5mg chol., 45mg sod., 21g carb. (20g sugars, 0 fiber), 1g pro.

PRINCESS LEIA CHOCOLATE CINNAMON ROLLS

These are different from regular cinnamon rolls. When I take them to my morning bowling league, they are quickly devoured!
—*Myrna Sippel, Thompson, IL*

PREP: 30 MIN. + RISING • **BAKE:** 25 MIN.
MAKES: 20 ROLLS

- 2 pkg. (¼ oz. each) active dry yeast
- 1½ cups warm water (110° to 115°), divided
- ½ cup butter, softened
- ½ cup sugar
- 1 tsp. salt
- 4½ to 4¾ cups all-purpose flour
- ⅔ cup baking cocoa

FILLING
- 2 Tbsp. butter, melted
- ⅓ cup sugar
- ½ tsp. ground cinnamon
- 1 cup miniature semisweet chocolate chips
- ⅔ cup finely chopped nuts, optional

ICING
- 2 cups confectioners' sugar
- ½ tsp. vanilla extract
- 2 to 3 Tbsp. 2% milk
  Additional miniature semisweet chocolate chips, optional

1. In a large bowl, dissolve yeast in ½ cup warm water. Add the butter, sugar, salt and remaining water. Stir in 2½ cups flour and the cocoa. Beat on medium speed for 3 minutes or until smooth. Stir in enough remaining flour to form a soft dough.
2. Turn dough onto a lightly floured surface; knead until smooth and elastic, 6-8 minutes. Place in a greased bowl, turning once to grease top. Cover and let rise in a warm place until doubled, about 1 hour.
3. Turn onto a lightly floured surface; divide in half. Roll each portion into a 12x10-in. rectangle; brush with melted butter. Combine the sugar, cinnamon, chocolate chips and, if desired, nuts; sprinkle over the dough to within ½ in. of edges.
4. Roll up each jelly-roll style, starting with a long side; pinch seams to seal. Cut each into 10 slices. Place cut side down in a greased 15x10x1-in. baking pan. Cover and let rise until doubled, about 45 minutes.
5. Bake at 375° for 25-30 minutes or until lightly browned. Meanwhile, in a small bowl, combine the confectioners' sugar, vanilla and enough milk to reach desired consistency. Spread over the rolls while slightly warm; sprinkle with additional chocolate chips if desired.

1 roll: 284 cal., 9g fat (5g sat. fat), 15mg chol., 161mg sod., 49g carb. (25g sugars, 2g fiber), 4g pro.

HAN ROLOS

Kids can help make these easy candies. Top each Rolo with a whole pecan or walnut or another kind of candy.
—*Taste of Home* Test Kitchen

PREP: 20 MIN. • **BAKE:** 5 MIN. + STANDING
MAKES: 4½ DOZEN

- 54 pretzel snaps or miniature pretzels
- 54 Rolo candies (about 11 oz.)
- 54 white candy coating disks or peanut butter M&M's

1. Preheat oven to 250°. Place pretzels 1 in. apart on foil-lined baking sheets. Top each pretzel with a Rolo candy.
2. Bake until the Rolos are softened, 3-4 minutes. (Rolos will still retain their shape.) Immediately top each with a candy coating disk or M&M's candy, pressing to spread Rolo into pretzel. Let stand until set.
1 piece: 41 cal., 2g fat (1g sat. fat), 1mg chol., 37mg sod., 6g carb. (5g sugars, 0 fiber), 0 pro.

DARTH TATERS

Indulge in just one of these scrumptious bacon-wrapped goodies and you'll know why they're always a hit. They'll go fast, so you may want to double the recipe!
—Joni Hilton, Rocklin, CA

PREP: 30 MIN. • **BAKE:** 15 MIN.
MAKES: 32 APPETIZERS

- 16 bacon strips, halved lengthwise
- ½ cup maple syrup
- 1 tsp. crushed red pepper flakes
- 32 frozen Tater Tots, thawed

1. Preheat oven to 400°. Cook bacon in a large skillet over medium heat until partially cooked but not crisp. Remove to paper towels to drain; keep warm.
2. Combine syrup and pepper flakes. Dip each bacon piece in syrup mixture, then wrap around a Tater Tot. Secure with toothpicks.
3. Place on a greased rack in a foil-lined 15x10x1-in. baking pan. Bake until bacon is crisp, 12-15 minutes.
1 appetizer: 52 cal., 3g fat (1g sat. fat), 4mg chol., 123mg sod., 6g carb. (3g sugars, 0 fiber), 2g pro.

BB-8 CAKE

This 3D droid cake is easy to assemble and decorate. A cake mix gives you a jump-start so you can spend more time arranging the decorations.
—*Taste of Home* Test Kitchen

PREP: 40 MIN. • **BAKE:** 1 HOUR + COOLING
MAKES: 40 SERVINGS

- 2 pkg. (16 oz. each) pound cake mix
- 1 cup shortening
- 1 cup butter, softened
- 8 cups confectioners' sugar
- 2 tsp. vanilla extract
- 4 to 6 Tbsp. 2% milk
- 2 cups orange and 1 single brown Reese's Pieces
  Silver nonpareils
- 1 mini Oreo cookie
- 2 pretzel sticks

1. Preheat oven to 350°. Prepare cake mixes according to package directions. Pour the batter into 2 greased 1.5-qt. ovenproof bowls and 2 greased 10-oz. custard cups.
2. Bake until a toothpick inserted in center of each cake comes out clean; 40-45 minutes for the custard cups and 60-65 minutes for the bowls. Cool in pans for 5 minutes before removing to wire racks to cool completely.
3. For the frosting, beat shortening and butter in a bowl. Beat in confectioners' sugar, vanilla and enough milk to achieve spreading consistency.
4. Use a serrated knife to level the cakes. Place 1 large cake flat side up on an 8-in. serving plate. Frost the top of the cake. Place the remaining large cake on top with the flat side down and edges even. Frost top and sides.
5. For the head, place 1 custard-cup cake flat side up on a plate. Frost the top of the cake. Place the remaining custard-cup cake on top with flat side down and edges even. Frost the top and sides. Trim 1 side of the assembled head so it is flat, then place head above the body, using extra frosting to adhere.
6. To decorate the cake, use orange Reese's Pieces to create four 3-in. circles randomly placed on the body. Arrange silver nonpareils and additional Reese's Pieces in decorative patterns inside each circle. Use additional Reese's Pieces and nonpareils to form parallel lines at the top and bottom of the head. Place 1 mini Oreo and 1 brown Reese's Pieces candy outlined with nonpareils in between the parallel lines to make cameras. Insert pretzel sticks into the head for antenna, leaving 1 longer than the other.
1 piece: 318 cal., 13g fat (6g sat. fat), 22mg chol., 140mg sod., 49g carb. (39g sugars, 1g fiber), 2g pro.

WOOKIEE COOKIES

Who wouldn't want a Chewie cookie? These adorable cutouts will be a fan favorite at any Star Wars party.
—*Taste of Home* Test Kitchen

PREP: 45 MIN. + CHILLING
BAKE: 10 MIN./BATCH + COOLING
MAKES: ABOUT 1½ DOZEN

- ⅓ cup butter, softened
- ¾ cup packed dark brown sugar
- ½ cup molasses
- 1 large egg, room temperature
- 2 tsp. vanilla extract
- 3 cups all-purpose flour
- 3 tsp. ground ginger
- 1½ tsp. baking powder
- 1¼ tsp. ground cinnamon
- ¾ tsp. baking soda
- ¼ tsp. salt
- ¼ tsp. ground cloves
- 1 cup semisweet chocolate chips, melted
- 1 cup white baking chips, melted

1. In a large bowl, beat the butter and brown sugar until light and fluffy, 5-7 minutes. Beat in molasses, egg and vanilla. In another bowl, whisk the flour, ginger, baking powder, cinnamon, baking soda, salt and cloves; gradually beat into creamed mixture. Divide the dough in half. Shape each into a disk. Cover and refrigerate 1 hour or until easy to handle.

2. Preheat oven to 350°. On a lightly floured surface, roll each portion to ¼-in. thickness. Cut with a floured 3-in. gingerbread man cookie cutter.

3. Place 2 in. apart on greased baking sheets. Create lines in each cutout with tines of a fork to look like fur. Bake until edges are firm, 7-9 minutes. Remove from pans to wire racks to cool completely.

4. To decorate, pipe melted semisweet chocolate for eyes, nose and weapon belt, then pipe melted white chocolate for mouth and bullets. Let stand until icing is set.

1 cookie: 202 cal., 6g fat (4g sat. fat), 19mg chol., 154mg sod., 34g carb. (19g sugars, 1g fiber), 3g pro.

APPRENTICE POPCORN

Whenever I take this sweet mix somewhere, I bring copies of the recipe—people always ask for it. Once you start munching, it is hard to stop!
—Cheryl Bull, Blue Grass, IA

PREP: 15 MIN. + CHILLING
MAKES: ABOUT 6 QT.

- 14 cups popped popcorn
- 2 cups salted peanuts
- 2 cups crisp rice cereal
- 2 cups miniature marshmallows
- 1 lb. white candy coating, coarsely chopped
- 3 Tbsp. creamy peanut butter

1. In a large bowl, combine popcorn, peanuts, cereal and marshmallows. In a microwave-safe dish, melt candy coating and peanut butter; stir until smooth. Pour over popcorn mixture; toss to coat.

2. Spread mixture onto waxed paper-lined baking sheets; refrigerate for 15 minutes or until set. Break into pieces. Store in an airtight container in the refrigerator.

1 cup: 241 cal., 15g fat (6g sat. fat), 0 chol., 152mg sod., 24g carb. (16g sugars, 2g fiber), 4g pro.

STORMTROOPER TREATS

When my daughter was just 7 years old, she had the brilliant idea of adding Oreo cookies to cereal treats. Now an adult, she still asks for them on occasion; they're that good.
—Tammy Phoenix, Ava, IL

PREP: 10 MIN. • **COOK:** 10 MIN. + COOLING
MAKES: 2 DOZEN

- ¼ cup butter, cubed
- 8 cups miniature marshmallows
- 6 cups Rice Krispies
- 2½ cups double-stuffed Oreo cookies (about 16), chopped, divided
- 1⅓ cups white baking chips, melted

1. In a Dutch oven, melt the butter over medium heat. Add marshmallows; cook and stir until melted. Remove from heat. Stir in cereal and 2 cups Oreos. Press into a greased 13x9-in. baking pan.

2. Spread melted baking chips over the top; sprinkle with the remaining Oreos, pressing gently to adhere. Cool to room temperature. Cut into bars.

1 bar: 189 cal., 7g fat (4g sat. fat), 6mg chol., 123mg sod., 31g carb. (19g sugars, 0 fiber), 2g pro.

WRAPPING UP BABY

Guests will love this Yoda-green beverage—even more so when it's all dressed up and ready for the party in a decorative glass!

Wrap a linen napkin or cloth around the stem of a champagne or margarita glass (fold over at top as needed to fit the length of the glass). Use a toothpick to secure the cloth in back. Fill the glass with Yoda Soda. Thread 2 blueberries onto a wooden skewer to resemble eyes. Attach lime wedges on each end to resemble ears. Rest the skewer on top of the glass and serve.

YODA SODA

It takes only three ingredients to create this jazzed-up party punch. Instead of vanilla ice cream, try it with lime sherbet for a tropical twist.
—*Taste of Home* Test Kitchen

TAKES: 5 MIN. • **MAKES:** 36 SERVINGS

1 gallon green berry rush Hawaiian Punch, chilled
1 bottle (2 liters) lemon-lime soda, chilled
2 pints vanilla ice cream
Optional: Fresh blueberries and lime wedges

In a punch bowl, combine Hawaiian Punch and soda. Top with scoops of ice cream. If desired, garnish each serving glass with fresh blueberries and lime wedges.

¾ cup: 82 cal., 2g fat (1g sat. fat), 6mg chol., 64mg sod., 16g carb. (15g sugars, 0 fiber), 1g pro.

Holiday Celebrations

Football Party

When it comes to cheering for your favorite team on the day or night of the big game, a celebration is never quite the same without food that's equally deserving of your applause. From delectable dips and wonderfully tasty wings to perfect pinwheels and touchdown desserts, these recipes for game-day grub will make your team's winning moments even more memorable.

QUICK TORTILLA PINWHEELS

Prepare these easy, cheesy pinwheels several days in advance if desired. Serve with your choice of mild or hot salsa, or picante sauce.

—Barbara Keith, Faucett, MO

PREP: 15 MIN. + CHILLING
MAKES: ABOUT 5 DOZEN

- 1 cup sour cream
- 1 pkg. (8 oz.) cream cheese, softened
- ¾ cup sliced green onions
- ½ cup finely shredded cheddar cheese
- 1 Tbsp. lime juice
- 1 Tbsp. minced seeded jalapeno pepper
- 8 to 10 flour tortillas (8 in.), room temperature
  Salsa or picante sauce

Combine the first 6 ingredients in a bowl. Spread on 1 side of each tortilla and roll up tightly. Cover and refrigerate for at least 1 hour. Slice into 1-in. pieces. Serve with salsa or picante sauce.
1 pinwheel: 47 cal., 3g fat (2g sat. fat), 6mg chol., 51mg sod., 4g carb. (0 sugars, 0 fiber), 1g pro.

ORANGE CRANBERRY PUNCH

Skip sugary soft drinks and serve this tangy citrus-flavored punch instead. It has just the right amount of sweetness.

—Brook Hickle, Enumclaw, WA

PREP: 10 MIN. + CHILLING
MAKES: 24 SERVINGS (ABOUT 4½ QT.)

- 4 qt. cranberry juice
- 2 cups orange juice
- 2 medium oranges, sliced
- 2 medium lemons, sliced
- 2 medium limes, sliced

In a large container, combine juices and fruit; cover and refrigerate overnight. Serve in pitchers or a large punch bowl.
¾ cup: 93 cal., 0 fat (0 sat. fat), 0 chol., 4mg sod., 24g carb. (23g sugars, 0 fiber), 1g pro.

EASY TACO CUPS

These zesty little cups rank high on my list of favorites because they're fast, easy and delicious! They make a fantastic finger food for parties, and guests have fun selecting their desired toppings.

—Ashley Jarvies, Manassa, CO

PREP: 30 MIN. • **BAKE:** 15 MIN.
MAKES: 12 SERVINGS

- 1 lb. ground beef
- ½ cup chopped onion
- 1 envelope taco seasoning
- 1 can (16 oz.) refried beans
- 2 tubes (8 oz. each) refrigerated seamless crescent dough sheet
- 1½ cups shredded cheddar cheese
  Optional toppings: Chopped tomatoes, sliced ripe olives, shredded lettuce, sour cream, guacamole and salsa

1. Preheat oven to 375°. In a large skillet, cook the beef and onion over medium heat 6-8 minutes or until no longer pink, breaking the meat into crumbles; drain. Stir in taco seasoning and refried beans; heat through.
2. Unroll each tube of dough into a long rectangle. Cut each rectangle into 12 pieces; press lightly onto bottom and up sides of 24 ungreased muffin cups.
3. Fill each muffin cup with a rounded tablespoon of the beef mixture; sprinkle each with 1 Tbsp. cheese. Bake until dough is golden brown, 14-16 minutes. Cool taco cups in pans for 10 minutes before removing. Serve with toppings as desired.
2 taco cups: 291 cal., 15g fat (7g sat. fat), 37mg chol., 819mg sod., 25g carb. (4g sugars, 2g fiber), 15g pro.

MAPLE SAUSAGE SLIDERS WITH SLAW

These dynamite coleslaw-topped sliders are sure to score with hungry fans. Small in size but big in flavor, they're a welcome change from usual game-day fare.
—Lisa Huff, Wilton, CT

PREP: 25 MIN. • **COOK:** 10 MIN./BATCH
MAKES: 1½ DOZEN

- 2 cups coleslaw mix
- 1 cup shredded peeled apple
- 1 cup crumbled blue cheese
- ¼ cup finely chopped red onion
- 3 Tbsp. olive oil
- 2 Tbsp. cider vinegar
- 1½ tsp. maple syrup
- ½ tsp. Dijon mustard
- ⅛ tsp. salt
- ⅛ tsp. pepper

SLIDER
- 1 cup finely chopped walnuts, toasted
- ½ cup finely chopped red onion
- 2 Tbsp. minced fresh thyme or 2 tsp. dried thyme
- ½ tsp. salt
- ¼ tsp. pepper
- 2 lbs. bulk maple pork sausage
- 18 dinner rolls, split and lightly toasted

1. In a large bowl, combine coleslaw mix, apple, blue cheese and red onion. In a small bowl, whisk the oil, vinegar, maple syrup, mustard, salt and pepper. Pour over coleslaw mixture; toss to coat. Chill until serving.

2. In a large bowl, combine walnuts, onion, thyme, salt and pepper. Crumble sausage over mixture and mix well. Shape into 18 patties.

3. In a large skillet, cook the patties in batches over medium heat, 3-4 minutes on each side or until a thermometer reads 160°.

4. Top each bottom roll with a burger and 2 Tbsp. coleslaw mixture. Replace roll tops.

1 slider with 2 Tbsp. slaw: 331 cal., 22g fat (6g sat. fat), 50mg chol., 678mg sod., 23g carb. (4g sugars, 2g fiber), 12g pro.

BEER DIP

Shredded cheddar cheese stars in this fast-to-fix mixture that's made to go with pretzels. Once you start eating it, you won't be able to stop! The dip can be made with any type of beer, including nonalcoholic.
—Michelle Long, New Castle, CO

TAKES: 5 MIN. • **MAKES:** 3½ CUPS

- 2 pkg. (8 oz. each) cream cheese, softened
- ⅓ cup beer or nonalcoholic beer
- 1 envelope ranch salad dressing mix
- 2 cups shredded cheddar cheese Pretzels

In a large bowl, beat the cream cheese, beer and dressing mix until smooth. Stir in cheddar cheese. Serve with pretzels.

2 Tbsp.: 89 cal., 8g fat (5g sat. fat), 26mg chol., 177mg sod., 1g carb. (0 sugars, 0 fiber), 3g pro.

GAME-DAY BOURBON-GLAZED CARAMEL CORN

Here's a grown-up version of a favorite kid's treat. The bourbon and ginger combination that is so good in cocktails now has a home in a munchie that's perfect for snacking.
—Sally Sibthorpe, Shelby Township, MI

PREP: 20 MIN. • **BAKE:** 1 HOUR • **MAKES:** 5 QT.

- 6 qt. air-popped popcorn
- 3 cups mixed nuts (pecan halves, unblanched almonds, hazelnuts and unsalted cashews)
- 2 cups packed brown sugar
- 1 cup butter, cubed
- ½ cup dark corn syrup
- ½ cup bourbon
- 1 tsp. salt
- 1 tsp. ground ginger
- 1 tsp. vanilla extract
- ½ tsp. baking soda

1. Place the popcorn and nuts in a large bowl. In a large heavy saucepan, combine the brown sugar, butter, corn syrup, bourbon, salt and ginger. Bring mixture to a boil over medium heat, stirring occasionally; cook and stir for 6 minutes.

2. Remove from the heat; stir in vanilla and baking soda (mixture will foam). Quickly pour over popcorn and nuts; mix well.

3. Transfer to 2 greased 15x10x1-in. baking pans. Bake at 250° for 1 hour, stirring every 15 minutes. Remove to waxed paper to cool completely. Store in airtight containers.

1 cup: 514 cal., 38g fat (8g sat. fat), 24mg chol., 244mg sod., 43g carb. (30g sugars, 5g fiber), 7g pro.

SPINACH & TURKEY PINWHEELS

Here's an awesome snack for game day. My kids love these easy four-ingredient turkey pinwheels. Go ahead and make them the day before—they won't get soggy!
—Amy Van Hemert, Ottumwa, IA

TAKES: 15 MIN. • **MAKES:** 8 SERVINGS

- 1 carton (8 oz.) spreadable garden vegetable cream cheese
- 8 flour tortillas (8 in.)
- 4 cups fresh baby spinach
- 1 lb. sliced deli turkey

Spread cream cheese over tortillas. Layer with spinach and turkey. Roll up tightly; if not serving immediately, cover and refrigerate. To serve, cut rolls crosswise into 1-in. slices.
6 pinwheels: 307 cal., 13g fat (6g sat. fat), 52mg chol., 866mg sod., 31g carb. (1g sugars, 2g fiber), 17g pro.

MICHELADA

Like your drinks with a south-of-the-border vibe? Try this kicked-up beer cocktail that's a zesty mix of Mexican lager, lime juice and hot sauce. There are many variations, but this recipe is perfect for rookie mixologists.
—Ian Cliffe, Milwaukee, WI

TAKES: 5 MIN. • **MAKES:** 2 MICHELADAS

Coarse salt
Lime wedges
Ice cubes
- 6 dashes hot sauce, such as Valentina or Tabasco
- 3 dashes Maggi seasoning or soy sauce
- 1 to 3 dashes Worcestershire sauce
- ¼ to ⅓ cup lime juice
- 1 bottle (12 oz.) beer, such as Corona, Modelo or Tecate

Place coarse salt in a shallow dish; run a lime wedge around rims of 2 cocktail glasses. Dip rims of glasses into salt, shaking off excess. Fill each glass with ice. In a small pitcher, combine the hot sauce, Maggi seasoning, Worcestershire sauce and lime juice. Add the beer. Pour into glasses over ice. Garnish with lime wedges. Serve immediately.
1 drink: 165 cal., 0 fat (0 sat. fat), 0 chol., 137mg sod., 17g carb. (12g sugars, 0 fiber), 1g pro.

SPICY SWEET POTATO CHIPS & CILANTRO DIP

This irresistible combo could become your new signature snack food. Park the spicy baked chips next to a bowl of the cool, creamy dip and let the gang have at it. What a fabulous twist on traditional chips and dip!
—Elizabeth Godecke, Chicago, IL

PREP: 20 MIN. • **BAKE:** 25 MIN./BATCH
MAKES: 12 SERVINGS (1½ CUPS DIP)

- 2 to 3 large sweet potatoes (1¾ lbs.), peeled and cut into ⅛-in. slices
- 2 Tbsp. canola oil
- 1 tsp. chili powder
- ½ tsp. garlic powder
- ½ tsp. taco seasoning
- ¼ tsp. salt
- ¼ tsp. ground cumin
- ¼ tsp. pepper
- ⅛ tsp. cayenne pepper

DIP
- ¾ cup mayonnaise
- ½ cup sour cream
- 2 oz. cream cheese, softened
- 4½ tsp. minced fresh cilantro
- 1½ tsp. lemon juice
- ½ tsp. celery salt
- ⅛ tsp. pepper

1. Preheat oven to 400°. Place sweet potatoes in a large bowl. In a small bowl, mix oil and seasonings; drizzle over potatoes and toss to coat.
2. Arrange half the sweet potatoes in a single layer in 2 ungreased 15x10x1-in. baking pans. Bake until golden brown, 25-30 minutes, turning once. Repeat with remaining sweet potatoes.
3. In a small bowl, beat dip ingredients until blended. Serve with chips.

½ cup chips with about 1 Tbsp. dip: 285 cal., 16g fat (4g sat. fat), 8mg chol., 217mg sod., 33g carb. (14g sugars, 4g fiber), 3g pro.

NACHO WINGS

I love wings. I love nachos. Together, they're the perfect pairing! This recipe earned an award in a wings and ribs contest we held at our summer cottage.
—Lori Stefanishion, Drumheller, AB

PREP: 20 MIN. • **COOK:** 1 HOUR
MAKES: 2 DOZEN

- 24 chicken wing sections
- ½ cup butter, melted
- 1 pkg. (15½ oz.) nacho-flavored tortilla chips, crushed
- 2 cups shredded Mexican cheese blend or shredded cheddar cheese
- 1 can (4 oz.) chopped green chiles
- 1 cup chopped green onions
  Seeded jalapeno pepper slices, optional
  Optional toppings: Salsa, sour cream and guacamole

1. Preheat the oven to 350°. Dip wing sections in butter, then roll in crushed nacho chips. Bake wing sections in a greased 15x10x1-in. baking pan until juices run clear, 45-50 minutes. Remove from oven.
2. Top wings with cheese, chiles, green onions and, if desired, jalapeno slices. Bake until the cheese is melted, about 15 minutes. Serve wings with toppings as desired.

1 piece: 188 cal., 13g fat (5g sat. fat), 45mg chol., 317mg sod., 8g carb. (1g sugars, 1g fiber), 9g pro.

TEST KITCHEN TIP

Disjoint chicken wings to make your own wingettes. Place each chicken wing on a cutting board; with a sharp knife, cut through the joint at the top of the tip end. Take the remaining portion of the wing and cut through center of the joint. Proceed with recipe as directed. (Discard tips or use for making chicken broth.)

TOUCHDOWN COOKIES

With some simple touches, you can transform regular sugar cookies into a special sweet treat for football fans.
—Sister Judith LaBrozzi, Canton, OH

PREP: 25 MIN. + CHILLING
BAKE: 10 MIN./BATCH + COOLING
MAKES: 4½ DOZEN

- 1 cup butter, softened
- 1 cup sugar
- 2 large eggs, room temperature
- 1 tsp. vanilla extract
- 3 cups all-purpose flour
- 2 tsp. cream of tartar
- 1 tsp. baking soda

GLAZE
- 4 cups confectioners' sugar
- 8 to 10 Tbsp. hot water
  Black paste food coloring
- 6 to 8 tsp. baking cocoa

1. In a large bowl, cream the butter and sugar until light and fluffy, 5-7 minutes. Add eggs, 1 at a time, beating well after each addition. Beat in vanilla. Combine the flour, cream of tartar and baking soda; gradually add to creamed mixture and mix well. Cover and refrigerate for 3 hours or until easy to handle.

2. On a lightly floured surface, roll out dough to ⅛-in. thickness. Cut with a football-shaped cookie cutter and a small person-shaped (gingerbread) cookie cutter. Place cutouts 2 in. apart on ungreased baking sheets.

3. Bake at 350° for 8-10 minutes or until lightly browned. Remove to wire racks to cool.

4. In a large mixing bowl, combine the confectioners' sugar and enough hot water to achieve spreading consistency; beat until smooth. Divide the glaze into thirds. Leave a third white; set aside. Stir black food coloring into another third; set aside. Add cocoa to the last third; stir until smooth. Spread brown glaze over football cookies. Pipe white glaze for the football laces. Spread or pipe white glaze over people shapes to make shirts. Pipe black stripes over the white shirts for referee stripes.

1 cookie: 108 cal., 4g fat (2g sat. fat), 16mg chol., 53mg sod., 18g carb. (12g sugars, 0 fiber), 1g pro.

GRIDIRON CAKE

Celebrate any big game with this easy-to-make cake with cream cheese frosting.
—Sarah Farmer, Waukesha, WI

PREP: 45 MIN. • **BAKE:** 25 MIN. + COOLING
MAKES: 20 SERVINGS

CAKE
- ⅔ cup butter, softened
- 1¾ cups sugar
- 1 Tbsp. vanilla extract
- 2 large eggs, room temperature
- 2½ cups all-purpose flour
- 2½ tsp. baking powder
- ½ tsp. salt
- 1¼ cups 2% milk

FROSTING
- 1 pkg. (8 oz.) cream cheese, softened
- ½ cup butter, softened
- 3¾ cups confectioners' sugar
- 1 Tbsp. 2% milk
- 1 tsp. vanilla extract
  Green paste food coloring

DECORATION
- 2 goals posts (made from yellow bendable straws)
  Large gumdrops

1. Preheat oven to 350°. Grease a half sheet foil cake pan (17x12x1 in.).

2. In a bowl, cream butter and sugar until light and fluffy, 5-7 minutes. Add vanilla and eggs, 1 at at time, beating well after each addition. In another bowl, whisk flour, baking powder and salt; beat into creamed mixture alternately with the milk. Transfer to prepared pan.

3. Bake until a toothpick inserted in the center comes out clean, 25-30 minutes. Place on a wire rack; cool completely.

4. For frosting, beat cream cheese and butter. Add the confectioners' sugar, milk and vanilla. Reserve ¼ cup of frosting for field markings. Tint the remaining frosting green; spread over top of cake. Pipe white yard lines and numbers accordingly. Decorate field with goal posts and gumdrops for football players.

1 piece: 365 cal., 16g fat (9g sat. fat), 60mg chol., 255mg sod., 54g carb. (41g sugars, 0 fiber), 4g pro.

TEST KITCHEN TIP

This cream cheese frosting can be made ahead and refrigerated so you always have some on hand for desserts or a last-minute treat. Just bring it to room temperature and beat it again to fluff it before using.

BUILD A SNACK STADIUM

When it comes to sports and snacks, go big or go home! This stadium is easy to assemble and sure to get people talking. Just fill disposable aluminum pans and trimmed cardboard soda-can boxes wrapped in paper with tasty eats and treats. Here are a few suggestions for a memorable spread.

THE FIELD: A GAME-DAY CAKE
Recipe: Gridiron Cake (p. 330)
Just as in the real game, all eyes are on the field. To make this snack stadium pop, you need a centerpiece. Though we've seen snack stadiums with fields made of guacamole or green serving trays, we love this showstopping cake.

The bright green frosting and clean yard lines—not to mention the gumdrop players (in the colors of your favorite teams!)—truly make this cake look like the real deal. Pop on a few yellow bendy straws as goal posts and you're ready for kickoff. If you don't have time to create an entire snack stadium, this sheet cake is impressive on its own.

THE END ZONES: PARTY-STARTING SPIRALS
Recipes: Quick Tortilla Pinwheels (p. 324) and Spinach & Turkey Pinwheels (p. 327)
The snack stadium deserves its fair share of savory treats, too. We loaded the end zones full of spiraled tortilla roll-ups in two flavors. These pack all the flavors of favorite sandwiches but are easier to make for a crowd.

THE SKYBOXES: DIPS AND DESSERTS
Recipes: Beer Dip (p. 326) and Touchdown Cookies (p. 330)
If you ask us, it's not a party without a few good dips. Fill the skyboxes full of Beer Dip and a favorite salsa. There's no need to take sides on which one is yummier. Just don't dribble on the cake—that's the wrong sport!

For those craving more sugar than a cake can offer, fill a few boxes with candies or decorated football and

referee cookies. If your guests can't manage to finish all these snacky confections, the boxes make adorable to-go gifts. Wrap them up at the end of the game and send your pals home with something sweet.

THE STANDS: STORE-BOUGHT MUNCHIES
To complement those delicious dips, you'll need lots of nibbles. We're in favor of filling the stands with snack-aisle favorites like pretzels, crackers, popcorn and chips.

Pro tip: Don't go it alone! Draft friends and family to bring their favorite noshes to help fill the stadium.

THE TOWERS: HEALTHY OPTIONS
This snack stadium isn't all about indulgence (though, we do admit, much of it is!). On the exterior towers, we filled disposable dishes with a store-bought creamy veggie dill dip and packed cups full of crunchy veggie sticks.

In the end, this snack stadium is such a fun and festive way to celebrate any big game, such as the Super Bowl, the Rose Bowl or even homecoming. Filled with loads of treats and sweets, the stadium is a one-stop destination for game-day snackers.

CHALKBOARD
TABLE RUNNER

Keep a play-by-play account of your game-day buffet with this creative runner. Use it to label foods or simply sketch out a few moves for the defense. However you use it, this is one table topper you'll turn to time and again!

MATERIALS
☐ 72x18-in. chalkboard table runner or chalk fabric

☐ Chalk

☐ Scissors or rotary cutter

STEP 1:
Roll out chalk fabric on a work surface. Using scissors or rotary cutter, trim to desired size.

STEP 2:
Lay runner on serving or buffet table. Use chalk to label recipes or sketch as desired.

FOOTBALL CAKE POPS

My son loves football! For his eighth birthday, I made cake pops with a rich chocolate cake center and a yummy peanut butter coating. These are sure to be winners at parties, bake sales, tailgates and other sports-watching events.
—Jenny Dubinsky, Inwood, WV

PREP: 2 HOURS + CHILLING
BAKE: 35 MIN. + COOLING
MAKES: 4 DOZEN CAKE POPS

 1   chocolate cake mix (regular size)
 1   cup cream cheese frosting
 1   cup dark chocolate chips
 1   cup peanut butter chips
 1   Tbsp. shortening
 48 4-in. lollipop sticks
 ¼   cup white decorating icing

1. Bake cake according to the package directions; cool completely. In a large bowl, break cake into fine crumbles. Add the frosting and stir until fully incorporated, adding more frosting if needed, until mixture maintains its shape when squeezed together with palm of hand. Shape 1 Tbsp. into a ball, then mold into shape of a football. Repeat with remaining mixture. Place on parchment-lined baking sheets; refrigerate until firm, about 30 minutes.
2. Meanwhile, place chocolate chips, peanut butter chips and shortening in a microwave-safe bowl. Microwave 30 seconds and stir; repeat, stirring every 30 seconds until melted and smooth, adding more shortening if needed. Do not overheat.
3. Dip a lollipop stick into chocolate mixture; insert halfway through a football shape, taking care not to break through the other side. Return to baking sheet until set; repeat to form remaining cake pops. Coat each cake pop with the chocolate mixture, allowing excess to drip off; reheat and stir chocolate mixture as needed. Return cake pops to baking sheets, ensuring they do not touch one another. Allow chocolate coating to set until firm to the touch. To decorate, use icing to draw laces onto cake pops.

1 cake pop: 132 cal., 7g fat (3g sat. fat), 12mg chol., 96mg sod., 17g carb. (12g sugars, 1g fiber), 2g pro.

SPICY ALMONDS

These scrumptious spiced nuts make a nutritious snack for camping and hiking trips, and they are a must for nervous munching when your team is battling on the gridiron.
—Gina Myers, Spokane, WA

PREP: 10 MIN. • **BAKE:** 30 MIN. + COOLING
MAKES: 2½ CUPS

 1   Tbsp. sugar
 1½   tsp. kosher salt
 1   tsp. paprika
 ½   tsp. ground cinnamon
 ½   tsp. ground cumin
 ½   tsp. ground coriander
 ¼   tsp. cayenne pepper
 1   large egg white,
      room temperature
 2½   cups unblanched almonds

Preheat oven to 325°. In a small bowl, combine the first 7 ingredients. In another small bowl, whisk egg white until foamy. Add almonds; toss to coat. Sprinkle with the spice mixture; toss to coat. Spread almonds in a single layer in a greased 15x10x1-in. baking pan. Bake for 30 minutes, stirring every 10 minutes. Spread on waxed paper to cool completely. Store almonds in an airtight container.

¼ cup: 230 cal., 20g fat (2g sat. fat), 0 chol., 293mg sod., 9g carb. (3g sugars, 4g fiber), 8g pro.

Elf on the Shelf Party

Whether welcoming the elf's arrival or sending him on his merry way, this fun Christmas tradition is the perfect opportunity to host a holiday party for kids. Have fun whipping up some easy, sweet surprises to make this rosy-cheeked Christmas icon the life of your party— and your dessert tray!

CHEESY PEPPERONI BUNS

A pizza version of the sloppy joe, this hot and melty open-faced sandwich is a surefire kid pleaser. Adults love them, too!

—Tanya Belt, Newcomerstown, OH

TAKES: 25 MIN. • **MAKES:** 12 SERVINGS

- 1   lb. lean ground beef (90% lean)
- 2   cups pizza sauce or pasta sauce
- 1   pkg. (3½ oz.) sliced pepperoni, chopped
- 4   slices American cheese, chopped
- 12 mini buns, split
- 2   cups shredded part-skim mozzarella cheese

1. Preheat oven to 350°. In a large skillet, cook the beef over medium heat until no longer pink, 5-7 minutes, breaking into crumbles; drain. Stir in pizza sauce, pepperoni and American cheese. Cook and stir until cheese is melted, 4-5 minutes.

2. Place the buns on a baking sheet, cut sides up. Spoon the meat mixture onto buns; top with mozzarella cheese. Bake until cheese is melted, about 5 minutes. If desired, serve with additional warmed pizza sauce.

2 open-faced sandwiches: 280 cal., 14g fat (6g sat. fat), 46mg chol., 612mg sod., 18g carb. (4g sugars, 1g fiber), 18g pro.

PB&J CHEX MIX

As a kid, I loved to add crunchy textures, like chips or popcorn, to my PB&J sandwiches. This mix has all the necessary components of that childhood favorite: sweet jelly, rich peanut butter, a little saltiness from peanuts and, finally, that irresistible crunch from the Chex mix.

—Shelley Ward, Isle of Palms, SC

PREP: 10 MIN.
COOK: 5 MIN./BATCH + COOLING
MAKES: 5 CUPS

- 5   cups Rice Chex
- ¼   cup strawberry jelly
- 2   Tbsp. butter
- 1   Tbsp. light corn syrup
- ½   cup peanut butter chips
- ⅓   cup salted peanuts
     Freeze-dried strawberries, optional

1. Place cereal in a large bowl. In a small bowl, combine jelly, butter and corn syrup. Microwave until smooth; pour over cereal. Toss to coat.

2. Microwave in batches on high for 4 minutes, stirring once every minute. Spread onto a parchment-lined baking sheet to cool. Stir in chips, peanuts and, if desired, strawberries. Store in an airtight container.

¾ cup: 284 cal., 13g fat (5g sat. fat), 10mg chol., 275mg sod., 38g carb. (18g sugars, 2g fiber), 6g pro.

ABC SWEET SALAD TOSS UP

Getting kids to eat their veggies, fruit and protein is as easy as ABC—that's apples, bananas and cheese. This slightly sweet salad appeals to kids' taste buds while still delivering lots of healthy benefits.

—Christine Maddux, Council Bluffs, IA

TAKES: 25 MIN. • **MAKES:** 16 SERVINGS

- 1   pkg. (12 oz.) broccoli coleslaw mix
- 1   pkg. (8 oz.) ready-to-serve salad greens
- ½   cup mayonnaise
- 1   Tbsp. sugar
- 2   tsp. olive oil
- 8   oz. Colby-Monterey Jack cheese, cut into ½-in. cubes
- 1   medium apple, chopped
- 1   cup seedless red grapes, halved
- ¼   cup raisins
- 1   medium banana, sliced

In a large bowl, combine coleslaw mix and salad greens. Whisk together the mayonnaise, sugar and oil; stir in cheese, apple, grapes and raisins. Pour over salad; toss to coat. Top with banana slices.

1 cup: 143 cal., 10g fat (4g sat. fat), 14mg chol., 135mg sod., 10g carb. (6g sugars, 1g fiber), 4g pro.

READER REVIEW

"Loved the crunch and the combination of sweet flavors. Came together quickly, and chilled it in the fridge before serving. Will make this often!"

—WENDY, TASTEOFHOME.COM

WHAT IS ELF ON THE SHELF?

Carol V. Aebersold and her daughter Chanda A. Bell published *The Elf on the Shelf: A Christmas Tradition* in 2005, sharing their family's experience with a holiday visitor from the North Pole. The idea quickly caught the imaginations of families everywhere as they welcomed their own elves into their homes.

As the story goes, scout elves are sent out from the North Pole to keep an eye on children to make sure they're being nice—or to see if they're being naughty! Some elves arrive on December 1, while others arrive when the Christmas tree goes up, signaling that the house is ready to welcome the elf. Each day, the elf sits motionless, watching. Every night, he disappears on a journey back to the North Pole to report to Santa. In the morning he returns to a different spot, leading to lots of fun as kids find the elf in his new hiding place.

Children can choose a name for their elf and leave out treats and small presents, but they should never touch the elf—it'll drain the little magical creature's energy, preventing him from making the trip back up north. If a child gives in to temptation, all can be put right with a sprinkling of cinnamon beside the elf before bedtime.

An elf-themed party to welcome the visitor or to bid farewell is a delightful way to celebrate the season!

CHICKEN PARMESAN PIZZA

This tasty pizza is the perfect combo—quick and simple to make, and a winner with even picky eaters. It's a handy option for a family dinner on a busy night or for the center of the table at a kids party.
—Karen Wittmeier, Parkland, FL

PREP: 25 MIN. • **BAKE:** 15 MIN.
MAKES: 6 SLICES

- 8   frozen breaded chicken tenders
- 1   loaf (1 lb.) frozen pizza dough, thawed
- ½   cup marinara sauce
- ¼   tsp. garlic powder
- 2   cups (8 oz.) shredded part-skim mozzarella cheese
- ¼   cup shredded Parmesan cheese
- 2   Tbsp. thinly sliced fresh basil
      Additional warmed marinara sauce

1. Bake the chicken tenders according to package directions. Remove from oven; increase oven setting to 450°.
2. Meanwhile, grease a 12-in. pizza pan. Roll the dough to fit pan. In a small bowl, mix marinara sauce and garlic powder; spread over dough.
3. Cut the chicken into 1-in. pieces. Top pizza with the chicken and mozzarella cheese. Bake on a lower oven rack until the crust is golden brown and cheese is melted, 12-15 minutes. Sprinkle with the Parmesan cheese and basil. Serve with additional marinara.
1 slice: 440 cal., 17g fat (6g sat. fat), 35mg chol., 774mg sod., 48g carb. (4g sugars, 3g fiber), 23g pro.

ELF PARTY PUNCH

I loved the punch some friends served at their wedding—but they wouldn't give out the recipe! I spent many Saturdays figuring out just the right combination to make a beverage that tastes just like it.
—Annette Lee, Lepanto, AR

PREP: 10 MIN. + CHILLING
MAKES: 20 SERVINGS

- 8   cups (64 oz.) lemonade
- 1   can (46 oz.) unsweetened pineapple juice
- ¾   cup water or coconut water
- ½   cup sugar
- 2   Tbsp. coconut extract

In a large pitcher or punch bowl, combine all ingredients. Refrigerate until serving. Garnish as desired.
¾ cup: 109 cal., 0 fat (0 sat. fat), 0 chol., 8mg sod., 26g carb. (23g sugars, 0 fiber), 0 pro.

MAKE YOUR OWN ELF COOKIES

Use your favorite sugar cookie recipe to make these adorable elves. Enjoy them as cookies or set them atop cupcakes for a fun topper (see photo on opposite page). The decorating tools and ingredients can be found in craft stores or online.

STEP 1: To decorate the cookies, use royal icing in a pastry bag with a fine tip. First, outline the elf's collar and hat brim. (Setting the outline first helps keep the colors from running together.) Then "color in" the open space. For the open spaces, add water to the icing to reach a flooding consistency.

STEP 2: Switch to bright red icing, and outline the elf's tunic and hat. Once the outline is done, fill in the open space with solid red.

STEP 3: Make the elf's face next—again, outline first and then fill in the area with a solid color. Adjust the proportions of food coloring to make the face the exact shade you want.

STEP 4: Using a clean tweezers, set round sprinkles precisely in place as eyes. Then let the cookies sit overnight to allow the icing to set and harden completely.

STEP 5: Using a cotton swab dipped in edible pink luster dust, add a spot of rosy color to each of the elf's cheeks.

STEP 6: Switch the tip on the pastry bag to a leaf-shaped tip. Using icing in the same shade as the face, pipe the ears. Use the small round tip to add a single dot of icing for the nose.

STEP 7: Using an edible color marker, draw a mouth. Or use an ultra-fine tip on your pastry bag to pipe the mouth with royal icing.

STEP 8: Using a star-shaped tip on the pastry bag, add the elf's hair. We used store-bought chocolate frosting, but you can tint more royal icing to create whatever hair color you'd like!

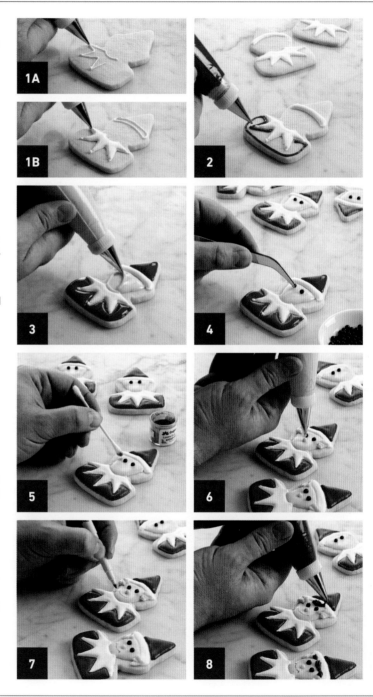

KID-MADE COCOA CUPCAKES

I'm only a kid, and this is the first recipe I've created. I spent a year perfecting these cupcakes, asking advice from owners of local bakeries and my baker friends. I make them for every special occasion in my family and sometimes just for fun. If you want the cupcakes to taste more like hot cocoa, double the amount of hot cocoa mix. This recipe works well with multiple frosting flavors: mint, maple syrup, vanilla, marshmallow and buttercream. Decorate them any way you want!
—Maia Hubscher, South Orange, NJ

PREP: 20 MIN. • **BAKE:** 25 MIN. + COOLING
MAKES: 2 DOZEN

- 2 cups all-purpose flour
- 1½ cups sugar
- 2 Tbsp. baking cocoa
- 2 Tbsp. instant hot cocoa mix
- ¼ tsp. baking soda
- 3 large eggs, room temperature
- ⅔ cup whole milk
- ⅓ cup water
- ½ tsp. vanilla extract
- ½ cup butter, softened
- 1 milk chocolate baking bar (4 oz.), melted
  Whipped topping, thawed, optional

1. Preheat oven to 375°. Line 24 muffin cups with paper liners.
2. Combine the first 5 ingredients. In another bowl, mix eggs, milk, water and vanilla. Add egg mixture to dry ingredients, beating on medium until smooth. Beat in butter; add melted chocolate and beat just until blended.
3. Fill the prepared muffin cups half full. Bake until a toothpick inserted in center comes out clean, 25-30 minutes. Cool in pans 10 minutes before removing to wire racks to cool completely. If desired, top with whipped topping. Decorate as desired.
1 cupcake: 162 cal., 6g fat (4g sat. fat), 36mg chol., 64mg sod., 25g carb. (16g sugars, 1g fiber), 3g pro.

MAC & CHEESE DINNER

Don't settle for ordinary mac and cheese. This version is my kids' favorite, so I always make a huge pot. It's an easy recipe to cut down or double (or triple!). It can also be made into a low-fat recipe if you use nonfat milk, reduced-fat cheeses and lean ham.
—Raymond James, Port Orchard, WA

TAKES: 25 MIN. • **MAKES:** 6 SERVINGS

- 2 cups uncooked elbow macaroni
- 4 medium carrots, thinly sliced
- 1 pkg. (10 oz.) frozen peas
- 1 cup cubed fully cooked ham
- ⅔ cup 2% milk
- ¼ cup cream cheese, softened
- 1 cup (4 oz.) shredded part-skim mozzarella cheese
- 2 Tbsp. grated Parmesan cheese
- 1 tsp. dried basil
- ⅛ tsp. salt
- ⅛ tsp. pepper

1. Cook macaroni in boiling water for 3 minutes. Add carrots and peas; return to a boil. Cook until macaroni is tender, 5-6 minutes longer. Drain; add ham.
2. In a 1-qt. microwave-safe dish, combine the milk and cream cheese. Cover and microwave at 50% power for 3 minutes; stir. Cook until cream cheese is melted, 2-3 minutes longer. Stir in mozzarella, Parmesan, basil, salt and pepper. Pour over the pasta and toss to coat.
1½ cups: 284 cal., 10g fat (5g sat. fat), 40mg chol., 609mg sod., 32g carb. (7g sugars, 4g fiber), 18g pro.

MAKE-AHEAD CREAMY FRUIT SALAD

We love fruit salads for our holiday dinners. I experimented and came up with this delicious medley—it reminds us of the tropics in the middle of winter! I sometimes add sliced bananas just before serving. Feel free to use your own favorite fruits.
—Joan Hallford, North Richland Hills, TX

PREP: 20 MIN. + CHILLING • **MAKES:** 6 CUPS

- ¾ cup pina colada yogurt
- ¾ cup Key lime yogurt
- ½ cup heavy whipping cream, whipped
- 1 Tbsp. Key lime juice
- 2 cups mandarin oranges, drained
- 1 can (15 oz.) peach halves in light syrup, drained and sliced
- 1 cup miniature marshmallows
- 1 cup unsweetened crushed pineapple, drained
- ½ cup sweetened shredded coconut
- ½ cup pitted dark sweet cherries, drained and halved
- ¼ cup chopped pecans, toasted

In a large bowl, combine the yogurts, whipped cream and lime juice. Gently fold in the remaining ingredients. Refrigerate, covered, until serving.
¾ cup: 250 cal., 11g fat (6g sat. fat), 19mg chol., 56mg sod., 38g carb. (35g sugars, 2g fiber), 4g pro.

CHRISTMAS ELF CAKE POPS

Happy elves that happen to taste like PB&J can easily be part of the party decor—until dessert, when they'll magically disappear!
—*Taste of Home* Test Kitchen

PREP: 1 HOUR • **BAKE:** 35 MIN. + FREEZING
MAKES: 4 DOZEN

- 1 pkg. yellow cake mix (regular size)
- ½ cup seedless strawberry jam
- 48 lollipop sticks
- 1 can (16 oz.) vanilla frosting
- ¼ cup creamy peanut butter
- 1½ cups canned chocolate fudge frosting
  Additional vanilla frosting, red paste food coloring, and dark chocolate and candy cane-flavored kisses

1. Prepare and bake cake according to the package directions using a greased 13x9-in. baking pan. Cool completely on a wire rack.
2. Crumble cake into a large bowl. Add the jam and mix well. Shape into 1½-in. balls. Place on baking sheets; insert sticks. Freeze for at least 2 hours or refrigerate for at least 3 hours, until cake balls are firm and easy to handle.
3. Insert cake pops into a plastic foam block to stand. In a microwave, warm vanilla frosting and peanut butter; stir until smooth. Spoon over cake pops.
4. Using fudge, additional vanilla and red frostings (tint desired amount of additional vanilla frosting red), pipe hair and faces; use leaf tip for ears. Top each with a chocolate or candy cane-flavored kiss hat. Let stand until set.

1 cake pop: 164 cal., 8g fat (2g sat. fat), 13mg chol., 125mg sod., 22g carb. (17g sugars, 0 fiber), 1g pro.

ITALIAN CHOCOLATE SPICE COOKIES

I recently found this old family recipe in my mom's kitchen. I made a few adjustments to streamline the process, and the end result was perfect.
—*Shawn Barto, Winter Garden, FL*

PREP: 30 MIN. • **BAKE:** 10 MIN. + COOLING
MAKES: 5 DOZEN

- ¾ cup shortening
- 1 cup sugar
- 4 large eggs, room temperature
- ½ cup 2% milk
- 1 tsp. vanilla extract
- 4 cups all-purpose flour
- ½ cup baking cocoa
- 2 tsp. ground cinnamon
- 2 tsp. baking soda
- 1 tsp. baking powder
- 1 tsp. ground cloves
- ½ cup chopped walnuts

GLAZE
- 2¼ cups confectioners' sugar
- 2 tsp. light corn syrup
- 3 to 4 Tbsp. 2% milk
  Sprinkles, optional

1. Preheat oven to 350°. In a large bowl, cream shortening and sugar until light and fluffy, 5-7 minutes. Beat in eggs, milk and vanilla. In another bowl, whisk the flour, cocoa, cinnamon, baking soda, baking powder and cloves; gradually beat into creamed mixture. Stir in nuts.
2. Shape level tablespoons of the dough into balls; place 1 in. apart on ungreased baking sheets. Bake 10-12 minutes or until bottoms are light brown. Remove from the pans to wire racks to cool completely.
3. For glaze, in a large bowl, mix confectioners' sugar, corn syrup and enough milk to reach desired consistency. Dip tops of cookies into the glaze; if desired, decorate with sprinkles. Let stand until set. Store between pieces of waxed paper in airtight containers.

1 cookie: 99 cal., 4g fat (1g sat. fat), 13mg chol., 57mg sod., 15g carb. (8g sugars, 0 fiber), 2g pro.

Gingerbread Decorating Party

Bring friends together for a little light construction—building and decorating all things gingerbread, from houses to cookies. Feed your creativity with these delicious snacks and gingerbread-flavored treats.

GINGERBREAD CARAMEL CRUNCH

If you love gingerbread, you won't be able to resist this crispy, crunchy popcorn. Munch it yourself or share it as a tasty gift!

—Lynne Weigle-Snow, Alexandria, VA

PREP: 25 MIN. • **BAKE:** 1 HOUR
MAKES: 3½ QT.

14	cups air-popped popcorn
¾	cup packed brown sugar
½	cup butter, cubed
¼	cup light corn syrup
¼	cup molasses
1½	tsp. ground ginger
½	tsp. ground cinnamon
¼	tsp. salt
½	tsp. baking soda
½	tsp. vanilla extract

1. Place the popcorn in a large bowl coated with cooking spray; set aside. Butter the sides of a small heavy saucepan; add the brown sugar, butter, corn syrup, molasses, ginger, cinnamon and salt. Bring to a boil over medium heat, stirring constantly. Boil without stirring for 5 minutes.
2. Remove from the heat; stir in baking soda (mixture will foam). Stir in vanilla. Quickly pour over popcorn and mix well.
3. Transfer to 2 greased 15x10x1-in. baking pans. Bake at 250° for 1 hour, stirring every 10 minutes. Remove from pans and place on waxed paper to cool. Store in an airtight container.
1 cup: 167 cal., 7g fat (4g sat. fat), 17mg chol., 144mg sod., 27g carb. (16g sugars, 1g fiber), 1g pro.

CRISP CARAWAY TWISTS

This appetizer is always a hit when I serve it on holidays or special occasions. The flaky cheese-filled twists (made with convenient puff pastry) bake to a crispy golden brown. When our big family gets together, I make two batches.

—Dorothy Smith, El Dorado, AR

TAKES: 30 MIN. • **MAKES:** ABOUT 1½ DOZEN

1	large egg
1	Tbsp. water
1	tsp. country-style Dijon mustard
¾	cup shredded Swiss cheese
¼	cup finely chopped onion
2	tsp. minced fresh parsley
1½	tsp. caraway seeds
¼	tsp. garlic salt
1	sheet frozen puff pastry, thawed

1. In a small bowl, beat egg, water and mustard; set aside. In another bowl, combine the cheese, onion, parsley, caraway seeds and garlic salt.
2. Unfold pastry sheet; brush with egg mixture. Sprinkle the cheese mixture lengthwise over half the pastry. Fold pastry over filling; press edges to seal. Brush top with remaining egg mixture. Cut widthwise into ½-in. strips; twist each strip several times.
3. Place 1 in. apart on greased baking sheets, pressing ends down. Bake at 375° for 15-20 minutes or until golden brown. Serve warm.
1 twist: 90 cal., 5g fat (2g sat. fat), 15mg chol., 91mg sod., 8g carb. (0 sugars, 1g fiber), 3g pro.

DID YOU KNOW?

Dijon, a town in eastern France's famous Burgundy wine-growing region, is the home of Dijon mustard. Mustard is commonly grown as a cover crop among grape vines. The plants attract beneficial insects and give nutrients back to the soil. Not to mention, the scores of tiny mustard seeds mean the crop replants itself year after year. Dijon mustard contains white wine instead of vinegar.

GINGERBREAD HOUSE COOKIES

Here is my favorite molasses cookie. I use the recipe not only to create little houses for Christmas but also to make bunnies for Easter and stars for the Fourth of July.
—Karen Haen, Sturgeon Bay, WI

PREP: 40 MIN. + CHILLING
BAKE: 10 MIN./BATCH + COOLING
MAKES: 4 DOZEN

- 1 cup shortening
- ½ cup sugar
- ½ cup packed brown sugar
- 2 large eggs, room temperature
- 1 cup molasses
- 1 to 1½ tsp. grated orange zest
- 5½ cups all-purpose flour
- 3 tsp. baking soda
- ¾ tsp. salt
- ¾ tsp. ground ginger
- ¾ tsp. ground cinnamon
- ½ tsp. ground nutmeg
- ½ cup water
  Optional: Royal Icing or frosting and food coloring of your choice

1. In a large bowl, cream shortening and sugars until light and fluffy, 5-7 minutes. Add eggs, 1 at a time, beating well after each addition. Beat in molasses and orange zest. Combine flour, baking soda, salt and spices; add to creamed mixture alternately with water, mixing well after each addition. Cover and refrigerate for 3 hours or until easy to handle.

2. On a lightly floured surface, roll out the dough to ¼-in. thickness. Cut with a 3½-in. gingerbread house cookie cutter dipped in flour. If desired, create windows using very small cutters of various shapes.

3. Place 1 in. apart on greased baking sheets. Bake at 350° for 8-10 minutes or until edges are firm. Cool 2 minutes before removing to wire racks. Use icing or frosting and food coloring to decorate cooled cookies as desired.

1 cookie: 127 cal., 4g fat (1g sat. fat), 9mg chol., 85mg sod., 20g carb. (9g sugars, 0 fiber), 2g pro.

Royal Icing: Beat 2 cups confectioners' sugar, 8 tsp. water, 4½ tsp. meringue powder and ¼ tsp. cream of tartar on low speed just until combined. Beat on high 5 minutes or until stiff peaks form. Tint with food coloring if desired.

GINGERBREAD TRUFFLES

I never received compliments on my baking until I brought my gingerbread truffles to a party. Every Christmas, family, friends and even co-workers ask me to make these.
—Angela Randjelovic, Independence, OH

PREP: 50 MIN. • **COOK:** 10 MIN. + CHILLING
MAKES: 3 DOZEN

- 14 oz. white baking chocolate, chopped
- ½ cup heavy whipping cream
- 1 tsp. ground cinnamon
- ½ tsp. ground ginger
- ¼ tsp. ground cloves
- 1 pkg. (10 oz.) dark chocolate chips
- 5 tsp. shortening
- 3 Tbsp. chopped crystallized ginger

1. Place the white chocolate in a small bowl. In a small saucepan, bring the whipping cream just to a boil. Pour over the white chocolate; whisk until smooth. Stir in the cinnamon, ginger and cloves. Cool to room temperature, stirring occasionally. Cover and refrigerate until firm, about 3 hours.

2. Shape mixture into ¾-in. balls. Place on waxed paper-lined baking sheets. Refrigerate for at least 1 hour.

3. In a microwave, melt chocolate chips and shortening; stir until smooth. Dip truffles in chocolate; allow excess to drip off. Place on waxed paper. Sprinkle with crystallized ginger. Store in an airtight container in the refrigerator.

1 truffle: 113 cal., 7g fat (5g sat. fat), 4mg chol., 12mg sod., 13g carb. (12g sugars, 1g fiber), 1g pro.

GINGERBREAD BUDDIES

A classic gingerbread man cookie cutter doesn't have to make cookie-cutter cookies! With a little imagination (and colored icing), you can make your cookies into almost anything—even a yeti!

CHOCOLATE GINGERBREAD TOFFEE CAKE WITH GINGER WHIPPED CREAM

This cake literally stands above the rest—it is exactly what you need for a special-occasion dessert. With notes of ginger coming though in both the frosting and cake, it is absolutely delicious and worth the extra steps involved.
—Marie Rizzio, Interlochen, MI

PREP: 45 MIN. + CHILLING
BAKE: 30 MIN. + COOLING
MAKES: 16 SERVINGS

- 2 cups heavy whipping cream
- 5 slices fresh gingerroot (⅛ in. thick)

CAKE
- 1½ cups dark chocolate chips
- ½ cup butter, softened
- 1½ cups packed brown sugar
- 3 large eggs, room temperature
- 2 tsp. vanilla extract
- 2¾ cups all-purpose flour
- 1 tsp. baking soda
- ¾ tsp. ground ginger
- ¾ tsp. ground cinnamon
- ½ tsp. salt
- ¼ tsp. ground allspice
- ¼ tsp. ground nutmeg
- 1 cup sour cream
- 1 cup hot water
- ½ cup molasses

GANACHE
- 1 pkg. (10 oz.) dark chocolate chips
- ¼ tsp. salt
- 1 can (14 oz.) sweetened condensed milk
- 2 Tbsp. butter
- 1 tsp. vanilla extract
- 2 Tbsp. heavy whipping cream

ASSEMBLY
- 6 Tbsp. confectioners' sugar
- 1 cup brickle toffee bits

1. In a small heavy saucepan, heat cream and ginger until bubbles form around sides of pan. Remove from the heat; let cool slightly. Cover and refrigerate for 8 hours or overnight.

2. Meanwhile, in a microwave, melt chocolate; stir until smooth. Set aside. In a large bowl, cream butter and brown sugar until blended. Add the eggs, 1 at a time, beating well after each addition. Beat in the melted chocolate and the vanilla. Combine the flour, baking soda, ginger, cinnamon, salt, allspice and nutmeg; add to the creamed mixture alternately with sour cream, beating well after each addition.

3. In a small bowl, combine the hot water and molasses; beat into batter. Transfer to 3 greased and floured 8-in. round baking pans.

4. Bake at 350° until a toothpick inserted in center comes out clean, 30-35 minutes. Cool for 10 minutes before removing from pans to wire racks to cool completely.

5. Meanwhile, for ganache, place the chocolate and salt in a double boiler or metal bowl over simmering water; cook and stir until melted, 2-3 minutes. Stir in condensed milk until smooth. Remove from the heat; stir in butter and vanilla until butter is melted.

6. Cool, stirring occasionally, to room temperature or until the ganache reaches a spreading consistency, about 45 minutes. Add cream; beat chocolate mixture until smooth, 2-3 minutes.

7. Strain ginger-cream mixture into a large bowl, discarding ginger slices. Beat until cream begins to thicken. Add confectioners' sugar; beat until stiff peaks form.

8. To assemble, place 1 cake layer on a serving plate; spread with half the ganache. Sprinkle with half the toffee bits. Repeat layers once. Top with the remaining cake layer; spread ginger whipped cream over top and sides of cake. Refrigerate at least 2 hours. Store leftovers in the refrigerator.

1 piece: 765 cal., 42g fat (25g sat. fat), 107mg chol., 409mg sod., 96g carb. (76g sugars, 3g fiber), 9g pro.

WARM SPICED NUTS

I like to set out bowls of spiced nuts when hosting holiday parties. Sometimes I stir in M&M's for a sweet and salty snack.
—Jill Matson, Zimmerman, MN

PREP: 5 MIN. • **BAKE:** 30 MIN.
MAKES: 3 CUPS

- 1 cup pecan halves
- 1 cup unblanched almonds
- 1 cup unsalted dry roasted peanuts
- 3 Tbsp. butter, melted
- 4½ tsp. Worcestershire sauce
- 1 tsp. chili powder
- ½ tsp. garlic salt
- ¼ tsp. cayenne pepper

1. In a large bowl, combine pecans, almonds and peanuts. Combine butter and Worcestershire sauce; pour over nuts and toss to coat.
2. Spread in a single layer in an ungreased 15x10x1-in. baking pan. Bake at 300° until browned, about 30 minutes, stirring occasionally.
3. Transfer warm nuts to a bowl. Combine chili powder, garlic salt and cayenne; sprinkle over nuts and stir to coat. Serve warm, or allow to cool before storing in an airtight container.
¼ cup: 231 cal., 22g fat (4g sat. fat), 8mg chol., 123mg sod., 7g carb. (2g sugars, 3g fiber), 6g pro.

SNAPPY COCKTAIL MEATBALLS

A German friend gave me this recipe more than 20 years ago. The meatballs are easy to prepare and can be made ahead of time.
—Nancy Means, Moline, IL

TAKES: 30 MIN. • **MAKES:** ABOUT 5 DOZEN

- 2 large eggs, lightly beaten
- 1¼ cups soft bread crumbs
- 1 tsp. salt
- ½ tsp. garlic salt
- ½ tsp. onion powder
- ½ tsp. pepper
- 2 lbs. lean ground beef (90% lean)

SAUCE
- 1 can (28 oz.) diced tomatoes, undrained
- ½ cup packed brown sugar
- ¼ cup vinegar
- ½ tsp. salt
- 1 tsp. grated onion
- 10 gingersnaps, finely crushed

1. In a large bowl, combine the first 6 ingredients. Crumble the beef over mixture and mix well. Shape into 1¼-in. balls. Place the meatballs on a greased rack in a shallow baking pan. Bake at 450° for 15 minutes. Drain meatballs on paper towels.
2. Meanwhile, for sauce, combine the tomatoes, brown sugar, vinegar, salt and onion in large saucepan. Bring to a boil. Stir in gingersnaps, continuing to boil until sauce is thick and clear. Reduce heat to a simmer; add the meatballs. Heat through.
1 meatball: 43 cal., 2g fat (1g sat. fat), 16mg chol., 118mg sod., 4g carb. (3g sugars, 0 fiber), 3g pro.

GINGERBREAD AMARETTI COOKIES

The classic Italian cookie gets a new gingerbread twist! Don't overbake— they should be slightly chewy.
—Tina Zaccardi, Eastchester, NY

PREP: 20 MIN. • **BAKE:** 10 MIN./BATCH
MAKES: 2 DOZEN

- 1 can (8 oz.) almond paste
- ¾ cup sugar
- 1 Tbsp. baking cocoa
- 1 tsp. ground ginger
- ½ tsp. ground cinnamon
  Dash ground cloves
- 2 large egg whites, room temperature
- 2 Tbsp. molasses
- 1 cup pearl or coarse sugar

1. Preheat oven to 375°. Crumble the almond paste into a food processor; add sugar, baking cocoa and spices. Pulse until combined. Add egg whites and molasses; process until smooth.
2. Drop by tablespoonfuls into pearl sugar; roll to coat. Place 2 in. apart on parchment-lined baking sheets. Bake until set, 10-12 minutes. Cool 1 minute before removing from pans to wire racks. Store in an airtight container.
1 cookie: 107 cal., 3g fat (0 sat. fat), 0 chol., 6mg sod., 21g carb. (19g sugars, 1g fiber), 1g pro.

BUILDING MEMORIES

Invite your favorite amateur architects over to design customized gingerbread cabins with creative candy decor.

THE BLUEPRINT FOR SWEET SUCCESS

Baking your own gingerbread base is the classic way to begin, but it can be time-consuming. Make it easier by starting with a kit, like the A-frame version we used here.

Let it snow! Blanket the surface around your gingerbread house with shredded coconut. Add a sweet snowman or two.

Search your pantry for building material inspiration. Grab a bag of pretzels or a box of cereal, or raid your secret candy stash. Get creative adding fun details to your edible edifice.

DETAILS, DETAILS

1. Edible chocolate rocks make your house feel lifelike. Use them to craft a facade, door frame or walking path.

2. Careful snipping turns sour gummy strips into bricks.

3. Use graham crackers to create custom additions, like a dormer, an entryway or a chimney.

4. Meringues make the perfect snowy peaks on rooftops.

5. Pretzels of various shapes frame the windows and doors, and cereal squares make fool-the-eye shingles.

6. Populate your town with cute snowman buddies made with skewered marshmallows. Decorate with tinted Royal Icing (recipe on p. 348).

MULLED GRAPE CIDER

I came up with this recipe one year when I attempted to make grape jelly and ended up with 30 jars of delicious grape syrup instead. I simmered the syrup with spices to make this pretty autumn drink.
—Sharon Harmon, Orange, MA

PREP: 20 MIN. • **COOK:** 3 HOURS
MAKES: 12 SERVINGS (3 QT.)

5	lbs. Concord grapes
8	cups water, divided
1½	cups sugar
8	whole cloves
4	cinnamon sticks (4 in. each)
	Dash ground nutmeg

1. In a large saucepan, combine the grapes and 2 cups water; bring to a boil, stirring constantly. Press through a strainer; reserve juice and discard skins and seeds.
2. Pour juice through a double layer of cheesecloth into a 5-qt. slow cooker. Add the sugar, cloves, cinnamon sticks, nutmeg and remaining water. Cover and cook on low for 3 hours. Discard cloves and cinnamon sticks.
1 cup: 231 cal., 1g fat (0 sat. fat), 0 chol., 4mg sod., 59g carb. (56g sugars, 0 fiber), 1g pro.

GARLIC-PARMESAN CHEESE BALL

This is one of our entertaining mainstays. It complements most meals and is so easy to prepare and dress up with a variety of garnishes.
—Susan Seymour, Valatie, NY

PREP: 10 MIN. + CHILLING
MAKES: ABOUT 2 CUPS

11	oz. cream cheese, softened
⅓	cup grated Parmesan cheese
¼	cup mayonnaise
½	tsp. dried oregano
¼	tsp. garlic powder or ½ to 1 tsp. minced garlic
¾	cup chopped walnuts, optional Assorted fresh vegetables and/or crackers

In a large bowl, combine the first 5 ingredients. Shape into a ball. Roll in walnuts if desired. Wrap tightly; chill 2 hours. Serve with vegetables and/or crackers.
2 Tbsp.: 98 cal., 10g fat (5g sat. fat), 21mg chol., 109mg sod., 1g carb. (1g sugars, 0 fiber), 2g pro.

Ugly Sweater Party

The ugly Christmas sweater would be nothing more than a piece of bad fashion without the ugly Christmas-sweater party! Join the holiday craze by hosting an epic event that's nothing short of big, bold and tacky. This delectable assortment of appetizers and drinks will round out the hideously fun and festive merrymaking.

CRANBERRY PARTY PUNCH

Cranberry-filled ice cubes float atop this refreshing five-ingredient fruit punch. It is easy to stir up and serve right away.
—*Taste of Home* Test Kitchen

PREP: 20 MIN. + FREEZING
MAKES: 20 SERVINGS

     Fresh or frozen cranberries
     Crushed ice
  4 cups chilled cranberry juice
  4 cups chilled pineapple juice
1½ cups sugar
  1 Tbsp. almond extract
  2 liters ginger ale, chilled

1. Line bottom of snowflake or other shaped molds with cranberries; top with crushed ice. Fill molds carefully with cold water; freeze until solid, about 2 hours.
2. To serve, combine juices, sugar and extract in a punch bowl; stir until sugar is dissolved. Stir in ginger ale. Invert ice molds onto a large plate; cover with a hot damp cloth to release. Transfer to punch. Serve immediately.
¾ cup: 145 cal., 0 fat (0 sat. fat), 0 chol., 9mg sod., 37g carb. (35g sugars, 0 fiber), 0 pro.

PEPPERMINT PATTY HOT COCOA

A hint of cool mint makes this rich sipper a nice change of pace from traditional hot cocoa. Add a dollop of whipped cream and crushed peppermint candies.
—Sue Gronholz, Beaver Dam, WI

TAKES: 20 MIN.
MAKES: 12 SERVINGS

1½ cups hot water
  1 cup sugar
  ½ cup baking cocoa
  ⅛ tsp. salt
  9 cups 2% milk
  1 cup peppermint schnapps liqueur or ¾ tsp. peppermint extract with additional 1 cup milk
     Whipped cream and crushed peppermint candies

1. In a large saucepan, combine water, sugar, cocoa and salt; bring to a boil over medium heat, stirring constantly. Cook and stir 2 minutes. Add milk; heat through, stirring constantly.
2. Remove from heat; add liqueur. Cook and stir over medium heat until heated through. Top servings with whipped cream and peppermint candies.
¾ cup: 213 cal., 4g fat (2g sat. fat), 15mg chol., 111mg sod., 28g carb. (26g sugars, 1g fiber), 7g pro.

APPLE-GOUDA PIGS IN A BLANKET

For New Year's, I used to make beef and cheddar pigs in a blanket, but now I like apple and Gouda for an even better flavor combination.
—Megan Weiss, Menomonie, WI

TAKES: 30 MIN. • **MAKES:** 2 DOZEN

  1 tube (8 oz.) refrigerated crescent rolls
  1 small apple, peeled and cut into 24 thin slices
  6 thin slices Gouda cheese, quartered
24 miniature smoked sausages
     Honey mustard salad dressing, optional

1. Preheat oven to 375°. Unroll crescent dough and separate into 8 triangles; cut each lengthwise into 3 thin triangles. On the wide end of each triangle, place 1 slice apple, 1 folded piece cheese and 1 sausage; roll up tightly.
2. Place 1 in. apart on parchment-lined baking sheets, point side down. Bake until golden brown, 10-12 minutes. If desired, serve with dressing.
1 appetizer: 82 cal., 6g fat (2g sat. fat), 11mg chol., 203mg sod., 5g carb. (1g sugars, 0 fiber), 3g pro.

TEST KITCHEN TIP
Honey mustard is a perfect dressing to serve alongside these appetizers, but you can also try ranch, creamy Parmesan or blue cheese.

UGLY SWEATER COOKIES

Perhaps the most amazing thing about Ugly Sweater Cookies is how cute they are. Try these classic gingerbreads on for size.
—Christy Thelen, Kellogg, IA

PREP: 1 HOUR + CHILLING
BAKE: 10 MIN./BATCH + COOLING
MAKES: ABOUT 5 DOZEN

- ¾ cup butter, softened
- 1 cup packed brown sugar
- 1 large egg
- ¾ cup molasses
- 4 cups all-purpose flour
- 1½ tsp. baking soda
- ¼ tsp. salt
- 2 tsp. ground ginger
- 1½ tsp. ground cinnamon
- ¾ tsp. ground cloves

ROYAL ICING

- 4½ cups confectioners' sugar
- ⅓ cup water
- 4 tsp. meringue powder
- ¼ tsp. cream of tartar
- ⅛ tsp. salt
- 1 to 3 Tbsp. heavy whipping cream
  Optional: Food coloring and assorted sprinkles

1. Cream butter and brown sugar until light and fluffy, 5-7 minutes. Beat in the egg and molasses. In another bowl, whisk together the flour, baking soda, salt and spices; gradually beat into the creamed mixture. Divide dough in half; shape each half into a disk. Cover and refrigerate until firm enough to roll, 4 hours or overnight.

2. Preheat oven to 350°. On a lightly floured surface, roll each portion of the dough to ⅛-in. thickness. Cut with floured 3½-in. sweater-shaped cookie cutters. Place 2 in. apart on ungreased baking sheets.

3. Bake cookies until edges are firm, 8-10 minutes. Remove to wire racks; cool completely.

4. Place the first 5 icing ingredients in a small bowl; beat on low speed just until blended. Beat on high until stiff peaks form, 4-5 minutes. Thin with cream to desired consistency. If desired, tint with food coloring.

5. Pipe icing onto cookies and decorate as desired. (Keep any unused icing covered at all times with a damp cloth. If necessary, beat again on high speed to restore texture.) Let cookies stand at room temperature several hours or until frosting is dry and firm.

1 cookie: 113 cal., 2g fat (2g sat. fat), 9mg chol., 70mg sod., 22g carb. (15g sugars, 0 fiber), 1g pro.

SWISS CHEESE CHICKEN PUFFS

My neighborhood has a progressive dinner before Christmas each year, and every house provides a course. These delightful puffs were served one year to everyone's enjoyment. The cheesy flavor and creamy texture of the chicken salad mixture are wonderful inside the tender puffs.
—Donna Kittredge, Westborough, MA

PREP: 35 MIN. • **BAKE:** 20 MIN./BATCH
MAKES: 3 DOZEN

1¼ cups water
¼ cup butter, cubed
½ tsp. salt
1 cup all-purpose flour
4 large eggs, room temperature
1 cup shredded Swiss cheese
FILLING
2 cups finely chopped
cooked chicken
1 cup shredded Swiss cheese
¾ cup chopped celery
½ cup mayonnaise
½ tsp. salt
½ tsp. prepared yellow mustard
⅛ tsp. pepper
Minced chives, optional

1. In a large saucepan, bring the water, butter and salt to a boil. Add the flour all at once and stir until a smooth ball forms. Remove from the heat; let stand for 5 minutes. Add the eggs, 1 at a time, beating well after each addition. Continue beating until the mixture is smooth and shiny. Stir in the cheese.
2. Drop by tablespoonfuls 2 in. apart onto greased baking sheets. Bake at 400° until golden brown, 20-25 minutes. Remove to wire racks. Immediately split puffs open; remove tops and set aside. Discard the soft dough from inside the puffs. Cool puffs.
3. Meanwhile, in a large bowl, combine the first 7 filling ingredients. Spoon into the puffs and, if desired, sprinkle with chives; replace tops. Serve immediately.
1 serving: 92 cal., 7g fat (3g sat. fat), 40mg chol., 124mg sod., 3g carb. (0 sugars, 0 fiber), 5g pro.

TIPS FOR AN EPIC UGLY CHRISTMAS-SWEATER PARTY

Someone's got a case of the uglies—and it's your Christmas sweater! Celebrate the worst knitted works in town with a bash everyone will remember. It's easy with these ideas.

DECK THE HALLS

Ambiance is everything. Sure, tinsel and twinkling lights bring warmth and cheer this time of year, but pretty things aren't exactly keeping with the ugly sweater vibe. Here's your chance to unearth those ornamental monstrosities banished to the basement. When it comes to decorating, opt for anything kitschy, weird, hilarious or just plain bad. The tackier, the better!

MUSIC

Now we don our bad apparel! It wouldn't be a Christmas party without Christmas music, right? Create your own party playlist with everything from gather-round-the-fire classics to pop-star holiday hits. Guests will love a game of Name That Tune, where you play a snippet of a Christmas song and see who can guess it! Or have a No-Talent Christmas Karaoke Show, where partygoers give their worst renditions of Christmas songs.

GAMES & ACTIVITIES

Have a roundup of fun games and activities to keep the party going all night long. Play a game of Christmas movie trivia or ask guests to bring a small, inexpensive gift to swap in a White Elephant gift exchange.

UGLIEST SWEATER AWARDS

Create people's choice awards for the best (or worst) sweaters in assorted categories, and let your guests vote. Category ideas include:

All-Around Ugliest

Most Original

Most Outrageous

Funniest

Best Couple

Most Festive

Most Likely to Go Viral
on Social Media

THREE-CHEESE CRAB & ARTICHOKE DIP

This is my absolute favorite go-to recipe for parties, potlucks and family events. Have plenty of bread and veggies for dipping, otherwise people will eat it with a spoon.
—Jasmin Baron, Livonia, NY

PREP: 25 MIN. • **BAKE:** 20 MIN.
MAKES: 24 SERVINGS

- 2 cups sour cream
- 1 pkg. (8 oz.) cream cheese, softened
- ½ cup grated Parmesan cheese
- ½ cup mayonnaise
- ½ tsp. garlic powder
- ½ tsp. cayenne pepper
- ¼ tsp. pepper
- 1 can (14 oz.) water-packed artichoke hearts, rinsed, drained and coarsely chopped
- 2 cups shredded Monterey Jack cheese, divided
- 2 cups shredded sharp white cheddar cheese, divided
- 8 oz. fresh or frozen crabmeat, thawed
- 1¼ cups finely chopped green onions, divided
  Assorted fresh vegetables and toasted baguette slices

1. Preheat the oven to 375°. In a large bowl, mix the first 7 ingredients. Stir in artichokes, 1½ cups Jack cheese, 1½ cups cheddar cheese, crab and ¾ cup green onions. Transfer to a greased 13x9-in. baking dish. Sprinkle with remaining cheeses.
2. Bake, uncovered, until edges are golden brown, 20-25 minutes. Sprinkle with remaining green onions. Serve warm with vegetables and toasted baguette slices.

¼ cup dip: 199 cal., 17g fat (9g sat. fat), 43mg chol., 287mg sod., 3g carb. (1g sugars, 0 fiber), 8g pro.

WHISKEY-BRANDY SLUSH

It may be cold outside, but we like to serve this icy citrus drink for Christmas gatherings at our house. It is fantastic for parties and large gatherings, and it keeps well in the freezer.
—Joan Shoebottom, Lexington, MI

PREP: 10 MIN. + FREEZING
MAKES: 32 SERVINGS

- 7 **green tea bags**
- 4 **cups boiling water**
- 7 **cups water**
- 2 **cups sugar**
- 1 **can (12 oz.) frozen orange juice concentrate**
- 1 **can (12 oz.) frozen lemonade concentrate**
- 1 **cup brandy**
- 1 **cup whiskey**
- 2 **liters lemon-lime soda, chilled**
  Optional: Cranberries and assorted citrus slices

1. Place the tea bags in a 4-cup glass measuring cup. Add the boiling water; steep 3-5 minutes according to taste. Discard tea bags. Cool tea slightly.
2. In a 6-qt. stockpot, combine 7 cups water and sugar; bring to a boil, stirring to dissolve sugar. Remove from heat; cool slightly. Stir in the orange juice and lemonade concentrates, brandy, whiskey and cooled tea. Transfer to freezer containers, allowing headspace for expansion; freeze at least 12 hours.
3. To serve, place ½ cup slush in each glass; top each with ½ cup soda. If desired, garnish with cranberries and citrus slices.
1 cup: 146 cal., 0 fat (0 sat. fat), 0 chol., 10mg sod., 29g carb. (27g sugars, 0 fiber), 0 pro.

PUCKER UP

Looking for a fun, inexpensive party favor? Create your own homemade lip balm. It makes an excellent stocking stuffer, too.

PEPPERMINT LIP BALM
Combine the following ingredients in a microwave-safe bowl: 1 Tbsp. shea butter, 1 Tbsp. beeswax pellets, 1 Tbsp. sweet almond oil and 4 drops food-grade peppermint essential oil. Heat in the microwave for 30 seconds or until completely melted. Using a clean dropper, fill empty lip balm tubes. Let cool completely. Adhere patterned paper to empty lip balm tubes.

ARGYLE CAKE

This wacky cake will be the star of your ugly Christmas-sweater party. Have fun with the decorations, choosing the colors and patterns you like best.
—*Taste of Home* Test Kitchen

PREP: 1 HOUR • **BAKE:** 40 MIN. + COOLING
MAKES: ABOUT 50 SERVINGS

2¼ **cups butter, softened**
12 **oz. cream cheese, softened**
4½ **cups sugar**
12 **large eggs, room temperature**
1½ **tsp. vanilla extract**
4½ **cups cake flour**
FROSTING
1½ **cups butter, softened**
8 **cups confectioners' sugar**
3 **tsp. vanilla extract**
8 **to 10 Tbsp. 2% milk**
1 **cup seedless raspberry jam**
1 **pkg. (24 oz.) ready-to-use rolled green fondant**
1 **pkg. (24 oz.) ready-to-use rolled blue fondant**
Red gel food coloring

1. Preheat the oven to 325°. Line two 13x9-in. baking pans with parchment; grease paper.
2. In a large bowl, beat butter, cream cheese and sugar until light and fluffy. Add eggs, 1 at a time, beating well after each addition. Beat in vanilla. Add flour; mix well. Transfer to prepared pans. Bake until a toothpick inserted in the center comes out clean, 40-45 minutes. Cool completely on a wire rack; gently remove paper.
3. For the frosting, in a large bowl, beat the butter until light and fluffy. Beat in the confectioners' sugar and vanilla. Add enough milk to achieve desired consistency.
4. Using a serrated knife, level tops of cakes if necessary. Place 1 cake layer on a cake board. Frost top with frosting; spread raspberry jam to within ½ in. of edges. Top with the remaining layer. Frost top and sides of cake with the remaining frosting, reserving 1 cup frosting for decoration.
5. For fondant argyle, on a work surface dusted with confectioners' sugar, roll out green fondant into an ⅛-in.-thick rectangle. Using a 4-in. diamond cutter, cut out 10 diamonds. Repeat with blue fondant. Place fondant diamonds in alternating colors on the top and sides of cake, cutting in half to fit the ends.
6. Color reserved frosting red with gel food coloring and place in a piping bag fitted with a #2 piping tip. Pipe dashed lines diagonally across the fondant diamonds to create an argyle pattern.
1 piece: 426 cal., 18g fat (11g sat. fat), 88mg chol., 150mg sod., 63g carb. (53g sugars, 0 fiber), 3g pro.

BROKEN GLASS DESSERT

This decidedly vintage, kitschy dessert may sound dangerous, but it's actually fun to make and eat. When it's cut, it looks like stained glass windows!
—Kathy Crow, Cordova, AK

PREP: 30 MIN. + CHILLING
MAKES: 15 SERVINGS

1 **pkg. (3 oz.) lime gelatin**
4½ **cups boiling water, divided**
1 **pkg. (3 oz.) strawberry gelatin**
1 **pkg. (3 oz.) orange gelatin**
1½ **cups graham cracker crumbs**
½ **cup sugar**
½ **cup butter, melted**
1 **envelope unflavored gelatin**
¼ **cup cold water**
1 **cup pineapple juice**
1 **carton (8 oz.) frozen whipped topping, thawed**

1. Combine lime gelatin and 1½ cups boiling water; stir until the gelatin is dissolved. Pour into a lightly greased 8x4-in. loaf pan; chill until very firm. Repeat to make the strawberry and orange gelatins in separate pans. Combine crumbs, sugar and butter; press into a greased 13x9-in. dish. Chill.
2. Meanwhile, in a small bowl, soften unflavored gelatin in cold water for 5 minutes. In a small saucepan, bring the pineapple juice to a boil. Stir in the unflavored gelatin until dissolved. Transfer to a large bowl; set aside until room temperature, 20-30 minutes.
3. When the flavored gelatins are firm, cut into ½-in. cubes. In the large bowl, whisk whipped topping into pineapple juice mixture. Gently fold ⅔ of the cubes into whipped topping mixture. Spoon over the crust; top with the remaining cubes. Chill for at least 2 hours.
1 piece: 183 cal., 4g fat (3g sat. fat), 0 chol., 86mg sod., 35g carb. (29g sugars, 0 fiber), 3g pro.

2. Preheat oven to 350°. On a lightly floured surface, roll each portion of dough to 1/8-in. thickness. Cut with a floured 3½-in. sock monkey-shaped cookie cutter. Place 2 in. apart on ungreased baking sheets.

3. Bake cookies until the edges are firm, 8-10 minutes. Remove to wire racks; cool completely.

4. Place the first 5 icing ingredients in a small bowl; beat on low speed just until blended. Beat on high until stiff peaks form, 4-5 minutes. Thin with cream to desired consistency. Divide icing into thirds. Tint 1 portion red and 1 portion gray; leave remaining portion white.

5. Pipe icing onto cookies and decorate with black sprinkles as desired. (Keep unused icing covered at all times with a damp cloth. If necessary, beat again on high speed to restore texture.) Let cookies stand at room temperature several hours or until frosting is dry and firm. Store in an airtight container.

1 cookie: 143 cal., 3g fat (2g sat. fat), 12mg chol., 88mg sod., 28g carb. (19g sugars, 0 fiber), 1g pro.

SOCK MONKEY COOKIES

Bring on Christmas and good luck with these adorable cookies. What's not to love about these little sock monkeys?
—Christy Thelen, Kellogg, IA

PREP: 1 HOUR + CHILLING
BAKE: 10 MIN./BATCH + COOLING
MAKES: ABOUT 4 DOZEN

- ¾ cup butter, softened
- 1 cup packed brown sugar
- 1 large egg, room temperature
- ¾ cup molasses
- 4 cups all-purpose flour
- 1½ tsp. baking soda
- ¼ tsp. salt
- 2 tsp. ground ginger
- 1½ tsp. ground cinnamon
- ¾ tsp. ground cloves

ROYAL ICING
- 4½ cups confectioners' sugar
- ⅓ cup water
- 4 tsp. meringue powder
- ¼ tsp. cream of tartar
- ⅛ tsp. salt
- 1 to 3 Tbsp. heavy whipping cream
  Food coloring and black sprinkles

1. In a large bowl, cream the butter and brown sugar until light and fluffy, about 5-7 minutes. Beat in egg and molasses. In another bowl, whisk the flour, baking soda, salt and spices; gradually beat into creamed mixture. Divide dough in half; shape each into a disk. Cover and refrigerate until firm enough to roll, 4 hours or overnight.

CRAZY SOCK PARTY

In the time-honored tradition of the Ugly Sweater Party, it's time for the Crazy Sock Party! Exchange socks as presents, award prizes for the gaudiest footwear and offer treats in holiday-themed stockings. And, of course, pull out all the stops with a spectacular spread of colorful and downright fun food!

Cookie Exchange

There's nothing like a warm, freshly baked cookie to make a moment memorable. From rum balls to classic gingerbreads, these melt-in-your-mouth cookie creations let you indulge in the sweetness of the season. If you are joining a cookie swap, giving some as gifts or simply wanting a big platter to share with the family, let these recipes and packaging ideas be your inspiration.

ITALIAN HORN COOKIES

My family has been making these delicate fruit-filled cookies for generations. They are light and flaky, with the look of an elegant old-world pastry.
—Gloria Siddiqui, Houston, TX

PREP: 30 MIN. + CHILLING
BAKE: 10 MIN./BATCH
MAKES: ABOUT 5 DOZEN

- 1 cup cold butter, cubed
- 4 cups all-purpose flour
- 2 cups vanilla ice cream, softened
- 1 can (12 oz.) cherry cake and pastry filling
  Sugar
  Confectioners' sugar, optional

1. In a large bowl, cut butter into flour until mixture resembles coarse crumbs. Stir in ice cream. Divide into 4 portions. Cover and refrigerate for 2 hours.
2. On a lightly floured surface, roll each portion to ⅛-in. thickness. With a fluted pastry cutter, cut into 2-in. squares. Place about ½ tsp. filling in the center of each square. Overlap 2 opposite corners of dough over the filling and seal. Sprinkle lightly with sugar.
3. Place on ungreased baking sheets. Bake at 350° for 10-12 minutes or until bottoms are light brown. Cool on wire racks. If desired, dust the cookies with confectioners' sugar before serving.
1 cookie: 79 cal., 4g fat (2g sat. fat), 10mg chol., 32mg sod., 10g carb. (3g sugars, 0 fiber), 1g pro.

ORANGE TWISTS

These soft and sweet twists have a long shelf life. You can make a number of flavor variations with this recipe, including lemon, cherry and almond. I sometimes add a confectioners' sugar glaze.
—Raine Gottess, Lantana, FL

PREP: 25 MIN. + CHILLING
BAKE: 10 MIN./BATCH
MAKES: ABOUT 3 DOZEN

- 1 cup butter, softened
- 1½ cups confectioners' sugar
- 1 large egg, room temperature
- 1 tsp. vanilla extract
- 2½ cups all-purpose flour
- ½ cup cake flour
- ½ tsp. salt
- 2 tsp. grated orange zest
- 4 drops yellow food coloring
- 2 drops red food coloring

1. In a large bowl, cream the butter and confectioners' sugar until blended. Beat in the egg and vanilla. In another bowl, whisk flours and salt; gradually beat into creamed mixture.
2. Divide dough in half. Mix orange zest and food colorings into 1 half; leave the remaining dough plain. Cover each half and refrigerate 1 hour or until firm enough to roll.
3. Preheat oven to 350°. Divide each half into 8 portions. Roll each portion into a 15-in. rope. Place 1 plain rope and 1 orange rope side by side; press together lightly. Cut rope crosswise into 3-in. pieces. Twist each piece several times; place 2 in. apart on ungreased baking sheets. Repeat with remaining dough. Bake 7-9 minutes or until the bottoms are golden brown. Cool on pans 2 minutes. Remove to wire racks to cool.
1 cookie: 95 cal., 5g fat (3g sat. fat), 17mg chol., 68mg sod., 12g carb. (4g sugars, 0 fiber), 1g pro.

HARDWORKING LAZY SUSAN

Use a lazy Susan for your next cookie-decorating extravaganza. It's a handy way to keep icings, sugars, sprinkles and other supplies within easy reach. It keeps the mess at bay, too.

COCONUT RUM BALLS

My mom has made rum balls for as long as I can remember. They look beautiful on a dessert spread and can be packaged in a decorative tin as a gift. I swapped coconut rum for the traditional rum and added shredded coconut.
—Jana Walker, Macomb, MI

PREP: 25 MIN. + STANDING
MAKES: ABOUT 4½ DOZEN

- 1 pkg. (12 oz.) vanilla wafers, finely crushed
- 1 cup confectioners' sugar
- 2 Tbsp. baking cocoa
- 1 cup sweetened shredded coconut
- 1 cup chopped pecans
- ½ cup light corn syrup
- ¼ cup coconut rum
- Additional confectioners' sugar

1. Whisk crushed wafers, confectioners' sugar and cocoa. Stir in coconut and pecans. In a separate bowl, whisk corn syrup and rum; stir into wafer mixture. Shape into 1-in. balls; let stand 1 hour.
2. Roll in additional confectioners' sugar. Store in an airtight container.
1 cookie: 73 cal., 3g fat (1g sat. fat), 1mg chol., 31mg sod., 10g carb. (8g sugars, 1g fiber), 0 pro.

READER REVIEW
"Yummy! I will use a little more rum next time, but really tasty!"
—KARLA, TASTEOFHOME.COM

CHOCOLATE CHIP PEPPERMINT BISCOTTI

My family loves peppermint. When I pair it with chocolate in crunchy biscotti, we know that the Christmas season has arrived. Dunk these in a glass of cold milk, hot chocolate or coffee—oh, so divine!
—Katherine Wollgast, Troy, MO

PREP: 10 MIN. • **BAKE:** 45 MIN. + COOLING
MAKES: ABOUT 3½ DOZEN

- ½ cup butter, softened
- 1⅓ cups sugar
- 3 large eggs, room temperature
- ½ tsp. peppermint extract
- 4 cups all-purpose flour
- 1 tsp. baking powder
- ½ tsp. salt
- ½ cup crushed peppermint candies
- ½ cup miniature semisweet chocolate chips

1. Preheat oven to 350°. In a large bowl, cream butter and sugar until light and fluffy, 5-7 minutes. Beat in eggs and extract. In another bowl, whisk flour, baking powder and salt; gradually beat into creamed mixture. Stir in crushed candies and chocolate chips.
2. Divide dough in half. On a parchment-lined baking sheet, shape each portion into a 10x3-in. rectangle. Bake until light brown, 30-35 minutes. Cool on pans on wire racks 15 minutes or until firm.
3. Transfer the baked rectangles to a cutting board. Using a serrated knife, cut diagonally into ½-in. slices. Place on baking sheets, cut side down.
4. Bake 15-18 minutes or until crisp and golden brown. Remove from pans to wire racks to cool completely. Store between pieces of waxed paper in an airtight container.
1 cookie: 102 cal., 3g fat (2g sat. fat), 18mg chol., 60mg sod., 17g carb. (8g sugars, 0 fiber), 2g pro.

STORING COOKIES

Before storing, allow cookies to cool completely and allow icing on cookies to dry completely.

To keep cookies and other baked goods soft and moist when storing, add a slice of white bread to the container. The cookies will absorb the moisture from the bread so you don't have treats that are too hard and crunchy to eat.

Store soft cookies and crisp cookies in separate airtight containers. If stored together, the moisture from the soft cookies will soften the crisp cookies.

Flavors can blend in storage; don't store strong-flavored cookies in the same container as treats that have a more delicate flavor.

Store cookies with waxed paper between layers.

Store unfrosted cookies in a cool, dry place in airtight containers for about 3 days. Cookies that are topped with cream cheese frosting should be stored in the refrigerator.

For longer storage, stack unfrosted cookies in an airtight container, seal and freeze up to 3 months. Thaw cookies at room temperature before frosting and serving.

If crisp cookies become soft during storage, crisp them up by heating them in a 300° oven for 5 minutes.

WAFFLE IRON COOKIES

The recipe for these cookies is the easiest to find in my book because the page is a beautiful mess covered with fingerprints, flour smudges and memories of more than 30 Christmases! I made these with my daughters, and now I make them with my granddaughters.

—Judy Taylor, Quarryville, PA

PREP: 10 MIN.
BAKE: 5 MIN./BATCH + COOLING
MAKES: 32 COOKIES (8 BATCHES)

- ½ cup butter, softened
- 1 cup sugar
- 2 large eggs, room temperature
- 1 tsp. vanilla extract
- 1½ cups all-purpose flour
- 1 tsp. baking powder
- ½ tsp. salt
  Confectioners' sugar

1. In a large bowl, cream butter and sugar until light and fluffy, 5-7 minutes. Beat in the eggs and vanilla. In another bowl, whisk flour, baking powder and salt; gradually beat into the creamed mixture (mixture will be thick).

2. Drop the dough in batches by tablespoonfuls 3-4 in. apart onto a greased preheated waffle iron. Bake until dark brown, 2-3 minutes.

3. Remove to wire racks to cool completely. Sprinkle with the confectioners' sugar.

1 cookie: 76 cal., 3g fat (2g sat. fat), 19mg chol., 79mg sod., 11g carb. (6g sugars, 0 fiber), 1g pro.

COLORFUL CANDY BAR COOKIES

No one will guess these sweet treats with the candy bar center start with store-bought dough. Roll them in colored sugar or just dip the tops for even faster assembly. Instead of using miniature candy bars for the centers, you can also slice regular-size Snickers candy bars into 1-inch pieces.

—*Taste of Home* Test Kitchen

PREP: 35 MIN. • **BAKE:** 10 MIN./BATCH
MAKES: ABOUT 3 DOZEN

- 1 tube (16½ oz.) refrigerated sugar cookie dough, softened
- ⅔ cup all-purpose flour
- 40 miniature Snickers candy bars
  Red and green colored sugar

1. Preheat oven to 350°. Beat cookie dough and flour until combined. Shape 2 tsp. dough around each candy bar. Roll in colored sugar.

2. Place 2 in. apart on parchment-lined baking sheets. Bake until set, 9-11 minutes. Cool on pans 1 minute. Remove to wire racks to cool.

1 cookie: 93 cal., 4g fat (1g sat. fat), 4mg chol., 65mg sod., 13g carb. (7g sugars, 0 fiber), 1g pro.

IRONING BOARD = COOLING RACK

Remove the cover from an ironing board to use it as a cooling rack when you're doing a lot of baking. The air circulation from both the top and bottom helps baked goods cool evenly. An added advantage is that it frees up counter space in the kitchen. Just be sure to use pans, paper liners, parchment or some other barrier between the baked goods and the rack.

PRETTY PACKAGING IDEAS

You don't have to spend a fortune or valuable time at the mall in search of perfect Christmas gifts. Often the most priceless treasures are your own homemade cookies, brownies or treats presented in decorative tins or in one of the pretty packages suggested below.

At Christmastime, craft and variety stores sell papier-mache boxes perfect for gift giving. You can stack star-shaped sugar cookies in a star-shaped papier-mache box that's been lined with wax-coated tissue paper.

Decorative tins, plates and candy dishes can often be found at bargain prices throughout the year at stores, yard sales and after-Christmas sales. Keep them on hand for last-minute gifts.

Stack cookies in a wide-mouth canning jar, cover the lid with fabric and screw on the band. You may also want to include the recipe for the cookies.

Instead of discarding potato chip cans, coffee tins or shortening cans, wash them, decorate the outsides with wrapping paper or contact paper, and fill them with cookies or candies. Attach a bow to each lid and close.

Wrap cookies in paper, place a bow on top, and tuck the package inside a pretty coffee mug or teacup.

CHOCOLATE ALMOND WAFERS

When my children were younger, we'd make dozens of cookies and candies each season. Then we would pack up assortments and deliver them to our friends and family. These wafers were always a favorite.
—Phyl Broich-Wessling, Garner, IA

PREP: 20 MIN. + CHILLING
BAKE: 10 MIN./BATCH
MAKES: ABOUT 4½ DOZEN

- ¾ cup butter, softened
- ¾ cup sugar
- 1 large egg, room temperature
- 1 tsp. vanilla extract
- 1¼ cups all-purpose flour
- ⅔ cup baking cocoa
- 1 tsp. baking powder
- ¾ cup sliced almonds
- ⅔ cup ground almonds

1. In a large bowl, cream the butter and sugar until light and fluffy, 5-7 minutes. Beat in egg and vanilla. Combine flour, cocoa and baking powder; gradually add to creamed mixture and mix well. Stir in sliced almonds.
2. Shape dough into a 14-in. log; roll in ground almonds. Wrap in waxed paper. Refrigerate 2 hours or until firm.
3. Unwrap and cut into ¼-in. slices. Place 1 in. apart on ungreased baking sheets. Bake at 375° for 9-11 minutes or until set. Remove to wire racks.
1 cookie: 60 cal., 4g fat (2g sat. fat), 10mg chol., 26mg sod., 6g carb. (3g sugars, 1g fiber), 1g pro.

PISTACHIO PALMIERS

My family loves palmiers from the bakery, so I created my own recipe. These have a Middle Eastern twist with the addition of rosewater, honey and a touch of cardamom. They are light and crisp—a special treat for the holidays.

—Deborah Hinojosa, Saratoga, CA

PREP: 30 MIN.+ CHILLING
BAKE: 10 MIN./BATCH
MAKES: ABOUT 5 DOZEN

- 1½ cups all-purpose flour
- ¾ cup cake flour
- ¾ tsp. salt
- 1¼ cups cold butter, cubed
- ⅓ cup ice water
- 1 Tbsp. lemon juice

FILLING
- ⅓ cup sugar
- 1 tsp. ground cinnamon
- ¼ tsp. ground cardamom
- ¼ cup butter, melted
- 2 Tbsp. honey
- 1 Tbsp. rosewater or water
- 1 cup chopped pistachios

1. Place the flours and salt in a food processor; pulse until blended. Add butter; pulse until butter is the size of peas. While pulsing, add ice water and lemon juice to form crumbs. Turn onto a floured surface; knead gently 8-10 times.

2. Roll dough into a 12x8-in. rectangle. Starting with a shorter side, fold dough in half. Repeat rolling and folding. Place folded dough in an airtight container and freeze 20 minutes.

3. Roll dough into a 12x8-in. rectangle. Starting with a shorter side, fold dough into thirds, forming a 4x8-in. rectangle. Place the folded dough with longer side facing you; repeat rolling and folding twice, always ending with a 4x8-in. rectangle. (If at any point the butter softens, chill after folding.) Cover the folded dough and refrigerate overnight.

4. Preheat oven to 400°. In a small bowl, mix sugar, cinnamon and cardamom. In another bowl, mix butter, honey and rosewater. Turn the dough onto a lightly floured surface; cut in half. Roll 1 half dough into a 12x10-in. rectangle. Brush with half the butter mixture; sprinkle with half each of the following: sugar mixture and pistachios.

5. Starting with a long side, roll up the left and right sides toward the center, jelly-roll style, until rolls meet in the middle. Repeat with the remaining dough, butter mixture, sugar mixture and pistachios. Refrigerate the rolls 20 minutes or until firm enough to slice.

6. Cut rolls crosswise into ¼-in. slices. Place 2 in. apart on parchment-lined baking sheets. Bake 8-10 minutes or until golden brown. Cool on the pans 2 minutes. Remove to wire racks to cool.

1 cookie: 72 cal., 5g fat (3g sat. fat), 11mg chol., 70mg sod., 6g carb. (2g sugars, 0 fiber), 1g pro.

DATE-FILLED PINWHEELS

My mom made these family favorites when I was growing up. Sliced thin, these cookies are crispy and chewy; sliced thick, they have a cakelike texture. They make an attractive baked gift.

—Kathryn Wilkins, Norfolk, VA

PREP: 20 MIN. + CHILLING • **BAKE:** 10 MIN.
MAKES: ABOUT 2½ DOZEN

- ¾ cup firmly packed chopped dates
- ⅓ cup sugar
- ⅓ cup water
- ⅓ cup chopped pecans
- ⅓ cup shortening
- ⅔ cup packed brown sugar
- 1 large egg
- ¼ tsp. vanilla extract
- 1⅓ cups all-purpose flour
- ¼ tsp. salt
- ⅛ tsp. baking soda

1. In a large saucepan, combine the dates, sugar and water. Cook and stir over medium heat 10 minutes until very soft. Add pecans; cool. In a large bowl, cream shortening and brown sugar. Beat in the egg and vanilla. In another bowl, whisk flour, salt and baking soda; gradually beat into the creamed mixture. Refrigerate, covered, 1 hour or until easy to handle.

2. On a lightly floured surface, roll out dough into an 8-in. square. Spread with the date mixture; roll up jelly-roll style. Wrap in waxed paper. Refrigerate 4 hours or until firm.

3. Preheat oven to 400°. Unwrap and cut dough crosswise into ¼-in. slices. Place 2 in. apart on greased baking sheets. Bake 8-10 minutes or until golden brown. Remove from pans to wire racks to cool.

1 cookie: 181 cal., 7g fat (1g sat. fat), 14mg chol., 58mg sod., 29g carb. (20g sugars, 1g fiber), 2g pro.

GINGERBREAD SNOW GLOBE

I make a big batch of these gingerbread cookies every Christmas to give to co-workers and family. For a festive decoration, arrange cutouts in a large clear jar to look like a snow globe.
—Kelly Kirby, Mill Bay, BC

PREP: 1¼ HOURS + CHILLING
BAKE: 10 MIN./BATCH + COOLING
MAKES: ABOUT 12 DOZEN (2-IN. COOKIES)

½ cup warm water
2 Tbsp. white vinegar
1 cup shortening
1 cup sugar
1 cup molasses
6 cups all-purpose flour
3 tsp. ground cinnamon
3 tsp. ground ginger
2 tsp. baking soda
1 tsp. salt
½ tsp. ground cloves
    Light corn syrup
    Coarse sugar
    Assorted sprinkles

1. Mix the water and vinegar. In a large bowl, cream shortening and sugar until light and fluffy, 5-7 minutes. Beat in the molasses. In another bowl, whisk the flour, cinnamon, ginger, baking soda, salt and cloves; add to the creamed mixture alternately with water mixture, beating well after each addition.
2. Divide dough into 6 portions. Shape each into a disk; cover and refrigerate 2 hours or until firm enough to roll.
3. Preheat oven to 350°. On a lightly floured surface, roll each portion of dough to ¼-in. thickness. Cut dough with assorted holiday cookie cutters. Place 2 in. apart on ungreased baking sheets. Bake 10-12 minutes or until set. Cool on pans 1 minute. Remove to wire racks to cool completely.
4. Using a new paintbrush, brush corn syrup onto edges of cookies; dip into coarse sugar. Decorate with sprinkles. Let stand until set.
5. For snow globe, place coarse sugar in a decorative glass jar. Arrange the cookies in jar. Decorate jar with ribbon.

1 (2-in.) cookie: 87 cal., 3g fat (1g sat. fat), 0 chol., 70mg sod., 14g carb. (6g sugars, 0 fiber), 1g pro.

TEST KITCHEN TIP

We love the simplicity of these plain gingerbread cookies decorated with just a touch of whimsy, but you can go all out and decorate with icing, too. For a simple look, pipe the icing as an outline around the edge of the cookies. Or sponge some thinned frosting on the cookies with a trimmed piece from a new, clean sponge. Add other edible decorations as desired.

FROSTED RED VELVET COOKIES

My student job in college was in the bakery. These dreamy morsels take me back to that special place and time. Red velvet lovers will appreciate this fun take on the cake.
—Christina Petri, Alexandria, MN

PREP: 20 MIN.
BAKE: 10 MIN./BATCH + COOLING
MAKES: 5 DOZEN

- 2 oz. unsweetened chocolate, chopped
- ½ cup butter, softened
- ⅔ cup packed brown sugar
- ⅓ cup sugar
- 1 large egg, room temperature
- 1 Tbsp. red food coloring
- 1 tsp. vanilla extract
- 2 cups all-purpose flour
- ½ tsp. baking soda
- ½ tsp. salt
- 1 cup sour cream
- 1 cup semisweet chocolate chips
- 1 can (16 oz.) cream cheese frosting
  Sprinkles, optional

1. In a microwave, melt unsweetened chocolate; stir until smooth. Cool.
2. In a large bowl, cream the butter and the sugars until light and fluffy, 5-7 minutes. Beat in egg, food coloring and vanilla. Add cooled chocolate; beat until blended. In another bowl, mix flour, baking soda and salt; add to creamed mixture alternately with sour cream, beating well after each addition. Stir in chocolate chips.
3. Drop by tablespoonfuls 2 in. apart onto parchment-lined baking sheets. Bake at 375° for 6-9 minutes or until set. Remove to wire racks to cool completely. Spread with frosting. If desired, decorate with sprinkles.
1 cookie: 103 cal., 5g fat (3g sat. fat), 8mg chol., 62mg sod., 14g carb. (10g sugars, 0 fiber), 1g pro.

Holiday Movie Marathon

Relive your favorite Christmas movie memories with recipes inspired by famous holiday flicks. These dishes are perfect for a jolly potluck with friends, or enjoy them with the family while wrapping presents and decorating the tree. From the Grinch's roast "beast" to Clark Griswold's eggnog, these foods are sure to make your movie night cozy.

PEANUT BUTTER SNOWBALLS

Inspired by edible snowballs from
The Nightmare Before Christmas

These creamy treats are a nice change from the typical milk chocolate and peanut butter combination. I once prepared them for a bake sale at my granddaughter's school, and I've also put them in gift boxes to share with neighbors at Christmas.
—Wanda Regula, Birmingham, MI

PREP: 15 MIN. + CHILLING
MAKES: 2½ DOZEN

1 cup confectioners' sugar
½ cup creamy peanut butter
3 Tbsp. butter, softened
1 lb. white candy coating, coarsely chopped
Chopped peanuts, optional

1. In a bowl, combine sugar, peanut butter and butter. Chill in freezer for 30 minutes or until the mixture is easy to handle. Shape into 1-in. balls and place on a waxed paper-lined baking sheet. Freeze for 30 minutes or until firm.
2. Meanwhile, melt the candy coating in a microwave-safe bowl. Dip each ball and place on waxed paper to harden. If desired, sprinkle with chopped peanuts.
1 piece: 132 cal., 8g fat (5g sat. fat), 3mg chol., 27mg sod., 16g carb. (15g sugars, 0 fiber), 1g pro.

OLD-FASHIONED EGGNOG

Inspired by Clark's eggnog from
National Lampoon's Christmas Vacation

Celebrating the holidays with eggnog is an American tradition that dates back to Colonial days. I toast the season with this smooth and creamy concoction that keeps family and friends coming back from more.
—Pat Waymire, Yellow Springs, OH

PREP: 40 MIN. + CHILLING
MAKES: 16 SERVINGS (ABOUT 3 QT.)

12 large eggs
1½ cups sugar
½ tsp. salt
2 qt. whole milk, divided
2 Tbsp. vanilla extract
1 tsp. ground nutmeg
2 cups heavy whipping cream
Optional: Whipped cream, additional nutmeg and cinnamon sticks

1. In a heavy saucepan, whisk together the eggs, sugar and salt. Gradually add 1 qt. milk. Cook and stir over low heat until a thermometer reads 160°, about 25 minutes. Pour into a large bowl; stir in vanilla, nutmeg and remaining milk. Place bowl in an ice-water bath; stir frequently until cool. If the mixture separates, process in a blender until smooth. Cover and refrigerate at least 3 hours.
2. When ready to serve, beat the cream in a bowl on high until soft peaks form; whisk gently into cooled mixture. Pour eggnog into a chilled 5-qt. punch bowl. If desired, top with dollops of whipped cream, sprinkle with additional nutmeg and serve with cinnamon sticks.
¾ cup: 308 cal., 18g fat (10g sat. fat), 186mg chol., 188mg sod., 26g carb. (26g sugars, 0 fiber), 9g pro.

GINGERBREAD FRUITCAKE COOKIES

Inspired by gingerbread cookies
from Jingle All the Way

Here's a recipe that combines two holiday classics—gingerbread and fruitcake—into one yummy favorite. I spread on a simple glaze made from confectioners' sugar and orange juice.
—Jamie Jones, Madison, GA

PREP: 20 MIN.
BAKE: 10 MIN./BATCH + COOLING
MAKES: 3 DOZEN

- 1 pkg. (14½ oz.) gingerbread cake/cookie mix
- ¼ cup butter, melted
- ¼ cup water
- 1 container (8 oz.) chopped mixed candied fruit
- ½ cup chopped pecans
- ½ cup raisins
- 1¼ cups confectioners' sugar
- 1 to 2 Tbsp. orange juice

1. Preheat the oven to 350°. In a large bowl, mix the cookie mix, melted butter and water to form a soft dough. Stir in candied fruit, pecans and raisins. Drop dough by tablespoonfuls 2 in. apart onto ungreased baking sheets.

2. Bake 8-10 minutes or until set. Cool on pans 1 minute. Remove from pans to wire racks to cool completely.

3. In a small bowl, mix confectioners' sugar and enough orange juice to reach desired consistency. Spread or drizzle over cookies. Let stand until set.

1 cookie: 111 cal., 4g fat (1g sat. fat), 3mg chol., 91mg sod., 19g carb. (15g sugars, 1g fiber), 1g pro.

FAMILY HOLIDAY TRADITION:
HOST 12 HOLIDAY MOVIE NIGHTS

Baby, it's cold outside. Light a fire, flip on the TV and plan a fun night in with your loved ones. Make each evening extra-special with easy decorating ideas, a merry popcorn mix and a classic holiday flick.

SET THE SCENE

Get the excitement started a few days early by slipping under each family member's bedroom door an invite that lists movie title, show time and requested attire (comfy pajamas only, please).

It's movie night! Cozy up the viewing area with plenty of pillows and fleece blankets to share. Or invite the kids to build a fort in the middle of the living room.

Prop up a chalkboard on a nearby serving table that notes the evening's showing.

Decorate the space with cute props that relate to your featured flick—yes, many stores sell replicas of that awesome leg lamp from *A Christmas Story*.

SERVE UP A SNACK BAR

Drizzle a fresh-popped batch of popcorn with melted white chocolate. Once the chocolate sets, make a merry mix by adding any of the following: red and green chocolate candies, chocolate-covered mini pretzels, gumdrops, dried cranberries, white chocolate chips or sugared nuts.

Wow them with a hot chocolate and coffee bar complete with flavored creamers, mini marshmallows, whipped cream, chocolate sauce, and candy cane or rock candy swizzle sticks.

Watching *How the Grinch Stole Christmas*? Make a Grinchy punch—a fizzy combination of white soda and lime sherbet. Serve with green sugar-rimmed glasses and ice cubes in fun holiday shapes (check online for seasonal silicone trays).

12 DAYS OF FA-LA-LA FLICKS

A Charlie Brown Christmas

A Christmas Carol

A Christmas Story

Elf

Home Alone

How the Grinch Stole Christmas!

It's a Wonderful Life

National Lampoon's Christmas Vacation

The Polar Express

Rudolph the Red-Nosed Reindeer

The Santa Clause

White Christmas

CREAMY MACARONI & CHEESE

Inspired by macaroni and cheese from *Home Alone*

This is the ultimate creamy mac and cheese. It's saucy, thick and rich, with a wonderful cheddar flavor. Once you taste it, you will be hooked.
—Cindy Hartley, Chesapeake, VA

PREP: 20 MIN. • **BAKE:** 35 MIN.
MAKES: 6 SERVINGS

2 cups uncooked elbow macaroni
½ cup butter, cubed
½ cup all-purpose flour
1½ to 2 cups 2% milk
1 cup sour cream
8 oz. cubed Velveeta
¼ cup grated Parmesan cheese
½ tsp. salt
½ tsp. ground mustard
½ tsp. pepper
2 cups shredded cheddar cheese

1. Cook the macaroni according to the package directions.
2. Meanwhile, preheat oven to 350°. In a large saucepan, melt butter. Stir in flour until smooth. Gradually add 1½ cups milk. Bring to a boil; cook and stir 2 minutes or until thickened. Reduce heat; stir in the sour cream, Velveeta, Parmesan cheese, salt, ground mustard and pepper until smooth and cheese is melted. Add additional milk to reach desired consistency.
3. Drain macaroni; toss with cheddar cheese. Transfer to a greased 3-qt. baking dish. Stir in cream sauce.
4. Bake, uncovered, 35-40 minutes or until golden brown and bubbly.
1 cup: 653 cal., 46g fat (30g sat. fat), 143mg chol., 1141mg sod., 35g carb. (8g sugars, 1g fiber), 25g pro.

PECAN FUDGE PIE

Inspired by Ma Bailey's pies from *It's a Wonderful Life*

This fudgy pie with a chocolaty twist is the perfect showcase for crunchy pecans. Top it with whipped cream, and you won't have to wait long for compliments!
—Jacquelyn Smith, Soperton, GA

PREP: 10 MIN. • **BAKE:** 55 MIN. + COOLING
MAKES: 8 SERVINGS

1¼ cups light corn syrup
½ cup sugar
⅓ cup baking cocoa
⅓ cup all-purpose flour
¼ tsp. salt
3 large eggs
3 Tbsp. butter, softened
1½ tsp. vanilla extract
1 cup chopped pecans
1 unbaked pastry shell (9 in.)
Whipped cream, optional

In a large bowl, beat first 8 ingredients until smooth. Stir in nuts; pour into crust. Bake at 350° for 55-60 minutes or until set. Cool completely. Garnish with whipped cream if desired.
1 slice: 512 cal., 24g fat (7g sat. fat), 96mg chol., 303mg sod., 73g carb. (40g sugars, 2g fiber), 6g pro.

HOMEMADE PIZZA

Inspired by cheese pizza from
Home Alone 2: Lost in New York

This recipe is a hearty, zesty main dish with a crisp, golden crust. Feel free to add your favorite toppings.
—Marianne Edwards, Lake Stevens, WA

PREP: 25 MIN. + RISING • **BAKE:** 25 MIN.
MAKES: 2 PIZZAS (3 SERVINGS EACH)

- 1 pkg. (¼ oz.) active dry yeast
- 1 tsp. sugar
- 1¼ cups warm water (110° to 115°)
- ¼ cup canola oil
- 1 tsp. salt
- 3½ to 4 cups all-purpose flour
- ½ lb. ground beef
- 1 small onion, chopped
- 1 can (15 oz.) tomato sauce
- 3 tsp. dried oregano
- 1 tsp. dried basil
- 1 medium green pepper, diced
- 2 cups shredded part-skim mozzarella cheese

1. In large bowl, dissolve the yeast and sugar in water; let stand for 5 minutes. Add oil and salt. Stir in flour, 1 cup at a time, until a soft dough forms.
2. Turn onto a floured surface; knead until smooth and elastic, 2-3 minutes. Place in a greased bowl, turning once to grease the top. Cover and let rise in a warm place until doubled, about 45 minutes. Meanwhile, cook beef and onion over medium heat until beef is no longer pink, breaking it into crumbles; drain.
3. Punch down dough; divide in half. Press each half into a greased 12-in. pizza pan. Combine tomato sauce, oregano and basil; spread over each crust. Top with beef mixture, green pepper and cheese.
4. Bake at 400° for 25-30 minutes or until crust is lightly browned.
2 slices: 537 cal., 19g fat (7g sat. fat), 40mg chol., 922mg sod., 64g carb. (5g sugars, 4g fiber), 25g pro.

HOME-STYLE GLAZED MEAT LOAF

Inspired by meat loaf from
A Christmas Story

Grated carrots and cheese add a hint of color to this down-home classic. If there are leftovers, we use them in meat loaf sandwiches the next day.
—Sandra Etelamaki, Ishpeming, MI

PREP: 15 MIN. • **BAKE:** 1 HOUR + STANDING
MAKES: 12 SERVINGS

- 2 large eggs, beaten
- ⅔ cup 2% milk
- 1½ cups shredded cheddar cheese
- 1 cup crushed saltines (about 30 crackers)
- 1 cup finely shredded carrots
- ½ cup finely chopped onion
- ½ tsp. salt
- ¼ tsp. garlic powder
- ¼ tsp. pepper
- 2 lbs. lean ground beef
- ½ cup packed brown sugar
- ½ cup ketchup
- 2 Tbsp. Dijon mustard
   Minced fresh parsley, optional

1. In a large bowl, combine the first 9 ingredients. Crumble beef over mixture; mix well. Shape into a loaf. Place in a greased 13x9-in. baking dish. Bake, uncovered, at 350° for 50 minutes.
2. For glaze, in a small saucepan, bring the brown sugar, ketchup and mustard to a boil. Reduce the heat; simmer, uncovered, for 3-5 minutes or until heated through. Spoon over meat loaf.
3. Bake 10-15 minutes longer or until the meat is no longer pink and a thermometer reads 160°. Drain; let stand for 10 minutes before slicing. If desired, top with minced fresh parsley.
1 slice: 266 cal., 12g fat (6g sat. fat), 100mg chol., 494mg sod., 18g carb. (12g sugars, 1g fiber), 20g pro.

READER REVIEW
"Fast and easy to make. Excellent finished result, and the glaze on top adds the perfect finishing touch."
—TREASURE13, TASTEOFHOME.COM

SPAGHETTI WITH ITALIAN MEATBALLS

Inspired by Buddy's spaghetti with maple syrup from *Elf*

My family enjoys this robust spaghetti dinner. The versatile sauce can be served over almost any type of pasta.
—Sharon Crider, Junction City, KS

PREP: 20 MIN. • **COOK:** 1¼ HOURS
MAKES: 10 SERVINGS

- ¾ cup chopped onion
- 1 Tbsp. olive oil
- 1 garlic clove, minced
- 1 can (28 oz.) Italian crushed tomatoes, undrained
- 1 can (6 oz.) tomato paste
- 1 cup water
- 1½ tsp. dried oregano
- ½ tsp. salt
- ½ tsp. pepper

MEATBALLS

- 4 slices white bread, torn
- ½ cup water
- 2 large eggs, lightly beaten
- ½ cup grated Parmesan cheese
- 1 garlic clove, minced
- 1 tsp. dried basil
- 1 tsp. dried parsley flakes
- ½ tsp. salt
- 1 lb. lean ground beef (90% lean)
- 2 Tbsp. olive oil, divided
- 1 pkg. (16 oz.) spaghetti

1. In a large saucepan, cook onion in oil until tender. Add garlic; cook 1 minute longer. Stir in tomatoes, tomato paste, water, oregano, salt and pepper. Bring to a boil. Reduce the heat; cover and simmer for 30 minutes.
2. Meanwhile, in a small bowl, soak the bread in water for 5 minutes. Squeeze out excess liquid. In a large bowl, combine the eggs, cheese, garlic, basil, parsley, salt and bread. Crumble beef over mixture and mix well. Shape into 1-in. balls.
3. In a large skillet, heat 1 Tbsp. oil over medium heat. In batches, brown the meatballs, adding more oil as needed. Remove to paper towels to drain. Add the meatballs to sauce; return to a boil. Reduce heat; simmer, uncovered, for 30 minutes or until meatballs are no longer pink.
4. Cook spaghetti according to package directions; drain. Serve with meatballs and sauce.

½ cup sauce with 3 meatballs and ⅔ cup cooked spaghetti: 385 cal., 11g fat (3g sat. fat), 69mg chol., 612mg sod., 49g carb. (7g sugars, 4g fiber), 21g pro.

ROAST BEEF WITH PEPPERS

Inspired by roast "beast" from *How the Grinch Stole Christmas!*

This moist, flavorful entree gets a bit of Italian flair from oregano and garlic. The sauteed peppers not only are a fresh-tasting accompaniment to the meat but look beautiful arranged on a platter around the sliced roast.
—Jeanne Murray, Scottsbluff, NE

PREP: 35 MIN. • **BAKE:** 3 HOURS + STANDING
MAKES: 10 SERVINGS

- 1 beef rump roast or bottom round roast (3 lbs.)
- 3 Tbsp. vegetable oil
- 3 cups hot water
- 4 tsp. beef bouillon granules
- 1 Tbsp. dried oregano
- 1 to 2 garlic cloves, minced
- ½ tsp. salt
- ½ tsp. pepper
- 3 medium bell peppers, julienned
- 3 Tbsp. butter
  Fresh oregano sprigs, optional

1. In a Dutch oven, brown the roast on all sides in oil over medium-high heat; drain. Combine the water, bouillon, oregano, garlic, salt and pepper; pour over roast.
2. Cover and bake at 350° for 3 hours or until meat is tender. Remove roast to a warm serving platter. Let stand 10 minutes before slicing.
3. Meanwhile, in a large skillet, saute the peppers in butter until tender. Serve peppers and pan juices with the roast. If desired, garnish with fresh oregano sprigs.

1 serving: 253 cal., 14g fat (5g sat. fat), 91mg chol., 512mg sod., 3g carb. (1g sugars, 1g fiber), 27g pro.

DID YOU KNOW?

Bell peppers add crunch, sweetness, color and vitamin C to recipes. Green bell peppers are actually unripened versions of sweeter-tasting red and orange peppers. Green peppers are less expensive because they're faster to market. Select firm peppers with little give when squeezed. Their surfaces should be bright and shiny. If they are dull, wrinkled, spotted or discolored, they are too old. Also check a store's salad bar for ready-chopped peppers.

White Elephant Party

One person's trash may be another person's treasure, but at a White Elephant party, the lines between trash and treasure blur completely! Also known as Yankee Swap or Dirty Santa, the all-in-good-fun gift exchange has become a hot holiday craze (see rules on page 394). As your guests are swapping, stealing and showing off their kitschy treasures, serve up any of these delicious party pleasers.

SNOW-TOPPED WHITE CHOCOLATE MACADAMIA COOKIES

These fluffy cookies will melt in your mouth. Include them as part of your cookie platter or serve them in decorative cupcake liners for extra visual appeal.
—*Taste of Home* Test Kitchen

PREP: 35 MIN.
BAKE: 15 MIN./BATCH + COOLING
MAKES: ABOUT 3 DOZEN

- 1 tube (16½ oz.) refrigerated sugar cookie dough
- ⅓ cup all-purpose flour
- ½ tsp. vanilla extract
- ¾ cup white baking chips
- ½ cup finely chopped macadamia nuts, toasted

GLAZE
- 1½ cups confectioners' sugar
- 3 Tbsp. 2% milk
- ½ tsp. lemon extract
- 1½ cups sweetened shredded coconut

1. Preheat oven to 350°. Place cookie dough in a large bowl; let stand at room temperature 5-10 minutes to soften.
2. Add flour and vanilla to dough; beat until blended (dough will be slightly crumbly). Stir in baking chips and nuts. Shape level tablespoons of dough into balls; place 2 in. apart on parchment-lined baking sheets.
3. Bake until the bottoms are lightly browned, 12-14 minutes. Remove to wire racks to cool completely.
4. For glaze, mix confectioners' sugar, milk and extract until smooth. Dip tops of cookies in the glaze. Sprinkle with coconut, patting gently to adhere. Let stand until set.

1 cookie: 171 cal., 9g fat (4g sat. fat), 7mg chol., 98mg sod., 22g carb. (13g sugars, 1g fiber), 2g pro.

APPETIZER TORTILLA PINWHEELS

A friend gave me the recipe for this tasty and attractive appetizer. You can prepare the pinwheels in advance and slice them just before serving to save time for other party preparations. The recipe couldn't be more convenient!
—Pat Waymire, Yellow Springs, OH

PREP: 20 MIN. + CHILLING
MAKES: ABOUT 4 DOZEN

- 1 pkg. (8 oz.) cream cheese, softened
- 1 cup shredded cheddar cheese
- 1 cup sour cream
- 1 can (4¼ oz.) chopped ripe olives
- 1 can (4 oz.) chopped green chiles, well drained
- ½ cup chopped green onions
  Garlic powder to taste
  Seasoned salt to taste
- 5 flour tortillas (10 in.)
  Salsa, optional

1. Beat cream cheese, cheese and sour cream until blended. Stir in olives, green chiles, green onions and seasonings.
2. Spread over tortillas; roll up tightly. Wrap each in plastic, twisting ends to seal; refrigerate several hours.
3. Unwrap. Cut into ½- to ¾-in. slices, using a serrated knife. If desired, serve with salsa.

1 pinwheel: 63 cal., 4g fat (2g sat. fat), 8mg chol., 119mg sod., 5g carb. (1g sugars, 0 fiber), 2g pro.

READER REVIEW
"I have made these for years. I am always getting asked to make them at our family and work functions."
—PALLSBURY, TASTEOFHOME.COM

WHITE CHEDDAR MAC & CHEESE

My mac and cheese is simple and has lots of flavor from the cheeses and ground chipotle chile. I use conchiglie pasta because its shape allows more melted cheese to pool inside. Yum!

—Colleen Delawder, Herndon, VA

TAKES: 25 MIN. • **MAKES:** 8 SERVINGS

- 1 pkg. (16 oz.) small pasta shells
- ½ cup butter, cubed
- ½ cup all-purpose flour
- ½ tsp. onion powder
- ½ tsp. ground chipotle pepper
- ½ tsp. pepper
- ¼ tsp. salt
- 4 cups 2% milk
- 2 cups shredded sharp white cheddar cheese
- 2 cups shredded Manchego or additional white cheddar cheese

1. In a 6-qt. stockpot, cook the pasta according to package directions. Drain; return to pot.

2. Meanwhile, in a large saucepan, melt butter over medium heat. Stir in flour and seasonings until smooth; gradually whisk in milk. Bring to a boil, stirring constantly; cook and stir until thickened, 6-8 minutes. Remove from heat; stir in cheeses until melted. Add to pasta; toss to coat.

1 cup: 650 cal., 35g fat (22g sat. fat), 101mg chol., 607mg sod., 55g carb. (8g sugars, 2g fiber), 27g pro.

PEPPERMINT WHITE HOT CHOCOLATE

My soothing white hot chocolate is a great warm-up after a wintry day spent sledding or ice skating. Or include it as a festive addition to brunch or an afternoon tea party.
—Darlene Brenden, Salem, OR

TAKES: 15 MIN.
MAKES: 6 SERVINGS

- 5½ cups 2% milk
- ⅓ cup heavy whipping cream
- 4 tsp. crushed peppermint candies, divided
- 12 oz. white baking chocolate, chopped
- ¾ tsp. peppermint extract
  Miniature marshmallows, optional

1. In a large saucepan, heat milk over medium heat until bubbles form around sides of pan. Meanwhile, in a small bowl, beat cream until stiff peaks form. Fold in 1 tsp. crushed candy.
2. Whisk chocolate into milk until smooth. Remove from heat; stir in extract. Pour into mugs; top with whipped cream. Sprinkle with remaining candy and, if desired, marshmallows. Serve immediately.

1 cup with about 1 Tbsp. whipped cream and ½ tsp. crushed candy: 519 cal., 32g fat (19g sat. fat), 54mg chol., 153mg sod., 46g carb. (44g sugars, 0 fiber), 11g pro.

TEST KITCHEN TIP
Before you begin beating the heavy whipping cream, make sure that your beaters and bowl are chilled. Cool tools will help the cream beat up more quickly. You can chill them by popping them in the fridge or freezer for 10 minutes before you start.

APRICOT WHITE FUDGE

This fudge is a family favorite and a nice change from typical dark or milk chocolate fudge. The blend of flavors and stained-glass look are hard to beat. It makes great Christmas gifts.
—Debbie Purdue, Westland, MI

PREP: 20 MIN. • **COOK:** 10 MIN. + CHILLING
MAKES: ABOUT 2 LBS. (81 PIECES)

- 1½ tsp. plus ½ cup butter, divided
- 2 cups sugar
- ¾ cup sour cream
- 12 oz. white baking chocolate, chopped
- 1 jar (7 oz.) marshmallow creme
- ¾ cup chopped dried apricots
- ¾ cup chopped walnuts

1. Line a 9-in. square pan with foil; grease foil with 1½ tsp. butter.
2. In a heavy saucepan, combine sugar, sour cream and remaining butter. Bring to a boil over medium heat, stirring constantly. Cook and stir until a candy thermometer reads 234° (soft-ball stage), about 5½ minutes. Remove from the heat.
3. Stir in chocolate until melted. Stir in marshmallow creme until blended. Stir in apricots and walnuts. Immediately spread into prepared pan. Refrigerate, covered, overnight.
4. Using foil, lift fudge out of pan. Remove foil; cut fudge into 1-in. squares.

1 piece: 54 cal., 2g fat (1g sat. fat), 5mg chol., 17mg sod., 8g carb. (7g sugars, 0 fiber), 0 pro.

SLOW-COOKED WHITE BEAN CHILI

My friend and I came up with an amazing chicken chili that simmers in the slow cooker. The Alfredo sauce base makes it stand apart from other white chilis. It's delicious served with warm homemade bread. Reduce the amount of cayenne pepper if you'd like a little less heat.
—Cindi Mitchell, St. Marys, KS

PREP: 15 MIN. • **COOK:** 3 HOURS
MAKES: 12 SERVINGS (3 QT.)

- 3 cans (15½ oz. each) great northern beans, rinsed and drained
- 3 cups cubed cooked chicken breast
- 1 jar (15 oz.) Alfredo sauce
- 2 cups chicken broth
- 1½ cups frozen gold and white corn (about 8 oz.), thawed
- 1 cup shredded Monterey Jack cheese
- 1 cup shredded pepper jack cheese
- 1 cup sour cream
- 1 small sweet yellow pepper, chopped
- 1 small onion, chopped
- 1 to 2 cans (4 oz. each) chopped green chiles
- 3 garlic cloves, minced
- 3 tsp. ground cumin
- 1½ tsp. white pepper
- 1 to 1½ tsp. cayenne pepper
  Optional: Salsa verde and chopped fresh cilantro

In a 5- or 6-qt. slow cooker, combine all ingredients except salsa and cilantro. Cook, covered, on low 3-4 hours or until vegetables are tender and flavors are blended, stirring once. If desired, serve with salsa and cilantro.

1 cup: 336 cal., 15g fat (9g sat. fat), 69mg chol., 772mg sod., 27g carb. (2g sugars, 7g fiber), 24g pro.

COUNTRY WHITE BREAD

Everyone loves a good slice of homemade bread, especially when it's spread with butter or jam. These loaves are especially nice because the crust stays tender. My husband makes most of the bread at our house, and this recipe is his favorite.
—Joanne Shew Chuk, St. Benedict, SK

PREP: 20 MIN. + RISING
BAKE: 25 MIN.
MAKES: 2 LOAVES (16 SLICES EACH)

- 2 pkg. (¼ oz. each) active dry yeast
- 2 cups warm water (110° to 115°)
- ½ cup sugar
- 2 tsp. salt
- 2 large eggs, room temperature
- ¼ cup canola oil
- 6½ to 7 cups all-purpose flour

1. In a large bowl, dissolve the yeast in warm water. Add sugar, salt, eggs, oil and 3 cups flour; beat on medium speed until smooth. Stir in enough remaining flour to form a soft dough.
2. Turn dough onto a floured surface; knead 6-8 minutes or until smooth and elastic. Place in a greased bowl, turning once to grease the top. Cover and let rise in a warm place until doubled, about 1 hour.
3. Punch down dough. Divide in half and shape into loaves. Place in 2 greased 9x5-in. loaf pans. Cover with kitchen towels; let rise in a warm place until doubled, about 1 hour. Preheat oven to 375°.
4. Bake 25-30 minutes or until golden brown. Remove from pans to wire racks to cool.

1 slice: 125 cal., 2g fat (0 sat. fat), 13mg chol., 226mg sod., 23g carb. (3g sugars, 1g fiber), 3g pro.

TEST KITCHEN TIP
Before you begin mixing and kneading, it's important to proof the yeast. This means ensuring the yeast is still alive and ready to create carbon dioxide, the gas that gives bread its lift. To proof, dissolve the yeast in a dish with a ½ tsp. of sugar and warm water, about 110°. Any hotter and you risk killing the yeast (and then you have to start again). You know the yeast is alive and ready when it starts to bubble and foam.

1. Pulse cookies in a food processor until fine crumbs form. Add melted butter; pulse just until combined. Press onto bottom of a 13x9-in. dish. Refrigerate while preparing filling.
2. Beat cream cheese, sugar and milk until smooth. Fold in 1 cup whipped topping and ½ cup crushed candies. Spread over crust.

3. Whisk the pudding mix and milk for 2 minutes; spread over cream cheese layer. Spread with remaining whipped topping. Refrigerate, covered, 4 hours. Sprinkle with remaining candies just before serving.

1 piece: 251 cal., 13g fat (7g sat. fat), 20mg chol., 250mg sod., 32g carb. (25g sugars, 1g fiber), 2g pro.

LAYERED CANDY CANE DESSERT

This chilled dessert has the magical flavor of candy canes plus the bonus of an Oreo cookie crust. And it looks like a winter wonderland, making it ideal for parties.
—Dawn Kreuser, Green Bay, WI

PREP: 25 MIN. + CHILLING
MAKES: 24 SERVINGS

1	pkg. (14.3 oz.) Oreo cookies
6	Tbsp. butter, melted
1	pkg. (8 oz.) cream cheese, softened
¼	cup sugar
2	Tbsp. 2% milk
1	carton (12 oz.) frozen whipped topping, thawed, divided
¾	cup crushed candy canes (about 7 regular size), divided
2	pkg. (3.3 oz. each) instant white chocolate pudding mix
2¾	cups cold 2% milk

WHITE ELEPHANT EXCHANGE RULES

Whether it's an office party or a gathering of friends, the white elephant has become a favorite holiday tradition. The rules can be whatever you want them to be, but the goal is to spark friendly competition and have a great time!

There are variations galore, but here's a rundown of the most widely accepted way to play:

STEP 1:
Every guest brings a wrapped gift. Set guidelines for gifts before the party. Put all the wrapped gifts in a central spot.

STEP 2:
Put numbered slips of paper—one for each participant—in a basket.

STEP 3:
Each guest draws a number from the basket. Guest #1 goes first, selects a gift from the table and opens it. Oohs and aahs all around!

STEP 4:
Guest #2 either selects a gift from the table and unwraps it or steals #1's gift. If #2 chooses to steal, guest #1 chooses another gift from the table and opens it.

STEP 5:
Guest #3 can either select a gift from the table and open it or steal a gift from either #1 or #2. Guests who have their gifts stolen will always choose a replacement gift—either from the table or stolen from another guest. (They can't directly steal their own gifts back in the same turn.)

STEP 6:
After a maximum of three swaps, the turn ends.

STEP 7:
After all players have taken a turn, guest #1 has a chance to steal a gift, making a direct swap with another guest. That guest can steal, and so on. There is no limit to the number of steals on the last turn— the exchange ends when a guest decides to keep the gift instead of stealing another guest's.

WHITE CHRISTMAS CAKE

"Wow!" is the reaction from family and guests when they see and taste this stunning three-layer cake. White chocolate, shredded coconut and chopped pecans make it so delicious.
—Nancy Reichert, Thomasville, GA

PREP: 35 MIN. + COOLING
BAKE: 25 MIN. + COOLING
MAKES: 16 SERVINGS

- 4 large eggs, separated
- ½ cup water
- 4 oz. chopped white candy coating or white baking chips
- 1 cup butter, softened
- 2 cups sugar
- 1 Tbsp. vanilla extract
- 2½ cups all-purpose flour
- ½ tsp. baking powder
- ½ tsp. baking soda
- 1 cup buttermilk
- 1 cup sweetened shredded coconut
- 1 cup chopped pecans

FROSTING
- 1 pkg. (8 oz.) cream cheese, softened
- ½ cup butter, softened
- 3¾ cups confectioners' sugar
- 1 Tbsp. 2% milk
- 1 tsp. vanilla extract

OPTIONAL DECORATIONS
- Melted white candy coating or white baking chips
- Red Sixlets candies and sprinkles

1. Place egg whites in a large bowl; let stand at room temperature 30 minutes. In a small saucepan, bring water to a boil. Remove from heat; stir in candy coating until blended. Cool 20 minutes.

2. Preheat oven to 350°. Line bottoms of 3 greased 8-in. square or 9-in. round baking pans with parchment; grease the paper.

3. Cream butter and sugar until light and fluffy, 5-7 minutes. Beat in egg yolks and vanilla. Beat in the candy coating mixture. In another bowl, whisk together the flour, baking powder and baking soda; add to creamed mixture alternately with buttermilk, beating after each addition. Fold in coconut and pecans. With clean beaters, beat egg whites on medium speed until stiff peaks form; fold into batter.

4. Transfer the batter to prepared pans. Bake until a toothpick inserted in center comes out clean, 25-30 minutes. Cool in pans 10 minutes before removing to wire racks; remove parchment. Cool cakes completely.

5. For the frosting, beat the cream cheese and butter until smooth. Beat in confectioners' sugar, milk and vanilla. Spread between layers and over top and sides of cake.

6. If desired, pipe leaf designs with candy coating onto a waxed paper-lined baking sheet; refrigerate until set. Decorate cake with Sixlets, sprinkles and leaves. Refrigerate leftovers.

1 piece: 622 cal., 33g fat (18g sat. fat), 107mg chol., 300mg sod., 79g carb. (62g sugars, 1g fiber), 6g pro.

Hanukkah

Light the menorah, spin the dreidel and celebrate the
eight-day winter holiday with traditional Hanukkah foods.
These special recipes, including latkes, sufganiyot,
brisket and kugel, are ready to further
brighten your Festival of Lights.

CHUNKY APPLE-CINNAMON CAKE

This is a nice change from apple pie. It's tasty and worthy of a special occasion—plus, it's easy to make.
—Ellen Ruzinsky, Yorktown Heights, NY

PREP: 25 MIN. • **BAKE:** 45 MIN. + COOLING
MAKES: 15 SERVINGS

- 2¾ lbs. McIntosh, Jonathan or Granny Smith apples, peeled and thinly sliced (11 cups)
- ½ cup packed brown sugar
- 3 tsp. ground cinnamon, divided
- 1 cup plus 1 Tbsp. sugar, divided
- 1 cup canola oil
- 4 large eggs, room temperature
- 3 Tbsp. orange juice
- 2 tsp. vanilla extract
- 2½ cups all-purpose flour
- 2 tsp. baking powder
- ½ tsp. kosher salt

1. Preheat oven to 425°. In a large bowl, toss apples with brown sugar and 2 tsp. cinnamon.
2. In another large bowl, beat 1 cup sugar, oil, eggs, orange juice and vanilla until well blended. In a third bowl, whisk flour, baking powder and salt; gradually beat into the sugar mixture.
3. Transfer half the batter to an ungreased 13x9-in. baking pan. Top with apples. Spread remaining batter over apples. Mix remaining cinnamon and sugar; sprinkle over top. Bake for 10 minutes.
4. Reduce oven setting to 375°. Bake until golden brown and apples are tender, 35-45 minutes. Cool on a wire rack.

1 piece: 349 cal., 17g fat (2g sat. fat), 56mg chol., 138mg sod., 47g carb. (30g sugars, 2g fiber), 4g pro.

BRAISED HANUKKAH BRISKET

My mother, Enid, always used the most marbled cut of brisket she could find to make this recipe, so she'd get the most flavor. When she added carrots to the pan, she threw in some potatoes, too.
—Ellen Ruzinsky, Yorktown Heights, NY

PREP: 25 MIN. • **COOK:** 2¾ HOURS
MAKES: 12 SERVINGS (4 CUPS VEGETABLES)

- 2 Tbsp. canola oil
- 1 fresh beef brisket (4 to 5 lbs.)
- 3 celery ribs, cut into 1-in. pieces
- 3 large carrots, cut into ¼-in. slices
- 2 large onions, sliced
- 1 lb. medium fresh mushrooms
- ¾ cup cold water
- ¾ cup tomato sauce
- 3 Tbsp. Worcestershire sauce
- 1 Tbsp. prepared horseradish

1. In a Dutch oven, heat the oil over medium heat. Brown the brisket on both sides. Remove from pan.
2. Add celery, carrots and onions to same pan; cook and stir 4-6 minutes or until crisp-tender. Stir in the remaining ingredients.
3. Return brisket to pan, fat side up. Bring mixture to a boil. Reduce heat; simmer, covered, 2½-3 hours or until meat is tender. Remove the beef and vegetables; keep warm. Skim fat from pan juices. If desired, thicken juices.
4. Cut the brisket diagonally across the grain into thin slices. Serve with the vegetables and pan juices.

4 oz. cooked meat with ⅓ cup vegetables and ½ cup juices: 247 cal., 9g fat (3g sat. fat), 64mg chol., 189mg sod., 8g carb. (3g sugars, 2g fiber), 33g pro. **Diabetic exchanges:** 4 lean meat, 1 vegetable, ½ fat.

READER REVIEW
"I love this recipe! I also put in ¼ cup of honey, and it really added another dimension of flavor!"
—GUCCI65, TASTEOFHOME.COM

ROASTED BRUSSELS SPROUTS WITH CRANBERRIES

There's practically nothing to this recipe—the preparation and cooking times are so quick. I sprinkle in a few dried cranberries, but you can let your imagination take over. Add a handful of raisins or walnuts or sliced oranges at the end. If your Brussels sprouts are large, cut them in half.
—Ellen Ruzinsky, Yorktown Heights, NY

PREP: 15 MIN. • **BAKE:** 20 MIN.
MAKES: 12 SERVINGS

- 3 lbs. fresh Brussels sprouts, trimmed and halved
- 3 Tbsp. olive oil
- 1 tsp. kosher salt
- ½ tsp. pepper
- ½ cup dried cranberries

Preheat oven to 425°. Divide Brussels sprouts between 2 greased 15x10x1-in. baking pans. Drizzle with oil; sprinkle with salt and pepper. Toss to coat. Roast until tender, stirring occasionally, 20-25 minutes. Transfer to a large bowl; stir in cranberries.

½ cup: 94 cal., 4g fat (1g sat. fat), 0 chol., 185mg sod., 14g carb. (6g sugars, 5g fiber), 4g pro. **Diabetic exchanges:** 1 vegetable, 1 fat.

LATKES WITH LOX

Lox, a salty smoked salmon, is a year-round delicacy. These crispy latkes, inspired by a recipe from the Jewish Journal, *use lox as a topping.*
—*Taste of Home* Test Kitchen

PREP: 20 MIN. • **COOK:** 5 MIN./BATCH
MAKES: 3 DOZEN

- 2 cups finely chopped onion
- ¼ cup all-purpose flour
- 6 garlic cloves, minced
- 2 tsp. salt
- 1 tsp. coarsely ground pepper
- 4 large eggs, lightly beaten
- 4 lbs. russet potatoes, peeled and shredded
- ¾ cup canola oil

TOPPINGS

- 4 oz. lox
   Optional: Sour cream and minced fresh chives

1. In a large bowl, combine the first 5 ingredients. Stir in the eggs until blended. Add potatoes; toss to coat.
2. Heat 2 Tbsp. oil in a large nonstick skillet over medium heat. Drop batter by ¼ cupfuls into the oil; press lightly to flatten. Fry in batches until golden brown on both sides, using remaining oil as needed. Drain on paper towels. Serve with lox; top with sour cream and chives if desired.

3 latkes with ⅓ oz. lox: 270 cal., 16g fat (2g sat. fat), 73mg chol., 610mg sod., 26g carb. (3g sugars, 2g fiber), 6g pro.

POTATO KUGEL

The secret to keeping your potatoes their whitest is to switch back and forth when grating the potatoes and onion in your food processor or box grater.
—Ellen Ruzinsky, Yorktown Heights, NY

PREP: 20 MIN. • **BAKE:** 40 MIN.
MAKES: 12 SERVINGS

- 2 large eggs
- ¼ cup matzo meal
- 2 tsp. kosher salt
  Dash pepper
- 6 large potatoes (about 4¾ lbs.), peeled
- 1 large onion, cut into 6 wedges
- ¼ cup canola oil

1. Preheat oven to 375°. In a large bowl, whisk the eggs, matzo meal, salt and pepper.
2. In a food processor fitted with the grating attachment, alternately grate potatoes and onion. Add to egg mixture; toss to coat. In a small saucepan, heat the oil over medium heat until warmed. Stir into the potato mixture. Transfer to a greased 13x9-in. baking dish. Bake 40-50 minutes or until golden brown.

1 serving: 210 cal., 6g fat (1g sat. fat), 35mg chol., 515mg sod., 36g carb. (3g sugars, 3g fiber), 5g pro.

TEST KITCHEN TIP
Matzo meal is ground matzo, a traditional Jewish unleavened bread also known as matzah. You can substitute matzo meal in almost any recipe that calls for regular bread crumbs. You can find prepared matzo meal at most grocery stores. Or you can make your own by grinding matzo bread.

YOUR GUIDE TO 8 TRADITIONAL HANUKKAH FOODS

From latkes (fried potato pancakes) to sufganiyot (fried jelly doughnuts), fried foods take center stage on the traditional Hanukkah table. Here's a guide to these and other popular Hanukkah foods, as well as their significance.

WHAT IS HANUKKAH?

Hanukkah, also known as the Festival of Lights, is a Jewish holiday that celebrates the ancient Jews' reclamation of their temple in Jerusalem after occupation by the Syrian-Greek empire.

As the story goes, the Jewish Maccabees reentered the temple and found only a tiny bit of oil—barely enough to burn their lamps for one day. Instead, the oil burned for eight days—a Hanukkah miracle.

Since Hanukkah typically falls in December, it's often considered the Jewish version of Christmas. But Hanukkah is actually a minor Jewish festival—far less significant than the Jewish High Holidays of Rosh Hashana and Yom Kippur.

Still, Hanukkah is a fun winter celebration—and it doesn't hurt that it's associated with lots of good food. There are dozens of Hanukkah recipes to make during the eight-day celebration, but here are some of the most traditional Hanukkah foods.

LATKES

Latkes are fried potato pancakes eaten to remember the oil miracle in the Hanukkah story. There are many variations, including sweet potato, zucchini, and cheese and red pepper.

APPLESAUCE & SOUR CREAM

Applesauce and sour cream are the most popular latke toppings. They can be playfully divisive—ask any Jewish person in your life which they prefer and they'll likely have strong opinions. Make sure you have both!

Whether you personally opt for applesauce or sour cream (or both!), these cool, smooth toppings provide the perfect contrast to piping hot, crispy latkes.

Editor's tip: Store-bought sour cream and applesauce work just fine, but take your latkes up a notch with homemade applesauce.

SUFGANIYOT

Fried jelly doughnuts are another reminder of the Hanukkah oil miracle. In Israel and many Jewish communities in the U.S., they're called sufganiyot, the Hebrew word for doughnuts. They're related to sfinge, which are Moroccan doughnuts also associated with Hanukkah.

GELT

Gelt refers to wrapped chocolate coins that are used to play dreidel, a traditional Hanukkah game. A dreidel is a top with four sides, each with a different Hebrew letter. Each letter represents a word in a Hebrew saying that means "a great miracle happened there" (referring to Israel, where the Hanukkah story took place).

To play the dreidel game, players each start with several pieces of gelt and take turns spinning the top. Depending on which letter the dreidel lands on, players have to give or take gelt from the center "pot." The game ends when one player wins all of the gelt.

Editor's tip: When playing the dreidel game, many people use store-bought gelt—it's readily available at many retailers in December. You can also play using pennies, M&M's or make your own homemade gelt.

HANUKKAH COOKIES

Hanukkah cookies may not be as traditional as latkes or sufganiyot, but they're a fun way to celebrate the holiday. Common cookie shapes for Hanukkah include dreidels, menorahs (the nine-branched Hanukkah candle holder) and stars of David.

Editor's tip: To mix up your sweets spread, include some other Hanukkah desserts, such as rugelach, babka and mandelbrot.

BRISKET

Brisket is a popular entree in many Jewish households for holidays including Hanukkah, Rosh Hashana and Passover. Different from Texas-style barbecue brisket, Jewish brisket is braised—often with carrots, potatoes and other vegetables.

Editor's tip: When you're buying brisket meat, look for a piece with lots of marbling—it'll make for a more flavorful dish.

KUGEL

Kugel is a traditional Jewish noodle casserole dish that can be either sweet or savory. Sweet versions often include cottage cheese, eggs, sugar, cinnamon and sometimes raisins. Savory versions may include garlic, onions and other vegetables.

CHOCOLATE-STUFFED DREIDEL COOKIES

These dreidel cookies are sure to spread some smiles this holiday season. Your friends and family will delight in the surprise chocolate filling.
—*Taste of Home* Test Kitchen

PREP: 15 MIN. + CHILLING
BAKE: 10 MIN./BATCH + COOLING
MAKES: 3 DOZEN

- 1 cup unsalted butter, softened
- 1 cup sugar
- 2 large eggs, room temperature
- 1 Tbsp. vanilla extract
- 3½ cups all-purpose flour
- 1 Tbsp. baking powder
- ½ tsp. salt
- 6 to 7 milk chocolate candy bars (1.55 oz. each), broken into 2-section pieces
- 2½ cups vanilla frosting
  White and light blue paste food coloring

1. Cream the butter and sugar until light and fluffy, 5-7 minutes. Beat in eggs and vanilla. In another bowl, whisk together flour, baking powder and salt; gradually beat into the creamed mixture. Divide dough in half; shape each into a disk. Cover and refrigerate until firm enough to roll, at least 1 hour.
2. Preheat oven to 350°. On a lightly floured surface, roll each portion of dough to ⅛-in. thickness. Cut with a floured 4-in. dreidel cutter. Place half the cutouts 1 in. apart on ungreased baking sheets; top with the candy bar pieces. Top with the remaining cutouts, pinching edges to seal.
3. Bake until bottoms are light brown, 10-12 minutes. Remove from pans to wire racks; cool completely.
4. Tint ⅔ cup frosting light blue. Spread remaining white frosting over cookies. Pipe 1 Hebrew letter on each cookie.
1 cookie: 236 cal., 11g fat (6g sat. fat), 26mg chol., 123mg sod., 32g carb. (20g sugars, 1g fiber), 2g pro.

HOMEMADE GELT

Giving chocolate coins to children, and sometimes to teachers, is a long-standing Hanukkah tradition. This homemade gelt uses a miniature muffin pan to mold the coins into shape. The sliced almonds add a nice crunch, but gelt can be left plain or topped with other ingredients like sprinkles, crushed peppermint candies or finely chopped candied ginger.
—*Taste of Home* Test Kitchen

PREP: 10 MIN. + CHILLING • **MAKES:** 3 DOZEN

- 2 tsp. canola oil
- 3 (3½ oz. each) dark chocolate candy bars, melted
- ¼ cup sliced almonds, finely chopped

Brush miniature muffin cups lightly with oil. Pour about 1 tsp. melted chocolate into each cup and bang on counter. Sprinkle with almonds. Refrigerate until set. Remove from muffin cups and blot off any excess oil, if needed.
1 piece: 42 cal., 3g fat (2g sat. fat), 1mg chol., 0 sod., 5g carb. (4g sugars, 1g fiber), 1g pro.

SUFGANIYOT

Sufganiyot are believed to have first come from Spain, adapted from a similar treat, the sopaipilla. Others say the sopaipilla was borrowed from the Jews. Either way, as a tradition, doughnuts are an easy (and tasty!) one to adopt.
—David Feder, Buffalo Grove, IL

PREP: 35 MIN. + RISING • **COOK:** 5 MIN./BATCH
MAKES: 1½ DOZEN

- ½ cup whole wheat flour
- 1 pkg. (¼ oz.) active dry yeast
- ¼ tsp. ground cloves
- 1½ to 2 cups all-purpose flour
- ½ cup water
- ¼ cup honey
- 2 tsp. canola or peanut oil
- 1 large egg, room temperature
- ½ tsp. vanilla extract
  Oil for deep-fat frying
- ¾ cup seedless raspberry preserves
  Confectioners' sugar

1. In a large bowl, mix the whole wheat flour, yeast, ground cloves and 1¼ cups all-purpose flour. In a small saucepan, heat water, honey and oil to 120°-130°. Add to the dry ingredients; beat on medium speed for 2 minutes. Add the egg and vanilla; beat 2 minutes longer. Stir in enough remaining flour to form a soft dough (dough will be sticky).
2. Turn onto a floured surface; knead until smooth and elastic, 6-8 minutes. Place in a greased bowl, turning once to grease the top. Cover and let rise in a warm place until doubled, about 1 hour.
3. Punch down dough. Turn onto a lightly floured surface; roll the dough to ¼-in. thickness. Cut with a floured 2-in. biscuit cutter.
4. In an electric skillet or deep fryer, heat oil to 375°. Fry the doughnuts, a few at a time, for 45 seconds on each side or until golden brown. Drain on paper towels.
5. Cut a small hole in the tip of a pastry bag or in a corner of a resealable bag; insert a small tip. Fill the bag with the raspberry preserves.
6. With a small knife, pierce a hole into the side of each doughnut; fill with the preserves. Dust with confectioners' sugar. Serve warm.

1 filled doughnut: 133 cal., 4g fat (0 sat. fat), 12mg chol., 5mg sod., 23g carb. (12g sugars, 1g fiber), 2g pro.

HANUKKAH COOKIES

Cream cheese adds richness to these holiday cutout cookies. Decorate with royal icing or your favorite buttercream frosting and toppings.
—*Taste of Home* Test Kitchen

PREP: 25 MIN. + CHILLING
BAKE: 10 MIN./BATCH + COOLING
MAKES: ABOUT 3½ DOZEN

- 2 cups butter, softened
- 1 pkg. (8 oz.) cream cheese, softened
- 2½ cups sugar
- 1 large egg, room temperature
- ½ tsp. almond extract
- 4½ cups all-purpose flour

ICING

- 3¾ cups confectioners' sugar
- ⅓ cup water
- 4 tsp. meringue powder
  Blue and yellow paste food coloring

1. In a large bowl, cream butter, cream cheese and sugar until light and fluffy, 5-7 minutes. Beat in egg and extract. Gradually beat flour into the creamed mixture. Divide dough in half. Shape each into a disk; cover and refrigerate until firm enough to roll, 2 hours.
2. Preheat oven to 350°. On a lightly floured surface, roll each portion of dough to ¼-in. thickness. Cut with floured 3-in. cookie cutters. Place cutouts 1 in. apart on greased baking sheets. Bake 10-12 minutes or until set (do not brown). Cool cookies on pans 5 minutes. Remove to wire racks to cool completely. For the frosting, in a small bowl, combine confectioners' sugar, water and meringue powder; beat on low speed just until combined. Beat on high 4 minutes or until soft peaks form. Cover the frosting with damp paper towels between uses.
3. Pipe the icing on the cookies as desired. Let stand until set. Store in an airtight container.

1 cookie: 236 cal., 11g fat (7g sat. fat), 33mg chol., 91mg sod., 33g carb. (23g sugars, 0 fiber), 2g pro.

TEST KITCHEN TIP
To make these cookies parve (which in this case means omitting the dairy), swap the butter and cream cheese for dairy-free alternatives that are labeled as plant-based or vegan. This is important if you follow kosher guidelines, as Jewish law does not allow meat and dairy products to be eaten together. A cookie that is parve, however, can be eaten following a meal that contains meat.

Christmas Morning Breakfast

The day you've anticipated all year long is finally here, so why not start the celebration as early as possible? Whether treating your family to a warm and cozy Christmas breakfast or hosting a holiday brunch for a larger group, you'll find the perfect dishes, beverages and eye-opening surprises right here. It's Christmas, so let's make it a merry morning!

CORNFLAKE-COATED CRISPY BACON

I've loved my aunt's crispy-coated bacon ever since I was a child. Now I've shared the super simple recipe with my own children. We still enjoy a big panful every Christmas morning—and on many other days throughout the year!
—Brenda Severson, Norman, OK

PREP: 20 MIN. • **BAKE:** 25 MIN.
MAKES: 9 SERVINGS

- ½ cup evaporated milk
- 2 Tbsp. ketchup
- 1 Tbsp. Worcestershire sauce
  Dash pepper
- 18 bacon strips (1 lb.)
- 3 cups crushed cornflakes

Preheat oven to 375°. In a large bowl, combine milk, ketchup, Worcestershire sauce and pepper. Add bacon strips, turning to coat. Dip strips in crushed cornflakes, patting to help the coating adhere. Place bacon on 2 racks; place each rack on an ungreased 15x10x1-in. baking pan. Bake until golden and crisp, rotating pans halfway through baking, 25-30 minutes.

2 bacon strips: 198 cal., 7g fat (3g sat. fat), 20mg chol., 547mg sod., 26g carb. (4g sugars, 0 fiber), 8g pro.

PEACHES & CREAM WAFFLE DIPPERS

I've prepared these for many brunches—peaches are my favorite fruit to add, but you can use strawberries or blueberries. People of all ages enjoy dunking crispy waffle strips into creamy dip.
—Bonnie Geavaras-Bootz, Chandler, AZ

PREP: 30 MIN. • **BAKE:** 5 MIN./BATCH
MAKES: 6 SERVINGS (2 CUPS SAUCE)

- 1 cup all-purpose flour
- 1 Tbsp. sugar
- 1 tsp. baking powder
- ¼ tsp. salt
- 2 large eggs, separated
- 1 cup 2% milk
- 2 Tbsp. butter, melted
- ¼ tsp. vanilla extract
- 1¼ cups chopped frozen peaches, thawed, divided
- 2 cups sweetened whipped cream or whipped topping
- ¾ cup peach yogurt
  Optional: Toasted pecans and ground cinnamon

1. In a large bowl, whisk flour, sugar, baking powder and salt. In another bowl, whisk egg yolks, milk, butter and vanilla until blended. Add to dry ingredients; stir just until moistened. Stir in 1 cup peaches.

2. In a small bowl, beat egg whites until stiff but not dry. Fold into batter. Bake in a preheated waffle maker according to manufacturer's directions until golden brown. Cut waffles into 1-in. strips.

3. In a small bowl, fold whipped cream into yogurt. Serve with waffle strips. Sprinkle with remaining peaches and, if desired, pecans and cinnamon.

8 waffle strips with ⅓ cup sauce: 341 cal., 21g fat (13g sat. fat), 122mg chol., 279mg sod., 30g carb. (14g sugars, 1g fiber), 8g pro.

TEST KITCHEN TIP
Save time on the big day by preparing the waffles ahead of time and storing them in the freezer. Simply reheat the waffles in the toaster, in the toaster oven or even in the air fryer.

SANTA BELT NAPKIN RINGS

Jolly up the table with red napkins that resemble Santa's suit. Just cinch them with napkin rings made of black ribbon and gold-glitter card stock.

For each ring, punch or cut a square from the card stock. Using a pencil, mark two slits in the center that are as long as the width of your ribbon. Use a craft knife to cut the slits, then thread the ribbon through the slits and tie it around a napkin.

PUMPKIN-CHOCOLATE CHIP PANCAKES

Who can resist a sky-high stack of golden, fluffy pancakes? Pumpkin and chocolate chips take them over the top!
—Elizabeth Godecke, Chicago, IL

PREP: 15 MIN. • **COOK:** 5 MIN./BATCH
MAKES: 15 PANCAKES

- 2⅓ cups pancake mix
- ½ tsp. ground cinnamon
- ¼ tsp. ground nutmeg
- ¼ tsp. ground cloves
- 2 large eggs, room temperature
- 1¼ cups buttermilk
- ⅓ cup canned pumpkin
- ¼ cup butter, melted
- 1 Tbsp. honey
- ½ cup miniature semisweet chocolate chips
  Additional miniature semisweet chocolate chips and honey

1. In a large bowl, combine pancake mix, cinnamon, nutmeg and cloves. In a small bowl, whisk eggs, buttermilk, pumpkin, butter and honey; stir into dry ingredients just until moistened. Fold in chocolate chips.
2. Lightly grease a griddle; heat over medium heat. Pour batter by ¼ cupfuls onto griddle. Cook until bubbles on top begin to pop and bottoms are golden brown. Turn; cook until second side is golden brown. Serve with additional chocolate chips and honey.

3 pancakes: 422 cal., 18g fat (10g sat. fat), 111mg chol., 844mg sod., 57g carb. (18g sugars, 5g fiber), 11g pro.

HOT COCOA WITH ALMOND MILK

Change up ordinary hot cocoa by stirring some dark baking cocoa into vanilla almond milk. Top it off with a plain large marshmallow or berry marshmallow creme, if you like, and add your favorite pretty sprinkles.
—Cindy Reams, Philipsburg, PA

TAKES: 15 MIN. • **MAKES:** 8 SERVINGS

- ½ cup sugar
- ½ cup dark baking cocoa or baking cocoa
- 2 cartons (32 oz. each) vanilla almond milk
- 1 tsp. vanilla extract
  Optional: Large marshmallows or strawberry marshmallow creme, and assorted sprinkles

In a large saucepan, combine sugar and dark baking cocoa; gradually whisk in almond milk. Heat until bubbles form around the sides of the pan, whisking occasionally. Remove from heat; stir in the vanilla. If desired, serve with large marshmallows or marshmallow creme, and sprinkles.

1 cup: 155 cal., 3g fat (0 sat. fat), 0 chol., 150mg sod., 32g carb. (28g sugars, 2g fiber), 2g pro.

BLUEBERRY CANTALOUPE SALAD

The simple citrus and poppy seed dressing in this fruit medley really dresses up the refreshing mix of berries and melon.
—R. Jean Rand, Edina, MN

TAKES: 10 MIN. • **MAKES:** 4 SERVINGS

¾	cup orange yogurt
1½	tsp. lemon juice
¾	tsp. poppy seeds
½	tsp. grated orange zest
2	cups diced cantaloupe
1	cup fresh blueberries

In a small bowl, mix yogurt, lemon juice, poppy seeds and orange zest. To serve, divide the cantaloupe and blueberries among 4 dishes; top with the yogurt dressing.
¾ cup with 3 Tbsp. dressing: 76 cal., 1g fat (0 sat. fat), 1mg chol., 24mg sod., 17g carb. (15g sugars, 1g fiber), 2g pro. **Diabetic exchanges:** 1 fruit.

MAPLE MORNING GRANOLA

Here, salty and sweet ingredients combine for an easy, wholesome breakfast or snack. Hosting a kids holiday party? Pack up the granola into treat bags and present them as take-home favors.
—Elizabeth Godecke, Chicago, IL

PREP: 15 MIN. • **BAKE:** 35 MIN. + COOLING
MAKES: 5 CUPS

3	cups old-fashioned oats
⅔	cup chopped pecans
⅓	cup salted pumpkin seeds or pepitas
½	cup maple syrup
4	tsp. butter, melted
1½	tsp. ground cinnamon
¼	tsp. salt
¼	tsp. ground nutmeg
½	cup dried apples, chopped
½	cup dried cranberries
	Plain yogurt

1. Preheat oven to 325°. In a large bowl, combine the oats, pecans and pumpkin seeds. In a small bowl, mix the maple syrup, butter, cinnamon, salt and nutmeg. Pour over the oat mixture and toss to coat.
2. Transfer to a 15x10x1-in. baking pan coated with cooking spray. Bake 35-40 minutes or until golden brown, stirring occasionally. Cool completely on a wire rack. Stir in the dried fruits; serve with the yogurt. Store granola in an airtight container.
½ cup: 268 cal., 12g fat (2g sat. fat), 4mg chol., 119mg sod., 37g carb. (16g sugars, 4g fiber), 7g pro. **Diabetic exchanges:** 2½ starch, 2 fat.

DOUBLE-CRUSTED SAUSAGE EGG CASSEROLE

This breakfast has become our Christmas tradition. I love being able to assemble and refrigerate the casserole the night before. Then I just pop it into the oven to bake while we open gifts in the morning.

—Lynne German, Buford, GA

PREP: 25 MIN. + CHILLING • **BAKE:** 35 MIN.
MAKES: 12 SERVINGS

2   lbs. bulk pork sausage
4   cups shredded
    Monterey Jack cheese
2   cans (8 oz. each) refrigerated
    crescent rolls
7   large eggs
¼   cup 2% milk
¼   tsp. salt
¼   tsp. pepper
¼   cup grated Parmesan cheese

In a large skillet, cook sausage over medium heat 8-10 minutes or until no longer pink, breaking it into crumbles; drain. Stir in Monterey Jack cheese.

2. Unroll 1 tube of crescent dough into a long rectangle; press perforations to seal. Press onto the bottom of a greased 13x9-in. baking dish. Top with the sausage mixture.

3. Separate 1 egg; reserve egg white for brushing the top. In a small bowl, whisk egg yolk, milk, salt, pepper and remaining eggs until blended; pour over the sausage mixture. Sprinkle with the Parmesan cheese.

4. On a lightly floured surface, unroll remaining crescent dough and roll into a 13x9-in. rectangle; cut crosswise into 13 strips. Twist each strip and place over filling; brush with reserved egg white. Refrigerate, covered, overnight.

5. Remove casserole from refrigerator 30 minutes before baking. Preheat oven to 350°. Bake 35-40 minutes or until golden brown. Let stand 5-10 minutes before serving.

1 piece: 511 cal., 38g fat (14g sat. fat), 185mg chol., 1092mg sod., 18g carb. (5g sugars, 0 fiber), 24g pro.

CRANBERRY-EGGNOG DROP SCONES

Round out a festive brunch menu with a fresh-baked treat from the oven. My tender scones feature a pleasant eggnog flavor and a nice crunch from pecans.

—Linda Hickam, Healdsburg, CA

PREP: 15 MIN. • **BAKE:** 10 MIN./BATCH
MAKES: ABOUT 1½ DOZEN

2   cups all-purpose flour
½   cup sugar
1½ tsp. baking powder
½   tsp. baking soda
¼   tsp. salt
⅓   cup cold butter, cubed
1   large egg, room temperature
½   cup eggnog
1½ tsp. vanilla extract
⅔   cup dried cranberries
½   cup chopped pecans

1. Preheat oven to 375°. Place the first 5 ingredients in a food processor; pulse to blend. Add butter; pulse until coarse crumbs form. In a bowl, whisk together egg, eggnog and vanilla. Add to food processor; pulse just until blended. Remove to a bowl; stir in cranberries and pecans.

2. Drop mixture by tablespoonfuls 2 in. apart onto greased baking sheets. Bake until golden brown, 10-13 minutes. Cool on a wire rack. Serve warm.

1 scone: 153 cal., 6g fat (3g sat. fat), 24mg chol., 143mg sod., 22g carb. (11g sugars, 1g fiber), 2g pro. **Diabetic exchanges:** 1½ starch, 1 fat.

NORTH POLE PARTY MASKS

Put on your best morning face—literally! These hand-held party masks add holly jolly to any meal. Start by looking online for simple ideas for various hats, beards and glasses, and create the patterns.

Next, trace the patterns onto colorful craft foam and cut out the pieces. Glue them together as needed; glue a thin wood dowel to the side of each mask for a handle. Then, grab your camera and let the fun begin!

LAYERED FRESH FRUIT SALAD

Fresh fruit flavor shines through in this combination, always welcome at potlucks. It's got a little zing from citrus zest and cinnamon—and is just sweet enough to feel like dessert.

—Paige Alexander, Baldwin City, KS

PREP: 20 MIN. + CHILLING
COOK: 10 MIN. + COOLING
MAKES: 12 SERVINGS

- 1/2 tsp. grated orange zest
- 2/3 cup orange juice
- 1/2 tsp. grated lemon zest
- 1/3 cup lemon juice
- 1/3 cup packed light brown sugar
- 1 cinnamon stick

FRUIT SALAD

- 2 cups cubed fresh pineapple
- 2 cups sliced fresh strawberries
- 2 medium kiwifruit, peeled and sliced
- 3 medium bananas, sliced
- 2 medium oranges, peeled and sectioned
- 1 medium red grapefruit, peeled and sectioned
- 1 cup seedless red grapes

1. Place the first 6 ingredients in a saucepan; bring to a boil. Reduce heat; simmer, uncovered, 5 minutes. Cool completely. Remove cinnamon stick.
2. Layer the fruit in a large glass bowl. Pour juice mixture over top. Refrigerate, covered, several hours.

1 serving: 110 cal., 0 fat (0 sat. fat), 0 chol., 5mg sod., 28g carb. (21g sugars, 2g fiber), 1g pro. **Diabetic exchanges:** 1 starch, 1 fruit.

RAINBOW QUICHE

With plenty of veggies and a creamy egg-cheese filling, this tasty quiche gets rave reviews every time I make it!

—Lilith Fury, Adena, OH

PREP: 30 MIN. • **BAKE:** 40 MIN. + STANDING
MAKES: 8 SERVINGS

- 1 sheet refrigerated pie crust
- 2 Tbsp. butter
- 1 small onion, finely chopped
- 1 cup sliced fresh mushrooms
- 1 cup small fresh broccoli florets
- 1/2 cup finely chopped sweet orange pepper
- 1/2 cup finely chopped sweet red pepper
- 3 large eggs, lightly beaten
- 1 1/3 cups half-and-half cream
- 3/4 tsp. salt
- 1/2 tsp. pepper
- 1 cup shredded Mexican cheese blend, divided
- 1 cup fresh baby spinach

1. Preheat the oven to 425°. Unroll the pie crust onto a lightly floured surface, roll to a 12-in. circle. Transfer to a 9-in. deep-dish pie plate; trim and flute edge. Refrigerate while preparing filling.
2. In a large skillet, heat the butter over medium-high heat; saute onion, mushrooms, broccoli and peppers until mushrooms are lightly browned, 6-8 minutes. Cool slightly.
3. Whisk together eggs, cream, salt and pepper. Sprinkle 1/2 cup cheese over crust; top with spinach and the vegetable mixture. Sprinkle with the remaining cheese. Pour in egg mixture.
4. Bake quiche on a lower oven rack 15 minutes. Reduce oven setting to 350°; bake until a knife inserted in the center comes out clean, 25-30 minutes. (Cover the edge loosely with foil if necessary to prevent overbrowning.) Let stand 10 minutes before cutting.

1 piece: 295 cal., 20g fat (10g sat. fat), 115mg chol., 482mg sod., 18g carb. (4g sugars, 1g fiber), 9g pro.

ORANGE JUICE SPRITZER

Here's a zippy twist on regular orange juice. It is not too sweet and is refreshing with any breakfast or brunch entree.
—Michelle Krzmarzick, Torrance, CA

TAKES: 5 MIN.
MAKES: 8 SERVINGS

- 4 cups orange juice
- 1 liter ginger ale, chilled
- ¼ cup maraschino cherry juice
  Optional: Orange wedges and maraschino cherries

In a 2-qt. pitcher, mix the orange juice, ginger ale and cherry juice. Serve over ice. If desired, top servings with orange wedges and cherries.
1 cup: 103 cal., 0 fat (0 sat. fat), 0 chol., 9mg sod., 25g carb. (23g sugars, 0 fiber), 1g pro.

RASPBERRY CHAMPAGNE COCKTAIL

At a restaurant, I often ordered a fizzy, fruity beverage. Then I decided to make it at home, giving mimosas a raspberry touch.
—Hillary Tedesco, Crofton, MD

TAKES: 5 MIN. • **MAKES:** 1 SERVING

- 1 oz. raspberry liqueur
- ⅔ cup chilled champagne
  Fresh raspberries

Place the raspberry liqueur in a champagne flute; top with the champagne. Top with raspberries.
¾ cup: 211 cal., 0 fat (0 sat. fat), 0 chol., 0 sod., 13g carb. (11g sugars, 0 fiber), 0 pro.

CHAMPAGNE COCKTAIL

This amber drink is a champagne twist on the traditional old-fashioned. Try it with extra-dry champagne.
—*Taste of Home* Test Kitchen

TAKES: 5 MIN. • **MAKES:** 1 SERVING

- 1 sugar cube or ½ tsp. sugar
- 6 dashes bitters
- ½ oz. brandy
- ½ cup chilled champagne
  Optional: Fresh rosemary sprig and fresh or frozen cranberries

Place sugar in a champagne flute or cocktail glass; sprinkle with bitters. Add brandy; top with champagne. If desired, top with rosemary and cranberries.
1 serving: 130 cal., 0 fat (0 sat. fat), 0 chol., 0 sod., 5g carb. (2g sugars, 0 fiber), 0 pro.

THE RIGHT WAY TO OPEN CHAMPAGNE

Curious about how to open a bottle of champagne without sending the cork flying? Popping the bubbly is far easier than many think.

STEP 1: CUT AND REMOVE THE FOIL

Using the serrated knife of a wine key, cut the metal foil. After removing the foil, cover the top of the bottle with a kitchen towel and place one hand on top of the bottle, with your thumb firmly over the cork.

STEP 2: OPEN THE BOTTLE

Before opening, be certain the bottle is pointed away from bystanders (or anything fragile). Untwist the metal cage and slowly rotate the bottle, not the cork. Use the hand on top of the bottle to help ease out the cork. By controlling how quickly the cork comes out, you can gradually allow gas to escape the bottle. The result should be a gentle hiss rather than a loud bang.

STEP 3: SERVE!

Put the cork and cage off to the side and get ready to pour. Again, take it easy and pour slowly to avoid causing overflow.

Remember these simple steps to pour your champagne like a pro with every pop of a cork. To your health or, as the French might say, *santé!*

Regal Christmas Dinner

The presents are wrapped, the cookies are baked and the lights on the tree are twinkling with a warm glow. Christmas is the time to break out your most impressive recipes and prepare a feast fit for the season. If you're looking for something elegant, try this menu's classic pairing of land and sea. Accompanied by succulent sides and a gorgeous dessert, this will be your most memorable holiday dinner yet.

Christmas Countdown

Your holiday season will shine brighter than ever this year with these festive and flavorful ideas. Use this handy guide to help plan the big feast!

A FEW WEEKS BEFORE
☐ Prepare two grocery lists—one for nonperishable items to buy now and one for perishable items to buy a few days before Christmas.

TWO DAYS BEFORE
☐ Buy remaining grocery items.
☐ Prepare jalapeno vodka for the Pomegranate Cocktail. Cover and refrigerate vodka for 2-3 days.
☐ Prepare the dressing for the Lemon Artichoke Romaine Salad. Refrigerate.
☐ Bake the cake layers for the Black Walnut Layer Cake. Freeze or store in an airtight container.
☐ Bake the Dinner Rolls. Freeze or store in an airtight container.
☐ Bake the Blue Cheese Thins. Store in an airtight container.

THE DAY BEFORE
☐ Prepare Greek Olive Tapenade. Cover and refrigerate.
☐ Prepare the Parsnip & Celery Root Bisque. Allow to cool completely and do not add garnishes. Cover and refrigerate.
☐ Prepare the Peppermint Patty Cream Pie. Cover and refrigerate until ready to serve.

CHRISTMAS DAY
☐ About 3-4 hours before dinner, remove the Dinner Rolls and Black Walnut Layer Cake layers from the freezer to thaw.
☐ About 3-4 hours before dinner, prepare the Gruyere Mashed Potatoes. Allow to cool. Cover and refrigerate.
☐ About 2 hours before dinner, prepare and bake the Seasoned Ribeye Roast. Keep warm until serving.
☐ About 45 minutes before dinner, prepare and broil lobster tails. Keep warm until serving.
☐ About 30 minutes before dinner, prepare Bacon-Wrapped Figs, Vegetable Brown Rice, and Bacon-Onion Green Beans. Keep dishes warm until serving.
☐ About 20 minutes before dinner, prepare the Rosemary Garlic Shrimp. Keep warm.

RIGHT BEFORE DINNER
☐ As guests arrive, prepare the Pomegranate Cocktail using the chilled jalapeno vodka.
☐ As guests arrive, toast baguette slices in the oven. Serve with Greek Olive Tapenade.
☐ Frost the Black Walnut Layer Cake. If desired, garnish with additional walnuts and orange slices. Remove pie from the refrigerator.
☐ Remove the salad dressing for the Lemon Artichoke Romaine Salad from the refrigerator and shake well. Prepare salad and toss with dressing. Sprinkle the salad with cheese.
☐ Remove mashed potatoes from the refrigerator and warm in the oven just before serving.
☐ Remove the bisque from the refrigerator and warm on the stovetop. Sprinkle with chives and pomegranate seeds just before serving.
☐ Warm dinner rolls in the oven just before serving.

LEMON ARTICHOKE ROMAINE SALAD

I created this dish when I was trying to duplicate a lemony Caesar salad. This version is not only delicious but more healthful, too.
—Kathy Armstrong, Post Falls, ID

TAKES: 15 MIN. • **MAKES:** 8 SERVINGS

- 10 cups torn romaine
- 4 plum tomatoes, chopped
- 1 can (14 oz.) water-packed quartered artichoke hearts, rinsed and drained
- 1 can (2¼ oz.) sliced ripe olives, drained
- 3 Tbsp. water
- 3 Tbsp. lemon juice
- 3 Tbsp. olive oil
- 2 garlic cloves, minced
- 1 tsp. salt
- 1 tsp. coarsely ground pepper
- ⅓ cup shredded Parmesan cheese

1. Place the first 4 ingredients in a large bowl. Place all the remaining ingredients except cheese in a jar with a tight-fitting lid; shake well. Pour over salad; toss to coat.
2. Sprinkle with cheese. Serve the salad immediately.

1½ cups: 105 cal., 7g fat (1g sat. fat), 2mg chol., 541mg sod., 8g carb. (2g sugars, 2g fiber), 4g pro. **Diabetic exchanges:** 2 vegetable, 1½ fat.

BLUE CHEESE THINS

I grew up in the South, where cheese straws are served at most potlucks and meals. This recipe uses blue cheese for a bit of a twist. These thins are wonderful to munch before the meal. They can also be crumbled and added to soups or salads.
—Kim Fabrizio, Burien, WA

PREP: 15 MIN. + CHILLING
BAKE: 15 MIN./BATCH + COOLING
MAKES: ABOUT 3 DOZEN

- 1¼ cups crumbled blue cheese
- ½ cup butter, softened
- 1½ cups all-purpose flour
- 3 tsp. poppy seeds
- ½ tsp. salt
- ½ tsp. garlic powder
- 3 to 6 tsp. water

1. In a large bowl, beat the blue cheese and butter until blended. Whisk together the flour, poppy seeds, salt and garlic powder; gradually beat into creamed mixture. Gradually stir in enough water to form a soft dough.
2. Divide dough in half; shape each into a 5½-in. long roll. Cover and refrigerate until firm, about 1 hour.
3. Preheat oven to 350°. Unwrap and cut the dough into ¼-in. slices. Place 2 in. apart on parchment-lined baking sheets. Bake until the edges are lightly browned, 13-15 minutes. Remove from pans to wire racks to cool.
1 appetizer: 60 cal., 4g fat (3g sat. fat), 10mg chol., 107mg sod., 4g carb. (0 sugars, 0 fiber), 2g pro.

GREEK OLIVE TAPENADE

Welcome to an olive lover's dream. Mix olives with freshly minced garlic, parsley and a few drizzles of olive oil to have the ultimate in Mediterranean bliss.
—Lisa Sojka, Rockport, ME

TAKES: 25 MIN.
MAKES: 16 SERVINGS (ABOUT 2 CUPS)

- 2 cups pitted Greek olives, drained
- 3 garlic cloves, minced
- 3 Tbsp. olive oil
- 1½ tsp. minced fresh parsley
  Toasted baguette slices

In a food processor, pulse olives with garlic until finely chopped. Add oil and parsley; pulse until combined. Serve with toasted baguette slices.
2 Tbsp. tapenade: 71 cal., 7g fat (1g sat. fat), 0 chol., 277mg sod., 2g carb. (0 sugars, 0 fiber), 0 pro.

DINNER ROLLS

My family loves the fragrance of these rolls as they bake, and each person has come to expect them whenever I make a special meal. Leftover rolls can be easily reheated. Just pop them in the microwave, or put them in a moistened paper bag and then place the bag in an oven on low heat.

—Anna Baker, Blaine, WA

PREP: 30 MIN. + RISING • **BAKE:** 20 MIN.
MAKES: 2 DOZEN

- 2 pkg. (¼ oz. each) active dry yeast
- ½ cup warm water (110° to 115°)
- 1¼ cups warm 2% milk (110° to 115°)
- ½ cup butter, softened
- 2 large eggs, room temperature
- ⅓ cup sugar
- 1½ tsp. salt
- 6 to 6½ cups all-purpose flour
  Melted butter, optional

1. In a small bowl, dissolve yeast in warm water. In a large bowl, combine milk, softened butter, eggs, sugar, salt, yeast mixture and 3 cups flour; beat on medium speed until smooth. Stir in enough remaining flour to form a soft dough.
2. Turn dough onto a floured surface; knead until smooth and elastic, about 6-8 minutes. Place in a greased bowl, turning once to grease the top. Cover; let rise in a warm place until doubled, about 1 hour.
3. Punch down dough. Turn onto a lightly floured surface; divide in half. Divide and shape each portion into 12 balls. Place rolls in 2 greased 13x9-in. baking pans. Cover with clean kitchen towels; let rise in a warm place until doubled, about 30 minutes. Preheat oven to 375°.
4. Bake 20-25 minutes or until golden brown. If desired, brush tops lightly with melted butter. Cool on wire racks. Serve warm.

1 roll: 173 cal., 5g fat (3g sat. fat), 27mg chol., 191mg sod., 28g carb. (4g sugars, 1g fiber), 4g pro.

PARSNIP & CELERY ROOT BISQUE

With its smooth texture and earthy flavors, this simple yet elegant soup makes a lovely first course. Add chives and pomegranate seeds on top for a pretty garnish.

—Merry Graham, Newhall, CA

PREP: 25 MIN. • **COOK:** 45 MIN.
MAKES: 8 SERVINGS (2 QT.)

- 2 Tbsp. olive oil
- 2 medium leeks (white portion only), chopped (about 2 cups)
- 1½ lbs. parsnips, peeled and chopped (about 4 cups)
- 1 medium celery root, peeled and cubed (about 1½ cups)
- 4 garlic cloves, minced
- 6 cups chicken stock
- 1½ tsp. salt
- ¾ tsp. coarsely ground pepper
- 1 cup heavy whipping cream
- 2 Tbsp. minced fresh parsley
- 2 tsp. lemon juice
- 2 Tbsp. minced fresh chives
  Pomegranate seeds, optional

1. In a large saucepan, heat the oil over medium-high heat; saute leeks 3 minutes. Add parsnips and celery root; cook and stir 4 minutes. Add garlic; cook and stir 1 minute. Stir in stock, salt and pepper; bring to a boil. Reduce heat; simmer, covered, until vegetables are tender, 25-30 minutes.
2. Puree the soup using an immersion blender. Or cool slightly and puree soup in batches in a blender; return to pan. Stir in cream, parsley and lemon juice; heat through. Serve with chives and, if desired, pomegranate seeds.

1 cup: 248 cal., 15g fat (7g sat. fat), 34mg chol., 904mg sod., 25g carb. (8g sugars, 5g fiber), 6g pro.

TEST KITCHEN TIP

Traditional bisque is a thick, creamy soup that's made with crustaceans, like lobster, shrimp or crab. The classic technique calls for the shells to be ground into a paste and stirred into the broth, but you can also thicken the soup by adding rice and straining. Nowadays, bisque recipes have evolved to be pretty much any soup that is creamy in texture and has its ingredients blended. This includes soups like butternut squash and tomato bisque, as well as this one made with root vegetables.

BROILED LOBSTER TAIL

No matter where you live, these succulent, buttery lobster tails are just a few minutes away. Here in Iowa, we use frozen lobster with delicious results, but if you're near the ocean, by all means use fresh!
—Lauren McAnelly, Des Moines, IA

PREP: 30 MIN. • **COOK:** 5 MIN.
MAKES: 4 SERVINGS

- 4 **lobster tails (5 to 6 oz. each), thawed**
- ¼ **cup cold butter, cut into thin slices**
  Salt and pepper to taste
  Lemon wedges

1. Preheat the broiler. Using kitchen scissors, cut a 2-in.-wide rectangle from the top shell of each lobster tail; loosen from lobster meat and remove.
2. Pull away edges of remaining shell to release lobster meat from sides; pry the meat loose from bottom shell, keeping tail end attached. Place in a foil-lined 15x10x1-in. pan. Arrange butter slices over lobster meat.
3. Broil 5-6 in. from heat until meat is opaque, 5-8 minutes. Season with salt and pepper to taste; serve with lemon wedges.

1 lobster tail: 211 cal., 13g fat (8g sat. fat), 211mg chol., 691mg sod., 0 carb. (0 sugars, 0 fiber), 24g pro.

READER REVIEW

"I never knew making lobster would be this easy!"
—ELLIE31773, TASTEOFHOME.COM

BUTTER UP!

Break out the bibs for some rich, velvety clarified butter. The ultimate lobster dunker is only a few minutes away.

1. SIMMER
Melt 1 cup of unsalted butter, cubed, in a heavy saucepan over low heat. Simmer until the solids and fat separate, about 10 minutes. Don't let it brown.

2. SKIM
Remove from heat; skim and discard the surface foam. What's left should be clear yellow liquid.

3. STRAIN
Pour liquid into a bowl through a fine-mesh or cheesecloth-lined strainer. Store in an airtight container in the fridge for up to three months or in the freezer for up to six months.

Q & A

Q: WHAT IS CLARIFIED BUTTER, EXACTLY?
A: It's butterfat—the stuff that's left over when you remove milk solids and water from butter.

Q: WHAT ELSE CAN I DO WITH IT?
A: Because of its high smoke point, clarified butter is fab in place of oil for sauteeing, frying and even popcorn popping. Adios, burnable milk solids!

Q: CAN I BRUSH IT OVER LOBSTER TAILS BEFORE BROILING?
A: Yup! But for more oomph, use compound butter. Process ¼ cup softened butter with any fresh herbs or flavorings you like. Roll it into a log, wrap it in waxed paper and refrigerate.

VEGETABLE BROWN RICE

Loaded with carrots, onions and peas, this rice makes a terrific side dish, but it can even stand on its own as a light main course. Raisins offer a slight sweetness, and pecans add a little crunch.
—Denith Hull, Bethany, OK

PREP: 10 MIN. • **COOK:** 30 MIN.
MAKES: 8 SERVINGS

- 2 cups water
- 1 cup uncooked brown rice
- ½ tsp. dried basil
- 2 Tbsp. olive oil
- 2 medium carrots, cut into matchsticks
- 1 medium onion, chopped
- 8 green onions, cut into 1-in. pieces
- ½ cup raisins
- 2½ cups frozen peas (about 10 oz.)
- 1 tsp. salt
- 1 cup pecan halves, toasted

1. In a small saucepan, bring the water to a boil; stir in rice and basil. Return to a boil. Reduce heat; simmer, covered, until the liquid is absorbed and rice is tender, 30-35 minutes.
2. In a large skillet, heat the oil over medium-high heat; saute the carrots, onions and raisins until vegetables are lightly browned and carrots are crisp-tender, 5-7 minutes. Add peas and salt; heat through. Stir in pecans and rice.
¾ cup: 305 cal., 13g fat (1g sat. fat), 0 chol., 397mg sod., 41g carb. (12g sugars, 7g fiber), 8g pro.

ROSEMARY GARLIC SHRIMP

Delicate shrimp take on fabulous flavor when simmered in a chicken broth mixed with garlic and ripe olives.
—*Taste of Home* Test Kitchen

...AKES: 20 MIN. • **MAKES:** 8 SERVINGS

- 1¼ cups chicken or vegetable broth
- 3 Tbsp. chopped ripe olives
- 1 small cayenne or other fresh red chili pepper, finely chopped
- 2 Tbsp. lemon juice
- 1 Tbsp. minced fresh rosemary or 1 tsp. dried rosemary, crushed
- 4 garlic cloves, minced
- 2 tsp. Worcestershire sauce
- 1 tsp. paprika
- ½ tsp. salt
- ¼ to ½ tsp. pepper
- 2 lbs. uncooked shrimp (31-40 per lb.), peeled, deveined

1. In a large skillet, combine all the ingredients except shrimp; bring to a boil. Cook, uncovered, until liquid is reduced by half.
2. Stir in shrimp; return just to a boil. Reduce heat; simmer, uncovered, until shrimp turn pink, 3-4 minutes, stirring occasionally.
½ cup: 110 cal., 2g fat (0 sat. fat), 139mg chol., 473mg sod., 3g carb. (1g sugars, 0 fiber), 19g pro. **Diabetic exchanges:** 3 lean meat.

GRUYERE MASHED POTATOES

Gruyere cheese and chives take mashed potatoes to a whole new level this holiday season! Don't have chives? Just use extra green onion instead.
—Preci D'Silva, Dubai, AE

TAKES: 25 MIN. • **MAKES:** 8 SERVINGS

- 2 lbs. potatoes, peeled and cubed
- ½ cup sour cream
- ⅓ cup 2% milk, warmed
- 1 garlic clove, minced
- ¼ cup butter, cubed
- ¼ cup shredded Gruyere or Swiss cheese
- ¼ cup minced fresh chives
- 2 green onions, chopped
- ½ tsp. garlic salt
- ¼ tsp. pepper

1. Place the potatoes in a 6-qt. stockpot; add water to cover. Bring to a boil. Reduce the heat; simmer, uncovered, until potatoes are tender, 10-15 minutes.
2. Drain; return to pot. Mash the potatoes, gradually adding sour cream, milk and garlic. Stir in the remaining ingredients.

¾ cup: 169 cal., 10g fat (6g sat. fat), 23mg chol., 206mg sod., 17g carb. (2g sugars, 1g fiber), 3g pro.

SEASONED RIBEYE ROAST

Here's an especially savory way to prepare a boneless beef roast. Gravy made from the drippings is exceptional.
—Evelyn Gebhardt, Kasilof, AK

PREP: 10 MIN.
BAKE: 1½ HOURS + STANDING
MAKES: 8 SERVINGS

- 1½ tsp. lemon-pepper seasoning
- 1½ tsp. paprika
- ¾ tsp. garlic salt
- ½ tsp. dried rosemary, crushed
- ¼ tsp. cayenne pepper
- 1 beef ribeye roast (3 to 4 lbs.)

1. Preheat oven to 350°. Mix seasonings. Place roast on a rack in a roasting pan, fat side up; rub with seasonings.
2. Roast, uncovered, until meat reaches desired doneness (for medium-rare, a thermometer should read 135°; medium, 140°), 1½-2 hours. Remove from oven; tent with foil. Let stand 10 minutes before slicing.

4 oz. cooked beef: 372 cal., 27g fat (11g sat. fat), 100mg chol., 321mg sod., 0 carb. (0 sugars, 0 fiber), 30g pro.

BACON-ONION GREEN BEANS

I threw together this recipe to give some color to the dinner plate. I knew all my relatives liked green beans, so I added onion, bacon, toasted sesame seeds and a little vinegar for a nice tang.
—Karen Darrell, Wood River, IL

TAKES: 25 MIN. • **MAKES:** 8 SERVINGS

- 6 bacon strips, chopped
- 1 medium onion, chopped
- 2 Tbsp. cider vinegar
- ¼ tsp. salt
- ⅛ tsp. pepper
- 1½ lbs. fresh green beans, trimmed
- 1 Tbsp. sesame seeds, toasted

1. In a large skillet, cook the bacon over medium heat until crisp, stirring occasionally. Remove with a slotted spoon; drain on paper towels. Pour off all but 1 Tbsp. drippings. Saute onion in drippings until tender. Stir in vinegar, salt and pepper.
2. Meanwhile, place beans in a large saucepan; add water to cover. Bring to a boil. Cook, covered, until crisp-tender, 4-7 minutes; drain.
3. Place the beans in a large bowl; toss with bacon and onion mixture. Sprinkle with sesame seeds.

1 serving: 84 cal., 5g fat (2g sat. fat), 8mg chol., 191mg sod., 8g carb. (3g sugars, 3g fiber), 4g pro.

POMEGRANATE COCKTAIL

This spicy and sweet sipper gives you a little fix of jalapeno flavor minus the heat. Start a couple of days ahead to flavor the vodka.
—Melissa Rodriguez, Van Nuys, CA

PREP: 10 MIN. + CHILLING
MAKES: 8 SERVINGS

- 2 jalapeno peppers, halved lengthwise and seeded
- 1½ cups vodka
- 6 to 8 cups ice cubes
- 3 cups pomegranate juice
- 3 cups Italian blood orange soda, chilled
  Lime wedges

1. For jalapeno vodka, place jalapenos and vodka in a glass jar or container. Refrigerate, covered, 2-3 days to allow flavors to blend. Strain before using.
2. For each serving, fill a cocktail shaker three-fourths full with ice. Add 3 oz. pomegranate juice and 1½ oz. jalapeno vodka; cover and shake until condensation forms on the outside of shaker, 10-15 seconds. Strain into a cocktail glass; top with 3 oz. soda. Serve with lime wedges.
1 cup: 184 cal., 0 fat (0 sat. fat), 0 chol., 12mg sod., 22g carb. (22g sugars, 0 fiber), 0 pro.

PEPPERMINT PATTY CREAM PIE

This dreamy chocolate cream pie with a touch of refreshing peppermint is the perfect way to cleanse the palate after a large meal. I first made this many years ago, not long after I got married. It was a winner then and is a winner now!
—Susan Simons, Eatonville, WA

PREP: 45 MIN. + CHILLING
COOK: 25 MIN. + COOLING
MAKES: 8 SERVINGS

- Pastry for single-crust pie (9 in.), baked (recipe at right)
- 2 oz. unsweetened chocolate, chopped
- 8 miniature chocolate-covered peppermint patties, unwrapped (about 4 oz.)
- 2 Tbsp. hot water
- 3 large eggs
- ¼ cup sugar
- ½ cup butter, softened
- 1 cup heavy whipping cream
  Chocolate curls

1. On a lightly floured surface, roll the pastry dough to a ⅛-in.-thick circle; transfer to a 9-in. pie plate. Trim crust to ½ in. beyond rim of plate; flute edge. Refrigerate 30 minutes. Preheat oven to 425°.
2. Line crust with a double thickness of foil. Fill with pie weights, dried beans or uncooked rice. Bake on a lower oven rack until edges are golden brown, 20-25 minutes. Remove foil and weights; bake until bottom is golden brown, 3-6 minutes. Cool completely on a wire rack.
3. In a small heavy saucepan, melt the chocolate and peppermint patties over low heat, stirring constantly (mixture will be thick). Remove from heat; stir in hot water until smooth. Remove to a bowl; cool.
4. Meanwhile, in a clean heavy saucepan, whisk together eggs and sugar. Cook and stir gently over low heat until a thermometer reads 160°, 12-14 minutes. Do not allow to boil. Immediately transfer to a bowl; cool about 10 minutes, stirring occasionally.
5. In a large bowl, beat butter until light and fluffy. Add cooled chocolate and egg mixtures; beat on high speed until light and fluffy, about 5 minutes.
6. In a small bowl, beat cream until soft peaks form. Fold into chocolate mixture. Spoon into crust. Refrigerate, covered, until set, about 2 hours. Top with chocolate curls.
1 piece: 525 cal., 40g fat (25g sat. fat), 164mg chol., 287mg sod., 36g carb. (17g sugars, 2g fiber), 7g pro.

PASTRY FOR SINGLE-CRUST PIE

Here's our basic recipe for homemade pie crust. Use it for any recipe that calls for pastry for a single-crust pie.
—*Taste of Home* Test Kitchen

TAKES: 10 MIN.
MAKES: 1 PASTRY SHELL (8 SERVINGS)

- 1¼ cups all-purpose flour
- ½ tsp. salt
- ⅓ cup shortening
- 4 to 5 Tbsp. cold water

1. In a large bowl, combine the flour and salt; cut in the shortening until crumbly. Gradually add water, tossing with a fork until a ball forms. Roll out pastry to fit a 9-in. or 10-in. pie plate.
2. Transfer crust to pie plate. Trim crust to ½ in. beyond edge of pie plate; flute edges. Fill or bake shell according to recipe directions. Double recipe for double-crust pies.
1 serving: 144 cal., 8g fat (2g sat. fat), 0 chol., 148mg sod., 15g carb. (0 sugars, 1g fiber), 2g pro.

4. For the frosting, beat butter and cream cheese until smooth. Beat in vanilla. Gradually beat in confectioners' sugar and enough buttermilk to reach spreading consistency.

5. Spread 1 cup frosting between the cake layers. Spread top of cake with an additional 1 cup frosting. Spread remaining frosting in a thin layer over side of cake. Top with additional walnuts and, if desired, orange slices.

1 slice: 630 cal., 30g fat (13g sat. fat), 92mg chol., 432mg sod., 84g carb. (60g sugars, 1g fiber), 9g pro.

BACON-WRAPPED FIGS

This is the first bacon-wrapped fig recipe I made. I like that the figs and walnuts have similar nutritional values, making this a high energy appetizer or snack.
—Shelly Bevington, Hermiston, OR

TAKES: 30 MIN. • **MAKES:** 2 DOZEN

- 24 dried figs, trimmed
- 24 walnut halves
- 12 bacon strips, halved crosswise
- ⅓ cup grated Parmesan cheese

1. Preheat oven to 375°. Cut a slit lengthwise down the center of each fig; fill each with a walnut half.
2. In a large skillet, cook bacon over medium heat until partially cooked but not crisp. Drain on paper towels.
3. Place cheese in a shallow bowl. Dip 1 side of bacon in cheese. Wrap each bacon strip around a stuffed fig, cheese side out; secure with a toothpick. Place on an ungreased 15x10x1-in. baking pan.
4. Bake 12-15 minutes or until bacon is crisp, turning once.

1 appetizer: 66 cal., 4g fat (1g sat. fat), 5mg chol., 86mg sod., 6g carb. (4g sugars, 1g fiber), 2g pro.

BLACK WALNUT LAYER CAKE

My sister gave me the recipe for this beautiful cake years ago. The thin layer of frosting spread on the outside gives it a chic modern look.
—Lynn Glaze, Warren, OH

PREP: 25 MIN. • **BAKE:** 20 MIN. + COOLING
MAKES: 16 SERVINGS

- ½ cup butter, softened
- ½ cup shortening
- 2 cups sugar
- 2 tsp. vanilla extract
- 4 large eggs, room temperature
- 3¾ cups all-purpose flour
- 2 tsp. baking soda
- ½ tsp. salt
- 1½ cups buttermilk
- 1¼ cups finely chopped black or English walnuts

FROSTING
- ½ cup butter, softened
- 1 pkg. (8 oz.) cream cheese, softened
- 1 tsp. vanilla extract
- 4½ cups confectioners' sugar
- 1 to 3 Tbsp. buttermilk
  Additional black walnuts
  Thin orange slices, optional

1. Preheat oven to 350°. Line bottoms of 3 greased 9-in. round baking pans with parchment; grease parchment.
2. Cream butter, shortening and sugar until light and fluffy, 5-7 minutes. Add vanilla and eggs, 1 at a time, beating well after each addition. In another bowl, whisk together the flour, baking soda and salt; add to creamed mixture alternately with buttermilk, beating after each addition. Fold in walnuts.
3. Transfer to prepared pans. Bake until a toothpick inserted in center comes out clean, 20-25 minutes. Cool in pans 10 minutes before removing to wire racks; remove paper. Cool completely.

New Year's Eve Party

There's no better way to kick off another trip around the sun than with an all-out New Year's Eve bash. This year, it's all about bubbles, bling and the best bites. So load up your plate, toss some confetti and raise your glass to the most epic party yet!

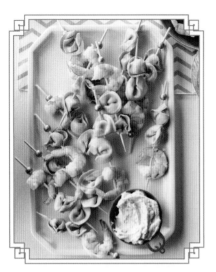

TORTELLINI & SHRIMP SKEWERS WITH SUN-DRIED TOMATO SAUCE

These fresh-tasting skewers with a creamy sauce will have guests nibbling all night.
—Cacie Biddle, Bridgeport, WV

PREP: 30 MIN. • **COOK:** 15 MIN.
MAKES: 32 APPETIZERS

- 1 pkg. (8 oz.) cream cheese, softened
- ½ cup sour cream
- ¼ cup fresh basil leaves
- ¼ cup oil-packed sun-dried tomatoes
- ¼ cup reduced-fat mayonnaise
- ¼ cup 2% milk
- 2 garlic cloves
- ½ tsp. Louisiana-style hot sauce
- ¼ tsp. salt
- ¼ tsp. pepper

SKEWERS

- 1 pkg. (9 oz.) refrigerated spinach tortellini
- 2 Tbsp. olive oil
- 1 lb. peeled and deveined cooked shrimp (31-40 per lb.)
- 32 frilled toothpicks

1. Combine first 10 ingredients in a food processor; pulse until blended. Remove to a small bowl; refrigerate, covered, until serving.
2. Cook tortellini according to package directions. Drain; rinse with cold water and drain again. Toss with oil. Thread tortellini and shrimp onto toothpicks. Serve with sauce.

1 appetizer with 1 Tbsp. sauce: 88 cal., 6g fat (3g sat. fat), 36mg chol., 112mg sod., 4g carb. (0 sugars, 0 fiber), 5g pro.

HORSERADISH MEATBALLS

Looking for a zippy twist on traditional meatballs? Try my recipe. When I'm not entertaining, I enjoy these meatballs with hot cooked rice and a fresh salad for a more substantial meal.
—Joyce Benninger, Owen Sound, ON

PREP: 30 MIN. • **BAKE:** 35 MIN.
MAKES: 3 DOZEN

- 2 large eggs
- ½ cup dry bread crumbs
- ¼ cup chopped green onions
- 1 Tbsp. prepared horseradish
- ½ tsp. salt
- ¼ tsp. pepper
- 1½ lbs. lean ground beef (90% lean)
- ½ lb. ground pork or ground turkey

SAUCE

- 1 small onion, finely chopped
- ½ cup water
- ½ cup chili sauce
- ½ cup ketchup
- ¼ cup packed brown sugar
- ¼ cup cider vinegar
- 1 Tbsp. Worcestershire sauce
- 1 Tbsp. prepared horseradish
- 1 garlic clove, minced
- 1 tsp. ground mustard
- ¼ tsp. hot pepper sauce

1. Preheat oven to 350°. Combine first 6 ingredients. Add beef and pork; mix lightly but thoroughly. Shape mixture into 1½-in. balls. Place on a greased rack in a 15x10x1-in. pan. Bake until a thermometer reads 160° (165° if using ground turkey), 35-40 minutes.
2. Meanwhile, in a large saucepan, combine sauce ingredients; bring to a boil, stirring frequently. Reduce heat; simmer, uncovered, 10 minutes. Gently stir in meatballs.

1 meatball: 68 cal., 3g fat (1g sat. fat), 26mg chol., 163mg sod., 5g carb. (3g sugars, 0 fiber), 5g pro.

TEST KITCHEN TIP

Horseradish is the root of a perennial plant in the brassica family (which also includes mustard, wasabi, broccoli, and cabbage). The plant's long, white root has almost no odor when it comes out of the ground, but its pungency is noticeable once you cut into it.

MANGO BELLINI

Simple yet delicious, this mango Bellini is made with mango nectar and your favorite champagne or sparkling wine—I usually choose Prosecco. You can easily turn it into a mocktail by using sparkling water in place of the champagne.
—Ellen Folkman, Crystal Beach, FL

TAKES: 5 MIN. • **MAKES:** 6 SERVINGS

- ¾ cup mango nectar or fresh mango puree, chilled
- 1 bottle (750 ml) champagne or other sparkling wine, chilled

Add 2 Tbsp. mango nectar to each of 6 champagne flutes. Top with champagne; gently stir to combine.
1 Bellini: 101 cal., 0 fat (0 sat. fat), 0 chol., 1mg sod., 6g carb. (4g sugars, 0 fiber), 0 pro.

GINGER-TUNA KABOBS

My elegant one-bite appetizers will be the talk of the party. Ginger and tuna are a delicious flavor combination, and the wasabi sauce adds a nice zing. If desired, serve on a watercress-lined platter.
—Mary Beth Harris-Murphree, Tyler, TX

PREP: 25 MIN. + MARINATING • **COOK:** 5 MIN.
MAKES: 16 KABOBS

- 1 lb. tuna steaks, cut into 16 cubes
- ¼ cup soy sauce
- 2 Tbsp. rice vinegar
- 1 Tbsp. sesame seeds
- 1 tsp. pepper
- 2 Tbsp. canola oil
- 16 pickled ginger slices
- 1 bunch watercress, optional
- ½ cup wasabi mayonnaise

1. Toss tuna with soy sauce and vinegar refrigerate, covered, 30 minutes.
2. Drain tuna, discarding marinade; pat dry. Sprinkle tuna with sesame seeds and pepper. In a large skillet, sear tuna until browned and center is medium rare or slightly pink; remove the tuna from skillet.
3. On each of 16 appetizer skewers, thread 1 ginger slice and 1 tuna cube. If desired, place on a watercress-lined patter. Serve with wasabi mayonnaise.
1 kabob with 1½ tsp. mayonnaise: 100 cal., 8g fat (1g sat. fat), 15mg chol., 186mg sod., 1g carb. (0 sugars, 0 fiber), 7g pro.

HONEY CHAMPAGNE FONDUE

This special fondue has a wonderful flavor from champagne and Swiss cheese, and a hint of sweetness from honey. It clings well to any kind of dipper.
—Shannon Copley, Upper Arlington, OH

TAKES: 30 MIN. • **MAKES:** 4 CUPS

- 1 Tbsp. cornstarch
- 1 tsp. ground mustard
- ¼ tsp. white pepper
- 1¼ cups champagne
- 1 tsp. lemon juice
- 2 Tbsp. finely chopped shallot
- 1 garlic clove, minced
- 1½ lbs. Swiss cheese, shredded
- 2 Tbsp. honey
  Pinch ground nutmeg
  Toasted French bread, asparagus, tart apple slices, endive spears or cooked shrimp

1. In a large saucepan, combine the cornstarch, ground mustard and white pepper. Whisk in champagne and lemon juice until smooth. Add the shallot and garlic; bring to a boil. Reduce the heat to medium-low; cook and stir until thickened, about 1 minute. Gradually stir in cheese until melted. Stir in honey. Sprinkle with nutmeg.

2. Keep warm in a fondue pot or small slow cooker. Serve with toasted bread, asparagus, apple slices, endive or cooked shrimp as desired.

¼ cup: 256 cal., 18g fat (10g sat. fat), 53mg chol., 107mg sod., 5g carb. (3g sugars, 0 fiber), 15g pro.

FRUIT & CHEESE BOARD

Who says cheese and sausage get to have all the fun? Make this board a party favorite with any fruits that are in season.
—*Taste of Home* Test Kitchen

TAKES: 25 MINUTES • **MAKES:** 14 SERVINGS

- 10 fresh strawberries, halved
- 8 fresh or dried figs, halved
- 2 small navel oranges, thinly sliced
- 12 oz. seedless red grapes (about 1½ cups)
- 1 medium mango, halved and scored
- ½ cup fresh blueberries
- 1 cup fresh blackberries
- ½ cup dried banana chips
- 2 large kiwifruit, peeled, halved and thinly sliced
- 12 oz. seedless watermelon (about 6 slices)
- ½ cup unblanched almonds
- 8 oz. Brie cheese
- 8 oz. mascarpone cheese
- ½ cup honey

On a large platter or cutting board, arrange fruit, almonds and cheeses. Place honey in a small jar; tuck jar among fruit.

1 serving: 304 cal., 17g fat (8g sat. fat), 36mg chol., 116mg sod., 36g carb. (30g sugars, 4g fiber), 7g pro.

FONDUE-MAKING TIPS

Cheese melts faster and easier if it is shredded, grated or cut into small cubes. Cooking spray keeps the cheese from sticking to the cheese grater, making cleanup easy.

Add a little cornstarch to the shredded cheese to help the cheese bind with the wine or broth.

Reduce the heat to low before setting the cheese into hot liquids one handful at a time. Keep the heat set at low while the cheese melts.

Cheese fondues are often made with white wine. If you don't wish to use wine, substitute vegetable or chicken broth.

Stir in seasonings, herbs or spices after all the cheese has melted to a smooth consistency.

CHEESE GRAPE APPETIZERS

These small bites are well worth the time. Serve them as part of an appetizer platter or charcuterie board alongside your favorite bottle of wine.
—Eleanor Grofvert, Kalamazoo, MI

PREP: 35 MIN. • **BAKE:** 10 MIN. + COOLING
MAKES: ABOUT 5 DOZEN

- 4 oz. sliced almonds (about 1 cup)
- 1 pkg. (8 oz.) cream cheese, softened
- 2 oz. crumbled blue cheese, room temperature
- 2 Tbsp. minced fresh parsley
- 2 Tbsp. heavy whipping cream, room temperature
   Appetizer skewers or toothpicks
- 1 to 1¼ lbs. seedless red or green grapes, rinsed and patted dry

1. Preheat oven to 275°. Pulse almonds in a food processor until finely chopped (do not overprocess). Spread in a 15x10x1-in. pan; bake the chopped almonds for 6-9 minutes, until golden brown, stirring occasionally. Transfer to a shallow bowl; cool slightly.
2. In another bowl, mix cream cheese, blue cheese, parsley and cream until blended. Insert a skewer into each grape. Roll grapes in cheese mixture, then in the almonds; place on waxed paper-lined baking sheets. Refrigerate, covered, until serving.

5 each: 146 cal., 11g fat (6g sat. fat), 28mg chol., 124mg sod., 8g carb. (7g sugars, 1g fiber), 4g pro.

HAM & CHEESE BISCUIT STACKS

I serve these mini sandwiches at holiday parties, showers and tailgates. Honey and stone-ground mustard add a sweet and savory taste to every bite.
—Kelly Williams, Forked River, NJ

PREP: 1 HOUR • **BAKE:** 10 MIN. + COOLING
MAKES: 40 APPETIZERS

- 4 tubes (6 oz. each) small refrigerated flaky biscuits (5 count each)
- ¼ cup stone-ground mustard
   ASSEMBLY
- ½ cup butter, softened
- ¼ cup chopped green onions
- ½ cup stone-ground mustard
- ¼ cup mayonnaise
- ¼ cup honey
- 10 thick slices deli ham, quartered
- 10 slices Swiss cheese, quartered
- 2½ cups shredded romaine
- 20 pitted ripe olives, drained and patted dry
- 20 pimiento-stuffed olives, drained and patted dry
- 40 frilled toothpicks

1. Preheat oven to 400°. Cut biscuits in half to make half-circles; place 2 in. apart on ungreased baking sheets. Spread mustard over tops. Bake until golden brown, 8-10 minutes. Cool completely on wire racks.
2. Mix the butter and green onions. In another bowl, mix the mustard, mayonnaise and honey. Split each biscuit into 2 layers.
3. Spread biscuit bottoms with butter mixture; top with ham, cheese, romaine and biscuit tops. Spoon mustard mixture over tops. Thread 1 olive onto each toothpick; insert into stacks. Serve immediately.

1 appetizer: 121 cal., 7g fat (3g sat. fat), 16mg chol., 412mg sod., 11g carb. (2g sugars, 0 fiber), 4g pro.

READER REVIEW
"This is a wonderful appetizer—easy and tasty. The first time I made it we actually ate them for dinner! You can, of course, substitute whatever meat and cheese combo you choose, but for us this was perfect as written."
—MARTHA, TASTEOFHOME.COM

COCONUT-RUM CAKE POPS

These coconut-coated cake pops with a hint of rum taste like paradise on a stick.
—*Taste of Home* Test Kitchen

PREP: 1½ HOURS + CHILLING
MAKES: 4 DOZEN

- 1 pkg. (16 oz.) angel food cake mix
- ¾ cup canned vanilla frosting
- 1 cup sweetened shredded coconut
- 1 tsp. coconut extract
- ½ tsp. rum extract
- 48 lollipop sticks
- 2½ lbs. white candy coating, melted
  Lightly toasted sweetened shredded coconut

1. Prepare and bake cake mix according to package directions. Cool completely on a wire rack.
2. In a large bowl, mix frosting, coconut and extracts. Tear cake into pieces. In batches, pulse cake in a food processor until crumbs form. Stir the crumbs into frosting mixture. Shape into 1-in. balls; place on baking sheets. Insert sticks. Freeze at least 2 hours or refrigerate at least 3 hours until firm.

3. Dip cake pops in the melted candy coating, allowing excess to drip off. Roll in toasted coconut. Insert cake pops in a Styrofoam block; let stand until set.
1 cake pop: 188 cal., 8g fat (7g sat. fat), 0 chol., 92mg sod., 29g carb. (25g sugars, 0 fiber), 1g pro.

MARINATED MOZZARELLA

Cheese is irresistible on its own, but with a light marinade of herbs and spicy red pepper flakes, it's out of this world. Try bocconcini (small, semi-soft round balls of fresh mozzarella) in place of the cubed mozzarella if you'd like a different shape.
—Peggy Cairo, Kenosha, WI

PREP: 15 MIN. + MARINATING
MAKES: 10 SERVINGS

- ⅓ cup olive oil
- 1 Tbsp. chopped oil-packed sun-dried tomatoes
- 1 Tbsp. minced fresh parsley
- 1 tsp. crushed red pepper flakes
- 1 tsp. dried basil
- 1 tsp. minced chives
- ¼ tsp. garlic powder
- 1 lb. cubed part-skim mozzarella cheese

In a large bowl, combine the first 7 ingredients; add cheese cubes. Stir to coat. Cover; refrigerate at least 30 minutes.
¼ cup: 203 cal., 16g fat (7g sat. fat), 24mg chol., 242mg sod., 2g carb. (trace sugars, trace fiber), 12g pro.

CHAMPAGNE BLONDIES

I was looking for a fun champagne recipe to take to a friend's bridal shower, but I couldn't find one. That's when I came up with this unique twist on blondies. The recipe calls for white chocolate chips, but I sometimes use butterscotch or chocolate instead.
—Heather Karow, Burnett, WI

PREP: 25 MIN. • **BAKE:** 25 MIN. + COOLING
MAKES: 16 SERVINGS

- ½ cup butter, softened
- 1 cup packed light brown sugar
- 1 large egg, room temperature
- ¼ cup champagne
- 1¼ cups all-purpose flour
- 1 tsp. baking powder
- ¼ tsp. salt
- ½ cup white baking chips
- ½ cup chopped hazelnuts, optional

GLAZE
- 1 cup confectioners' sugar
- 2 Tbsp. champagne

1. Preheat oven to 350°. Line an 8-in. square baking pan with parchment, letting ends extend up sides. In a large bowl, beat butter and brown sugar until crumbly, about 2 minutes. Beat in egg and champagne (batter may appear curdled). In another bowl, whisk flour, baking powder and salt; gradually add to butter mixture. Fold in baking chips and, if desired, nuts.

2. Spread into prepared pan. Bake until edges are brown and center is set (do not overbake), 25-30 minutes. Cool completely in pan on a wire rack.

3. Combine glaze ingredients; drizzle over blondies. Lifting with parchment, remove blondies from pan. Cut into bars. Store in an airtight container.

1 blondie: 203 cal., 8g fat (5g sat. fat), 28mg chol., 126mg sod., 32g carb. (24g sugars, 0 fiber), 2g pro.

Recipe Index

A

B

C

How-To's, Crafts & Extras